France since 1815

France since 1815 provides an accessible overview of the major socio-political changes in France during this period. Designed for area studies students studying French, it presents the historical context necessary for language students to understand the complexities of contemporary French society. Adopting a chronological approach, it surveys nearly two hundred years of French history, with events covered including the French Revolution, the Bourbon Restoration, the Third Republic, occupied France, the Fourth Republic, the Gaullist Revolution and France after 2003.

This revised edition includes new material that focuses on Chirac's second mandate (Iraq War, religion, suburbs and the inability/impossibility of carrying on with reform), an assessment of the controversial Sarkozy presidency, and a final chapter covering the last ten years, culminating in the results of the French presidential elections in 2012.

Features include:

- clear timelines of main events and suggested topics for discussion
- glossary inserts throughout of key terms and concepts
- the use of primary documents to re-create and understand the past
- free access to a website (www.port.ac.uk/francesince1815/) containing a wealth of complementary material

Drawing on the best scholarship, particular emphasis has been given to the role of political memory, the contribution of women and the impact of colonialism and post-colonialism. In this second edition the relationship between France and her European partners is analysed in greater depth and there are new sections explicitly situating France and the French within a wider transnational/global perspective.

Martin Evans is Professor of Modern European History at the University of Sussex, UK and **Emmanuel Godin** is Principal Lecturer in European Area Studies at the University of Portsmouth, UK.

Modern History for Modern Languages

Written in an accessible style and assuming no prior knowledge, the books in this series address the specific needs of students on language courses. Approaching the study of history from an interest in contemporary politics and society, each book offers a clear historical narrative and sets its region into a world context.

Titles in the series:

France since 1815, **Second Edition**
Germany and Austria 1814–2000
Latin America 1800–2000
Spain since 1812, **Second Edition**

France since 1815
Second Edition

**Martin Evans and
Emmanuel Godin**

LONDON AND NEW YORK

Second edition published 2014
by Routledge
2 Park Square, Milton Park, Abingdon, Oxon OX14 4RN
and by Routledge
711 Third Avenue, New York, NY 10017

Routledge is an imprint of the Taylor & Francis Group, an informa business

First published 2004
by Arnold, a member of the Hodder Headline Group

British Library Cataloguing in Publication Data
A catalogue record for this book is available from the British Library

Library of Congress Cataloging in Publication Data
Evans, Martin, 1964-
    France since 1815 : modern history for modern languages / Martin Evans,
    Emmanuel Godin. – Second edition.
        pages cm. – (Modern history for modern languages series)
    Previous edition published under title: France, 1815–2003.
    Includes bibliographical references and index.
I. France – History – 1789–2. France – Politics and government – 1789-I. Godin, Emmanuel.
II. Evans, Martin, 1964-France, 1815–2003. III. Title.
    DC251.E83 2014
    944 – dc23
    2013028588

ISBN: 978-0-415-73380-9 (hbk)
ISBN: 978-1-4441-7790-9 (pbk)
ISBN: 978-0-203-78469-3 (ebk)

Typeset in Lucida
by Phoenix Photosetting Ltd, Chatham, Kent

Printed and bound in Great Britain by
TJ International Ltd, Padstow, Cornwall

This book is dedicated with love to
Ken and Phyl Marshman,
Félix Gaido-Force and Eugénie Vallin

Contents

List of figures   x

List of maps   xi

Preface   xiii

Abbreviations   xv

1 The French Revolution: history, memory, politics   1

Causes 4
Phases 9
Legacy 17

2 The Bourbon Restoration, 1814–30   19

The Charter and the foundations of constitutional
   monarchy 20
1816–20: 'Union and forgetfulness'? 22
Charles X and the Ultras 23
Polarisation and the 1830 Revolution 26

3 The July Monarchy, 1830–48   33

A repressive liberal monarchy 35
The reign of the bourgeosie 37
Thiers and Guizot: from instability to stalemate 41
The 1848 Revolution 43

4 The Second Republic, 1848–52 and the
   Second Empire, 1852–70   47

A social and democratic republic? (February–June 1848) 48
A conservative republic, June 1848–December 1851 50
The authoritarian empire, 1852–60 52
Economic expansion 54
A new international role? 56
Towards a liberal empire, 1860–70 57

5 The Third Republic, 1870–1914   63

The Paris Commune, March–May 1871 63
The monarchist republic, 1871–79 64

The opportunist republic, 1879–99 66
Challenges from the right and the left 69
The Dreyfus Affair 72
The radical republic, 1899–1914 73

6 France, 1914–31   79

The international situation, 1871–1914 79
The outbreak of war 81
Union sacrée 82
Versailles Peace Treaty, 28 June 1919 85
Reparations 88
The Colonial Exhibition, May 1931 91

7 France, 1931–39   97

The impact of the Depression in France 98
The institutional crisis 99
The Popular Front 100
The Popular Front in power 103
Path to war, 1937–39 106

8 Occupied France, 1940–44   113

The Phoney War 113
The Vichy regime 115
Vichy and the Holocaust 121
Survival 122
Collaboration 123
Resistance 124
Liberation and the purge 127

9 The Fourth Republic, 1944–58   131

Fourth Republic politics 133
Economic and social change 138
Decolonisation and the end of the Fourth Republic 140

10 The Gaullist Revolution, 1958–69   149

Decolonisation and the end of the Algerian War 150
Constitutional reform 154
Foreign policy 155
Economic and social change 156
The roots of May 1968 158
The events of May 1968 161

11 After de Gaulle: Pompidou, 1969–74
and Giscard, 1974–81   165

From Gaullism to conservatism? France under
    Pompidou 166
La petite alternance under Giscard 169
Liberal reforms and their limits 170
Economic crisis and political polarisation 172
Foreign policy 174
Fin de règne 175

12 1981–2002: From *la grande alternance* to
normalisation?   179

La grande alternance, 1981–86 180
La cohabitation, 1986–88 185
Mitterrand's second term, 1988–95 188
Chirac's first term, 1995–2002 and *la gauche plurielle*,
    1997–2002 193

13 France since 2002   201

2002–7 Chirac's second term 202
Le Sarkozysme et la droite décomplexée 207

Further reading   221
Index   227

List of figures

3.1 Daumier, *Gargantua*, 1831   38
5.1 An anti-MacMahon caricature   66
5.2 Anti-Semitic cartoon from *Le Psst*, February 1898   73
6.1 Colonial postcard: exoticism and eroticism   92
8.1 Vichy propaganda: the *révolution nationale* and
the two Frances   119
9.1 Advertisement from *Paris-Match*, 1959   141
9.2 The representation of women in elected
assemblies, 1945–83   147
10.1 Underground student poster, May 1968   162

List of maps

1.1 The departments of France in 1790   12
1.2 Napoleon's empire, 1812   16
5.1 The French Republic, 1881   69
6.1 Military operations, 1914–18   85
6.2 The French Empire in 1930   90
8.1 Occupied France, 1940–44   116
8.2 The liberation of France   128

Preface

The aim of this book is to provide the historical context necessary to under-stand contemporary France. It is essentially an overview of the major politi-cal and social changes in France over the last two centuries. As such, the book provides students with a chronology and a framework of analysis which allows them to explore the connection between the past and present.

Each chapter is divided into four specific sections. First, there is a timeline which gives students a summary of the key dates and a starting point for understanding the past. Second, there is the main body of the chapter which explains not only the causes and consequences of major events but also the historical controversies these events have generated and still generate. Third, there are glossary boxes, which perform several purposes. They provide illustrative snapshots which complement the overall panorama presented in the text, giving a human face to complex and sometimes seemingly abstract social and political changes. They offer further definitions and explanations of events and concepts, thus refining students' understanding of specific issues. Finally, they draw attention to recurrent themes which cross the boundaries between chapters, such as the ongoing relationship between history and memory, as well as the place of France in the wider world. Fourth, there are the primary source documents, followed by topics for further discussion. The primary documents are wide-ranging and include popular songs, official declarations, diary extracts, excerpts from pamphlets and eyewitness accounts. These primary sources need to be distinguished from secondary sources, that is the various interpretations produced by historians when they retrospectively analyse the significance of the past. The primary documents illustrate themes raised in each chapter and give students the opportunity to confront these sources critically with the historical knowledge they have now acquired. As such, the documents provide students with an insight into the methods of the historian, that is how primary documents are used to re-create and understand the past. The questions set at the end of each chapter have been designed to encourage students to reflect on the relevance and nature of primary documents and how they relate to the overall chapter.

Finally, alongside the book there is a website, www.port.ac.uk/francesince1815/, which contains complementary materials such as interviews with key historians about specific events, further primary documents, and links to other websites.

This book is the result of twenty years of teaching French history in the School of Languages and Area Studies at the University of Portsmouth. It presents ideas and documents that we have used in lectures and seminars with area studies students following courses on European history, twentieth-century France and contemporary French politics and society. It is also the outcome of a specific research culture which has been fostered by the Centre for European Studies Research (CESR) at the University of Portsmouth. Working with colleagues in the research group specialising in the Francophone world has been vital in refining our ideas on contemporary French history, as has teaching on the MA Francophone Africa. In particular these exchanges have underlined the role of memory in history and the experience of colonialism, two essential themes of this book.

We would like to express our thanks to the following people for their patience and support during the writing of this book. First of all, we have a debt of gratitude toward Elena Seymenliyska, who first approached us with the idea for this project. Thereafter, we are grateful to Eva Martinez and Rada Radojicic at Arnold and the copy editor Alison Kelly whose support has been invaluable throughout the writing up process. The library at the University of Portsmouth has superb holdings on contemporary French history and we would like to thank our librarian Anne Worden, who has done so much to maintain the collection. Finally, we are particularly indebted to those who have been kind enough to give us their time, suggestions and assistance: Lucy Noakes, Calum Evans, Hannah Abbo, Christopher Lee, Jean Craggs, Rod Kedward, Tony Chafer, John Keiger, Susan Dunsmore, Geneviève Parkes, Neil Whitehead, Kenny Nicholson, Liz Clifford, Janet Blaikie, Irène and François Sullo, and Ruth Berry.

Abbreviations

AEF	*Afrique équatoriale française*
AOF	*Afrique occidentale française*
BBC	British Broadcasting Corporation
CD	*Centre démocrate*
CGT	*Confédération générale du travail*
CGTU	*Confédération générale du travail unifiée*
CNIP	*Conseil national des indépendants et paysans*
CNR	*Conseil national de la résistance*
CSU	*Couverture sociale universelle*
DATAR	*Délégation à l'aménagement du territoire et à l'action régionale*
ECSC	European Coal and Steel Community
EDC	European Defence Community
EDF	*Electricité de France*
EEC	European Economic Community
ENA	*Ecole nationale d'administration*
EU	European Union
FGDS	*Fédération de la gauche démocratique et socialiste*
FLN	*Front de libération nationale*
FN	Front national
FO	*Force ouvrière*
FTP	Francs-tireurs et partisans
GATT	General Agreement on Tariffs and Trade
GDF	*Gaz de France*
GDP	gross domestic product
IFOP	*Institut français de l'opinion publique*
JAC	*Jeunesse agricole chrétienne*
JCR	*Jeunesse communiste révolutionnaire*
JEC	*Jeunesse étudiante chrétienne*
JOC	*Jeunesse ouvrière chrétienne*
LVF	*Légion des volontaires français*
MDC	*Mouvement des citoyens*
MEDEF	*Mouvement des entreprises de France*
MLF	*Mouvement de libération des femmes*
MRP	*Mouvement républicain populaire*
NATO	North Atlantic Treaty Organisation
OAS	*Organisation de l'armée secrète*
PACS	*Pacte civil de solidarité*

PCF	*Parti communiste français*
POF	*Parti ouvrier français*
PPF	*Parti populaire français*
PS	*Parti socialiste*
PSF	*Parti social français*
PSU	*Parti socialiste unifié*
RMI	*Revenu minimum d'insertion*
RNP	*Rassemblement national populaire*
RPF	*Rassemblement du peuple français*
RPR	*Rassemblement pour la république*
SEA	Single European Act
SFIO	*Section française de l'internationale ouvrière*
SMIC	*Salaire minimum indexé sur la croissance*
SNCF	*Société nationale des chemins de fer*
STO	*Service du travail obligatoire*
UDCA	*Union de défense des commerçants et artisans*
UDF	*Union pour la démocratie française*
UDR	*Union pour la défense de la république*
UDV	*Union des démocrates pour la V*
UMP	*Union pour un mouvement populaire*
UNEF	*Union nationale des étudiants de France*
UNR	*Union pour la nouvelle république*
USDR	*Union démocratique et socialiste de la résistance*

CHAPTER 1

Timeline

1774
Accession of Louis XVI

1788
*8 August   Estates-General
convoked for 1789*

1789
*5 May   Estates-General
convenes
14 July   Bastille falls
4 August   Abolition of
feudalism
26 August   Declaration of
Rights of Man*

1790
*12 July   Civil Constitution of
the Clergy*

1791
*13 April   Pope condemns the
Civil Constitution
20–1 June   Louis XVI
captured trying to flee France*

1792
*20 April   War declared on
Austria
13 June   Prussia declares
war on France
10 August   Overthrow of
monarchy
20 September   French
victory at Valmy
22 September   Republic
proclaimed*

1793
*21 January   King executed
6 April   Committee of Public
Safety created
31 October   Girondins
executed*

1794
*27–8 July   Fall of
Robespierre
12 November   Jacobin Club
closed*

1795
*2 November   Directory
established*

The French Revolution: history, memory, politics

On the evening of 14 July 1989 1.5 million people congregated along the Champs-Elysées to celebrate the two-hundredth anniversary of the French Revolution. The centrepiece was the huge parade organised by the publicist and fashion photographer Jean-Paul Goude. At a cost of £10 million Goude's extravaganza was a provocative mixture of high camp and contemporary politics. His floats included Russians on a moving ice rink, British Dragoon Guards being drenched in an artificial rainstorm, as well as Chinese students being butchered, an explicit reference to the communist repression in Tiananmen Square in Beijing just five weeks before. The climax was the black opera virtuoso Jessye Norman on stilts singing *La Marseillaise*. For Goude the whole parade was premissed upon a rejection of purity. 'It will have an African rhythm, there will be Africans in it wherever possible. That is because I am against the purity of races. I am against the very idea of purity.' For him the French Revolution was a universal event which went beyond France to embrace the whole of humanity.

1796
11 April   Napoleon invades Italy

1799
9–10 November   Napoleon takes power

1804
21 March   Introduction of the Civil Code
18 May   Napoleon proclaimed emperor

1812
Napoleon invades Russia

1814–15
First Bourbon restoration

1815
20 March–22 June   The Hundred Days
18 June   French defeat at Waterloo

1989
July Bicentenary celebrations

Goude's daring spectacle was part of a week of celebrations which had opened on the morning of 11 July with a solemn reading of the Declaration of Human Rights in front of the Palais de Chaillot before 37 of the world's leaders. Backed by the well-amplified humming of a heavenly choir, actors and actresses, including Jane Birkin, read aloud from the works of great revolutionaries including Mirabeau and Condorcet. Thereafter the celebrations included the opening of a new opera house at the Bastille, a symposium of 900 historians from all over the world at the Sorbonne University on the meaning of the Revolution, as well as a meeting of the seven richest countries, the so-called G7.

Having won two presidential elections in 1981 and 1988, President François Mitterrand always had a strong historical consciousness and for him the Bicentenary became something of a personal crusade. The socialist president had taken a leading role in organising the events and from the outset the explicit intention was to celebrate 1789 in a manner which would underline its centrality not just in French history, but in the history of humanity as a whole. By foregrounding the ideas of universal fraternity and human rights Mitterrand wished to underline the enduring legacy of the French Revolution for the forthcoming millennium.

Yet, despite the desire to produce consensus on the meaning of Bicentenary, the celebrations provoked anger within certain quarters of French society. At the beginning of the year several royalist movements combined to form 'Anti-89'. They laid wreaths in the Place de la Concorde in Paris where Louis XVI was guillotined and said mass for the repose of the king's soul. One leading member, Abbé Aulagnier, denounced the Revolution as 'the negation of God and the triumph of rationalism'. In the same vein Philippe de Villiers, a right-wing opposition representative from the Vendée, condemned the celebrations in forthright terms. He characterised the brutal repression of the royalist-led peasant uprising, where an estimated 600,000 Bretons lost their lives, as nothing short of genocide. For de Villiers the Revolution was neither generous nor fraternal. Drawing on the historical research of Reynald Secher he condemned the Revolution as inherently brutal, a precursor of Hitler and Stalin, and he wrote to the president calling on him to remove the name of General Turreau, the man responsible for the 1793 punitive campaign in which one-quarter of Vendéens were killed, from the Arc de Triomphe. Significantly too the attacks on the Bicentenary did not just come from the right. The veteran left-wing commentator Jacques Juillard condemned Mitterrand's celebrations as highly selective. By focusing on the civil rights, freedom of worship for Protestants and Jews, and the Declaration of the Rights of Man and the Citizen, Mitterrand wanted to portray these values as the very essence of the

Revolution. However, in doing so, Juillard argued, he downplayed or ignored not only the questions of social equality but also the conflict between church and state, the regions and the centre, as well as the role of state power and the Terror.

This snapshot from the 1989 controversy is highly revealing and it illustrates some of the central concerns of this book. Firstly, it shows that history is deeply divisive. The French Revolution was a conflictual event which has continued to divide French society ever since. Thus there is no single truth or interpretation but several. Secondly, the Bicentenary highlights how far history is entangled with politics. 1789 inaugurated a long period of internal conflicts and, as we shall see, this civil war was to be constantly fuelled by appeals to the past. In this precise way the Bicentenary points towards the wider historical consciousness that exists beyond the confines of history writing as a professional discipline. Undoubtedly in the Vendée the memory of 1793 has been passed down from one generation to the next, a kind of past that is permanently present, and this explains why this region in the west of France has consistently voted for the right ever since. Thirdly, 1989 underlines why history is such a subversive subject: because it is not just about

history and memory

History as a professional discipline is concerned with the recreation of the past on its own terms using documentary evidence. Beyond the confines of the discipline a wider sense of the past exists within museums, monuments and the media, as well as more intimate cultural forms such as letters, diaries and family photograph albums. Within these different contexts there are different constructions of the past which are often at war with each other: some achieve centrality whilst others are marginalised. In the case of the Bicentenary, de Villiers's defence of an alternative Vendean memory was a direct challenge to the image of the Revolution produced within the official, state-sponsored commemorations. Significantly neither history nor the wider processes of memory are static. History is subject to constant reinterpretation, whilst memory, as it is transmitted from one generation to the next, is always evolving.

the past; it is also about the present and the future. So for some, the Revolution has been a dire warning, whilst for others it has been an inspiration for action, a blueprint for a future society. In this context Goude's belief that the rejection of purity was the message of the Bicentenary was a thinly veiled attack on the politics of Jean-Marie Le Pen's *Front national*. Finally, the Bicentenary reminds us that any understanding of the past is fashioned by the contemporary context. Clearly, by linking the French Revolution to Stalinism and Nazism, de Villiers was seeing 1789 through the prism of the twentieth century. In this way the Bicentenary provides a telling contrast with the hundred-and-fiftieth and hundredth anniversaries. In 1939 commemorations were dominated by the pending threat of war. Thus Jean Renoir's cinematic recreation of the Revolution, his 1938 film *La Marseillaise*, cast the revolutionary wars as a final struggle between free French people and enslaved Prussians, a warning to his compatriots that they must be ready to defend the same rights against Nazi Germany. Likewise 50 years earlier, the commemorations were about the establishment of the fledgling Third

Republic still vulnerable to the threat of royalism. In 1889, therefore, the tone was one of triumphalism where the Third Republic was held up as the political embodiment of the principles of the Revolution.

So, from whatever political angle you view it, the French Revolution is clearly a faultline. Put simply, the French Revolution plunged the continent into the most profound and protracted crisis that it had ever known. It divided the continent of Europe. For the champions of the Revolution it represented an attack on the forces of oppression enshrined in monarchy, nobility and organised religion. For its opponents, it was synonymous with the dangerous forces of mob rule. It is vital, therefore, to have an understanding not only of its causes and phases, but also of its legacy.

Causes

The precise causes of the Revolution have been the subject of endless controversy. Interpretations have not been fixed but have shifted and shifted again, underlining the complex interplay between history and politics. From 1920 until the 1970s the classic Marxist interpretation held sway. This conjured up the Revolution as a rupture in history whose fundamental cause was the transition from feudalism to capitalism. The motor of the Revolution was the revolt of a growing bourgeois capitalist class against the landed aristocracy. Once the bourgeoisie had swept absolutism away and replaced it with a new order supportive of their own economic interests, the stage was set for the titanic struggle between the forces of capitalism and the forces of socialism.

The fact that this mechanistic schema became something of an orthodoxy points to the enormous influence of Marxism within French academia. In 1928 the Sorbonne University in Paris established the prestigious chair in the history of the French Revolution and from the outset the post was a political appointment reserved for historians with a clear commitment to socialism. The first was Albert Mathiez, a champion of the Communist Revolution in Russia, who saw the principles of 1917 as a continuation of those of 1789. He was succeeded by Georges Lefebvre, whose *The Coming of the French Revolution*, published in 1939, argued that four separate movements characterised 1789. These were the aristocratic, bourgeois, peasant and popular revolutions, each of which, because they were motivated by narrow class interests, played their own distinctive role in bringing about the end of absolutism. Lefebvre's successor, Albert Soboul, continued, through his work on the crowd, to present 1789 as a bourgeois revolution.

By the time Soboul died in 1982 the monopoly of the Marxist interpretation was already under attack. The first challenges came from Anglo-Saxon historians. In 1964 Alfred Cobban, a British historian of France, claimed that the bourgeoisie, as understood in the Marxist sense as a class of capitalists, played a relatively small role in the Revolution. Likewise American historians began to decouple 1789 from 1917 and view the French Revolution as part of an Atlantic Revolution that had begun with the American War of Independence against the British in 1776. Within France the major assault on the Marxist interpretation came in the wake of the student rebellion of May 1968. In the intellectual climate of the late 1960s and early 1970s the orthodoxies of right and left were openly challenged. François Furet, himself a former member of the French Communist

Party (PCF), called for an interpretation that was more detached and less political. In doing so he argued that the French Revolution could not be reduced to class conflict. In truth, Furet continued, 1789–95 had less to do with class conflict and much more to do with political struggle between groups within the same class. As such, social continuity was far more significant. It is impossible to overplay the significance of Furet in opening up new interpretative pathways. The Marxist framework had been overturned and the 1970s and 1980s witnessed a mushrooming of research that tried to re-examine the French Revolution in a different light. In place of a narrow class analysis historians such as Keith Baker and Lynn Hunt in America now focused on the language of revolutionary politics, attempting to elucidate what it meant for contemporaries.

Much of this new framework was taken up by the British historian Simon Schama, whose book *Citizens* was published to coincide with the Bicentenary. Again and again, Schama attacked any mechanistic interpretation. For him the term *ancien régime* was a loaded category that implied the inevitability of 1789 when in reality there was much that was dynamic about the absolute monarchy. More than anything, Schama maintained, the Revolution had to be understood as the product of people and politics rather than impersonal historical forces. In this way Schama wanted to underline the significance of the contingent and the accidental, and also the reality of the choices facing the historical actors.

Stylistically *Citizens* was written as a chronological account of the Revolution whose basic message was the folly of undertaking revolution. As such, the impact of the book cannot be separated from the overthrow of communism in Eastern Europe in autumn 1989. The end of these regimes, which had presented themselves as the inheritors of the radical aspects of 1789, led to a general discrediting of the revolutionary tradition.

Inevitably, though, despite the new consensus on the primacy of politics the controversy on causality will continue. In 1774 Louis XVI acceded to the throne. The king was widely regarded as deriving his legitimacy from God, and he shared his power with nobody. In the affairs of state his decision was final even if he had to take advice. Fifteen years later such absolutism collapsed. Below we have identified the key factors in bringing this about, although it is important to underline that there was not one single trigger. Rather it is more accurate to talk about a series of causes stretching back across the century.

1. Economic pressures

Although the French economy witnessed economic growth during the eighteenth century, this growth was highly uneven geographically. Essentially it was limited to the coastal ports which benefited from the slave trade with French possessions in the West Indies. In contrast, interior France remained largely unaffected and experienced worsening deprivation during the course of the eighteenth century. In comparison with Britain, the major rival for Great-Power status, the French economy lacked dynamism in many key areas. Manufacturing was still at a relatively primitive stage. For example, in 1789 Britain had over two hundred factory-type mills whilst France had only eight.

Crucially too a 30 per cent increase in the population during the eighteenth century fragmented landholding and created a pauperisation process. By 1789 the French population stood at 28 million and this demographic pressure put an intolerable strain on the food supply, triggering price rises – they increased three times faster than wages between 1730 and 1789 – and dramatically increasing social tensions. These social tensions were pushed to breaking point with economic depression when the collapse of wine prices in 1778 was followed by a succession of failed grain harvests in the late 1780s. By spring 1789 nearly nine-tenths of an artisan's daily wage was being spent on bread which in turn depressed spending on textile goods and created large-scale rural and urban unemployment. During the spring and summer of 1789 France was gripped by a wave of food riots. Although economic rather than political in origin, these protests formed the backdrop to the calls for an end to absolutism. Significantly they seemed to demonstrate that the system was exhausted. The police force was unable to cope with such a breakdown in law and order, whilst troops made clear their reluctance to fire on ordinary people.

2. Financial crisis

The end of absolutism was also brought about by the financial bankruptcy of the regime. Traditionally absolutist France saw itself as the greatest European power. To defend this position against the challenge of the new powers – Prussia, Russia, but above all Great Britain – France became embroiled in a series of worldwide conflicts which ended in ruination. However, the organisation of society meant that the absolutist state could not unlock the necessary resources to sustain a challenge to British international dominance. The burden of taxation, for example, was haphazard and uneven, principally because the richest groups in society, notably the clergy and the nobility, had established powerful rationales for exemption.

After the Seven Years War (1756–63) not only was France driven out of India and North America, but the country was left with a colossal debt. Servicing it alone accounted for 60 per cent of tax revenues. Some pride was restored by the American War of Independence (1776–83) when the French intervened to support the North American colonists in their successful struggle for independence from the British. However, victory brought no territorial gains whilst on the other hand it precipitated the final fiscal paralysis of the regime. Disastrously the war had been financed by new loans rather than increases in taxation and this massive borrowing now continued into peacetime. It was this credit crisis which finally forced the king to give in to demands for a national body whose sanction was required for peacetime taxation and reform: the Estates-General.

The Estates-General was made up of three separate assemblies: the clergy, the aristocracy and the commoners, the so-called Third Estate. Although the Estates-General had not been summoned since 1614, it was hoped that this body would restore financial confidence. But from the outset there was conflict because the Paris **parlement** decreed that the Estates-General should meet according to the form of its last meeting, whereby each of the three orders had equal weighting. This immediately provoked opposition from the Third Estate, whose leaders demanded voting by head and not order and a doubling of the number of its own representatives. This anger was evident not only in the explosion of articles in the press during the winter of 1788–89, but also in the widespread debates that now took place in cafés and public spaces – testament to the way that politics had been so radically transformed since the seventeenth century. Now politics was no longer about manoeuvring within the confines of the royal court but about the assertion of public opinion. Far and away the most influential pamphlet was *What is the Third Estate?* by Abbé Sieyès. In answer to this provocative question Sieyès argued that in truth the Third Estate was everybody; it was the embodiment of the nation. Yet, in practice it counted for nothing and was excluded from government.

> ### *Parlements*
>
> There were 13 sovereign courts (*parlements*) under the *ancien régime*. Not only did they act as a supreme court of appeal in their particular area, but they also had to register royal edicts before they became law. Membership was made up of a legal elite that was ennobled by virtue of their office. The Paris *parlement* in particular became a major focus of opposition to what was seen as the despotic tendencies of absolutism.

In essence, therefore, 1789 was about the assertion of the Third Estate in a process that began with the election of the Estates-General from January onwards. Undoubtedly this politicised huge numbers of people and the drawing up of lists of grievances, the *cahiers des doléances*, intensified the expectation of change. Thus, when the Estates-General was finally convened on 5 May 1789, the economic crisis rapidly spilt over into a political crisis about royal authority because almost immediately the Third Estate transformed itself into a national representative assembly. In the eyes of the Third Estate it was this assembly, rather than the king, that now had the sovereign power to reform taxation in the name of the French nation. Absolutism was at an end.

3. Intellectual origins

The financial crisis was in turn intimately connected to the growth of public opinion and the intellectual origins of the Revolution. In 1720 the attempt to liquidate the huge royal debt through the creation of a commercial royal bank produced a financial crash that left thousands ruined. Thereafter the royal accounts were subject to increasing scrutiny from a watchful public. Previously monarchs had routinely renounced debts, but from now on this was no longer an option. Henceforth the monarch could not act with financial irresponsibility and in this sense absolutism was severely constrained by the need to maintain public confidence. François Furet links this growth of public opinion as a major factor to the emergence of new forms of political sociability. Since the beginning of the seventeenth century, Furet argues, absolute monarchs had set out to concentrate power in their own hands, thereby undermining traditional institutions such as the *parlements*, guilds and religious communities which had held in place the hierarchy of power extending from the king down to the people. However, as the traditional buffers between ruler and subject were swept aside, the eighteenth century witnessed the creation of a new social sphere, through such entities as masonic lodges,

---

Les Liaisons dangereuses

In 1782 Choderlos de Laclos, an officer in the artillery, published *Les Liaisons dangereuses*. Within the novel a pair of depraved aristocrats plot and achieve the seduction of a young convent girl. Such a frank depiction of a morally corrupt elite, 7 years before the outbreak of Revolution, was an example of the way in which literature was undermining the legitimacy of the absolutist regime.

---

coffee houses and philosophical societies, that allowed individuals to meet without regard to social rank. Within these spaces new democratic ideas began to circulate that challenged the basic precepts of absolutism. These ideas were hostile to what were seen as the despotic tendencies of absolutism, exemplified by any attempt to renounce the royal debt, and were increasingly sceptical about the traditional constitutional structures. In this precise sense, Furet argued, 1789 was about the assertion of this new society which wanted to establish a new political order based upon democratic principles rather than the monarchy and the church.

The growth of public opinion was closely connected to the dramatic rise in literacy. Ironically, this rise was in large part due to the work of church teachers and by 1789 roughly a third of the population could read. In this context the eighteenth century produced a rising demand for printed materials of all kinds. There was a proliferation not only of books, newspapers, periodicals and weeklies, but also of literary and reading societies which meant that the reading public could follow political developments closely. Significantly many of these publications took the form of scurrilous literature, in particular pamphlets and caricatures, which, relating as they did stories of sexual depravity on the part of Queen Marie-Antoinette, did much to damage the legitimacy of the monarchy.

Such a proliferation of reading also facilitated the circulation of the writings of Enlightenment thinkers. Although many were of aristocratic birth, these thinkers challenged the authority of the monarchy, the nobility and the church. Many, such as Montesquieu and Voltaire, were champions of the British system of liberty, toleration and parliamentary government. British success in the wars against the French had shown the strength of the system and what they wanted was a constitutional monarchy where the king would actively govern in partnership with the educated social elite. The clamour for reform was heightened by the American War of Independence in which the French were supporting the Americans, whose rebellion against the British monarchy was fuelled by the idea that George III, in attempting to impose taxation without representation, was acting like a despot. In the wave for all things American that swept France in the wake of victory, many began to argue that the same principles should be applied to France.

The establishment of censorship by Louis XVI shows how far absolutism was frightened by the impact of the printed word. Yet, by the 1780s attempts to control what reached the reading public were simply overwhelmed by market forces, at which point the absolute monarchy implicitly recognised the need to persuade opinion, publishing the first ever statement of royal accounts in 1781. However, although the king's 'ordinary' accounts reassured the public, the fact that they had to be published at all, points towards the way in which absolutism was increasingly constrained.

4. Cultural origins

Finally, Peter Campbell argues that there are two, though he admits not wholly separate, issues to analyse. It is important, he argues, to disentangle the collapse of the *ancien régime* from the Revolution because they are far from identical in their causes. The crisis of 1787–89 was essentially, in Campbell's view, about the breakdown of absolutism. The *ancien régime* was a delicate balancing act that contained many tensions. In the absence of a clear constitutional framework, conflicts between institutions and social groups had the potential to become very dangerous. For instance, during the eighteenth century the Paris and provincial *parlements* became involved in a series of bitter conflicts over the precise limits of monarchical power. The Paris *parlement* in particular began to cast itself as the defender of the nation against the encroachments of absolutism. Thus, when in 1771 de Maupeou, the chancellor, dissolved the Paris *parlement* and tried to restrict its functions to the merely judicial, the monarchy was instantly accused of despotism. In this sense, Campbell continues, 1787–89 has to be seen as the latest in a long series of standoffs. However, what differentiated it from the others was that it spiralled out of control and led to a fundamental questioning of the structures of absolutism. Thereafter it was to be the revolutionary situation itself that created that ideology of the Great Revolution as the terms of debate altered under the pressure of events. Thus the subsequent course of events is not a logical extension of 1787–89.

Phases

In the first instance the Revolution brought about the end of absolutism and what this created was a power vacuum. The task of the Estates-General was to fill this vacuum. However, under the pressure of events the Revolution underwent a relentless process of radicalisation.

1. Capitulation of the absolutist monarchy, May–October 1789

As we have seen, the depth of the financial crisis forced Louis XVI to recall the Estates, but when the Paris *parlement* declared that the three orders should meet and vote separately, the Third Estate rejected this because it would have been outvoted by the two privileged orders. The leaders of the Third Estate, drawn largely from the professional middle classes, in particular lawyers, demanded a doubling of Third Estate deputies and vote by head, thereby giving themselves a majority. The king agreed to doubling but not to voting by head, with the result that there was confusion when the Estates-General met on 5 May. For the leaders of the Third Estate it was self-evident that they represented the majority and on 17 June the Third Estate voted to call itself the National Assembly, claiming that, as the representative of the nation, it had the right to decide taxation. This direct challenge to the legitimacy of absolutism was reinforced by the Tennis Court Oath of 20 June, when the Third Estate took an oath not to disband until France had a constitution. Eventually the king backed down and on 7 July the Estates-General adopted the name National Constituent Assembly.

Bastille Day

Under the Third Republic 14 July became the national day, the focus of secular religion which bound the nation together. Initially Bastille Day was seen to symbolise the fight for political liberties but during the 1920s and 1930s it took on a strongly military and imperial aspect. Now one not only saw the Foreign Legion, with a goat as their mascot, and regiments from North Africa, West Africa and Indo-China, thereby reminding French people that they were at the centre of an immense empire.

However, this was only a tactical retreat on the part of the king. In the meantime he had surrounded Paris with troops with the clear intention of dissolving the Assembly in Versailles. Rumours of counter-revolution now began to circulate and at this point the artisans and workers of Paris, motivated by economic insecurity as well as the hope of reform, rose up on 14 July and attacked the **Bastille**, the huge state prison which dominated the east end of the city. With the help of military deserters they overran the prison and forced its surrender. Confronted with this violence the king ordered the withdrawal of his troops. Thus he lost control of Paris and the National Assembly was saved.

The king also lost control of the countryside. During late July and early August the fear of counter-revolution produced the Great Fear. Fuelled by rumours of aristocratic plots the peasants ransacked rural châteaux, burning manorial records and title deeds to feudal dues. The feudal system was no more and the wish to restore law and order led the politicians at Versailles to quickly recognise this *fait accompli*. On 4 August the Assembly abolished serfdom, the tithe (part of the harvest given to the church), the venality of offices and seigneurial courts. The August Decrees marked the end of noble powers and privileges and prepared the way for a national, uniform and representative system of administration for France. The foundations of this new system were enshrined within the Declaration of the Rights of Man and Citizen on 26 August which established the first principles of a constitutional monarchy. The Declaration stressed natural rights, religious toleration and civil equality. It also underlined freedom of thought and expression. For example, no one was to be imprisoned without a trial. Likewise taxation was to be 'borne equally by all citizens in proportion to their means'. Most importantly of all, political sovereignty now resided in the nation as opposed to the Divine Right of Kings.

However, Louis refused to sanction either the August Decrees or the Declaration of Rights. His intransigence provoked demands that he and the Assembly be brought back from there to Paris. Once again political demands fed off economic discontent – there were huge food shortages in the capital – and on 5 October 7,000 women set off on the five-hour march to Versailles. At Versailles they invaded the Assembly and forced the king to provide Paris with food and to approve the August Decrees and the Declaration of Rights. The following day the king and queen appeared on the balcony and were then escorted back to the Tuileries Palace in Paris, followed shortly after by the deputies. Undoubtedly this was a major turning point in the Revolution. Henceforth the Paris populace was to impose its will on both the king and the deputies.

2. The failure of constitutional monarchy, October 1789–September 1792

The August Decrees dismantled the *ancien régime* and paved the way for the creation of a national, uniform and representative administration for France. The reforms carried out by the Constituent Assembly freed internal trade, thereby creating a national market, and unified a legally diverse country through the introduction of a common constitution, a common coinage, a common metric system of weights and measures and the establishment of French as the common language. They were animated by an uncompromising individualism and in June 1791 laws were introduced which abolished workers' guilds and unions.

The Constitution of 4 September 1791 made France into a constitutional monarchy. The monarch, now defined as the 'king of the French', became a paid office of the state and legislative power now lay with an assembly elected by adult male taxpayers over 25. The aim was to replace a society based upon

Revolution

Through the experience of 1789–95 the word 'revolution' took on a new meaning. Previously it had meant the return to a point of origin as in the complete revolution of a wheel. Henceforth revolution was used to describe the violent transformation of the existing order whereby one type of society was replaced by a different type. Thus in October 1793, to underline the extent to which the French Revolution represented a new beginning for humanity, the revolutionary leaders introduced a new calendar beginning with the anniversary of the declaration of the Republic on 22 September. The names of the months, such as Thermidor, month of heat, and Brumaire, month of mist, evoked the seasons and remained in use until 1806.

birthright with one based upon talent, where merit and money would determine the social standing of any one individual. So when the Assembly talked about equality, they meant the equality of rights and opportunities and most definitely not social and economic equality. Thus people should be free to worship as they chose, as witnessed by the religious emancipation of the Jews and Protestants, and they should also have the same rights in law; but social inequalities were seen as a fundamental trait of society which could not be altered.

Within France there was little opposition to this reform process until the Civil Constitution of the Clergy in July 1790. Under this the priests and bishops were elected and became paid officials of the state. However, by rejecting papal authority over the church in France the Civil Constitution put the clergy into a terrible dilemma over whether or not to take the civic oath. Half of the lower clergy and all but seven of the bishops refused and, in March and April 1791, the pope, Pius V, condemned the Civil Constitution as well as the other reforms of the Revolution, above all the confiscation of church lands in November 1789. Crucially this papal opposition fuelled hostility to the Revolution in areas such as the ultra-Catholic Vendée and was to provide the counter-revolution with a popular base. Moreover, it stiffened the resolve of the king, who now tried to flee abroad in order to find support among the declared enemies of the Revolution. Late on the night of 20 June

Map 1.1   The departments of France in 1790
Source: *D.M.G. Sutherland,* France, 1789–1815: Revolution and Counter-Revolution.

despite his disguise he was recognised and stopped at Varennes. Returning to Paris he was received by the populace in icy silence. Psychologically it was a huge turning point. He had betrayed the nation and now people began to call openly for a republic, a view that was fuelled by the fierce repression of a pro-republican demonstration by the National Guard at the Champs de Mars, a meadow just outside of Paris.

Ultimately the fate of the monarchy was to be sealed by the French declaration of war on Austria and Prussia in April 1792. The immediate causes of conflict were the discredit of the king, the combined threats of the Prussian and Austrian monarchies (which wished to restore absolutism) and the increasingly aggressive tone of the Assembly. However, the fundamental cause was whether two forms of society based upon totally opposed principles could coexist side by side. In this very precise sense the French revolutionary wars were to be a new type of war because they were not about territory, but about political ideas.

In the Assembly the clamour for war was led by a group of deputies from the Gironde region, the Girondins, who believed that foreign conflict would rally support for the Revolution. In practice, war was to destroy the 1789 consensus by unleashing a process of ceaseless radicalisation. Soon the king was suspected of secretly desiring an Austrian victory, which in turn provoked a surge in support for the Jacobin party in the Assembly, so called because of the old Paris monastery where they met. Led by Danton and Robespierre, the Jacobins were fervent believers in a centralised republic, the extension of the vote and the introduction of state economic controls. The Jacobin power base was in Paris through their strong links with the **sans-culottes** and their assumption of leadership of the National Guard, and this was to prove decisive on 10 August 1792 when the

> ### sans-culottes
>
> These were Parisian shopkeepers, artisans and workers. The term, meaning literally without breeches, differentiated the ordinary people from the aristocracy. Through direct action the sans-culottes pushed the Revolution in a socially radical direction with legislation such as the Law of Maximum on 29 September 1793 which fixed prices and wages.

sans-culottes attacked the Tuileries Palace, intimidated the Assembly into imprisoning the king and demanded elections by universal male suffrage. The following day the Assembly also handed over executive power to an emergency committee of six ministers under the effective leadership of Danton which agreed to replace the Assembly with a Convention, elected by universal male suffrage. On 21 September, the Convention abolished the monarchy.

3. The popular revolution, September 1792–July 1794

The Prussian invasion caused a panic in Paris. The enemy was now at the gates and this triggered two days of massacres in early September where over a thousand royalist prisoners were slaughtered under the direction of the new revolutionary Paris Commune led by the Jacobin journalist Marat. The Prussians were defeated at Valmy on 20 September and from then on the French were on the offensive. On 19 November Convention proclaimed the 'Edict of Fraternity' calling on the peoples of Europe to overthrow their rulers. The Jacobins were now in the ascendancy and this radicalisation was related not just to the war, but also to economic deterioration. Confronted with widespread food shortages, the *sans-culottes*, through their control of the Paris municipal council or Commune, which in effect became a rival authority in the capital, looked to the Convention for measures to control prices. Furthermore, the king was put on trial, found guilty of treason and executed on 21 January 1793, but the following month the Convention declared war on Holland and Britain.

Within the Convention politics was now dominated by the bitter conflict between the Jacobins and the Girondins. Robespierre accused the Girondins of wishing to conspire with royalist forces and encouraged the *sans-culottes* to rise up against the Girondin deputies. On 2 June 1793 the *sans-culottes* surrounded the Convention and arrested leading Girondins. At this point the Revolution was under threat from all sides with military defeat against the Austrians, a rising in the Vendée against conscription, a federal revolt in the provinces against the dominance of the Paris Commune over the Convention and rampant inflation. In response the Convention set up a Revolutionary

La Marseillaise

On 30 July 1792 volunteers from Marseille arrived in Paris singing the 'Chant de guerre pour l'armée du Rhin', composed a few months earlier by Joseph Rouget de Lisle, a young army officer. The song was immediately called *La Marseillaise* and henceforth its rousing words would be sung whenever the revolutionary cause was in danger. The song eventually became the French national anthem. Initially associated with the left, it would also be appropriated by the right as a symbol. In 1979, the *enfant terrible* of French pop music, Serge Gainsbourg, recorded a reggae version of *La Marseillaise* with Jamaican producers Sly Dunbar and Robbie Shakespeare. The fact that Gainsbourg, a Jew, had the temerity to record the national anthem with two Rastafarians caused outrage on the right. The right-wing daily *Le Figaro* suggested that Gainsbourg should have his citizenship revoked and at a concert in Strasbourg Gainsbourg was attacked by a group of ex-paratroopers. Two years later Gainsbourg continued his provocation by purchasing the original Rouget de Lisle manuscript at a public auction.

Tribunal and a Committee of Public Safety which, after the fall of the Girondins, was dominated by Robespierre. From now on the Committee of Public Safety used extreme methods to defend the Republic, driving out the invaders, crushing the Federal revolt, controlling food prices and rooting out enemies. In what became known as the Terror, the Committee of Public Safety executed royalists, Girondins and profiteers. Then Hebert, who had wanted to go too far towards social revolution, and Danton, who wanted to end the Terror and the war, were also guillotined. In the meantime the new constitution provided for universal male suffrage and for an elected government. But as long as the Committee of Public Safety maintained its grip, this remained a dead letter.

Soon everyone in the Convention was so terrified that they dared not criticise the Committee, but in the end Robespierre over-reached himself. On 26 July 1794, which in the French Revolutionary calendar was 8 Thermidor, he accused colleagues on the Committee of Public Safety of conspiracy. In self-defence they turned against Robespierre and on 28 July he and 105 of his supporters were executed.

4.   From the Republic of the Thermidorians to Bonapartism, July 1794–June 1815

In September 1795 the new constitution replaced the Convention with the Directory. Now the democratic and egalitarian aspirations of 1793 were abandoned in favour of a return to the principles of 1791 as the electorate was reduced by means of a property qualification. Executive power was placed in the hands of a five-man directorate which tried to steer a middle path between Jacobinism, republicanism and the royalists. Thus the *sans-culotte* insurrection of May 1795 was brutally suppressed, as was the royalist revolt of the following October. In this context the Directory was increasingly forced to rely upon the army to maintain order, in particular the young General Napoleon Bonaparte who had enjoyed a string of remarkable military successes in Italy against Austria. By November 1799 the Directory was extremely unpopular and at this point Bonaparte carried out a coup in collusion with Sieyès and Ducos. Now the Directory was transformed into the Consulate, with executive power concentrated in a triumvirate of consuls in the persons of Sieyès, Roger Ducos and Napoleon himself.

Quickly Napoleon manoeuvred his way to unlimited power, using his position as first consul to restructure the police, local government and the criminal court system. Then in May 1803, flushed with the Peace of Amiens which brought temporary peace and confirmed France as the dominant force on the continent, he made himself consul for life, a move that was ratified by 3.5 million votes to 8,000 in a popular plebiscite. The constitution was quickly amended to give him dictatorial powers and then on 2 December 1804 he crowned himself emperor at Notre Dame.

In many respects the Bonapartist regime must be understood as a creation of the Revolution. Napoleon himself was from relatively humble origins, he was born in Corsica in 1769, the son of a lawyer of noble ancestry, and he was a fervent believer in meritocracy. From the outset, therefore, he sought to create a new and talented elite, where service to the state, especially in the army, was rewarded. During the Consulate Napoleon carried out major reforms, bringing the provinces under central control through the appointment of prefects, reforming the tax structure and creating a central Bank of France. Furthermore, after the religious tumult of the Revolution, he reached a settlement with Pope Pius VII, the famous

rights of women

Olympe de Gouges was a butcher's daughter from Montauban, born in 1748. From the late 1780s onwards she wrote pamphlets calling for greater rights for women. Angered by the way in which women had been excluded from the Constituent Assembly, de Gouges penned *Les Droits de la femme* as a retort to *Les Droits de l'homme*. Within it she proclaimed that women, no less than men, were members of the nation. After opposing the Terror de Gouges was guillotined in 1793.

slavery

In 1792 the French plantation colony of Saint-Domingue in the Caribbean witnessed a huge uprising by 450,000 black slaves. Led by Toussaint L'Ouverture and inspired by events in France, the rebellion led to the first abolition of slavery in modern times, a fact that was endorsed by the Convention in February 1794. Despite attempts to reintroduce slavery by Napoleon, the former slaves established the independent state of Haiti in 1804.

Concordat of 15 July 1801, which reaffirmed the public right of worship whilst simultaneously ratifying the nationalisation of church property. However, Napoleon's most enduring legacy was to be the Civil Code of 1804 which replaced the 360 local codes still in force in 1789. Under the Code, known from 1807 onwards as the Napoleonic Code, the decisive reforms of 1789 – equality before the law, religious toleration, the abolition of feudalism and freedom of enterprise – were safeguarded. The sale of *émigrés'* and church property was also confirmed, which placed property owners firmly behind Napoleon, as was the Revolutionary principle of the subdivision of estates between male heirs. Moreover, paternal authority within the family was restored and the rights of women, who were officially classed as minors, were severely curtailed.

Napoleon realised that he could not ignore the politicisation of the lower orders, a factor which he tried to institutionalise through plebiscites. In doing so he invoked the idea of the nation but in a way that was very different from the ideology that had fuelled the earlier revolutionary movement. Bonapartist definitions replaced the state for people, bureaucracy for democracy, passive obedience for active citizenship. The equation of the nation with the people now disappeared behind the imperatives of order and discipline. Obedience and authority were everything.

The peace of 1802 quickly gave way to war. Although on land Napoleon came to dominate continental Europe through successive defeats of Austria and Prussia, plans to invade Britain were thwarted by naval defeat at Trafalgar in 1805. Nonetheless by 1811 the Napoleonic Empire stretched from the Baltic to the Adriatic with client states in Germany, Italy and Poland. It was the high point of his power, but after the failure of his invasion of Russia in 1812 Napoleon was on the defensive, and in 1814 he was forced to abdicate and exiled to Elba. He escaped in March 1815 but after defeat at Waterloo on 18 June he spent the rest of his life as a prisoner on St Helena in the Atlantic.

Map 1.2   Napoleon's empire, 1812
This map is extracted from The Rough Guide History of France, *with permission from Rough Guides Ltd, published October 2002.*

Legacy

What was the legacy of 1789–1815? On the one hand, despite the enormous upheaval, there was little change in the social elite. In 1802 the vast majority of the wealthiest landowners were still the pre-1789 nobility. Amongst the lower orders the greatest social change took place in the peasantry, who, in ending feudalism, safeguarded itself and its landholdings.

In this sense the most potent legacy of 1789–1815 was in the realm of political ideas. It was a protean event that generated a whole series of reflexes, assumptions and structures. In the first place the definitions of left and right in politics were derived from the Estates-General, where the nobles positioned themselves to the right of the king, while the Third Estate sat on the left. These divisions became even more pronounced in the Convention after 1793 when the Jacobins occupied benches in the left and upper sections of the chamber. The opposition between right and left has dominated the French political mindset ever since.

In the same way the Revolution defined the ideologies of liberalism, socialism and conservatism. The essence of liberalism, the belief in the equality of rights and the equality of opportunities, is to be found in the Declaration of the Rights of Man, while the *sans-culottes*, with their belief in greater social and economic equality, can be seen as the harbingers of socialism. Equally, the counter-revolution with its adherence to God and the monarchy can be viewed as the fulcrum of conservatism. No less importantly, the Revolution fashioned the concept of national sovereignty and once this genie was out of the bottle, there was no turning back. Henceforth no regime could rely upon ideas of tradition, custom and divine right. The masses had intervened in politics and now legitimacy had to come from below through some element of popular consent. Likewise the introduction of military service in August 1793 was another innovation that had far-reaching consequences. By establishing the principle that the state has the right to command the service of all its citizens, this system led to the modern citizen army and transformed war from a battle between armies into a conflict between whole nations. As such, the Revolution has to be seen as a revolution in rationality and uniformity. It was an attempt to remodel France into a new set of arrangements and institutions. The efficiency of this new system was to provide a model of how modern states organise themselves.

If rationality has marked French political culture deeply ever since 1789–95, so too has universalism, a belief in the world historical mission that would soon justify colonial expansion. By the same token the Revolution established different spheres for men and women which became deeply embedded within republican culture. Women were excluded from citizenship and their political organisations were banned, a process that was virtually complete by autumn 1793. Essentially women were confined to the domestic sphere where they were expected to rear the children in republican principles. But, although marginalised politically, women came to be central symbolically. Marianne, the female allegory of liberty, was the embodiment of republican virtues.

Finally, however, it was a legacy that could be taken in many different, and often opposing, directions. So on 1 November 1954 Algerian nationalists justified their rebellion in terms of the right of the Algerian people to national self-determination. Twelve days later the interior minister, François Mitterrand, told the National Assembly, in a speech that was soaked in the imagery of 1793 revolutionary patriotism, that Algeria was an integral part of the Fourth Republic. In the face of rebellion, Mitterrand went on, the only possible negotiation was war.

Document 1a: Extract from *Les Droits de l'homme et du citoyen*, 26 August 1789

Les représentants du peuple français, constitués en Assemblée nationale, considérant que l'ignorance, l'oubli ou le mépris des droits de l'homme sont les seules causes des malheurs publics et de la corruption des gouvernements, ont résolu d'exposer, dans une déclaration solennelle, les droits naturels, inaliénables et sacrés de l'homme, afin que cette déclaration, constamment présente à tous les membres du corps social, leur rappelle sans cesse leurs droits et leurs devoirs; afin que les actes du pouvoir législatif et ceux du pouvoir exécutif, pouvant être à chaque instant comparés avec le but de toute institution politique, en soient plus respectés; afin que les réclamations des citoyens, fondées désormais sur des principes simples et incontestables, tournent toujours au maintien de la Constitution et au bonheur de tous.

En conséquence, l'Assemblée nationale reconnaît et déclare, en présence et sous les auspices de l'Être Suprême, les droits suivants de l'homme et du citoyen.

Article premier – Les hommes naissent et demeurent libres et égaux en droits. Les distinctions sociales ne peuvent être fondées que sur l'utilité commune.

Article 2 – Le but de toute association politique est la conservation des droits naturels et imprescriptibles de l'homme. Ces droits sont la liberté, la propriété, la sûreté et la résistance à l'oppression.

Article 3 – Le principe de toute souveraineté réside essentiellement dans la Nation. Nul corps, nul individu ne peut exercer d'autorité qui n'en émane expressément.

Article 4 – La liberté consiste à pouvoir faire tout ce qui ne nuit pas à autrui: ainsi, l'exercice des droits naturels de chaque homme n'a de bornes que celles qui assurent aux autres membres de la société la jouissance de ces mêmes droits. Ces bornes ne peuvent être déterminées que par la loi.

Topics
FOR DISCUSSION

1 Why did the Bicentenary provoke controversy? What does the controversy tell us about the nature of history?
2 What were the causes of the French Revolution?
3 According to Document 1a, what were the principles of the initial phase of the Revolution?
4 What were the phases of the Revolution?
5 What has been the legacy of the Revolution?

CHAPTER 2

Timeline

1815
June–September   Ultra-royalist forces institute a 'White Terror'
8 July   King Louis XVIII enters Paris
14–21 August   The ultra-royalists sweep to victory in elections
20 November   The treaty of Paris returns France to pre-1790 frontiers

1816
September   Louis dissolves the Chamber of Deputies
8 December   Marshal Ney is executed for having rallied to Napoleon

1819
November   The moderate Decazes forms a new government

1820
13 February   Duc de Berry, Louis XVIII's nephew, is assassinated by a Bonapartist

1821
5 May   Napoleon dies on St Helena

1823
April   France intervenes in Spain to restore Ferdinand VII, who had been faced with liberal revolt

1824
February–March   The Right wins elections
16 September   Louis XVIII dies

1825
29 May   Charles X crowned at Rheims

1827
April   The Dey of Algiers strikes the French consul with a flywhisk. The French blockade Algeria

The Bourbon Restoration, 1814–30

A major question dominated nineteenth-century France: what was to be done with the revolutionary-imperial heritage? The main problem was that there was no obvious agreement about the nature and value of this heritage. Memory of the Revolution could be highly selective. Some preferred to remember the liberal principles of 1789; others the egalitarianism of 1793; others still Jacobin nationalism, the Terror or the glory of the Napoleonic wars. These conflicting memories were constantly mobilised to inform political options. In such a polarised context, the search for a synthesis, or at least a balanced political solution, was to be a long and argumentative one. Constitutional instability became a salient feature of French political life. France tried out four different regimes from 1815 to 1870: the Restoration of the Bourbons (1814–1830), the July Monarchy (1830–1848), the Second Republic (1848–1852) and the Second Empire (1852–1870). Why did France fail to find an acceptable form of government over this period? In this chapter and the following one the failure to impose a constitutional monarchy will be addressed.

Nineteenth-century France also experienced substantial economic and social changes. The development of industry and capitalism, the rise

1828

January   Appointment of the more moderate Martignac government

1829

August   Charles X dismisses Martignac. He is replaced by de Polignac, a diehard ultra

1830

18 March   Standoff between Charles X and the liberal deputies
16 June   French force lands in Algeria
5 July   Algiers is taken
June–July   Elections reinforce the liberal majority
27–9 July   Revolution overthrows the Bourbon dynasty
9 August   Louis-Philippe is proclaimed king

of a bourgeois elite and the emergence of the working class will be treated in the next chapter. The relations between political instability and social conflicts generated by the industrial revolution are difficult to assess. The elite, whether monarchist or bourgeois, certainly feared the entrance of the masses and of socialism into politics. However, it is debatable whether class struggles were the prime reason for political instability. Initially, the 'dangerous classes', as they were portrayed by the elite, were not particularly responsive to socialism and could even support conservative solutions, as will be seen in Chapter 4. Instead of class struggle, political conflict was the primary dynamic, a conflict which opposed the principles of 1789, modernity, progress, liberalism and laicity to the values of tradition, authority and clericalism.

The Charter and the foundations of constitutional monarchy

The Restoration of the Bourbons was the first experience of **constitutional monarchy** in France. It was a testing time, witnessing the emergence of a parliamentary system. It also exemplified how difficult it was to find a lasting compromise between polarised memories of the Revolution.

The restored monarchy was supposed to be a moderate one. The organisation of the regime rested on the Charter granted by King Louis XVIII, brother of Louis XVI. It was not a constitution resulting from a debate about the nature of the pact which should have united the nation and the monarchy. It was a gift from the monarch who could at any time modify or suppress what he had conceded of his own free will. The Charter did not recognise national sovereignty. The preamble clearly stated that the king was king because 'divine Providence [had brought him] back to [his] realm after a long absence'. A direct link with pre-revolutionary France was thus maintained. The

Constitutional monarchy

As opposed to a monarchy of divine right, this system of government is rooted in a set of rules (constitution) which define the respective prerogatives and powers of the monarch and of the parliament, which may or may not be democratically elected.

powers of the king were central. His person was declared 'sacred and inviolable'. He disposed of the executive power, appointed ministers, had the sole right to initiate legislation and could dissolve parliament at will. Article 14 gave him emergency powers, so he could rule by decree. The Charter, however, integrated some constitutional principles inherited from the Revolution and the Empire. Equality before the law, personal liberties and freedom of expression were recognised as essential. Trial by jury guaranteed the rights of individuals. Property was declared inviolable, including property confiscated during the Revolution from the church and *émigrés*. Parliamentary consent was required for taxation. The Chamber of Deputies was to be elected by a wealthy minority. Only men older than 30 and paying at least 300 FF in direct tax had the right to elect men older than 40 and paying at least 1,000 FF in direct tax. The House of Peers was appointed by the king, but peers were first chosen among the Empire's civil servants. Both chambers could appeal to the king to introduce legislation. The Charter, thus, was supposed to keep at equal distance national sovereignty and the *ancien régime*.

Despite Louis' motto – union and forgetfulness – the Restoration started in an atmosphere of revenge. The fall of Napoleon at Waterloo triggered a wave of vicious punitive executions against Bonapartists, liberals and Protestants, all seen as the natural enemies of the Bourbons. In the South of France, in particular, royalist mobs, encouraged by the Comte d'Artois, the king's brother, lynched prominent officers who had rallied around the emperor during the Hundred Days. They also harassed Protestant communities, ransacking their homes and places of worship. This 'White Terror' was accompanied by official purges and trials organised by special courts. A large number of officers who had served the imperial armies were demoted or forced to retire. The death penalty passed against Marshal Ney, a glorious hero of the Empire, generated much public resentment. Seventy prefects were sacked. The Civil Service, the French Academy and the University were stripped of their 'subversive' elements. Fanatical aristocrats encouraged this wave of terror. One of their leaders, La Bourdonnaye, shouted: 'We need chains, executioners, torture: death, death!'

In this fearful atmosphere a new Chamber was elected. It was dominated by a massive majority of royalist deputies (350 out of 402), most of them ultra-royalist (*les Ultras*). Louis was surprised by this electoral result and thought it was a sign that the monarchy was popular. However, this chamber (*chambre introuvable*) soon became a thorn in his side. Whereas the king would have liked to appease strong feelings and unite the two Frances divided by the legacy of the Revolution, the Ultras derided his cautious approach. Insolently, they shouted 'Long live the king, even so!' Organised in secret societies, such as **Les Chevaliers de la Foi**, and enjoying the full support of the king's brother, their programme was drenched in the language of religious reaction. France had to expiate her revolutionary sins. Ostentatious religious processions were organised, hell-fire sermons were delivered by zealous missionaries and crosses were erected throughout the kingdom as a sign of collective repentance. Fearing that the excesses of the

Chevaliers de la Foi

Created under the empire, this secret society believed that a freemason conspiracy triggered the Revolution. Devoted to the alliance between the throne and the altar, it provided Ultra deputies with organisational and political support, under the leadership of Montmorency, a reactionary Catholic. Denounced by liberals as an occult government opposed to the king's government, it enjoyed the protection of Artois, the king's brother. Relying on some 100 deputies in the *chambre retrouvée*, it forced Villèle to introduce reactionary legislation.

Chamber would put his throne at risk, the king opted for its dissolution. The 1816 elections resulted in a majority conforming more to his views. Dominated by moderate royalists (*Ministériels*) without a clear doctrinal coherence, the majority was determined to make the Charter work. An influential but small group of intellectuals, known as *les Doctrinaires* (Guizot, Royer-Collard), strove to define the Charter as an ideal compromise between a strong king and a parliament exclusively composed of hereditary nobles and the wealthiest members of the bourgeoisie.

1816–20: 'Union and forgetfulness'?

From 1816 to 1820 the successive Richelieu and Decazes governments rejected both democracy and reaction: rather they tried to root the monarchy's legitimacy in the Charter. They cautiously implemented a moderate programme with the support of the king and the Chambers. In 1817 the Lainé law reformed the electoral system. One-fifth of the Chamber of Deputies was to be renewed each year and all taxpayers over 30 who paid at least 300 FF in taxes could vote. The electoral body was nearly doubled and more than 90,000 wealthy Frenchmen were given the right to vote. However, it also enfranchised part of the middle class which was more likely to favour liberal ideals. Legislation was introduced to liberalise the press. Censorship was gradually relaxed. Paradoxically, Ultras and liberals joined forces to defend press freedom and to protect their respective newspapers against censorship. Consequently, offences for which newspapers could be prosecuted were narrowed, trials by jury, rather than by a criminal court, were introduced and caution money was abolished. Finally, in 1818 the Gouvion Saint-Cyr law, aimed at reorganising the military forces after the dissolution of the imperial army, made new provisions for promoting officers. It enraged the Ultras, who believed that the profession of officers should remain the sole preserve of the nobility. Conscription was maintained but the sons of the wealthiest families were allowed to buy their way out. In reality, ill-trained nobles were often promoted at the expense of experienced imperial officers. This encouraged resentment towards the regime and revived Bonapartist nostalgia.

This moderate interpretation of the Charter met with mounting difficulties. The annual renewal of the Chamber of Deputies between 1817 and 1819 saw a rapid increase in the liberal opposition. In 1819 the so-called Independent group, made up of disparate elements, including liberals, Jacobins and Bonapartists, won 35 of the 55 renewable seats, whereas the Ultras won 6 seats and the *Ministériels* 14. The Ultras, haunted by the memory of the liberal concessions which had precipitated the fall of the *ancien régime*, violently opposed the conciliatory policy of the king's ministers. In February 1820 the assassination of the Duc de Berry, the only heir to the throne able to ensure the continuity of the dynasty, marked the end of moderation. The Ultras argued that the assassination was to be imputed directly to Decazes' leniency towards liberal ideas. Soon they regained the upper hand. Drastic measures were immediately introduced to limit public liberties and to muzzle the opposition. The press was to endure reinforced censorship. Newspapers could be suspended or suppressed by royal courts if they 'had a tendency to endanger law and order, the

respect due to the state religion, the authority of the king or the stability of constitutional government'. The Universities were to
be more strictly controlled and under the
growing influence of the Jesuits. Above all, a
new electoral law was introduced (*la loi du
double vote*), which allowed voters who paid
the highest amount of tax in a *département*
to vote twice. Prefects falsified electoral lists
and liberal deputies were constantly harassed
and intimidated. Manuel, a bourgeois deputy
elected against an aristocrat in the Vendée,
was expelled from the Chamber because he
had 'insulted' the memory of Louis XVI. Thus
the Ultras ignored the Charter which was supposed to protect deputies' freedom of
speech. Some Bonapartist officers and liberal
students, disillusioned with the regime, con-

> ### Spanish expedition (1823)
>
> With the backing of her previous
> 'enemies' (Russia, Austria and
> Prussia), French armies invaded
> Spain to crush the liberal forces in
> that country which opposed King
> Ferdinand's brutal rule. The king
> rejected any evolution of the
> regime towards constitutional
> monarchy, and uprisings were
> organised throughout Spain. The
> French troops crossed the border
> to save Ferdinand from
> 'revolutionaries', and remained in
> Spain until 1828 to guard the
> monarchy against its liberal
> enemies.

spired in a secret society, *la Charbonnerie*. Organised in some 60 *départements* and
numbering around 40,000 men, it launched a series of plots between 1820 and 1822,
aimed at overthrowing the regime. Its repeated failures had no result other than reinforcing government repression. For instance, individuals suspected of conspiracy
could be detained for three months without trial. Bonapartist officers, however, were
soon appeased and their patriotism rekindled by the successful **Spanish expedition
(1823)** when 100,000 men were sent to the rescue of the Spanish king, whose throne
had been endangered by a liberal rebellion. The romantic appeal of foreign expedi-
tions away from the boredom of provincial garrisons, the prospect of promotion
gained on the battlefield and the renewed prestige granted to the French armies, for a
time restored their loyalty to the Bourbons.

Charles X and the Ultras

These overtly anti-liberal measures successfully tamed the opposition and in the
1824 elections only 19 liberal deputies were elected. The Ultra majority was massive
(50 per cent of the deputies were former *émigrés*, 60 per cent belonged to the
noblesse). This *chambre retrouvée* was also more right-wing than the *chambre introuvable*. If ultracism was tolerated by the sick and bedridden Louis XVIII, it was actively
encouraged by Artois, who became King Charles X in 1824. Charles was crowned in
Rheims, following an archaic ceremony which celebrated the renewed alliance
between the throne and the altar. Indulging in the medieval rite of touching the scro-
fulous, and anointed by an archbishop whose sermon severely criticised the Charter,
the king clearly intended to reassert the divine nature of his power. **Chateaubriand**
noted in his *Mémoires d'Outre-Tombe*: 'I would have preferred to see no pomp today:
the king on horseback, the church unadorned [...] Today was to be the regeneration

(François-René) Chateaubriand (1768–1848)

Breton aristocrat, diplomat and leading romantic writer. Exiled in Britain (1793-1800) during the Great Revolution, he became convinced that constitutional monarchy was the best form of government. His early fictional work (*René*, 1802) celebrated the victory of Christianity over paganism. An acerbic critic of Napoleon, he supported the Bourbons and became a peer (1815), ambassador to London (1822), and foreign secretary (1823–24) before withdrawing from political life in 1830. He thought that the monarchy could recapture the fervour of the people by allying the defence of tradition with the need for more freedom.

of the monarchy: it could have restarted with religion and freedom: unfortunately, there was not much love for freedom.' The image of Charles prostrated at the feet of the archbishop encapsulated the clerical tone of the regime. The church was given a greater voice in state affairs, and in the field of education its influence was increased from primary schools to the universities. A ministry of ecclesiastical affairs was created. A new law concerning sacrilege in churches was introduced. It imposed long prison sentences and the death penalty for those who stole holy vessels and profaned the host. The domination of the church was often imputed to the Jesuits. Popular suspicion against the occult power of the clergy gained ground and conspiracy theories started to abound. The violence with which the clergy denounced the Revolution and its legacy, including freedom of consciousness, provoked derision and anger against a priest-ridden government. Anti-clericalism ran high amongst the enlightened bourgeoisie, the National Guard and the popular classes, who resented and ridiculed the clergy.

Further, the preferential treatment of landed aristocrats within the bureaucracy and the army gave the impression that it was not only the Bourbons, but the *ancien régime* which had been restored. The decision to compensate generously former *émigrés* whose land had been confiscated during the Revolution generated heated debates. Liberals stigmatised the *milliard des émigrés* (the *émigrés'* billion) financed by national debt, as an unfair and heavy burden on the nation, benefiting only the wealthiest noble families. Some Ultras called for the immediate restitution of 'stolen' properties to their rightful owners, thus ignoring the guarantees provided by the Charter. In this context the House of Peers played a moderating role. Concerned with the defence of civil liberties, peers rejected a plan voted by the Chamber which would have compelled newspapers to submit their articles for approval five days before they were published. It also prevented the restoration of an inheritance law for the sole benefit of the elder son, a plan which would have enraged the bourgeoisie by eroding the principle of equality before the law.

The Villèle ministry (1821–27) attempted to dilute the Ultras' demands into a more moderate programme. Villèle's lacklustre character and his constant scheming and hedging failed to satisfy his majority, which decidedly refused any form of compromise. In fact, it was hard to maintain discipline among the large Ultra majority. Although it had the support of the king, it was divided by personal rivalries and lacked political coherence. Montmorency and La Bourdonnaye, on the extreme right, led a 'counter-opposition' whose attacks on Villèle gradually became more violent. They wished to abolish a monarchy based on the Charter and rejected *en bloc* the heritage of the Revolution. 'What distinguishes the French Revolution', Joseph de Maistre wrote in his *Considérations sur la France*, 'and what makes it a unique event in history, is that it is radically bad [...] It is the highest level of corruption known.' They dreamt of restoring not so much the *ancien régime*, but a quasi-feudal system, based on clericalism and the decentralised power of the landed nobility. For them society rested on natural communities (families, parishes and provinces), organically organised and hierarchically ordered. Paradoxically, in insisting that ministers were also responsible to the 'Ultra Chamber', they enabled **parliamentarism** to take root. Conversely other Ultras, led by Chateaubriand, wished to find a compromise between the monarchy and modern liberties. They

> ### parliamentarism
>
> A political system based upon a necessary conformity of views between government and public opinion, expressed through parliamentary majority. It rests on the principle of political responsibility. Governments must resign if they lose the support of parliament. Because of the hereditary character of his function, the king should not dissolve parliament to impose his own views. Elections should be called to adjudicate between government and parliament. The Charter did not stipulate whether ministers were responsible to the king or to parliament. This was to be a major source of conflict. Gradually and empirically the principle of political responsibility was to impose itself.

fought for freedom of the press and argued that an extension of suffrage would rally the lower echelons of society to the monarchy. The monarchy had nothing to fear from freedom. To accelerate the natural movement towards progress would be disastrous, but to remain obsessed with obsolete ideas would be equally dangerous. In his *Monarchie selon la Charte*, Chateaubriand indeed argued: 'I see the salvation of the country [...] in the union of former mores and modern political institutions, our fathers' good sense and the advanced ideas of this century [and] in the alliance of religion and freedom rooted in the law.' Gradually, this group became known as the Defectors as their opposition to Villèle's obsession with political control grew.

The liberal opposition, harshly repressed in the early 1820s, started to re-emerge and formed the core of the opposition to the Bourbons. Gathered in a society named *Aide-toi, le Ciel t'aidera*, whose prime objective was to ensure electoral mobilisation, the opposition nevertheless remained very fragmented. Liberals, who claimed to be the heirs of 1789, strongly resented the prevalent clericalism and the reactionary orientation of the regime. They saw themselves as the standard-bearers of liberty. One of their leaders, Benjamin Constant, noted in 1829, 'I have defended the same principle for 40 years. Liberty in everything: in religion, philosophy, industry, and politics. By liberty I mean the triumph of the individual over powers trying to govern by despotism and over masses demanding the right to subjugate the minority to the majority. Despotism has no rights.' Although, initially, liberals wanted a change of policy, rather than a change of regime, they were ready to voice their opposition whenever the fundamental achievements of 1789 were jeopardised. They were joined by Bonapartists, especially officers, dismissed by the regime after Waterloo, who had no obvious leader after the death of the emperor in 1821. The *Doctrinaires*, who had defended the constitutional monarchy in the early years of the regime, were drawn towards the liberals because of the Ultras' excesses. Finally, the Republican opposition was still very weak and disorganised. So-called 'American' republicans, loosely gathered around General La Fayette, followed a strategy which respected the law, whereas 'Montagnard' republicans, led by General Cavaignac, were inspired by the Jacobin Revolution of 1793 and were willing to mount an insurrection.

Polarisation and the 1830 Revolution

The reliance on repressive measures, the unwillingness to build consensus, the introduction of reactionary policies, often marked by bigotry, the contempt in which the Charter was held and the failure to broaden the regime's social base encouraged further political polarisation which ultimately was to be fatal to the regime. Confronted with an increased opposition on his right and his left, Villèle thought he could reaffirm his authority by dissolving the Chamber in 1827. Despite much electoral manipulation the results were unfavourable to Villèle: 170 seats went to the liberal opposition, as many to the ministry and 75 to the extreme right. Grudgingly the king appointed Martignac, a moderate liberal, whose attempt to calm the political situation was persistently sabotaged by the king himself and his Ultra coterie. The Martignac ministry brought about an illusory truce, allowing political enemies to sharpen their knives. Charles had no intention of taking into account the makeup of the Chamber and in 1829 he dismissed Martignac to impose a ministry that was to his liking. For the king the choice of Prince Polignac was supposed to restore royal supremacy over so-called parliamentary anarchy. For most deputies and the liberal press the Polignac ministry was the surest sign that the king had chosen the path of reaction and clericalism. *Le Figaro* ironically remarked, 'Monsieur de Polignac pretends to serve the interests of the country. He knows only how to serve mass.' More importantly, this ministry blatantly questioned the virtues of the Charter, in particular the responsibility of ministers to Parliament. In the king's speech Charles haughtily asserted that the liberties granted by the Charter were second to the sacred rights of the crown. 'Be reassured about your rights: they are contained within mine.' The president of the Chamber, Royer-Collard, in an address to the king signed by a majority of deputies, reminded Charles that the Charter rested on agreement between the political views of the ministry appointed by the king and the wishes of the people expressed by Parliament. He concluded by saying, 'Sire, our loyalty and our devotion oblige us to tell you that no such agreement exists today.' Some newspapers, such as *Le National*, went further and called for a change of dynasty. Charles dissolved the Chamber on 16 May. There was now open conflict between the sovereignty of the king and the sovereignty of the nation represented by the Chamber. The elections produced a majority which was hostile to Polignac. Believing that any concession of his royal prerogatives would be a sign of weakness triggering a revolutionary movement, as had been the case in 1789, Charles opted for a *coup de force*. In July 1830, his authority boosted by the successful military **expedition to Algiers**, he used Article 14 of the Charter which gave him the right to rule by decree. Charles dissolved the new Chamber before it could even meet, drastically increased press censorship, modified the method of recruitment for deputies and reduced the franchise to the wealthiest portion of the landed aristocracy. By doing so he cut himself off from those who might have been inclined to support the monarchy, had it been willing to respect a moderate interpretation of the Charter.

The constitutional conflict between the king and those who defended liberty was to be settled in the streets on 27, 28 and 29 July: three days known as *les trois glorieuses*. The press and the bourgeoisie led the attack. Thiers in *Le National* claimed that 'The legality of the regime does not exist any more [. . .] Obedience ceases to be a duty.' Then barricades were erected in the popular quarters of Paris and a bloody battle ensued. Members of the National Guard joined workers and artisans. Different motives pushed people into the streets. Some accused the government of having done little to solve the economic crisis which had gripped the country since 1827. Others were infuriated by the clerical orientation of the regime. Only a minority held republican views. However, all were ready to rally around the liberal elite in defence of liberty. Some soldiers abandoned their posts

> **expedition to Algiers (May–July 1830)**
>
> In 1830, Algeria was a tributary 'regency' of the Ottoman Empire, but enjoyed great autonomy under the rule of a *dey*. In 1827 at a meeting aimed at settling a series of diplomatic and financial issues, the *dey* struck the French consul three times with his flywhisk and refused to accede to French demands. Three years later, one hundred warships were sent to Algiers, resulting in the capitulation of the *dey* (5 July) and the occupation of the Algerian coast by French troops. This punitive action to avenge French honour might have had other motives, such as curbing Algerian piracy in the Mediterranean or distracting public opinion from Charles's domestic problems. The naval victory may also have strengthened the king's resolve to pursue his *coup de force* against the liberal opposition. At first, the July Monarchy did not have a clear plan for Algeria and showed lukewarm support for costly military occupation of the Algerian coast. Until 1834, no effort was made to extend French control inland. Thus, the French colonisation of Algeria started with relative indifference and lack of foresight.

to fraternise with the insurgents. Charles abdicated and fled to England. The crowd, led by General La Fayette, who found himself in the same role he had played in 1789, took the Hôtel de Ville and was ready to proclaim the republic. However, liberal deputies, such as Thiers, bypassed the popular movement, fearing a republic supported by the masses. Thiers issued posters which clearly indicated that the republic could not be a viable alternative to the Bourbons and that it would lead into civil and foreign wars. He urged Louis-Philippe, Duc d'Orléans and cousin to the king, to accept the crown. For the liberals the duke had good credentials. His father had voted in favour of Louis XVI's execution and he himself had fought for the revolutionary armies in 1792. He had

The Foreign Legion

The Algerian invasion led to the creation of the Foreign Legion, one of the army's elite forces, in 1831. The Legion's headquarters were established at Sidi-Bel-Abbès in Algeria and thereafter it was to play a leading role in colonial expansion, drawing recruits from a wide variety of countries and from many different social backgrounds. No questions were asked about a *legionnaire*'s past but he had to swear an oath of allegiance to the legion. Algerian independence in July 1962 forced the legion's headquarters to be relocated to Corsica.

always distanced himself from the Ultras. The duke appeared to liberals to be 'a prince devoted to the Revolution', a potential 'citizen-king'. After deliberately procrastinating, the duke appeared on the balcony of the Hôtel de Ville with La Fayette, both draped in a single Tricolour, and declared his intention to respect the Charter. Having failed to impose himself as a republican president, La Fayette, it was rumoured, declared that this king was 'the best of republics'.

Charles had been anointed in Rheims at the feet of an archbishop but Louis-Philippe was elevated to the throne by the cheers of the crowd gathered at the Hôtel de Ville. His power was not derived from divine right, but was based on a contract with the nation. Thus, he was not king of France, but king of the French. The Chamber slightly revised the Charter in more liberal terms and Louis-Philippe had to swear on oath to respect it. The July Monarchy was born. However, it soon became clear that its legitimacy rested on a series of misconceptions.

Document 2a: La Charte constitutionnelle du 4 Juin 1814: Préambule rédigé par Louis XVIII

Le divine providence, en nous rappelant dans nos États après une longue absence, nous a imposé de grandes obligations. [. . .] Nous avons considéré que, bien que l'autorité toute entière résidât en France dans la personne du roi, ses prédécesseurs n'avaient point hésité à en modifier l'exercice, suivant la différence des temps [. . .].

Nous avons dû, à l'exemple des rois nos prédécesseurs, apprécier les effets des progrès toujours croissants des Lumières, les rapports nouveaux que ces progrès ont introduits dans la société, la direction imprimée aux esprits depuis un demi-siècle, les graves altérations qui en sont résultées: nous avons reconnu que le vœu de nos sujets pour une Charte constitutionnelle était l'expression d'un besoin réel; mais en cédant à ce vœu, nous avons pris toutes les précautions pour que cette Charte fût digne de nous et du peuple auquel nous sommes fiers de commander [. . .] En même temps que nous reconnaissons qu'une Constitution libre et monarchique devait remplir l'attente de l'Europe éclairée, nous avons dû nous souvenir aussi que notre premier devoir envers nos peuples était de conserver, pour leur propre intérêt, les droits et les prérogatives de notre couronne. Nous avons espéré qu'instruits par l'expérience, ils seraient convaincus que l'autorité suprême peut seule donner aux institutions qu'elle établit, la force, la permanence et la majesté dont elle est elle-même revêtue [. . .]

En cherchant ainsi à renouer la chaîne des temps, que de funestes écarts avaient interrompue, nous avons effacé de notre souvenir, comme nous voudrions qu'on pût les effacer de l'histoire, tous les maux qui ont affligé la patrie durant notre absence. [. . .] Sûrs de nos intentions, forts de notre conscience, nous nous engageons, devant l'Assemblée qui nous écoute, à être fidèle à cette Charte constitutionnelle, nous réservant d'en jurer le maintien, avec une nouvelle solennité devant les autels de celui qui pèse dans la même balance les rois et les nations. A ces causes, nous avons volontairement et par libre exercice de notre autorité royale, accordé et accordons, fait concession et octroi à nos sujets, tant pour nous que pour nos successeurs, et à toujours, de la Charte constitutionnelle qui suit. [. . .]

Document 2b: Gabriel Bourbon-Leblanc, *Les ultra-royalistes, les indépendants et les ministériels au tribunal de l'opinion publique* (Paris, 1817)

Les *ultra-royalistes* se composent de cette masse de chevaliers fidèles qui, voyant dans la royauté une institution divine, dans la noblesse son unique soutien, dans la religion, un obstacle insurmontable à l'introduction de la tyrannie, dans le dogme de la légitimité et de l'hérédité du pouvoir souverain, la seule garantie du bonheur des peuples et dans la monarchie ainsi constituée, le seul gouvernement qui assure la tranquillité publique, ont sacrifié et sont toujours prêts à sacrifier leur fortune, leur existence et leurs affections les plus chères au triomphe d'une cause qui leur paraît sacrée. La patrie est pour eux là seulement où le roi se trouve. Qu'une démocratie se fonde dans le pays qui les a vus naître, ou qu'un chef unique y commande, ils méconnaissent et cette démocratie et ce chef, parce qu'ils considèrent l'institution de l'une et l'avénement de l'autre comme un attentat aux lois fondamentales, qui ne peuvent être ni changées ni abrogées. Leur devise est Dieu et le Roi. [. . .]

Les *indépendants*, nés et formés pour la plupart, au milieu des tempêtes révolutionnaires, sont d'une activité, d'une persévérance et d'une énergie qui tiennent en quelque sorte de cet héroïsme de pensée des beaux temps de la république romaine. Leur devise est Liberté et Égalité. Suivant eux, nul ne peut exercer le pouvoir souverain que par une délégation formelle du peuple; suivant eux, une loi n'a son vrai caractère et n'est bonne qu'autant qu'elle est l'expression du vœu librement émis de la majorité des individus qu'elle concerne: les rois, les princes, les empereurs, [. . .] les prefets, les ministres [. . .] ne doivent sous aucun pretexte se soustraire aux devoirs imposés par la loi commune. [. . .] Le droit de commander aux hommes ne peut être justifié que par la supériorité des talents; [. . .] les fonctions publiques sont les domaines des plus instruits et des meilleurs, de même que la couronne de laurier est les bien propre des plus braves. [. . .] C'est à celui qui rend le plus de services qu'appartient le plus grand nombre de récompenses. [. . .] Ils veulent que le citoyen, libre de sa personne comme de sa pensée, ait le droit de soumettre à son examen particulier les actes de l'autorité et de reprocher au magistrat quelle que soit l'élévation de sa dignité, la fausseté

continued

de ses démarches, l'abus de son pouvoir et la nullité de son talent, si ce magistrat est incapable, s'il oublie ses devoirs, et si par ses mœurs, il ne sait pas commander le respect.

Les *ministériels* sont constamment admirateurs des actes de l'autorité et des personnes qui tiennent le pouvoir; et comme l'autorité est la source d'où découle toutes les grâces et toutes les faveurs, ils ont pour légende: 'obéïssance passive'. Ils ont pensé qu'en se rapprochant tour à tour des ultra-royalistes et des indépendants et surtout en les trompant également tour à tour, ils parviendraient à tout maîtriser [. . .]. Les ministeriels veulent des places et surtout qu'on les paye. [. . .] Comme Dieu n'a pas encore permis que la révolution française ait terminé son cours, elle marche constamment avec [ces] trois agents principaux.

Document 2c: *Petit Dictionnaire Ultras*, par un royaliste constitutionnel (Paris, 1823)

[Avec la Restauration], la France allait enfin se reposer à l'abri du trône constitutionnel. Cependant une race d'hommes singuliers par leur habitude et leur langage s'élève au milieu de nous. [. . .] Bientôt, aux regrets du temps passé et des vieux préjugés succèdent des plaintes contre les bienfaits du monarque: on accuse sa bonté, sa sagesse. Le nombre de ces mécontents se compose d'abord d'hommes devenus tout à fait étrangers à la France, se grossit d'anciens apôtres de la tyrannie aristocratique, féodale et religieuse. [. . .] Leurs écrits proclament déjà tous les avantages de l'ancien régime en chargeant le nouveau de calomnies, en insultant l'amour propre national, dans ce qu'il a de plus cher, c'est à dire sa gloire militaire. A ces sourds frémissements qui effraient la confiance publique, la France s'est émue et lève les yeux vers le trône constitutionnel, et quand le monarque, éclairé sur ces périls veut rassurer son peuple, il n'est plus temps: les fanatiques ont détruit son sublime ouvrage et rouvert toutes les plaies de la France. [. . .] La France qui avait eu tant à souffrir des novateurs de 1793 vit avec effroi ces terroristes. La dénomination d'ultra qui leur fut donnée ne fut qu'une bien faible vengeance des maux qu'ils avaient causés; mais du moins elle démasquait ce faux zèle qui sous des dehors de royalisme exagéré, prétendait légitimer des abus et des violences. Les vrais royalistes, ceux qui confondent dans leur affection le prince, la France et sa constitution, rejetèrent avec horreur de leurs rangs des hommes qui ne rêvaient que l'anarchie.

Topics
FOR DISCUSSION

1 What was the nature of Louis XVIII's regime? According to Document 2a, how did the new regime try to reconcile the revolutionary heritage with the traditions of the *ancien régime*?
2 What were the major political divisions in France between 1815 and 1824?
3 Using Documents 2b and 2c, define the political and religious ideology of the Ultras.
4 What was the nature of Charles X's regime? How did it differ from that of Louis XVIII?
5 What were the causes of the 1830 Revolution?

CHAPTER 3

Timeline

1831
Silk workers' uprising in Lyons is harshly repressed

1832
February   A legitimist conspiracy is foiled in Paris

1833
28 June   The education minister, François Guizot, establishes the principle of general primary education

1834
Workers' riots in Paris and Lyons

1836
October   Napoleon's nephew, Louis-Napoleon Bonaparte, stages a failed coup

1839
12 May   Unsuccessful insurrection led by Auguste Blanqui and Armand Barbès

1840
6 August   Another failed coup attempt by Louis-Napoleon, who is then imprisoned
15 December   Napoleon's ashes are deposited in Les Invalides

1846
25 May   Louis-Napoleon escapes from prison
Poor harvests lead to growing social unrest

1847
October   The subjugation of Algeria is now complete

1848
A ban on a large-scale political banquet scheduled for 22 February leads to demonstrations across Paris. Louis-Philippe abdicates
25 February   A Republic is proclaimed

The July Monarchy, 1830–48

What were the significance and the meaning of the 1830 July Revolution? Different interpretations at the time revealed a profound disagreement over the events of July 1830. The 1830 Revolution rested on three fundamental misconceptions that were ultimately to be fateful to the July Monarchy. The first misunderstanding was related to the legitimacy of the new regime. 'Who made you king?' Was Louis-Philippe really the king of the barricades? Were the hereditary principle and his indirect filiation with previous monarchs enough to justify the king's legitimacy? What was the meaning of his oath to the Chamber?

Liberal deputies argued that the king had been freely chosen by the representatives of the nation, even though he was a Bourbon. They insisted on the contractual nature of his power and thus implied that the nation that made him king could also take his crown away if he did not respect its will. There was hope for a new kind of constitutional monarchy: the king should reign, but not rule. Ministers should be responsible to a parliament whose electoral base should progressively be enlarged. For this *parti du mouvement*, July 1830 was a new start, the promise of a democratic modernisation of the monarchy. Conversely, the most fervent supporters of the king argued that *necessity*, not popular will, had put him on the throne. The crown had fallen;

the national interest required an immediate solution. Louis-Philippe had not been chosen, but was imposed by necessity. 'Who made you king?' 'Fate!' was Louis-Philippe's
answer, refusing a legitimacy rooted in divine providence or popular sovereignty. With
Charles having failed to make the Charter work properly, it was necessary to find a better king who would. If such were the case, what happened in 1830 was not a revolution,
but merely a change of dynasty. For the *parti de la résistance*, July 1830 was not a new
start, but the final act of the French Revolution. The July Monarchy was perceived to be
the best political solution to the series of crises that had affected the country since 1789;
liberty was legitimate only if strongly contained by order.

The second misconception concerned the social base of the regime. July 1830 could be
seen as an alliance between the bourgeoisie and the masses against the reactionary and anti-
quated power of an aristocratic clique. For the bourgeoisie, the 1830 Revolution was about
freedom: political freedom, aimed at limiting the arbitrary power of the king, but also freedom
of enterprise and trade, and freedom to organise working conditions as they deemed fit,
without interference from the state. For the masses, or rather their leaders, the revolution was
mainly about equality, an opportunity to redefine social relations, to improve the material
conditions of the worst off and to ensure their integration into the political body. Under such
circumstances, the alliance between the bourgeoisie and the masses could only be short-lived.
In September 1830 in Lyons, the **National Guard** organised a ball to honour the eldest son of
the king, the new heir to the throne. Tickets were issued, but the cheapest ones were with-
drawn at the last moment, making it impossible for workers and craftsmen to attend the
celebrations. One of them bitterly complained: 'Are we not good enough to attend a ball offered
to our prince? It appears that equality with the rich only works when there is a danger. We are
only their equals when our service is required to
defend their property.' From the outset, part of the
population felt that the insurgents of the barricades had died in vain and that they had been
robbed of their revolution. The July Monarchy was
to be the monarchy of the bourgeoisie, not of the
people.

The third misconception concerned the
foreign policy of the new regime. Before
appearing on the balcony of the Hôtel de Ville,
Louis-Philippe briefly met republican leaders,
who warned him that the revolution was not a
liberal but a national one. The sight of the
Tricolour had rekindled popular nationalism.
The masses were keen to take their revenge
against the European powers who had humili-
ated France at Waterloo. Memories of the Great
Revolution pushed them to support other
European peoples who, encouraged by the
French example, were ready to overthrow the
'tyrants' who ruled over them. Fraternity with

The National Guard

A national citizen militia, created
in 1789 to maintain order and
protect private property, to
defend revolutionary principles
and the National Assembly
against aristocratic conspiracy.
Under the July Monarchy, it
represented the bourgeoisie in
arms, ready to repress
insurrectionary movements. Tax-
paying requirements for
membership were lowered in
1837, opening its membership to
the petty bourgeoisie and
encouraging the Guard's reformist
leanings. Poorly equipped and
organised, it proved unable and
unwilling to defend the monarchy
in 1848, many guardsmen siding
with the revolution.

other European peoples against their king could arouse passions in a way that the somewhat abstract nature of Charles's *coup de force* could not. In Belgium, Poland and Italy, nationalist movements expected France to support their struggles against oppressive monarchs. However, the new king was determined to preserve peace in Europe. In August 1830 he declared: 'France will show the rest of Europe . . . that it cherishes peace as much as liberty and wishes only for the happiness and tranquillity of its neighbours.' In a letter addressed to the czar, he deplored the July Revolution as an 'accident' that could have been avoided. Anxious to have his throne recognised by other European powers, he quickly reassured the King of Naples, his brother-in-law, that he would not support the cause of Italian nationalists. Opting for cautious diplomatic solutions, Louis-Philippe became known as the 'Napoleon of peace'. His policy gave the impression that the 'king of the barricades' was all too ready to side with repressive European monarchs against their people. An Italian nationalist resentfully asked in 1831: 'Have the people of Paris risen to support the so-called rights of these tyrants and their atrocious crimes? Are you on the throne to sanction these horrible crimes?' Some felt that the new king had betrayed the spirit of July 1830 and of the Great Revolution.

A repressive liberal monarchy

Given these misunderstandings, it was not surprising that the new regime found it difficult to assert its authority. From 1830 to 1840, the July Monarchy had to fight difficult battles in order to survive. To uphold its self-proclaimed ambition, the rule of the 'golden mean' (*juste milieu*), it tried to reject extreme political solutions to maintain both liberty and order, but in fact it became an oppressive regime. For a short period of time, the *parti du mouvement*, led by Laffitte, obtained some limited but important changes. The franchise was extended. All men over 25 who paid more than 200 FF in tax could vote at general elections. The electoral body grew from 94,600 to 167,000 men. In 1833, 2 million men were allowed to vote at local elections and were thus initiated into political life. Peers lost their hereditary privilege. The National Guard opened its ranks to the petit-bourgeoisie.

However, some expected more radical measures to break with the past and the country was soon gripped by unrest motivated by political, social and anti-clerical agendas. Violence erupted in Paris during the trial of Charles's ministers when it appeared that they would not be sentenced to death. Throughout France, workers were angry at the lack of economic and social reform. The economic recession which had affected the country since 1827 had generated a sharp rise in unemployment. In manufacturing towns, workers broke machines, went on strikes and demanded higher wages. Finally, there were outbursts of anti-clericalism. For instance, in Paris the archbishopric was ransacked. As an act of revenge against the Ultras' bigotry, the National Guard in Brest refused to protect religious processions from hostile crowds. Laffitte seemed unable or unwilling to intervene to restore order and gave the impression that he had lost control.

In March 1831, *le parti de la résistance*, led by Périer, regained the upper hand. Suspicious about political democratisation and fearing a wave of social unrest, it introduced a series of laws designed to restore order and protect property. Périer successfully mobilised the National Guard and the army to foil political plots. First, in 1832, ultra-royalist attempts to mount a series of popular insurrections against the regime in the South and in the Vendée were frustrated. Charles's supporters – *les légitimistes* – were discredited. Aristocrats who had remained faithful to the Bourbons withdrew to their provincial estates and scornfully refused to participate in the regime's political life. Second, in 1836 and 1840, Louis-Napoleon, the emperor's nephew, tried to capitalise on popular Bonapartist nostalgia to mount a coup against the regime. Twice the regime managed to foil his plots. Finally, the republican opposition, weak in the Chamber but better organised in various clubs, such as *la Société des amis du peuple*, waged a constant war against the regime. Its newspapers, pamphlets and caricatures vigorously attacked the monarchy and offered, as an alternative, an outright Jacobin programme. Frequent press trials and restrictions imposed on the right of assembly compelled some republicans to resort to violent action. In 1832 Paris was in a state of insurrection. Barricades were erected in the name of the republic. The so-called 'citizen-king' appeared on his horse to organise the repression and the insurrection was successfully crushed.

The regime also had to face a period of vigorous social unrest. In 1831 Lyons witnessed the first insurrection, motivated by poor working conditions (*la révolte des canuts*). The Lyons prefect had successfully negotiated higher wages and better working conditions for the silk workers (*canuts*), whose standards of living had dramatically worsened over the past decade. This agreement was denounced by Périer as a serious infringement on freedom of enterprise. No public authority, Périer argued, should determine wages or working hours. Such decisions had to be left to employers. In November 1831, 15,000 *canuts*, who lived a life of misery, took up arms. Shouting 'live working or die fighting', they successfully occupied the city for four days. The troops and the National Guard were sent in and one of Louis-Philippe's sons actively participated in a savage repression. Gradually, social movements and the republican opposition started to link social and political demands. The republican clubs began to demand better wages for workers as well as further political rights. The regime intensified its repression against republicans and most of their leaders were arrested. When an insurrection broke again in Lyons and in Paris in 1834, the regime used the harshest methods: innocent people were massacred, more than 2,000 people were arrested and 121 republicans were put on trial for plotting against the state. The republican opposition was crushed. The bourgeoisie, scared by a revolution led by the 'dangerous classes', rallied around the king. An assassination attempt on the king in 1835 prompted the Chamber to pass the notorious 'September laws'. Press controls were reinforced and it became an offence to question the legitimacy and the nature of the regime or to profess republican allegiances. The judicial system was reformed to facilitate condemnations of seditious acts. In 1839 attempts to overthrow the regime by radical republican societies such as Blanqui's *Société des Saisons* came to nothing. By 1840, for want of legitimacy, the July Monarchy had asserted its authority as a repressive regime.

The reign of the bourgeoisie

In his *Souvenirs*, de Tocqueville wrote that 1830 represented the definitive triumph of the bourgeoisie, monopolising both political and economic power. Its leaders were chiefly recruited among the high bourgeoisie, notably from the world of finance (Laffitte, Périer), but also comprised liberal aristocrats (De Broglie), military and administrative dignitaries of the Empire (Soult, Maret) and university professors (Guizot, Cousin). Voltairean and Protestant personalities were also prominent within the new elite and a whiff of anti-clericalism surrounded the early years of the regime. Religious scepticism, inherent to any liberal creed and the importance attached to free will, could hardly accommodate the tenets of sectarian Catholicism. However, convinced that religion was a major pillar of social order, the regime avoided direct confrontations with the church. Further, the development of liberal Catholicism, more attached to rigorous moral values than equivocal dogmas, and critical of legitimist politics, presaged the impending reconciliation of the bourgeoisie with Catholicism.

The July Monarchy was often derided as the lacklustre reign of bourgeois opportunism tainted by greed, materialism and mediocrity. Ministers dined with bankers; rich merchants were invited to the court. Victor Hugo noted with irony that 'when Louis-Philippe falls from his throne, he will become a grocer'. *Légitimistes* deplored the bad taste of the regime and its *nouveau riche* pretensions whereas **Daumier**'s caricatures derided its cupidity and conceit. Yet, politically, the regime offered an original conception of the political order, known as Orleanism. Its ambition to respect *le juste milieu* was not a simple rejection of ultra-royalism and republican Jacobinism. It also had a positive content. It asserted the sovereignty of reason over popular sovereignty and a desire for moderation. Only men whose ideas and actions had been enlightened by reason had the 'political capacity' to participate in the government of the nation. Reason, however, was not a gift of nature, but a privilege derived from property and culture. Elections were not organised to take into account public opinion, always prey to excess and mindless judgements, but to select those who could best articulate reasonable ideas. Voting could not be a political right, but must be a function associated with the status given by property and culture. Parliament and the press were valued as a deliberative forum, provided that they remained in reasonable and safe hands. Representative government was nothing other

> **(Honoré) Daumier (1808–1879)**
>
> Republican artist and caricaturist, best remembered for his satirical political cartooning and his savage attacks on Louis-Philippe as a fat, bloated ogre devouring the wealth of the nation. Prison sentences, fines and accrued censorship (September laws, 1835) compelled him to abandon political satire for social criticism. He invented two famous characters. *Robert Macaire*, a brash, fraudulent, self-important stock-market speculator, personified the development of an unscrupulous capitalism under the July Monarchy. Later (1850s) *Ratapoil*, a sinister character in rags, armed with a club, symbolised the brutality of Napoleon III's regime and its ability to find support among the poorest sections of French society.

Figure 3.1 Daumier, Gargantua (1831). Daumier was imprisoned from September 1832 to January 1833 for this caricature of the king

than the representation of **les notables**, an elite defined by its fortune, its intellectual superiority or its ability to organise production. Nonetheless, a stake in politics could be acquired through education and thrift. The 1833 education law, prepared by Guizot, compelled every municipality to open a primary school, which was free of charge for the poorest children. The curriculum had to extol history as the triumphal march of bourgeois virtues. Education, although not compulsory, was perceived as a preparation for public life. It aimed to moralise the popular classes and to teach them to respect order and to value thrift. Guizot urged the French to get richer through hard work and saving, because this was the best way to enter the ranks of the virtuous bourgeoisie, to acquire

> ### Notables
>
> Familial lineage, property, wealth and, to a lesser extent, education and professional skills gave the *notable* a social status which legitimated his participation in public life. A representative mandate or the charge of a public office often allowed the *notable* to wield influence and power over his local or professional community, but also to defend its interests and to voice its concerns at the national level. An aristocrat or a bourgeois, the *notable* formed the backbone of the Orleanist system.

political influence and finally to side with the regime which would defend their interests. By 1846, 246,000 propertied Frenchmen had acquired the right to vote.

The July Monarchy also witnessed the expansion of capitalism and the development of industry. Scientific inventions fostered industrial production. Steam-activated machinery, chiefly powered by coal, transformed iron and steel production. From 1829 to 1847, coal production increased from 1.5 million to 5.2 million tonnes and iron production grew from 154,000 to 592,000 tonnes. New chemicals helped the diversification of textile products with the introduction of cheaper dyeing techniques. The development of mechanical looms transformed the textile industry. From 1830 to 1846 the amount of cotton processed by the textile industry grew from 32 to 65 million kilos. However, the mechanisation of production was not as swift as in Britain and industrial growth remained moderate: 1.6 per cent between 1830 and 1840, 2.2 per cent between 1840 and 1848. Various factors could explain this modest growth. Some companies were reluctant to invest in costly machinery. In western France, employers preferred to maintain manual looms and to employ rural workers, who accepted lower wages and were more docile than their urban counterparts. Most companies were run as family businesses, averse to the intrusion of outside capital. Banks were sometimes unwilling to grant loans for seemingly hazardous industrial ventures and preferred to invest in commercial undertakings. At a time when bankruptcy could be punished by imprisonment, some entrepreneurs favoured safer investment in landed properties, which also provided them with status. Further, internal demand remained weak. The large semi-autarkic peasant sector, still poorly equipped and prone to subsistence crises, offered limited prospects. Costly investments were recouped by lower wages, which deflated potential demand and generated misery among workers. For instance, the introduction of the Jacquard loom downgraded the specialised skills of tulle embroiderers who saw their daily wage reduce from 11 to 4 FF between 1825 and 1847.

However, far from embracing strict liberal principles, the regime's policies demonstrated that it knew how to intervene to enhance and protect the interests of the French bourgeoisie and to promote the development of industry. Having successfully tamed the opposition, debates centred increasingly on economic rather than political issues. The main concern of successive governments was to adjudicate between competing interests within the bourgeoisie. The regime first favoured protectionist policies. Whereas the importation of cheaper foreign goods could have benefited consumers, a coalition of powerful interests convinced the regime to maintain protective tariffs to shield their position from foreign competition. Until 1842, for instance, the importation of iron and steel was prohibited. The regime also intervened to promote the development of industry. It created commercial banks in major provincial centres to encourage credit. Through a vast public-works programme it provided industry with the necessary infrastructure for its expansion. In particular, realising that private capital alone could not support the construction of a national railway network, the regime devised a partnership between the state, local authorities and private companies for the development of railways. From 1831 to 1847, the length of the railway network grew from 31 to 1,511 kilometres and this venture proved to be very lucrative for private investors.

Industrial development, however, had a heavy social cost. Workers lived a life of misery. Lower wages, rising living costs, long working hours and insalubrious dwellings worsened their condition. In 1840 a parliamentary report showed that of 10,000 young men from the most industrialised *départements*, 9,000 had to be exempted from conscription due to their physical weakness. Between 1833 and 1847, the ranks of the needy poor swelled from 695,000 to 1,329,000. High infant mortality, alcoholism and prostitution plagued industrial workers, who often fell into delinquency and crime, threatening order and property. However, for most *notables*, poverty was the result of low moral standards rather than poor economic conditions and the regime did little to improve workers' well-being. In 1841 the majority of deputies showed little interest in a law regulating child labour in factories. In the name of freedom to work, the regime maintained a legal system protecting employers against workers' demands and it implemented strict anti-strike policies.

In this context, various theories against capitalism emerged. Some romantic writers rejected industrialism and dreamt of a return to craft production, away from the ugliness of factories. Some conservatives denounced the damaging consequences of economic liberalism: the destruction of the traditional social fabric and the rise of pauperism nourished dangerous revolutionary demands. Others proposed the reorganisation of industrial production. Inspired by the economist Sismondi or the political thinking of Saint-Simon, they heralded industrialisation as a source of economic and social progress if stripped of its capitalist logic. They argued that employers' profit did not result from the difference between production costs and selling price, but was extorted from the equitable wages that workers should normally have received. **Utopian socialists** claimed that the means of production had to be owned by self-regulating workers' communities or workers' associations. Private property and competition were perceived to be destructive. Fourrier, for instance, imagined society as a collection of workers' communities (*phalansteries*) where a methodical division of labour would make work a pleasurable activity and lead to the satisfaction of people's desires. Others, such as Buchez, inspired by evangelical ideas, stressed the importance of fraternity over private property and concluded that companies should be managed by workers themselves. However, the pacifist and moral approach of utopian socialists was also criticised for its political naivety, notably by Marx and Blanqui. Only violent action (strikes, uprising) led by the oppressed class and the constitution of a proletarian dictatorship could put an end to capitalist production and bourgeois domination. However, these ideas rarely reached the masses, whose class-consciousness remained weak and whose leaders, in most cases, had been successfully subdued.

Thiers and Guizot: from instability to stalemate

> **Utopian socialism**
>
> Term used to define a variety of theories opposed to capitalism and offering as an alternative an imagined and ideal society based on radically new principles. Criticised by 'scientific' socialists (e.g. Marx) for refusing to ground their ideas in the analysis of economic reality and for failing to provide any practical solutions to attain their ideal world, utopian socialists believed that the strength of their ideas would be enough to impose social change. They rejected both reformism, as an unacceptable form of compromise, and violence, which often made revolution an end in itself. The creation of small communities isolated from the 'real' world would serve as a model for an egalitarian and fraternal society. The multiplication of these communities would eventually ensure the conversion of the whole society to their ideal.

Politically, the first 10 years of the regime were marked by ministerial instability. Various ill-defined and shifting factions within the Orleanist majority fought against one another, often out of personal ambition, and the king himself encouraged rivalry between his ministers as a way to reinforce his personal authority. For Louis-Philippe, only the crown could govern, because deputies represented not the nation but sectoral or local interests. The king refused to be a mere figurehead and intended to govern.

However, a coalition of Orleanist deputies, led by Adolphe Thiers, argued that the king should rule but not govern. This coalition won the 1839 elections and soon after Thiers was appointed to lead the cabinet. Coming from a modest provincial background, Thiers, a lawyer and journalist, had played an active role in the 1830 Revolution. He was now a cunning politician and a brilliant orator with strong business connections. As a previous interior minister of the regime, he had resorted to fierce methods to curb social unrest. However, in 1840, with vociferous enthusiasm, he championed liberal and nationalist policies and his short leadership seemed to inject some passion into an otherwise depoliticised climate. He defended the rights of parliament against the crown and met ministers without Louis-Philippe. To flatter the petit-bourgeoisie, traditionally inclined to flag waving, he staged the transfer of Napoleon's ashes to the Invalides and deliberatedly stirred anglophobe feelings through his adventurous and belligerent foreign policy.

Until now, the regime had cultivated a good relationship with Britain. The cautious and pacifist approach of the July Monarchy had reassured London. However, since 1830 France had been engaged in the progressive conquest of Algeria and now seemed willing to extend further its influence in the Mediterranean. Thiers' ambition to use France's Egyptian ally, Mehemet Ali, to secure territorial superiority in Syria at the expense of the Ottoman Empire met with strong opposition from other European powers, in particular Britain and Russia. In July 1840, under the leadership of Palmerston, the four powers which had defeated France some 25 years earlier – Britain, Russia, Austria and Prussia – signed the Treaty of London aimed at halting French ambitions in Syria. The coalition of her previous enemies provoked an outbreak of nationalism in France, further encouraged by Thiers' belligerent gestures. In *Le Temps*, an editorialist echoing Thiers' ideas wrote: 'If Europe tries to play a terrible war game with us, we will play the game of revolution with her.' War was imminent. The king and the conservative elites feared French diplomatic isolation and dreaded a war which could damage business interests and generate further social unrest. Thiers' lack of moderation made him appear a dangerous revolutionary. Although he had constantly rejected demands to extend the franchise, his leadership awakened popular passions, encouraged nationalist agitation, triggered a wave of strikes and fostered further claims for political and social reforms. The intrusion of popular demands into politics was deemed highly dangerous by growing sections of the Orleanist elite, who soon withdrew their support. Thiers resigned. The king tried to appease European powers and appointed François Guizot as foreign minister, who *de facto* became the real leader of the cabinet for the next 7 years.

Guizot tried to convince other powers that France was not a threat to European order. He painfully rekindled the *entente cordiale* with London, showed little enthusiasm for colonial expansion and pursued a peaceful policy which offended nationalist feelings by appearing too subservient to Britain. His willingness to turn France into a bastion of social conservatism led him to support the autocratic Austrian emperor against liberals in Switzerland and Italy. For many, Guizot seemed more concerned to enhance the prestige of the dynasty with European courts than to defend national interests.

At home, Guizot's economic liberalism and willingness to promote free trade furthered capitalist modernisation, but his political conservatism and fierce defence of social order led the regime into stalemate. In 1842 he declared to parliament: 'All the great battles have been won, all the major interests are satisfied. Our first, indeed our only duty, is to preserve firmly and completely what has been conquered.' Impervious to criticism, Guizot stubbornly refused to meet growing demands to reform the electoral system and thus failed to enlarge the social base of the regime. Through intrigue and corruption, he sought to strengthen royal authority over parliament, notably by buying off hostile deputies into lucrative positions within the civil service. With a third of deputies on the government payroll, parliament was easily tamed. The 1846 election, marked by illegal practices, gave a clear majority to Guizot, but did not manage to dispel growing feelings of frustration and disgust, including those of conservative supporters of the regime. Petty scheming and corruption scandals affecting the higher echelons of the elite discredited its moral uprightness by revealing its hypocrisy. The press and prominent figures of the regime, such as de Tocqueville and Thiers, deplored the baseness of political mores.

From 1846, the economic and financial crisis which had started to affect the country, coupled with poor harvests, prompted social unrest and renewed fears of disorder. The petit-bourgeoisie, which relied on continued prosperity to acquire further political rights, became more critical of the regime's lack of economic intervention. Above all, Guizot's political *immobilisme* was to be fateful. In 1847 a deputy conservative summarised Guizot's political achievements by an ironic exclamation: 'Nothing, nothing, nothing!' and the poet Lamartine remarked 'France is bored' and called for a 'revolution of contempt'. At the same time, historians presented a new and positive interpretation of the Great Revolution. Michelet, somewhat romantically, replaced images of mob violence and tyranny with a celebration of the virtuous people as revolutionaries. Lamartine praised the moderate but decisive role played by the Girondins. He extolled their virtues: freedom, political representation, equality before the law, religious tolerance and the rejection of violence and political assassination as political means. Under their pens, the Revolution became a less fearful event. In any case, the king and Guizot failed to understand these various signals. In December 1847 Louis-Philippe formally rejected any project of political reform, being convinced that his constitutional monarchy was a harmonious regime which had achieved stability and was best able to fulfil the moral and material interests of the nation.

The 1848 Revolution

Since July 1847, throughout France, the opposition had organised a series of banquets (as a way of bypassing laws against political meetings) to expose the regime's refusal to introduce electoral reforms. Moderates wishing to extend the franchise by reducing tax qualifications were soon eclipsed by radicals, such as Ledru-Rollin, who demanded the introduction of universal suffrage and social reforms. But there was little talk of a revolution. The dismissal of Guizot would have satisfied the bulk of the opposition. At best, some envisaged the abdication of the king, but not the overthrow of the regime. No conflict opposed parliament to the crown and the regime still enjoyed a strong majority. The climate of discontent, exasperation and pessimism which gripped France made the 1848 Revolution possible but not predictable.

The fall of the constitutional monarchy in February 1848 seemed to result from a fateful spiral of localised events. First, on 22 February, the government forbade a banquet in Paris which should have been attended by some 100 deputies. This sparked off sporadic clashes in the streets between students, craftsmen and the police. The National Guard was called by Guizot, but, instead of re-establishing order, it manifested its opposition to the conservative policies of the government. Guizot resigned on 23 February, but a shooting incident near his office triggered a popular uprising. Thinking that orders had been given to shoot on the crowd, workers and students took up arms and barricades were erected. The military defence of the capital proved to be particularly ineffective and Louis-Philippe himself was reluctant to solve the crisis by provoking a bloodbath. To save the monarchy, the king abdicated in favour of his grandson. On 24 February this solution was rejected by the National Assembly, now besieged by street rioters, and the republic was proclaimed. Rather than being crushed, the July Monarchy crumbled. For the third time since 1792, the constitutional monarchy had been discredited as a regime. 1848 symbolised the revenge of 1830 over conservatism and the victory of democracy over *les notables*. Crucially, the republic also heralded the hope for major social reforms.

Document 3a: 1830, une révolution liberale?

Nous, Conseiller d'Etat, Préfet de Police,

Considérant que des ouvriers en grand nombre parcourent, depuis quelques jours, et sous divers prétextes, les rues de la capitale,

Que si, fidèles aux sentiments qui animent l'héroïque population parisienne, ils ne commettent aucun acte de violence, leurs réunions plus ou moins tumultueuses sont elles-mêmes un désordre très grave; qu'elles alarment les habitants paisibles; qu'elles tendent à altérer la confiance que la nation française doit au gouvernement institué par elle et pour elle; que ces réunions causent aux ouvriers une perte onéreuse de temps et de travail au moment où des ateliers publics leur sont ouverts; qu'enfin elles peuvent offrir des moyens de troubles que les malveillants ne manqueraient pas de saisir.

Que le maintien de l'ordre et de la sécurité publique confié à notre responsabilité exige impérieusement qu'un tel état de chose cesse.

Considérant que, si les ouvriers de Paris ont à élever des réclamations fondées, c'est individuellement et dans une forme régulière qu'elles doivent être présentées aux autorités compétentes qui s'occupent sans relâche de toutes les mesures qui peuvent concourir à la prosperité de l'industrie.

[. . .]Ordonnons ce qui suit:

Art 1: Défenses sont faites à toutes personnes de former des réunions ou attroupements sur la voie publique, sous quelque prétexte que ce soit.

Art 2: Conformément à l'article 415 du code pénal, il est défendu aux ouvriers de se coaliser pour interdire le travail dans l'atelier, empêcher de s'y rendre et d'y rester avant ou après certaines heures et en général pour empêcher, suspendre ou enchérir les travaux.

Art 3: Aucune demande à nous adressée pour que nous intervenions entre le maître et l'ouvrier au sujet de la fixation du salaire ou de la durée du travail journalier ou du choix des ouvriers, ne sera admise comme étant formée en opposition aux lois qui ont consacré le principe de la liberté de l'industrie.

Art 4: Les commissaires de police, le chef de la police centrale, les officiers de paix, les préposés de la Préfecture de Police, la Garde nationale et les autres corps militaires assureront par tous les moyens qui sont en leur pouvoir l'exécution de la présente ordonnance.[. . .]

Le Préfet de Police de Paris, Girot de l'Ain, *Gazette des tribunaux*, 28 août 1830

Document 3b: La monarchie de François Guizot

La révolution de juillet n'avait soulevé que des questions politiques, que des questions de gouvernement; par ces questions la société n'était nullement menacée. Des questions sociales se sont élevées. [. . .] Il y a aujourd'hui des attaques contre les classes moyennes, contre la propriété, contre les sentiments de famille. Des questions sociales, des troubles intérieurs, des questions de société sont venus se joindre aux questions politiques et nous sommes aujourd'hui en presence de cette difficulté d'un gouvernement à construire et d'une société à défendre.

F. Guizot, *le Moniteur Universel*, 22 décembre 1831

Document 3c: F. Guizot, *Chambre des députés*, 15 février 1847

Nous avons trois grandes choses à fonder: une société nouvelle, la grande démocratie moderne, jusqu'ici inconnue dans l'histoire du monde; des institutions nouvelles, le gouvernement représentatif jusqu'ici étranger à notre pays; et enfin une dynastie nouvelle. Il n'est certainement jamais arrivé à aucune une époque d'avoir une pareille tâche à remplir; jamais!

Cependant, messieurs, nous approchons beaucoup du but. La société nouvelle est aujourd'hui prépondérante, victorieuse; elle a fait ses preuves; elle a pris possession du terrain social; elle a conquis en même temps et les institutions et la dynastie qui lui conviennent et qui la servent. Oui, toutes les grandes conquêtes sont faites, tous les grands intérêts sont satisfaits.

Document 3d: La question sociale

Entend-on parler de révolution *violente* qui détruirait sans transition tous les rapports existants et contre la volonté des individus? [. . .] C'est précisément parce que l'on a vu l'inéfficacité des révolutions violentes [qu'il faut préparer] une révolution d'un genre nouveau. [. . .]

D'ailleurs sans même parler des malheurs directement causés par les grandes commotions politiques, le système compétitif ne fait-il pas naître une source de calamités qui équivalent à celles des révolutions? La classe industrielle ne doit-elle pas regarder comme d'affreuses révolutions, toujours renaissantes, cette infinité de maux qui viennent fondre sur elle dans tant de circonstances? Mais les malheureux qui en sont victimes ont à peine une voix pour gémir et ils sont accoutumés à regarder eux-mêmes ces maux comme l'œuvre inévitable du destin, sans remonter à leurs veritables causes. [. . .] chaque jour ils souffrent la plus cruelle incertitude sur leur subsistance et celle de leur famille [. . .] chaque jour ils sont repoussés du sanctuaire de la justice par l'énormité des frais judiciaires ou l'absurdité des règles de procédures; chaque jour on enlève leurs fils pour ces

continued

boucheries régulières qu'on nomme la guerre [. . .] chaque jour on emprisonne, on mutile, on exécute des milliers d'entre eux que la société force à devenir vicieux et criminels; mais chacun regarde en silence et presque sans émotion ce tableau continuel des malheureux de la classe qui crée tous les biens! Et c'est cela qu'on ose appeler *l'ordre social*! Et c'est pour conserver un pareil ordre qu'on nous fait sans cesse un si grand épouvantail de toute reforme politique!

Joseph Rey, *Appel au ralliement des socialistes,* Paris: Librairie Phalansterienne, 1847, p. 17

Topics
FOR DISCUSSION

1   What does Document 3a reveal about the nature of the 1830 Revolution?
2   What was the nature of the July Monarchy? Describe its governing principles. How do Documents 3b and 3c help us to understand the nature of the July Monarchy? To what extent can the July Monarchy be qualified as 'liberal'?
3   Where did the political and social opposition to the July Monarchy come from?
4   How and why did society change between 1830 and 1848? What does Document 3d tell us about these changes?
5   What caused the downfall of the July Monarchy?

CHAPTER 4

Timeline

1848
23 April   Elections give a clear majority to moderate republicans
21 June   Ateliers nationaux are disbanded
21–6 June   Savage repression of workers' uprising in Paris
10 December   Louis-Napoleon Bonaparte wins presidential elections

1849
13 May   Legislative elections see swing to the right

1851
December   Louis-Napoleon carries out a coup

1852
2 December   The Second Empire is proclaimed

1854
27 March   Napoleon declares war on Russia

1856
Treaty of Paris marks the end of war with Russia

1858
14 January   Napoleon survives assassination attempt

1859
3 May   Declaration of war on Austria
24 June   Franco-Piedmontese army defeats Austrians at Solferino

1861
Expedition to defend French interests in Mexico

1863
11 April   Cambodia becomes a protectorate

1864
25 May   Right to strike is recognised in law

The Second Republic, 1848–52 and the Second Empire, 1852–70

The Second Republic was born out of a revolution (February 1848) and died of a *coup d'état* (December 1851). Since 1840, apparent political stability and economic prosperity had masked the rise of new aspirations. A growing part of the bourgeoisie called for liberal and democratic reforms. A new working class, not yet fully conscious of itself, but harshly affected by unemployment and poverty, demanded social reforms. In February 1848 the people of Paris, suffering massive unemployment and gripped by a revolutionary fever, drove the king out of the country and proclaimed the republic. A regime based on *notables* and supported by a wealthy oligarchy was replaced by a democratic and representative republic grounded in universal male suffrage, thus establishing the participation of the masses in politics. Was the rest of the

1866 *Prussia defeats Austria* **1867** *June   Humiliating defeat in Mexico* **1870** *19 July   France declares war on Prussia* *2 September   Napoleon captured with his army at Sedan* *4 September   Proclamation of the Third Republic*

country ready to accept a republic imposed by the Parisian revolutionary crowd? And above all, what kind of republic was it to be? The acquisition of democratic rights produced unexpected results: the Frenchmen who had just acquired the right to vote used it to legitimise the destruction of the republic (December 1851) and the instauration of a Bonapartist empire (December 1852). Did the republic prove itself unable to fulfil the aspirations which brought it into being in February 1848?

A social and democratic republic? (February–June 1848)

1848 was more than the successful repetition of 1830. Political motives alone could not explain the lyrical enthusiasm of the crowds and the explosion of joy which gripped the streets of Paris. Whereas 1830 reeked of anti-clericalism, the republican celebrations of 1848 were imbued with a fraternal Christian mysticism. Some priests, appalled by the prevalent pauperism and irritated by the materialist rationalism of the previous regime, blessed trees of freedom planted to commemorate the 1789 Revolution. Lacordaire, a noted Dominican, launched his newspaper *L'Ere nouvelle* and called the clergy to devote its efforts to the improvement of social justice and the defence of liberty, equality and fraternity. Freedom of speech and of association having been immediately restored, numerous low-priced newspapers flourished, public debates were organised and new societies were formed, including some devoted to the emancipation of women. Romantic exaltation of 'the people' and citizenry, quasi-religious love of humankind and social utopia defined the atmosphere of 1848. People expected democratic reforms and hoped that French national pride, badly damaged by Guizot's dynastic policy, would be restored. But above all, they aspired to a republic which would bring about a new type of society based on social justice and fraternity.

Remembering the mistakes made in 1830, the insurgents did not wish to leave the National Assembly to decide the fate of the revolution. Once the republic had been proclaimed, they forced the formation of a provisional government, which remained under their constant watch. The composition of the provisional government reflected both a spirit of conciliation and a major ambiguity. Arago, the renowned physicist, and Lamartine, the distinguished romantic poet, gave the prestige of their names to the government. But, on the whole, it was dominated by liberal, moderate republicans (Marie, Garnier-Pagès) whose ambition was restricted to the introduction of universal suffrage. Their economic and social liberalism precluded support for social reforms, although they favoured workers' associations as the best way to alleviate poverty. Socially-minded democrats (or *radicaux*, Ledru-Rollin, Flocon), critical of free enterprise, wished to reform labour production and introduce social legislation. Finally, the Parisian insurgents managed to impose the socialist Louis Blanc and symbolically

Martin Albert, a mechanical worker, who were less interested in the nature of the regime than in the need to transform the economic and social system. Both remained very much isolated in the provisional government. Therefore, it was not clear whether the republic would be a liberal or a social one.

Nevertheless, the first decisions taken by the provisional government gave the republic a fraternal image. It repealed the 1835 laws and abolished corporal punishment, slavery and the death penalty for political crimes. The Second Republic intended to be generous and reassuring by distancing itself from the horrifying memory of the First Republic, in particular *la Terreur*. The republic was also responsive to social demands. Working hours were regulated and limited to 10 hours per day. Although it did not formally recognise the right to work demanded by Parisian workers,

> ### *Ateliers nationaux*
>
> A traditional relief programme which committed the government to guaranteeing an income to the unemployed through the launch of public-works projects. Louis Blanc would have preferred the creation of *ateliers sociaux*, a form of producers' cooperative based on the free association of workers sharing 'the legitimate fruit of their labour'. Marx denounced the *ateliers nationaux* as bourgeois subterfuge to rally workers to the new regime, whereas conservatives pointed out that they helped workers to organise themselves and encouraged the propagation of revolutionary ideas.

it created **les Ateliers nationaux** aimed at providing public work for the unemployed. Socialists would have liked to turn the *ateliers* into productive models for a new society, based on equitable social relations, but they essentially fulfilled a charitable role. A new 'labour parliament' (*Commission du Luxembourg*), made up of 699 workers' delegates and 231 employers, was set up to resolve social conflicts on a corporatist basis. Finally, the new republic intended to be a democratic one: it introduced universal male suffrage, increasing the electoral body from 240,000 to 9 million voters. Throughout the country, celebrations were organised to acclaim this new political freedom. The election of an assembly to draft a new constitution was to be organised in April 1848. Socialists, however, argued that without preliminary education of the masses, democracy could be manipulated by conservative forces. Stressing the political immaturity of most voters and the persistent influence of *notables* on the peasantry, they asked, in vain, for the elections to be postponed.

The rest of the country did not display the same lyrical enthusiasm for the revolution. Most of the *notables* believed that the republic was a transitional step towards the restoration of a monarchy of some sort. Fearing above all social disorder, which erupted in few urban centres and poorer rural areas, they preferred to adopt an opportunist position and declared themselves republican. These *républicains du lendemain* soon outnumbered the committed *républicains de la veille*, but despite their anxious and ambiguous support, they did not contest the legitimacy of the republic. However, the drastic policies introduced by the provisional government to curb an economic crisis worsened by the revolutionary context, such as an increase of 45 per cent in direct tax, harshly affected the peasantry. Thus, its support for the republic remained lukewarm. The election of the Constituent Assembly in April 1848 reflected the victory of *les républicains du lendemain.* Of 851 representatives, only 285 could be considered committed republicans, including some 55 socialists and radicals. The vast majority was made up of rural *notables* and monarchists. The first experience of universal male suffrage delivered a conservative assembly, which immediately replaced the provisional government with an executive commission of five members (*Pentarques*) excluding socialists and dominated by moderate republicans.

Socialists, radicals and workers were deeply disappointed by the results of the election. Images of rural communities herded by a priest or a *notable* to the polling station reinforced the idea that the democratic process had been distorted. On 15 May a demonstration of 150,000 discontented Parisians ended up with a tumultuous occupation of the Assembly and the proclamation of an insurrectional government in the Hôtel de Ville. The legitimacy of the Assembly was directly questioned by the crowds. Socialist leaders (Blanc, Albert, Blanqui) were arrested and the movement disbanded. The peasantry and the republican bourgeoisie now feared radical action. Moderate republicans were ready to harden the repression against social movements and decided to dissolve the *Ateliers nationaux*, which had become a centre of political radicalism, but which for the majority of workers remained the only hope of escaping misery. This led to a massive insurrection in eastern Paris in June 1848 and the erection of more than 400 barricades. The Assembly declared a state of siege, dismissed the *Pentarques* and appointed General Cavaignac as a temporary dictator to restore order. This was done with a remarkable efficiency and cruelty: 1,500 insurgents were shot, 11,000 people were imprisoned and 4,300 were to be deported to Algeria. Cavaignac completed the military repression with a series of reactionary measures. He restricted individual and political freedom, increased press control and extended the legal limit for working hours. Part of the bourgeoisie, which sincerely believed in the republic, refused to accept that the streets had defied a legally and legitimately elected government. Cavaignac, a true republican who could not be suspected of monarchist leanings, imposed a conservative republic. In June 1848 the dream of a social republic disappeared. Yet the event revealed the importance of class struggles as a permanent feature of modern French politics.

A conservative republic, June 1848–December 1851

Once order was re-established, the Assembly drafted a constitution for the new republic, adopted on 4 November 1848. Its preamble reasserted republican values (*Liberté, Egalité, Fraternité*) and expressed a willingness to improve the well-being of the people, notably through education. But it also included strong conservative elements. The regime reasserted the primacy of hard work, family, property and public order. There was no mention of the right to work, denounced as an economic and social heresy by conservatives. The new institutional framework gave legislative power to an assembly of 750 members elected for three years. However, a president, directly elected by the people for a non-renewable 4-year term, enjoyed strong executive prerogatives. He could not dissolve the Assembly, but the Assembly could not censure the government he alone appointed. The principle of parliamentary responsibility was ignored. Thus, the conservative republic was also to be a presidential rather than a parliamentary one and the first president of the republic elected by the French in December 1848 was a prince: Louis-Napoleon Bonaparte, Napoleon's nephew. The prince was an enigmatic character, with no clear programme. His greatest asset was his name, easily recognisable, and the patriotic glory it symbolised. The peasantry saw him as the heir of the Great Revolution, which redistributed lands previously owned by the aristocracy and the clergy, and massively voted for him. His willingness to defend order and authority reassured conservatives. His advanced social views made him popular among workers, now disillusioned with republicans. Monarchists considered him a weak and spiritless character, who twice had failed to overthrow the Orleanist regime. They believed he could easily be manipulated. The result was that while the republican candidates, such as Cavaignac, failed abysmally to gather support, Louis-Napoleon won 74 per cent of the vote. Thus, the conservative and presidential republic was not to be governed by republicans.

Ignoring the parliamentary majority, the president chose the members of his government among the monarchist elite. Under military pressure, he compelled the Assembly to vote its own dissolution. The legislative elections in May 1849 gave a clear majority (53 per cent) to the *parti de l'ordre*, essentially consisting of monarchists. Moderate republicans were crushed, but the Radicals, who defended a social and demo-cratic conception of the republic, obtained more than 25 per cent of the votes. A politically polarised France emerged, based on a clearer left–right cleavage. Radicals were active in industrial centres (Paris, Lyon), poorer rural regions (Limousin) and the republican bastions of the Southwest and the Alps. They organised demonstrations against the government which sometimes degenerated into riots and were severely repressed. The monarchist majority, fearing the 'red peril', implemented reactionary policies. It manipulated electoral rules to restrict universal suffrage, introduced legisla-tion to increase the influence of the church on the education system (*loi Falloux*) and used repressive measures to tame the radical opposition and its press. Abroad, it supported the counter-revolutionary military expedition of General Oudinot, aimed at restoring the temporal powers of the pope against the Roman liberal republic.

The president, however, had personal ambitions and progressively dissociated himself from the *parti de l'ordre*. He disapproved of the Oudinot expedition, criticised the attempt to restrict universal suffrage, blamed the anti-democratic drift of the regime, and denounced its inability to resolve the persistent economic and social crisis. He presented himself as a providential saviour who could rescue the country from radical turmoil and at the same time restore democracy. To orchestrate his propaganda, he financed anti-parliamentary newspapers and appointed prefects devoted to his cause. When the reactionary assembly refused to modify the constitution to allow him to bid for a second term, he masterminded a *coup d'état* on 2 December 1851 with the support of the army. The Assembly was dissolved, political leaders arrested and universal suffrage restored. Paris feebly resisted: most Parisian workers could not moti-vate themselves to defend a republic which had betrayed their aspirations. A plebiscite ratified the coup in December 1851: 75 per cent of voters approved. A new constitution claimed to respect the principles of 1789. It maintained universal suffrage to elect an assembly with limited prerogatives. The assembly was renamed the *Corps législatif* to stress its technical rather than political function. Although it voted on laws and approved the budget, it was not supposed to represent the French people. The president alone, now elected for 10 years, was the holder of popular legitimacy. He controlled legislative, executive, judiciary and military powers and appointed his ministers, individually and directly responsible to him. He chose members of the Senate, which was defined as 'the guardian of the constitution'. The principle of parliamentary democracy was definitely abolished. As early as January 1852, the republican motto – *Liberté, Égalité, Fraternité* – was stripped from public buildings and the president was to be addressed as '*Monseigneur*'. Following a tour of major French 'republican' cities (Bourges, Lyons, Marseilles, Bordeaux) to convince his potential opponents, the president asked the Senate to prepare a text restoring the Empire. It was approved by more than 7 million citizens, through a plebiscite (250,000 voted against it). On 2 December 1852, the president was crowned as Napoleon III.

Following the example of his uncle some 50 years earlier, Louis-Napoleon was called to save the republic before overthrowing it. However, the success of the coup should not lead us to dismiss the Second Republic as a failure and to ignore its enduring effects on French political culture. Universal suffrage and electoral contests helped to crystallise democratic principles. The growing salience of social conflicts and the strong, even violent, political polarisation which ensued would also become a permanent feature of French politics over the next 150 years.

The authoritarian empire, 1852–60

The first decade of the empire was marked by a complete control over the political and social life of the nation. The emperor's government was chosen from a small circle of men, chosen for their docility and devotion or their professional skills (Fould, a banker, Rouher, a lawyer, and Baroche, a top civil servant). Napoleon alone defined the government's agenda, mostly dominated by technical issues. Political options were rarely debated and foreign policy remained his exclusive and personal prerogative. Ministers were only the instrument of the emperor's personal will. At the local level, the regime maintained its grip on the country through the deployment of an army of dedicated civil servants who had to take an oath of allegiance to the emperor. In particular, in each *département*, the regime gave extended powers to *préfets*, faithful henchmen of the empire. They appointed and if necessary sacked local civil servants, police officers, primary school teachers and mayors of smaller communes. As such, they became more powerful than the traditional *notables*, and furthered the centralisation of the country. The *préfets* also controlled and manipulated public opinion. Public meetings and associations, although not always forbidden, came under their close scrutiny. The press was subjected to pernickety constraints, which prevented it from criticising the regime. For each election campaign, the *préfets* mobilised all available resources to support the official candidate of the regime, resorting to fraudulent practice, intimidation and violence if necessary. They could count on police officers, whose numbers more than doubled under the empire, and on an efficient network of informers. Therefore, it was hardly surprising that of the

267 members of the *Corps Législatif*, only 8 opposed the regime in 1852 and 12 in 1857. A wave of assassination attempts against the emperor led the regime to intensify its repression against republican milieux and to pass a law (*loi des suspects*, 1858), which allowed the police to jail, without trial, anyone who had already been condemned for political reasons. An atmosphere of suspicion prevailed and the opposition was successfully muzzled.

The empire was anxious to charm the traditional elites of the county. In particular, Napoleon sought the support of the Catholic church, as a pillar of social order. The clergy were invited to official ceremonies, saw an increase in the budget devoted to religion and benefited from subsidies for the construction of new churches. The regime stimulated the creation of new congregations which increased their control over primary and secondary education. The empire particularly cajoled Brittany, where the support for the coup had been lukewarm and where monarchist feelings were deep-rooted. A bishopric was created in Laval, Rennes was given its first archbishop and the expansion of congregations in the Morbihan was actively supported. The church, however, remained under state control. The emperor, fortifying the **Gallican** tradition, could reprimand or suspend bishops and still controlled the implementation of papal decisions. Nevertheless, even **Ultramontain** Catholics were seduced by his authoritarian rule and his willingness to tame social unrest. The vast majority of the clergy rallied to the regime.

> ### Gallicans and Ultramontains
>
> Gallican Catholics rejected the pope's supremacy within the church, and rejected his right to intervene in secular matters and believed that the state had a role to play in the organisation of the national church, notably the appointment of bishops. Ultramontain Catholics defended the leadership of the pope, supported his crusade against national and liberal ideals and claimed that education should be the preserve of the church alone. Ultramontains increased their influence under the Second Empire. Anxious to conciliate the church as a bulwark of social order, Napoleon maintained French troops in Rome to protect the temporal papal powers against the Italian nationalist and republican armies, but refused to relax his control over bishops or to extend the influence of the church on education.

Repression alone could not explain the ability of the regime to control public opinion. In 1857 more than 5.5 million Frenchmen voted for official candidates. Such a majority could not have been entirely 'manufactured'. The authoritarian empire was also a popular one. Its appeal partly rested on the equivocal nature of 'Bonapartism'. In the name of national unity, Bonapartism rejected the polarisation of political life. To the self-serving interests of political parties and the parliamentary squabbling of the *notables* it opposed the authority of one leader, directly and personally supported by the nation. Attached to the principle of national sovereignty, ideally expressed through plebiscites, Bonapartism appeared as a nationalist, democratic and popular ideology. Against aristocratic ambitions, Bonapartism warranted the major reforms of the Revolution, including the redistribution of land. Against the stifling powers of the *notables*, it promised democratic emancipation, and this might explain the massive support it received from the peasantry, ready to assert its independence against the traditional local elites. Against social turmoil, it defended order and property. Against poverty, it developed the vision of a modern industrial society, rich enough to eradicate misery. Against isolation in Europe, it offered to make France the arbiter of powers on the continent. The ambiguous political nature of Bonapartist synthesis was, therefore, its strength because Louis-Napoleon was able to bring together different social groups around a common national project at home and abroad.

Economic expansion

Economic modernisation and the industrialisation of the nation were at the heart of Napoleon's project. What characterised economic and industrial expansion in France was the proactive role played by the state in encouraging prosperity, promoting technical progress and mobilising resources to bring material well-being to the nation. Napoleon considered economic expansion as a prerequisite to solving social tensions and integrating the working class into the nation. First, the state encouraged partnership and cooperation between various decision-makers, through the creation of the Agriculture, Trade and Public Works High Council. Ministers, civil servants, industrialists and bankers together defined economic priorities. Second, the state stimulated economic activities with a considerable reform of the banking sector. Due to the reluctance of the traditional banking system to invest in capitalist ventures, the state supported the development of commercial banks, which were ready to grant long-term loans and to invest in new commercial undertakings. *Le Crédit mobilier*, for instance, rapidly acquired an international stature. It gave a decisive boost to the development of railways, not only in France, but also in Russia, Austria and Spain. It financed the creation of the *Compagnie générale transatlantique*, stimulating trading relations with the American continent. It participated in the modernisation of major ports, such as Marseilles, facilitating relations with Algeria and the emerging colonial empire. At the regional level, the state also promoted the creation of deposit banks, such as *le Crédit Lyonnais*, in order to drain off

Haussmann and Paris

Baron Haussmann (1809–91), *préfet* of the Seine, was in charge of carrying out the emperor's plans to turn Paris into a symbol of modernity. Paris became a gigantic construction project financed by the state, the city, private companies and supported by *le Crédit foncier*. Two hundred thousand workers were employed to demolish and rebuild some 3,800 buildings, thus absorbing part of the unemployed population. Styling himself as *un artiste démolisseur*, Haussmann replaced the insalubrious narrow streets of central Paris with elegant and large avenues. This made the erection of barricades more difficult. Paris was embellished with fountains, public squares, public buildings (*Opéra Garnier*), two railway stations (*Gare du Nord, Austerlitz*), new bridges, churches and schools, and equipped with a new water and sewage system. The limits of the capital were extended to embrace the inner suburbs, but working-class housing received little attention, the administration being essentially preoccupied with building for the wealthy.

savings into productive activities. Third, the state undertook a series of major public works to modernise agriculture (extension of arable lands, irrigation of Provence) and to improve communications. The telegraph network reached more than 40,000 kilometres in 1870, and the railway network grew from 3,250 to 17,000 kilometres between 1851 and 1870. Railway construction had a beneficial impact on other industries, such as steel and iron. Powerful new companies, such as Schneider in Le Creusot or Wendel in Hayange, employed

> ### Les grands magasins
>
> The first department store in Paris – *le Bon Marché* – was opened in 1852, followed by the *Printemps* in 1865 and *la Samaritaine* in 1870. Shopping in these stores became a symbol of wealth and prestige, as described by Emile Zola in his novel *Au Bonheur des Dames*.

some 10,000 workers to produce railway tracks and trains. The improvement of communication boosted the volume of domestic trade, which doubled under the empire. Twenty-four chambers of commerce were created throughout the country, transactions were made easier by the use of cheques, authorised in 1865, and departmentments (**les grands magasins**) became fashionable. The architecture of major cities was deeply altered by urban renovation, sponsored by the state. Finally, the state encouraged international trade. It signed a trading treaty with Britain (1860) removing prohibition on raw materials and lowering customs tariffs, notably on textiles and wines. A series of similar treaties, aimed at improving free trade between nations, were signed with most European powers in the 1860s, often against the desire of the Orleanist *notables*, who were deeply attached to protectionism. The empire witnessed a three-fold increase in the value of foreign trade.

However, economic results remained uneven. Despite the progressive mechanisation of agriculture and the use of chemical fertilisers, especially in the Beauce region, productivity remained low in large parts of the country. Peasants of poorer regions (Alps, Brittany, Limousin) migrated to big industrial centres or found part-time jobs in local industries to supplement their income. Around Rouen or Lyons, peasants, mostly women, worked in their own homes to produce garments for wool and silk companies, whose production methods often remained those of cottage industry. Small companies still dominated French industry, and owing to their lack of capital, were prone to crises. Companies which traded internationally remained the exception. Workers' conditions were still precarious. Paternalistic industrialists, such as Dollfus in Mulhouse, offered their employees decent lodgings, schools and contingent funds to alleviate their misery, but required them to distance themselves from political activities. The emperor himself attempted to reconcile the working class with the regime. In 1859, working-class leaders (Blanqui, Barbès) were granted amnesty. In 1862 Napoleon authorised a workers' delegation to travel to London to study the organisation of British trade unions. In 1864 the right to strike was legally recognised. But workers refused to be lured into the emperor's game. They opposed the regime and its paternalism, launching numerous strikes and setting up employees' associations. Progressively they became convinced that only a revolution could impose a social and democratic republic.

A new international role?

In 1852 Napoleon promised that the empire would mean peace in Europe. However, his prime ambition was to raise France to the rank of a great European power, a position that was lost with the 1815 treaties. The Crimean War (1854) gave him the opportunity to break the alliance formed against his uncle. The expansionist policy of the czar in the Black Sea, aimed at opening the Mediterranean to Russian influence and bringing the Holy Land under Orthodox control, met with the hostility of London and Paris. Britain could not accept Russian control of Constantinople, a key position on the road to India. France claimed to be the protector of Catholics in the Holy Land. In 1854, both declared war on Russia. The war cost many lives. Fifty-five thousand French soldiers were killed either by the enemy, epidemics or the freezing Crimean winter. During the long siege of Sebastopol, two-thirds of the French troops were slain. But the Crimean War fulfilled Napoleon's objectives. France and Britain had fought together, Prussia and Austria had remained neutral and Russia was vanquished. The 1815 Alliance against France was broken. In 1856 Napoleon invited European powers to Paris to solve their disputes. France wanted to be a chief mediator in Europe to recover its prestige.

Napoleon's foreign policy was also influenced by what has been called the 'theory of nationalities'. This rested on the idea that all people had the right to self-determination. France's historic mission was to assist European peoples to achieve this objective. Thus, France supported the creation of an independent Rumania (1856–66) against the Ottoman Empire. Above all, the victorious French military intervention in Italy (1859) was decisive in ousting Austria from Italy (except in the Veneto) and uniting the country under the Sardo-Piedmontese crown. The pope lost most of his territories and this generated resentment against the empire among French Catholics. Nevertheless, the emperor who led the troops in Italy returned triumphantly to Paris, giving the impression that France was powerful enough to shape the European map.

Yet the 'theory of nationalities' was not a coherent one. The abortive military attempt to crush republican forces in Mexico and place an Austrian archduke on a Mexican throne (1861–67) was dictated by commercial interests and diplomatic transactions which directly contradicted Napoleon's support for nationalism. Likewise, in its failed attempt to check Prussia's rise, the empire was ready to sponsor the creation of a Rhenish buffer state, to acquire Luxemburg and to question the independence of Belgium. In all cases, it showed that the theory was easily sacrificed in favour of French national interests.

Outside of Europe, colonial expansion, which resulted from *ad hoc* opportunist decisions rather than a well-defined policy, gave France great prestige. It derived economic advantages from the annexation of New Caledonia (1853), rich in nickel, gained further access to the Chinese market (1858) and brought Madagascar and the Gabonese coast under its economic influence (1862). France asserted its sovereignty over Indochina and made Cambodia a protectorate (1863). The strengthening of its presence in Senegal and the military submission of Algeria (1858) helped France to pursue its penetration of the African continent. Napoleon tried to develop an original policy in Algeria. The reconciliation of settlers' and indigenous interests was perceived as the necessary prerequisite for the valorisation of the territory. In 1865 he declared to the indigenous population that 'France has not come here to destroy your people and your national culture ... I want to increase your well-being, to associate you further with the administration of your country and to bring you the benefits of civilisation.' Through a policy of association, rather than assimilation, he returned part of the land to the tribes (1860) and gave Muslims the possibility of acquiring French nationality (1865). However, the 'emperor of the Arabs' met with the determined opposition of settlers, who wished to pursue the colonisation of Algeria without taking into account the fate of the Arab population. In the end the settlers were too powerful and the emperor's failure in Algeria reflected a general weakening of the regime at the end of the 1860s.

Towards a liberal empire, 1860–70

The 1860s witnessed a liberal evolution of the regime. Once his powers had been strengthened and the opposition had been tamed, the emperor was not opposed in principle to a progressive but limited liberalisation of the regime. The *Corps législatif* was allowed to discuss the general orientation of the regime (1860), to control part of the budgetary process (1861), to amend legislation (1866) and above all to criticise the government (1867). However, these concessions encouraged rather than disarmed the opposition. Catholics, already critical of Napoleon's Italian policy, criticised the growing interference of the state in the education system, which curtailed the church's influence on schools. The bourgeois elite rediscovered the liberal virtues it had forgotten when threatened by the red peril and asked for political reforms. In 1864 Thiers called for the regime to respect fundamental rights and to restore the parliamentary system which was abolished in 1852. Republican ideas, purged of their 1848 idealism, gained ground in rationalist and anti-clerical circles and were echoed by a combative but often muzzled press. Gambetta, a lawyer and talented orator, was able to rally the middle class, the petty bourgeoisie and part of the working class to the republican cause, calling for social reforms and the separation of church and state. Socialists maintained the pressure on the regime, regularly organising strikes and demonstrations. The alliance between liberals and republicans in 1869 gave them enough seats in the *Corps législatif* to call for the restoration of a parliamentary system. Napoleon reluctantly agreed to return some parliamentary prerogatives to the *Corps législatif*, providing that the direct link uniting the emperor with the French people was not severed. Cunningly, in 1870 he organised a plebiscite (in itself the negation of parliamentary principles) to ratify the liberal evolution of the regime and to reinforce his personal prestige. An overwhelming majority (82 per cent) fortified his authority. Both the new

Baudelaire and Flaubert

In 1857 Charles Baudelaire published a collection of poems, *Les Fleurs du Mal*, which explored the complexities of love with unprecedented frankness. One year earlier Gustave Flaubert's first novel, *Madame Bovary*, shocked readers with his story of a provincial doctor's wife who is bored with marriage and seeks fulfilment through adultery. Both were prosecuted for offending public morals, an example of the illiberal nature of the early years of the Second Empire.

parliamentary majority *and* the emperor thought that they had strengthened their respective position. Five months later, the empire collapsed.

By 1867, the international prestige of the regime had been seriously eroded by a series of diplomatic and military mistakes, which left France rather isolated in Europe. Specifically, in remaining neutral in the conflict opposing Austria and Prussia for the domination of the German states, France failed to check Prussian military and political ambitions. After the Austrian defeat in Sadowa (1866), the Prussian chancellor Bismarck took the lead in an enlarged federation of German states. Bismarck thought that a war with France could stir up German nationalist feelings, overcome the reluctance of some southern German states to rally to Prussia and finally achieve German unification under his leadership. When the chancellor released a truncated letter from the Prussian king, which seemed insulting to France, French public opinion, the press and the *Corps légis-latif* called for war. Napoleon thought that a war could both stop Prussian ambitions and unite the country behind him. French diplomatic isolation and its military inferiority led to a crushing defeat. The emperor, who commanded the French army, capitulated in Sedan and was imprisoned by the enemy. Paris responded to the military capitulation by abolishing the empire and proclaming a republic (4 September 1870). With nationalist fervour, Paris declared its willingness to carry on fighting the Prussian army.

The emperor was released by the Prussians (1871) and died in exile in Chislehurst, in England (1873) to general indifference in France. However, Bonapartist ideas became a major feature of the French right. A belief in the authority of the state, a lack of enthu-siasm for parliamentary democracy and political parties, the role played by a providential saviour to redeem France from its own divisions and to provide her with international *grandeur*, all found in de Gaulle, some 80 years later, a convincing heir. The empire did not entirely fulfil Napoleon III's ambitions. Social tensions had not been diffused but polarised and France did not acquire a predominant diplomatic role in Europe. However, the empire rooted universal suffrage in French political culture, provided the country with the necessary structures for the development of a modern industrial system and laid the foundations for French colonial expansion. All these achievements would be further developed by the new republic.

Document 4a: Un républicain marseillais

Circulaire électorale de Louis Langomazino, ouvrier mécanicien chaudronnier de Marseille pour les élections à l'Assemblée constituante (mars–avril 1848).

CITOYENS,

J'ai été, je suis et serai toujours Républicain. Je l'ai été car toutes les actions de ma vie ont toujours tendu vers les grands principes égalitaires, car tous mes écrits antérieurs respirent l'esprit de la Démocratie; car alors qu'il y avait au moins de l'audace à proclamer cette opinion, je n'ai pas hésité à le faire. [. . .] je fus porté à l'étude des questions sociales par ce besoin d'aimer et d'être aimé qui est selon moi, l'expression la plus vraie du Républicanisme. Sans l'Egalité, pas d'amour. [. . .]
      Je considère la guerre comme un fléau. La paix est l'état normal de la nature;

mais la paix glorieuse qu'on n'achète pas au prix de son honneur. [. . .] le jour où des despotes voudraient en profiter pour enchaîner les peuples et neutraliser leurs efforts vers la liberté, je mêlerais ma voix à la voix des milliers de citoyens qui se lèveraient comme un seul homme pour frapper à coups redoublés sur l'hydre de la tyrannie. [. . .] Que la France [. . .] respecte toutes les nationalités; qu'elle leur souffle l'air vivifiant et pur qu'elle respire; qu'elle rende enfin à celles qui se tordent dans une longue agonie la vie et la liberté.

Une fusion bien franche et bien sincère doit s'opérer dans toutes les classes de la société; plus de ligne de démarcation parmi les enfants de la grande famille humaine; égalité de droits, de devoirs, de condition, de considération [. . .] Que la justice n'ait pas deux poids dans sa balance; que son temple soit accessible à tous; que la clé d'or ne soit plus la seule qui ouvre ses portes. Que tous les emplois scientifiques, littéraires, administratifs, etc., ne soient accordés qu'au mérite [. . .] et pour arriver à ce résultat, qu'on n'accorde de place qu'à celui qui sort victorieux d'un concours où chacun soit appelé à donner la mesure de ses aptitudes.

La conscience d'un citoyen est un tabernacle sacré dans lequel il ne doit pas être permis de fouiller; que chacun professe sa religion et manifeste ses croyances en toute liberté; mais que l'Etat soutienne également tous les cultes et ne permette pas à l'un d'absorber tous les autres, [. . .] Qu'on fasse disparaître des temples de la prière tout ce qui peut rappeler à l'esprit l'amour des choses matérielles; que la prière ne soit plus mise à contribution, ce qui n'a pas peu contribué à l'indifférence en matière religieuse dans l'esprit d'un grand nombre de Citoyens; que le luxe effréné en soit banni pour faire place à l'humilité que toute religion commande [. . .]. Que les couvents soient abolis [. . .] Cette réclusion volontaire n'est ni dans les lois de Dieu ni dans les lois de la nature [. . .] chacun est nécessaire à tous; c'est donc désobéir à la loi divine que de vivre dans cette solitude. La retraite cloîtrée décèle plutôt de la lâcheté qu'un véritable amour de Dieu.

Mais surtout ce qui doit être pour tous l'objet des plus vives sollicitudes, c'est l'organisation du travail [. . .] par ce moyen, la République s'établira sur des bases inébranlables. La souffrance aigrit et divise; que chacun des membres du corps social reçoive, en retour de son travail, la rémunération proportionnée à ses besoins présents et à venir, afin que tous viennent se rallier autour du gouvernement qui la leur aura donnée. [. . .] L'Etat doit avoir à sa charge les impotents et les invalides, non pas traités comme des malfaiteurs, mais bien comme des malheureux dont il faut adoucir les douleurs [. . .].

Dominique Lecoeur, 'Du socialisme ouvrier à la République des paysans, l'itinéraire de Louis Langomazino', in *Provence 1851: Une insurrection pour la République Association 1851–2001*, Les Mées, 2000, pp. 82–90

Document 4b: Le Bonapartisme et le parti de l'ordre

La France ne veut ni le retour à l'Ancien régime, quelle que soit la forme qui le déguise, ni l'essai d'utopies funestes et impraticables. C'est parce que je suis l'adversaire de l'un et de l'autre qu'elle a placé sa confiance en moi [. . .] Si mon gouvernement n'a pas pu réaliser toutes les améliorations qu'il avait en vue, il faut s'en prendre aux manœuvres des factions. Depuis trois ans on a pu remarquer que j'ai toujours été secondé par l'Assemblée quand il s'est agi de combattre le désordre par des menaces de compression; mais lorsque j'ai voulu faire le bien, améliorer le sort des populations, elle m'a refusé son concours.

Discours du Prince-Président à Dijon, 1 juin 1851

Document 4c: Les objectifs de l'empire

[. . .] Je le dis avec franchise aussi éloignée de l'orgueil que de la fausse modestie, jamais un peuple n'a témoigné d'une manière plus directe, plus spontanée, plus unanime, la volonté de s'affranchir des préoccupations de l'avenir, en consolidant dans la même main un pouvoir qui lui est sympathique. [. . .] Il sait qu'en 1852 la société courait à sa perte, parce que chaque parti se consolait d'avance du naufrage général par l'espoir de planter son drapeau sur les débris qui pourraient surnager. Il me sait gré d'avoir sauvé la vaisseau en abordant seulement le drapeau de la France. [. . .] Je ne suis pas de la famille des idéologues. Pour faire le bien du pays, il n'est pas besoin d'appliquer de nouveaux systèmes; mais de donner avant tout confiance dans le présent, sécurité dans l'avenir. Voilà pourquoi la France semble vouloir revenir à l'Empire. [. . .] Par esprit de défiance, certaines personnes se disent: 'l'Empire, c'est la guerre.' Moi je dis: 'l'Empire, c'est la paix.' C'est la paix car la France le désire et lorsque la France est satisfaite, le monde est tranquille. [. . .] J'en conviens, cependant, j'ai, comme l'empereur, bien des conquêtes à faire. Je veux, comme lui, conquérir à la conciliation les partis dissidents et ramener dans le courant du grand fleuve populaire les dérivations hostiles qui vont se perdre sans profit pour personne. Je veux conquérir à la religion, à la morale, à l'aisance, cette partie encore si nombreuse de la population qui, au milieu d'un pays de foi et de croyance, connaît à peine les précepts du Christ; qui au sein de la terre la plus fertile du monde, peut à peine jouir de ses produits de première nécessité. Nous avons d'immenses territoires incultes à défricher, des routes à ouvrir, des ports à creuser, des rivières à rendre navigables, des canaux à terminer, notre réseau de chemin de fer à compléter. Nous avons en face de Marseille, un vaste royaume à assimiler à la France. Nous avons tous nos grands ports de l'ouest à rapprocher du continent américain par la rapidité de ces communications qui nous manquent encore. Nous avons partout enfin des ruines à relever, de faux dieux à abattre, des vérités à faire triompher. Voilà comment je comprends l'empire, si l'empire doit se rétablir.

Discours du Prince-Président prononcé à Bordeaux le 9 octobre 1852 (*Le Moniteur universel*, 12 octobre 1852)

Topics
FOR DISCUSSION

1   What were the principles upon which the Second Republic was established? How does Document 4a illustrate the original spirit of the Second Republic? To what extent has this spirit been fulfilled?

2   What were the causes of the June 1848 Revolution?

3   What was the popular appeal of Louis-Napoleon Bonaparte? How does Document 4b help us to understand this appeal?

4   What sort of regime was the Second Empire? How does Document 4c help us in understanding the nature of the Second Empire?

5   How did the Second Empire evolve in the 1860s?

6   What was Louis-Napoleon's foreign policy? How successful was this policy?

CHAPTER 5

The Third Republic, 1870–1914

Timeline

1870
4 September   Proclamation of the Republic

1871
18 January   Proclamation of a united Germany
March–May   the Paris Commune

1877
16 May   President MacMahon dissolves the Assembly

1879
MacMahon resigns

1882
Laws establishing free primary school education

1894
Dreyfus court-martialled for spying

1899
Establishment of the government of republican defence under Waldeck-Rousseau

1901
1 June   Establishment of the Radical Party

1905
Creation of the Socialist Party
9 December   Separation of church and state

1906
Clémenceau government comes to power

1907
Repression of protests by winegrowers in Languedoc

The Franco-Prussian War was a humiliation for French society. The proclamation by Bismarck of a united Germany in the Hall of Mirrors at the Palace of Versailles on 18 January 1871, followed closely by the loss of Alsace-Lorraine, demonstrated in an emphatic manner that France was no longer the most powerful country on the continent, a position of pre-eminence which the French had enjoyed since the mid-seventeenth century. Henceforth the lost provinces would be an open wound in French politics, fuelling anti-German hatred for decades to come. In the short term, however, the threat of revolution produced a large-scale swing to conservatism.

The Paris Commune, March–May 1871

Initially the provisional, republican government of national defence tried to stiffen French resistance but it quickly proved incapable of stemming the Prussian invasion. From 19 September 1870 Paris was under siege and after a long, harsh winter – the coldest in living memory – the capital finally capitulated on 28 January 1871. Thereafter elections in February 1871 led to a monarchist National Assembly which made the now arch-conservative Adolphe Thiers, an Orleanist, head of government. Thiers immediately negotiated the Treaty of

les pétroleuses

In the face of the army advance the Communards set fire to buildings and right-wing commentators were horrified by what they saw as mindless acts of mob violence. In particular they singled out working women – dubbed *les pétroleuses* – as the principal culprits. They were disgusted by the way in which these women, through participation in the Commune, were transgressing the boundaries of conventional, bourgeois femininity. Thereafter the female revolutionary, encapsulating the threat of the 'dangerous classes', was to become a familiar figure of fear and loathing within the right-wing press.

Frankfurt under which France surrendered Alsace-Lorraine – thus losing vital iron ore reserves and agricultural land – and was forced to accept an indemnity of 5,000 million FF. In Paris there was outrage at the indignity of these terms and this was compounded still further by the unsuccessful attempt on 18 March to disarm the National Guard, the citizens' militia formed to defend Paris against the Germans. Fearing an uprising, Thiers now moved the government and army to Versailles, but if he hoped this would intimidate the Parisian populace, their response was unequivocal. Rather than submit, they elected a Commune by universal male suffrage to run the city.

Practically speaking, the Commune had few concrete goals beyond preservation of the Republic. Likewise only one member out of 81 was a self-proclaimed Marxist, whilst only 35 members could be properly described as working class. Thus, the Commune was neither revolutionary nor socialist. Yet Thiers saw it as such and on 21 May dispatched troops commanded by Marshal MacMahon to attack Paris. What followed became known in left-wing folklore as the 'bloody week'. Twenty-five thousand communards were killed, 10,000 convicted and 5,000 deported to the penal colony of New Caledonia in the Pacific. The political significance of this repression was enormous. It was the foundation stone of the new regime because it demonstrated that the Republic was not synonymous with revolution. In the wake of the Commune, large numbers of the propertied classes rallied to the Third Republic.

The monarchist republic, 1871–79

Thiers was now convinced that a republic was the best guarantee of law and order. 'The Republic will be conservative or will not be' was his dictum and on this basis he set out to win support for the new regime. Firstly, he quickly paid off the war indemnity. This meant that all German troops had gone by September 1873 and allowed him to cast himself as the 'liberator of the territory'. Secondly, he maintained administrative continuity, leaving prefectoral power largely intact. Thirdly, he followed a policy of financial prudence, ensuring conservative and middle-class support through the rejection of income tax. However, in November 1872 Thiers went too far when he openly declared support for republicanism. This conversion provoked outrage amongst the royalist majority, which, faced with dwindling numbers because of by-elections in 1871 when republicans had won 99 out 114 seats, now took decisive action. The upshot was that in May 1873

Thiers was replaced as president by Marshal MacMahon and as prime minister by the Duke de Broglie, an Orleanist. As the man who had crushed the Commune, MacMahon was the personification of Catholic ultra-conservatism and what followed was a right-wing aristocratic government which combined extravagant displays of religious fervour with a purge of republican mayors, the closure of subversive cafés and the banning of public celebrations of the French Revolution on 14 July.

At this point a royalist restoration seemed a likely scenario. Yet in time-honoured fashion the royalists remained bitterly divided. The legitimists backed the Comte de Chambord, Charles X's grandson, as the most obvious candidate for the throne, whilst the Orleanists backed the Comte de Paris, grandson of Louis-Philippe. One possible solution was that the Comte de Paris would accept Chambord, who was childless, as king if he could then succeed him, but Chambord rejected any talk of compromise. To make matters worse, he continued to insist that the white flag of the Bourbons should replace the Tricolour as the national flag and with such intransigence went all hopes of a restoration.

> ### Sacré-Cœur
>
> In July 1873, shortly after MacMahon came to power, the Assembly approved the building of the Sacré-Cœur basilica on the Montmartre hilltop, the spot where two generals had been shot by the Communards. Dominating the Paris skyline, the Sacré-Cœur served the symbolic purpose of asking for forgiveness for the sins of the atheist Commune. However, for republicans it came to stand for the worst excesses of clerical domination.

Despite this impasse the royalist majority fought a fierce rearguard action. The constitutional settlement of 1875 established a 7-year presidency with strong executive powers, and a part nominated, part indirectly elected Senate, both of which were designed to limit the powers of a chamber of deputies based upon universal male suffrage. Indeed, the fact that the presidential powers, which included the right to appoint ministers and dissolve the Assembly, bore such a strong resemblance to those enjoyed by Louis-Philippe under the July Monarchy was indicative of the way in which royalists were playing a waiting game, still hoping to engineer a restoration at a later date.

The stage was now set for the 1876 elections which saw the return of 340 republicans, elected principally in the east, southeast and Paris regions, alongside 155 monarchists. Given this arithmetic MacMahon was forced to accept the moderate republican Jules Simon as prime minister, but, from the outset, confrontation was just a matter of time. MacMahon could not stomach the anti-clericalism of the new government and on 16 May 1877 he dismissed Simon and dissolved the parliament despite its clear republican majority. Republicans accused MacMahon of trying to carry out a coup and on this platform they won another resounding majority in the October elections. Once more MacMahon had a republican government foisted upon him and in this precise sense the political importance of 16 May cannot be overstated. Henceforth presidential powers would be weak. Never again would the power of dissolution be used nor would the president be allowed to pick ministers. From now on the Chamber of Deputies would dominate the political life of the Third Republic. In effect, it would come to dictate the composition of governments and in the absence of clearly

Figure 5.1   An anti-MacMahon caricature

organised parties, this would lead to chronic instability. In the first 40 years of the Third Republic there were to be no less than 50 changes of government.

The opportunist republic, 1879–99

In 1879 not only did the Senate fall to republicans but MacMahon finally resigned over attempts to purge army officers. He was replaced by Jules Grévy, an elderly republican lawyer, and at this point it was clear that the republicans had definitively won out over the monarchists. To symbolise this political victory parliament was moved from Versailles to Paris, the Marseillaise was adopted as the national anthem and the anniversary of 14 July was made into a national holiday. Sociologically 1879 represented the defeat of the traditional social elite, in particular noble and non-noble landowners, although it is important not to overplay this sense of a definitive social rupture. In practice, a large section of the economic elite now came to the view that a conservative republic would be the regime best designed to defend their interests.

The year 1879 now ushered in a long period of conservative republican rule as politics was dominated by moderates who came to be known as opportunists. With no formal parties in the modern sense political tendencies were organised around meetings and informal networks and, in the case of the opportunists, they were to find their unity and direction in two particular personalities, Thiers and Gambetta. The one-time monarchist and the one-time firebrand radical were an unlikely couple. Nonetheless, Thiers' reassuring conservatism and Gambetta's fierce anti-clericalism were to be a powerful combination. Forgetting their previous differences, both underlined their common belief in science, progress and an attachment to patriotic values; both upheld the principles of individual liberty; and both came to support a moderate republic which aimed to introduce a liberal-democratic system and hold the centre ground against the monarchists on the right and the socialists on the extreme left. In electoral terms their programme found support amongst shopkeepers, café owners, the peasantry, lawyers, school teachers – what Gambetta called the new strata (*couches nouvelles*) – as well as the established middle classes and the nobility. As he strove to build this broad consensus of support for the Third Republic, Gambetta studiously avoided all talk of class conflict and social reform, preferring to speak in more general terms about the little people against the big interests, in particular the church and the wealthy conservative elite.

To cement this consensus the 1880s witnessed a whole spate of reforms. To begin with, there was the invention of a secular religion as a whole range of republican symbols and ceremonies were introduced into daily French life. The bust of Marianne was prominently displayed in each town hall; the revolutionary triptych of liberty, equality and fraternity was enshrined as the slogan of the Third Republic. Yet, in doing all this the opportunists were careful to underline that the goals of 1789 had been realised and social change was no longer on the agenda, a further example of the way in which the Republic was being disentangled from Revolution. At the same time restrictions on the press and public meetings were lifted, trade unions were legalised and work schemes were introduced for the unemployed, whilst concrete attempts were made to remove inequalities and open careers to talent. For example, life senators were abolished in 1884 and replaced by elected ones and, in the diplomatic service, competitive examinations were introduced to determine recruitment. In 1881 the Communards were amnestied in a symbolic gesture of reconciliation and national unity.

cafés

Because cafés were the traditional place to talk, they had been subjected to stringent restrictions under the Second Empire. However, when laws passed in 1881 relaxed these restrictions, there was an explosion of café culture and cafés became vital public arenas for the dissemination of republican ideas. Now in countless villages across France the local café and the local church stood in defiant opposition to one another. Invariably marked by a strong drinking culture, the café, along with the game of *boules*, was to become a traditional male reserve. In Paris the hill of Montmartre was dotted with cafés and café-concerts where poets read their writings and mingled with artists trying to sell their work.

However, the greatest energy was reserved for a concerted attack on clerical power. In republicans' eyes the church – with its reactionary politics, its immense wealth and, above all, its control of the education of the masses – was the greatest barrier to the principles of 1789. Gambetta had been the leading voice of anti-clericalism but with his death in November 1881 this mantle was passed to Jules Ferry, who, as minister of education for most of the time from 1870 to 1885, unveiled a state education system which aimed to take on and break the power of the priesthood. As from March 1882 education was to be free and obligatory for everybody aged 6 to 13. Through mass primary education the Third Republic would wrest control of minds and bodies from the church and this explains why teachers came to assume such a truly heroic status within republican imagery. They were the foot soldiers of the Republic, the guardians of 1789, spreading civilisation and battling against obscurantism. In this way the Ferry revolution was uncompromisingly secular. Consequently the Jesuit order was dissolved in 1880, all religious education was removed from the curriculum and in 1886 all clerics in state schools were replaced by lay personnel. Now children would be taught to be good citizens. They would be inculcated with a secular frame of mind which stressed loyalty and patriotism along with a healthy respect for law and order.

The struggle against clericalism went hand in hand with the desire to end illiteracy and create a strong sense of national identity. By teaching geography and history and by teaching in French, rather than Occitan or Breton, Ferry wanted to eradicate regional and local identities and instil loyalty to the Third Republic. Primary schools, therefore, would turn the peasantry into loyal French citizens and between 1875 and 1914 school numbers increased by 1 million. Within republican circles these figures were held up as a triumph, illustrating the way in which the generous republic had liberated the minds of ordinary people. There was much truth in this, but it was also true that primary education illustrated the extent to which the Third Republic was shot through with divisions of class, race and gender. Secondary education, for example, remained a middle-class privilege. In Algeria, formally divided into three departments in 1881, the majority of Muslims were denied basic education until well into the 1950s. Likewise in primary schools, girls were taught that nature predestined them to a subordinate role to men. Thus public space, the domain of the active citizen, was exclusively masculine, whilst private space was feminine. This sense of exclusion was reinforced by conscription. Women, it was argued by moderate republicans, could not be considered true citizens, and hence have the right to vote, because they had not forged a bond with the nation through military service.

Not only was Jules Ferry the architect of the godless school; he was also the most powerful advocate of imperial expansion. Ferry was the moving force behind the annexation of Tunisia in 1881 and the completion of the conquest of Indo-China in 1883. He also sanctioned the acquisition of the Congo and Madagascar. To those who opposed this aggressive expansion Ferry offered up a triple justification. Firstly, there was an economic argument. By providing markets and raw materials, the empire would insulate France from economic depression. Secondly, there was a humanitarian aspect. France was embarking upon a civilising mission which would raise inferior cultures to the level of French civilisation. Finally, there was the importance of national prestige.

Possession of colonies proved that France was still a great power. Ferry's arguments illustrated the way in which the empire, which hitherto had been acquired largely by accident, was being given greater purpose and direction by the Third Republic. They also represented a fusion of the 1789 principles and imperial expansion that in turn was reflected in the changing tone of the Bastille Day ceremonies. With each passing year of the Third Republic the 14 July celebrations increasingly blended republicanism with displays of military and imperial might. Nonetheless, in the short term imperialism was Ferry's undoing. Ferry was attacked as a dupe of Bismarck, who was diverting France away from the reconquest of Alsace-Lorraine, and in 1885, fearful that military forces in Tonkin were on the verge of defeat, Ferry's enemies engineered his downfall. Yet, in the end Ferry's arguments won out. As all the major powers became involved in the scramble for colonies, France could not lose out and between 1880 and 1895 the empire grew dramatically from 1 million to 9.5 million square kilometres. Thereafter the momentum was unstoppable, with the result that by 1914 France was the ruler of an immense empire, second in size only to the British one.

Map 5.1   The French Republic, 1881. Schoolchildren were taught that Algeria was comprised of three départements and that the Mediterranean separated France like the Seine separated Paris
Reproduced with permission from L. Lanier, A. Laborde, C. Rogeaux, La France et ses Colonies, *Cours Elémentaire, © Librairie Belin, 1920*

Challenges from the right and the left

The world economic downturn of 1873, symbolising as it did the extent to which France was locked into a global, capitalist economy, produced a general mood of discontent. Workers, peasants, small traders and manufacturers were all hit very hard, and as the downward spiral continued, they became more and more disgruntled at the failure of the new republic to combat the depression. Politicians were increasingly dismissed as instinctively corrupt and self-serving. In particular, people were frustrated at the instability of the system and this anger was to fuel political challenges from the right and the left.

On the right new political movements found support from within the ranks of disgruntled Catholics. Here the most dynamic force was Paul Déroulède's *Ligue des patriotes,* founded in 1882. Initially sympathetic to the Third Republic, by 1885 Déroulède had moved to a position of outright hostility. An instinctive rabble-rouser, his language laced clericalism, opposition to social reform and a mystical belief in the army with hatred of the Third Republic and a rejection of its electoral system. Déroulède first shot to national prominence during the so-called Boulanger affair, the roots of which can be traced to the 1885 elections when the opportunists lost their majority and were forced to depend upon the radicals to survive. Ironically, given the subsequent turn of events, the radicals insisted upon the appointment of Georges Boulanger, a veteran of the Franco-Prussian War and well known as a republican general, as minister of war. Yet Boulanger quickly won huge popularity with the wider public, calling for a more authoritarian government and styling himself as the one man capable of standing up to Germany. Alarmed by the burgeoning cult of Boulanger, and fearing an anti-parliamentary coup, the government dismissed him from the army in 1887. Now, however, Boulanger was free to stand as a political candidate and in alliance with Déroulède he won a series of stunning by-elections, including Paris in January 1889. Financed by wealthy royalists this was the first mass campaign in French politics and the country was flooded with statues and posters of Boulanger. In a rising tide of street violence Boulanger's followers urged him to seize power. Sensing danger, the government now took resolute action, banning the *Ligue des patriotes* and threatening Boulanger with prosecution for treason. At this crucial point Boulanger lost his nerve and fled to Belgium. Two years later he committed suicide on the grave of his mistress.

Although disappointed by the immediate outcome, the Boulanger episode was a vital political apprenticeship for the likes of Déroulède. It allowed Déroulède to sharpen his anti-parliamentary arguments, and if the ideas of this new populist right continued to gain ground, this was in large part due to a series of high-profile political scandals which sapped the legitimacy of the Third Republic. In 1887 Daniel Wilson, the son-in-law of President Jules Grévy, exploited his connections to sell the Legion of Honour to the highest bidder. It was a sordid affair, symbolising just how far high ideals were being soiled by greed and self-interest. Five years later the Third Republic was shaken by the Panama scandal when Ferdinand Lesseps, who had already built the Suez Canal, set up the Panama Canal Company to finance the linking of the Pacific Ocean with the Caribbean. When difficult terrain and malarial conditions caused financial problems, the Company bribed members of the Chamber of Deputies to approve a large loan to rescue the project. Despite this, in 1889 the Company still went bankrupt whereupon more than half a million investors lost their money. Three years later Edouard Drumont's daily *La Libre Parole* broke the scandal, revealing just how the Company had spun a web of deceit, duping ordinary investors. Drumont was already infamous as the leading propagandist of anti-Semitic racism. In *La France juive*, published in 1886 and selling over 100,000 copies, he had already denounced the Third Republic as a Jewish plot. Jews, he claimed, might only be 80,000 out of a population of 40 million but they had untold influence and were cynically manipulating the regime to line their pockets. The fact that two of the directors of the Panama Canal Company were Jewish fuelled this rabid anti-Semitism and Drumont took delight in uncovering all the unsavoury details of the case. When all but one of the accused was acquitted in 1893, Drumont's appeal was strengthened.

As scandals engulfed it, the moderate Republic was not only threatened on the right but also the left. During the 1890s the socialist movement emerged as a powerful political force. In the 1893 election the number of socialist deputies increased from 12 to 49, while in 1895 the establishment of the *Confédération générale du travail* (CGT) set out to unify the trade-union movement. There were waves of strikes – rising from 100 per year in the 1880s to over 1,000 in the 1900s – and in 1894 President Sadi Carnot was assassinated by an anarchist. Yet socialists remained splintered over substantive issues of doctrine and practice. Was capitalism to be overthrown by reform or revolution, electoral politics or extra-parliamentary action? Disagreements of this nature fragmented the socialist movement and weakened it as a political force. The *Parti ouvrier français* (POF) of Jules Guesde, founded in 1880, proclaimed itself to be a hard-line class-based Marxist party. Any talk of compromise with the parliamentary system was treachery. All social reforms were dismissed as attempts to buy off the workers and divert them from the overthrow of capitalism. In contrast, the followers of Paul Brousse, known as 'Possibilists' because they rejected the all-or-nothing principles of Guesde, focused on immediate problems, trying to transform working-class lives through reform at the municipal level. Alongside these movements there was an influential group of middle-class intellectuals and individual parliamentarians calling themselves independents. The most important of these was Jean Jaurès, who began his career as a supporter of Ferry but steadily moved to the left. A former schoolmaster and professor of philosophy at the University of Toulouse, he entered parliament in 1893 as the socialist candidate for Carmaux. A brilliant orator, he drew inspiration not just from Marx but also from the utopian socialist tradition, believing that spiritual and economic liberation had to go hand in hand. His goal was the unification of the socialist movement but for the time being this remained elusive. The question of participation in a 'bourgeois' government split the movement into two in May 1901 with Guesde's *Parti socialiste de France* on one side and Jaurès's *Parti socialiste français* on the other.

Given the militancy of socialist discourse, old moderate republicans took fright and became increasingly conservative. They sought cooperation with Catholics and were encouraged by the *ralliement*, a movement of reconciliation on the part of the church which had begun when Cardinal Lavigerie toasted the Third Republic in 1890. In 1892 the call for Catholics to accept the Republic and share power came from Pope Leo XIII himself and although many on principle remained enemies of the atheist Republic, some stood as republicans in 1893. On this basis the moderate governments of 1893–94 and 1896–98 actively sought out their support and, even if there was no relaxation of the anti-clerical legislation, many middle-class Catholics warmed to the clamp-down on socialism.

The Dreyfus Affair

In 1894 Alfred Dreyfus, a young Jewish staff officer born in Alsace, was court-martialled for passing military secrets to Germany and sentenced to life imprisonment on Devil's Island off French Guiana. Over the next 3 years, as doubts about the case began to surface, the Dreyfus Affair was to mushroom into a huge scandal. In January 1898 the celebrated novelist Emile Zola wrote an open letter, 'J'Accuse', in *L'Aurore* in which he accused the army of an anti-Semitic conspiracy. Dreyfus, Zola claimed, was innocent but other officers had fabricated evidence to cover up the injustice and preserve the honour of the army. Eventually, and amid great controversy, a retrial was ordered in 1898 which found Dreyfus still guilty but with 'extenuating circumstances'. Immediately he was pardoned by President Loubet, although not formally declared innocent and reinstated as an officer until 1906.

The Dreyfus Affair had enormous consequences for the Third Republic, polarising public opinion and realigning party politics. For the anti-Dreyfusards the order and stability of the state were under attack from a Jewish conspiracy. For them Dreyfus's innocence was irrelevant, his 'guilt' lay in the fact that the whole affair had undermined the army. This new integral nationalism, nurtured by the Boulanger episode, was most fiercely espoused by Charles Maurras and *Action française*. Finding their inspiration in concepts of blood and soil, Maurras and his supporters wanted to take France back to pre-1789. Their ideal was a hierarchical society reserved for French people alone. The significance of Dreyfus for Maurras was that it illustrated how Jews were trying to destroy France from the inside. By definition, Maurras claimed, Jews could not be trusted because they were rootless, a race apart. In Maurras's view they, along with Protestants and freemasons, did not belong and had to be expelled from positions of influence within the French state. With his emphasis on religion, race and milieu – the values of the eternal France – Maurras's ideas were a striking reformulation of the language of nationalism. No longer was nationalism equated with the 'people' and the 'nation', the struggle for emancipation from the *ancien régime*. Instead it was identified with the conservative institutions of order and discipline – the army, the church and the state.

The Dreyfusards, meanwhile, believed that the most cherished republican principles were under attack. A miscarriage of justice was being tolerated for reasons of state – this was the essence of Zola's argument. In this way the Dreyfus Affair cemented a working alliance between moderate republicans, radicals and socialists like Jaurès. When

the Fourth Estate

By 1890 *Le Petit Journal* had a circulation of 1 million, making it the largest daily in the whole world. Such figures are an indication of the spectacular growth of the mass media, itself facilitated by print technology, transport for distribution and the spread of primary education. The power of the press to mould public opinion was even more evident during the Dreyfus Affair, arguably the first mass-media event. With the anti-Dreyfusard Catholic daily *La Croix* selling 170,000 copies a day at one point, commentators began to talk of the press as being the Fourth Estate.

Figure 5.2   Anti-Semitic cartoon from Le Psst, *February 1898*

large-scale anti-Semitic riots in France and Algeria in January and February 1898 were followed by an attempted coup led by Dérouède, they were convinced that the Republic was in danger and in June 1899 René Waldeck-Rousseau formed a government of republican defence. The way was now open for an anti-clerical backlash which would mark the end of the *ralliement.*

The radical republic, 1899–1914

In June 1901 an alliance of 155 masonic lodges, 215 newspapers, 476 republican committees, along with numerous free-thought groups came together to form the Radical Party. Radicals spearheaded by Clémenceau had long been frustrated by the conservatism of the opportunists and thereafter the party was to become the driving force behind reform. The Dreyfus Affair had only reinforced the conviction that the

nuns

In France the cult of the Virgin Mary was a major factor in the feminisation of religion, with the result that by the 1890s more women than men were apt to go to church, whilst nuns accounted for almost 60 per cent of the clergy. On the republican side the nun was to become a standard hate figure and in part this explains their opposition to female emancipation.

freemasons

Freemasonry was a cornerstone of the radical frame of mind. Based upon values of freethinking, positivism and anti-clericalism, the various lodges formed a network of contacts for their clientele of teachers, lawyers, doctors, shopkeepers and artisans. In 1900 membership totalled 30,000 and freemasons played a key role in mobilising support for radicalism at election time. Like the café, the lodge was a masculine space. All members of the Combes ministry of 1902 had masonic connections.

stranglehold of Catholicism had to be finally broken and with this end in mind the Combes administration 1902–5 dissolved many religious orders and prohibited their teaching. Angrily the Pope broke off diplomatic relations in 1904, but such condemnation only served to harden the radical resolve and pave the way for the formal separation of church and state in December 1905. The fact that for radicals this was a momentous event, the final victory over the *ancien régime*, illustrates just how far anti-clericalism was the cornerstone of their credo. It explains too why so many leading radicals were bitterly opposed to votes for women. They believed that women were dominated by the Catholic church and that female emancipation would in effect hand over a block vote to reaction.

Now radicalism became the political establishment, the upholder of the status quo. What, therefore, were the tenets of the radical doctrine? Apart from an instinctive anti-clericalism, radicals talked about the sanctity of the electorate and sought the primacy of parliament over government. They posed as the defender of the little people against entrenched interests, calling for a progressive income tax which would finance pensions for the aged and sick. In the economic sphere radicalism strove to find a middle way between capitalism and socialism, balancing social reform with the defence of the free market. In terms of support, such a programme drew votes from the provincial middle classes and large parts of the peasantry, particularly in the south and centre. By 1914 the Radical Party had 200,000 members.

Yet, despite its espousal of the egalitarian ideals of the Revolution, radicalism was increasingly defined by its opposition to militant socialism. On a fundamental level radicalism was committed to a property-owning society and this made all talk of an end to property anathema. Thus, although the socialist independent Millerand had been the minister of labour in Waldeck-Rousseau's cabinet, and although there was a parliamentary coalition between radicals and socialists during the Combes government of 1902–5, by 1905 the radical–socialist alliance had broken down. The various strands of the socialist movement came together to form the *Section française de l'internationale ouvrière* (SFIO) and moved into open opposition. Jaurès was the architect of unification and the ideology of the party reflected his blend of Marxism and the French revolutionary tradition. For him the French Revolution was still an unfinished revolution and he saw socialism as the translation into the economic sphere of the egalitarian ideals of 1789–95. By July 1914 the SFIO had 104 deputies in the Assembly.

The growth of socialism was not just evident in party politics. There was also the emergence of a revolutionary trade-union movement. In 1906 the CGT Amiens Charter refused to affiliate to the newly unified socialist party. Espousing a deep distrust of the parliamentary process, the CGT leadership talked instead of the capacity of the working class itself, through autonomous action, to challenge the capitalist system. Socialist revolution, they claimed, could only be achieved through direct action. The weapon was to be the general strike, not the ballot box. The growth of a self-conscious working-class movement was testament to the economic transformation of the country. The rise in coal and iron production and the emergence of the chemical industry illustrated the way in which artisanal forms of production were being replaced by factory production. By 1914 there were 4.5 million industrial workers – including 600,000 in metallurgy alone – and many suffered from miserable conditions. Poor pay, long hours, the harsh discipline of factory work: all these created a strong sense of grievance and were the root cause of a huge wave of strikes between 1906 and 1909. Significantly this strike action was not just urban. The largest protests took place in June 1907 in Montepellier in the south of France when 500,000 vineyard owners and workers, confronted with a regional wine crisis, called on the government to save their industry.

The radicals were alarmed by this upsurge of action and followed a policy of outright repression. Clémenceau became prime minister in 1906 and during his 3-year reign he was uncompromising. Again and again he broke the strikes by deploying troops and arresting union leaders, to such an extent that he was soon dubbed '*le premier flic de France*' (France's first cop). In government propaganda, strikers were vilified as the enemy within. Not only did they take orders from the socialist international movement, but their pacifism and anti-war agitation played into the hands of German militarism. Such language revealed how far radicalism had moved to the right, now that the issue related to the nature of the regime (monarchy or republic) had become redundant and had been replaced by the social question. The viciousness of Clémenceau's policies left no doubt that radicalism was now fundamentally committed to the defence of the economic status quo.

Document 5a: Popular song

L'enfant crucifié

C'etait tout au fond de l'Alsace
Sous les toits d'un pauvre hameau
Où l'Aigle noir a pris la place
Des couleurs de notre drapeau
Là vivaient l'époux et sa femme
Avec leur fils bambin charmant
Mais le père comme un infâme
Acceptait le joug allemand.
Et malgré son enfance,
En dépit du vainqueur
L'enfant aimait la France
De tout son petit cœur.

La mère avait l'âme française
A son enfant en l'endormant
Elle apprenait la Marseillaise
Lorsque le père était absent.
Elle lui disait d'une voix fière:
– 'Quand tu seras grand, mon Louis
Tu repasseras la frontière
Pour servir ton ancien pays!'
– 'Ah! Oui mère chérie'
Disait-il tendrement
'J'aime tant ma patrie
C'est aussi ma Maman.'

Un jour rentrant à l'improviste
Le père dans un coin obscure
Vit son fils en petit artiste
Faisant des dessins sur le mur.
Et c'étaient des braves et des braves
Qu'il dessinait le cher enfant

Des turkots, des chasseurs, des
    zouaves
– 'Ah!' dit-il – 'que fais tu là, brigand?'
L'enfant répond au traître:
– 'Ces soldats triomphants
C'est ce que je veux être,
Lorsque j'aurai vingt ans!'

L'homme d'une voix abrutie
Dit: 'Je suis Allemand, tu sais!
Tu vas voir comme je châtie
Quiconque ose aimer les Français.'
L'attachant avec une corde,
Ce vil serviteur des Germains
Contre un mur sans miséricorde
Lui cloua les pieds et les mains.
Et bravant la souffrance
L'enfant malgré ses pleurs
Criait : 'Vive la France!
France pour toi je meurs!'

Enfin à ses appels suprêmes
La cohorte accourut – Oh! Stupeur!
Les soldats allemands eux-mêmes
Etaient pétrifiés d'horreur!
Le couvrant de baisers sa mère
Dans ses bras l'emporte en pleurant
Mais l'enfant fermant la paupière
Disait encore en expirant:
– Adieu France que j'aime,
Adieu je vais mourir
Mais je t'aime quand même
Jusqu'au dernier soupir!'

Cahier de chansons d'Eugénie Vallin, Givors, 1910–29

Topics

1   Why was the Franco-Prussian War so important for France? What does Document 5a reveal about popular attitudes towards Germany?

2   What was the significance of 16 May 1877? How does Figure 5.1 help us to understand the 16 May crisis?

3   What was the purpose of the Ferry reforms?

4   Why was there increasing disenchantment with the Third Republic? Where did the challenges to the political system come from?

5   What was the significance of the Dreyfus Affair? How did it divide France politically? How does Figure 5.2 help us to understand the nature of these political divisions?

6   What was the nature of radicalism as a political ideology?

CHAPTER 6

Timeline

1891
Franco-Russian alliance

1904
Entente cordiale *between Britain and France*

1905
First Moroccan crisis

1908
Annexation of Bosnia and Herzegovina

1911
Second Moroccan crisis

1914
28 June   Assassination of Franz-Ferdinand at Sarajevo
3 August   Germany declares war on France
6–13 September   Battle of the Marne

1915
Italy enters the war on the Allies' side

1916
February–December   Battle of Verdun

1917
6 April   America declares war on Germany
16 April   Nivelle offensive
October   Communists take power in Russia
November   Clémenceau becomes prime minister

1918
March   German offensive
August   Allied counter-attack
11 November   Armistice

1919
28 June   Signing of Versailles Treaty
14 November   Election landslide for the bloc national

1920
1 May   Strikes on the railways

France, 1914–31

World War I marks the end of what the historian Eric Hobsbawm has called the long nineteenth century, the period 1815–1914 that was characterised by peace, material progress and the dominance of Europe throughout the world. Now Europe was to enter 31 years of bloodshed and instability which ended in 1945 with the dwarfing of the continent by the two superpowers – America and the Soviet Union.

The international situation, 1871–1914

After 1871 the foundation stone of the Bismarck system was the diplomatic isolation of France achieved through the Treaty of The Three Emperors (Germany, Russia, Austria–Hungary) in 1881 and by the Triple Alliance (Germany, Austria–Hungary, Italy) in 1882. In tandem with this strategy Bismarck encouraged colonial rivalry between Italy, Britain and France as a further way of diverting French attention from a war of revenge. However, in March 1890 Bismarck clashed with the new emperor, Wilhelm II, and resigned as chancellor. His departure precipitated a major diplomatic realignment that allowed France to progressively break out of the German straitjacket. First of all, in 1891, France signed a treaty with Russia. Under it each country pledged to support the other if attacked by Germany. Now France could threaten Germany with the possibility of war

December   Creation of the Parti communiste français *(PCF) at the Congress of Tours*
1923 *Occupation of the Ruhr by French troops*
1924 *11 May   Election victory of the* cartel des gauches
1926 *Poincaré returns as prime minister*
1928 *25 June   Franc is returned to the gold standard*
1929 *Young Plan drastically reschedules German reparations*
1931 *16 May   Colonial Exhibition opens in Paris*

on two fronts and henceforth this would be pivotal to French diplomacy. Never again would France experience solitary defeat, a pattern of thinking which explains why there was so much large-scale French investment in the czarist economy. Then France tried to detach Italy from the Triple Alliance, concluding an agreement in 1902 which guaranteed neutrality if either was attacked. Finally, there was a rapprochement with Britain. Traditionally Britain had stood aloof from the continent, but military and industrial rivalry with Germany forced Britain to look for allies. Once France had renounced imperial ambitions in Egypt, a rivalry that had brought the two countries to the brink of war in 1898, the way was open for closer relations and 1904 witnessed the signing of the *entente cordiale* (friendly agreement). Although not a formal treaty, the *entente* cast aside old enmities and laid the basis for an understanding of common interests. In particular it allowed France to act as a mediator for the 1907 rapprochement between Russia and Britain when the countries agreed to recognise different spheres of influence in Persia.

By 1907 European peace was already beginning to look precarious. The division of Europe into two hostile blocks was clearly discernible and thereafter a succession of crises would tighten the ties within each group, leading to a steady deterioration in international relations. The first of these was over Morocco, when Wilhelm II visited the Moroccan sultan in 1905. Through the visit Wilhelm II wanted to block French expansion, but in practice his sabre-rattling badly backfired. Not only did the Algeciras conference in 1906 recognise Morocco as a sphere of French influence, the whole crisis bound Britain and France more closely together. Still smarting from this humiliation, Wilhelm II sent a gunboat to Agadir on the Moroccan coast in July 1911. The outcome was a second climb down for the Germans and the recognition of a French protectorate in Morocco. The fact that after the second Moroccan standoff the British fleet agreed to focus upon the Channel coastline whilst the French navy covered the Mediterranean was equally significant. It indicated how far the security of the two countries was interdependent by this point.

The second flashpoint was to be the Balkans, which directly affected France because of the close alliance with Russia. There the dramatic decline of the Ottoman Empire led to a conflict of interests between Russia and Austria as both strove to fill the power vacuum. In essence the confrontation was between pan-Slavism and pan-Germanism. Austria and Germany were fearful of Slav expansion into Central Europe and large parts of the Ottoman Empire. They believed that, as the champion of pan-Slavism, Russia was trying to establish a series of Slavic client states which would act as magnets for Slav minorities in the Habsburg empire. Above all, Austrian hardliners saw the principal threat as coming from Serbia, whose king, Peter I, was resolutely pro-French and pro-Russian. They were itching to teach the Serbs a lesson and this was the reasoning behind the annexation of Bosnia and Herzegovina in October 1908. Not only did the Austrians want to prevent Bosnia and Herzegovina, which they had occupied since 1878, from returning to Ottoman rule, they also wanted to antagonise the Serbs, who constituted most of the population in Bosnia, and the Russians, who resented any increase in Austrian power in the Balkans. The crisis deepened in January 1909 when Germany called for the immediate and unconditional acceptance of Austrian demands, at which point Russia and Serbia gave way, resentfully. Although the Bosnian crisis appeared to be a triumph for Austria and Germany, in effect it would lead Russia to forge even greater links with France and Britain. Likewise the memory of humiliation would determine Russia's uncompromising stance in July 1914.

The desire to stymie further Austrian advance southwards led Russia to bring Serbia and Bulgaria together in February 1912. The first Balkan war pitted the Balkan League against the Ottoman Empire, a traditional German ally, and was a spectacular success for the League. Indeed the extent of this success alarmed the Great Powers, who hastily convened a peace conference in London in 1913. The resultant treaty recognised the expulsion of the Ottoman Empire from Europe, but Austrian pressure led to the creation of Albania, a buffer state to block Serbia from reaching the Adriatic. By way of compensation Serbia demanded a larger share of Macedonia and this brought the Serbs into conflict with Bulgaria, who declared war on Serbia and Greece in June 1913. The second Balkan war led to another quick and emphatic victory for Serbia and inevitably this provoked renewed consternation in Austria. Serbia had doubled in size and could field a force of 400,000. Increasingly Austria was convinced that the very stability of southeastern Europe was at stake and that Serbia needed another lesson along the lines of 1908–9.

The outbreak of war

In France the two Moroccan crises and the Balkan wars produced a hardening of attitudes amongst the political elite. Many believed that war was inevitable and the nomination of the conservative republican Raymond Poincaré as head of government in January 1912 and as president in May was symbolic of the new national mood. The war issue now dominated politics and from the beginning the need to stand up to the German threat was the linchpin of Poincaré's policies. Abroad he reinforced the alliance with Russia, floating another huge loan to bolster the czarist state. At home, military service was lengthened from 2 to 3 years and extended to Algeria. Such a strengthening of resolve was welcomed by the right, but bitterly opposed by a number of socialists and radicals. The socialists campaigned against the 3-year conscription law and here the themes of anti-militarism and internationalism did strike a popular chord. Many on the left were sincere in the hope that German and French workers would refuse to fire upon fellow proletarians and this anti-war feeling was bolstered by two further factors – firstly, the way in which the army had been used to repress strikes and, secondly, the alliance with Russia, whose authoritarian monarchy was widely detested. In the April–May 1914 elections the socialists made significant gains, advancing from 76 to 103 seats in the National Assembly. Even so, the new radical-dominated government backed away from revoking the 3-year law.

The immediate cause of war was the Balkans. On 28 June 1914 the heir to the Austrian throne, Archduke Franz Ferdinand, was assassinated by a Serb nationalist during a state visit to Sarajevo, the capital of Bosnia–Herzegovina. During July Germany pushed Austria into war against Serbia, knowing full well that this would trigger Russian mobilisation. This in turn gave Germany the pretext to declare war on Russia on 1 August and on France on 3 August. When Germany immediately invaded Belgium, Britain, the guarantor of Belgian independence since 1839, declared war on 4 August. Both sides expected a short war that would be over by Christmas.

During the July crisis Poincaré, himself on an official visit to Russia, encouraged the czar's ministers to take a hard line. He insisted that French security depended on standing by the Russians and on 1 August a general mobilisation was ordered. Once Germany had declared war, the anti-war movement was quickly marginalised. Internationalist arguments were fatally undermined by the support of German socialists for the war, leading many of their French counterparts to adopt a fall-back position, namely that this was a defensive war to preserve democracy and safeguard the future progress of the French working class in the face of naked aggression. Furthermore, there was the inevitable pull of nationalism and chauvinism. Even on the left the majority could not countenance any activity that might be construed as anti-patriotic and pro-German. Consequently only a tiny minority – less than 2 per cent – evaded the call-up. The final isolation of anti-militarism was symbolised by the assassination on 31 July in Paris of Jean Jaurès, who had been working tirelessly to avoid war, and the decision of the CGT not to antagonise public opinion by calling a general strike. Now war was inevitable.

Union sacrée

Although war was greeted with resignation rather than enthusiasm, most supported the view that this was a just war against German militarism. Temporarily social and political differences were put to one side and the outward expression of this consensus was the so-called *union sacrée*. Spanning from left to right, the fact that the government included the veteran revolutionary Jules Guesde as well as the archbishop of Paris was a measure of the spirit of national unity.

Germany set out to defeat France in 6 weeks before the Russians could fully mobilise, but after initial successes the German advance was thrown back at the Battle of the Marne (6–13 September). By the end of 1914 there was deadlock on the Western Front as each side dug in behind a line of trenches stretching from Switzerland to the Channel. In 1915 France tried to break the stalemate with offensives at Artois and Champagne. Each ended in costly failure with 1,292,000 killed or wounded, and during the following 3 years the two lines were hardly to move. For the ordinary soldier, trench life was to become very hard. Not only was there the unending cycle of cold, mud, hunger and thirst, but they were also forced to endure the impact of new weapons such as poison gas, flame throwers and aerial warfare. The only solace was the entry into the war of Italy on the Allied side.

In the French consciousness the Battle of Verdun in 1916 was to become the indelible symbol of World War I. The German decision to attack Verdun was based upon a crude logic. The town lay in an exposed position in the south of the French line and the German plan was to draw the French army to where it would be destroyed by artillery. Through a battle of attrition the aim of the German high command was to 'bleed France white'. They reasoned that because of the lower birth rate France could not afford to lose as many soldiers as Germany and that a protracted offensive, where it was calculated that France would lose five men for every two German soldiers killed, would soon bring the French to their knees. The battle began on 21 February when the Germans fired a million shells on the first day – the heaviest bombardment the world had ever seen – and lasted until December. The losses on both sides were horrendous: France suffered 540,000 casualties and Germany 430,000. When the French line was close to collapse, Joffre, the French commander, rushed up reinforcements and sent General Philippe Pétain to take command. At Verdun Pétain proved himself to be a brilliant commander. With the railways destroyed by constant shelling, Pétain organised an effective route by road which became popularly known as the *voie sacrée* (sacred road). He also introduced the rotation of front-line units, a system which reassured ordinary soldiers (**poilus**) that they were not being treated like cannon fodder and stiffened their resolve to fight. Under Pétain's leadership, therefore, the French clung on desperately and by July, when the British launched an offensive at the Somme to relieve Verdun, the Germans were on the defensive. With phrases like *on les aura* (we will get them) and *ils ne passeront pas* (they will not pass), Pétain became a national hero. Henceforth he would be known as the 'victor of Verdun', the living embodiment of the fight against Germany.

In April 1917 the new French supreme commander, General Robert Nivelle, launched what he believed would be the decisive

Douaumont

Verdun became a place of pilgrimage after 1918. On Armistice Day, on Bastille Day and, above all, on 21 February, veterans, *ceux de Verdun*, came in their thousands to remember their fallen comrades. The concrete fortress of Douaumont was pivotal in the fighting and for this reason was chosen as the site for a vast ossuary which, with its tower of four crosses, stands over the remains of 130,000 unidentified soldiers from both sides. For families of those missing in action, visiting Douaumont was a way of coming to terms with their sense of loss. On 11 November 1984, President Mitterrand and Chancellor Kohl participated at Verdun in a ceremony of reconciliation. The way in which they linked hands symbolised their determination to build a new Europe based on Franco-German friendship.

poilu

Popular term for ordinary French soldier.

War and memory

Twenty-seven men were eventually shot for their part in the 1917 mutiny. On 6 November 1998 Lionel Jospin, the socialist prime minister, called for the rehabilitation of the mutineers within the national memory. If these men mutinied, Jospin argued, it was only because they did not want to be sacrificed senselessly. Immediately Jospin's remarks provoked outrage on the right. President Chirac judged his comments to be inappropriate, whilst Philippe Séguin, a traditional Gaullist politician, deemed any talk of understanding or rehabilitation to be an insult to the millions who died loyally during World War I.

offensive. It was a bloody catastrophe, but in the face of no immediate gains Nivelle refused to break off the attack and, as the losses continued to mount, huge numbers of ordinary soldiers were pushed past breaking point. They saw the tactics as senseless – some units even bleated like sheep as they moved up to the front line – and from the end of April there was a mutinous mood in the French army. Now 68 divisions refused to go into battle and this pessimism quickly spread to the home front which witnessed strikes and the rise of pacifist ideas. The French war effort seemed to be on the brink of collapse, at which point Pétain was called in to replace the now disgraced Nivelle. Pétain immediately dealt with the mutinies in a humane manner. Not only did he make sure that the lot of the ordinary soldiers was improved, with better food and more leave granted, but he was also lenient, carefully limiting the number of court martials meted out to the mutineers. Tactically speaking he underlined that there would be no more wasteful offensives. Instead the French army would sit tight and wait for the Americans.

Until November 1917 the French government was marked by chronic instability. Briand succeeded Viviani as prime minister in October 1915 and was himself replaced in March 1917 by Alexandre Ribot, who in turn resigned in September. The new government, led by Paul Painlevé, contained no socialists and in effect represented the end of the *union sacrée*. Two months later Painlevé was forced to stand down for Clémenceau, who, at the age of 76, was the leader to the end of the war. Determined, resolute, intransigent, Clémenceau immediately quashed any thought of a negotiated peace. Speaking in the National Assembly, he summed up his policy in strident terms. From now on it would be war, war and nothing but war. To underline this message defeatists were imprisoned, the primacy of civilian leadership over the military was re-established and the war effort organised in a thorough and systematic way. Through drastic measures not only did Clémenceau mobilise women and the empire, he also introduced greater state intervention to fix prices, distribute raw material and organise production.

In 1917 two events altered the course of the war. Firstly, America entered the conflict. After the sinking in 1915 of the British cruise liner *Lusitania*, which was carrying American passengers, the Germans abandoned unrestricted submarine warfare. However, when in February 1917 the German high command returned to this strategy, seeing it as the last hope of knocking Britain out of the war, this led America to declare war on 6 April. Secondly, in October there was a communist revolution in

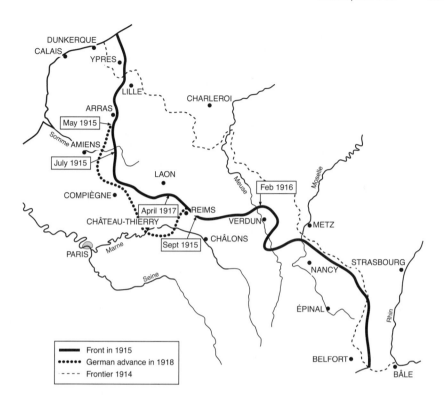

Map 6.1   Military operations, 1914–18
Reproduced with permission from Antoine Prost, Petite Histoire de la France du XXe siècle.

Russia. The communists, led by Lenin, hoped that the Russian Revolution would ignite a world revolution, transforming the imperialist war into a class war. Thus they took Russia out of the conflict, concluding the peace of Brest–Litovsk in 1918. The prospect of fresh American troops, in addition to the transfer of men from the Eastern Front, led the Germans to launch a final assault in March 1918. At one point the Germans were 40 miles from Paris but by July the offensive was exhausted and the Allies counter-attacked. On 8 August – the 'Black Friday of the German Army' – 456 British tanks recaptured 8 of the lost 35 miles in one day. It was a decisive turning point and although the German line did not break, the weight of American soldiers, together with the collapse of Austria–Hungary, Bulgaria and Turkey and the threat of communist revolution at home, led Germany to seek an armistice. Fighting stopped on 11 November 1918 and was followed by the Versailles Peace Conference.

Versailles Peace Treaty, 28 June 1919

From whatever vantage point you choose, the impact of the war was disastrous. Of the 8 million Frenchmen who were mobilised, more than 1.3 million had been killed and 3 million wounded. In terms of the infrastructure of the country, 220,000 houses, 9,000 factories, 200 coal mines and 1,490 miles of railway track had been destroyed,

pauvres couillons du front

(Poor cretins from the front) was the popular slang for ex-servicemen. Many veterans, particularly the war wounded, found it too difficult to reintegrate into the peacetime world. One group, *les gueules cassés* (the smashed faces), felt so alienated that they formed their own specific ex-servicemen's organisation. Through it they bought beach homes in order to hide away from society.

surrealism

The surrealists were a group of avant-garde artists and writers led by André Breton, who had worked in a psychiatric hospital at the end of the war. Motivated by a hatred of bourgeois society, whose values in their opinion were the root cause of World War I, they set out to shock established opinion. Heavily influenced by Freud, Breton's 1924 *Manifesto of Surrealism* rejected the limitations of logic and celebrated the unconscious as a source of freedom. Initially sympathetic to the PCF, the surrealists became fierce opponents of imperialism, protesting against the repression in Morocco in 1925 and organising opposition to the Colonial Exhibition of May 1931. This anti-colonialism carried on into the post-1945 period when the likes of Breton, André Masson and Jean Schuster supported illegal opposition to the Algerian War.

destruction which had been deliberately increased by the scorched-earth policy of the retreating Germans. Huge tracts of agricultural land lay waste, particularly in those areas in the north and northeast that had borne the brunt of the fighting. Economically the war had been ruinous too. The decision to finance the war through foreign borrowing left France with a deficit of 26 billion FF and when America refused to cancel French war debts, this transformed the country into a debtor nation.

These bald statistics explain why Clémenceau, backed by French public opinion, wanted a punitive peace. Throughout the peace negotiations he was absolutely determined that Germany should be made to pay for the war. In contrast, the American president, Woodrow Wilson, was guided by the desire to make the 'world safe for democracy'. He saw the dangers of a harsh settlement and wanted a new era of peace based upon the principle of national self-determination, the framework of which was to be provided by the League of Nations. Based in Geneva, the League would uphold collective security, resolving disputes by arbitration and guaranteeing the territorial integrity of all member states. Although Wilson did much to restrain the French, who wanted the Rhineland to be an independent state, the Saar annexed to France and Danzig given to Poland, during the long months of negotiations, Clémenceau's intransigence gradually won.

Drawn up by Britain, America, Italy and France and then imposed upon Germany, the treaty, symbolically signed in the Hall of Mirrors in Versailles where German unity had been proclaimed in 1871, was harsh, and provoked huge resentment amongst Germans, many of whom came to see it as a diktat and not morally binding. Under the Versailles settlement Alsace and Lorraine were returned to France. The Rhineland was demilitarised and occupied by the Allies for 15 years. France was given control of the rich coal and iron mines of the Saar border for 15 years. In addition, Germany lost all its colonies. The disarmament clauses restricted the German army to 100,000 men and prohibited the production of artillery, aircraft and tanks. Finally, by the 'war guilt cause', article 231 of the treaty, Germany had to take the blame for the war and admit to a 'crime against humanity'.

Away from Versailles the return to peacetime was fraught with difficulties. Given their years of suffering on the front line, how could the millions of demobilised soldiers possibly piece their lives back together? Such tensions were perhaps clearest in respect to gender relations. Between 1914 and 1918, 8 million women were mobilised to replace men in factories and offices and undoubtedly this gave many greater self-confidence and economic independence. Indeed it was often women who were the most militant in the workplace because they did not run the risk of being sent to the front if they threatened to strike. After 1918 large numbers of women's pressure groups, ranging from feminists within the *Conseil national des femmes françaises* through to Catholic women within the *Ligue patriotique des françaises*, campaigned for the vote. Yet the immediate post-war period saw a reassertion of traditional values. Conservative deputies, many of them wartime veterans, talked about the need to turn the clock back to 1914. More than anything, they argued, society had to return to normal male–female relations, to the way they had been before the war had started. For this reason the bill to give women the vote, passed by the National Assembly in 1919, was thrown out by the Senate in 1922. Rejection was based not only on the now familiar argument that women's suffrage would give a numerical advantage to the clerical enemies of the Third Republic, but also on the belief that, if France was to maintain Great-Power status, the country needed to be repopulated. Pro-natalism was the order of the day, and legislation such as the July 1920 law outlawing birth control underlined that, in the eyes of the state, women were expected to produce children and be good mothers.

Tensions were also very apparent in terms of class relations. In 1919–20 the country was gripped by political and social instability. There were widespread strikes and this militancy, much of it inspired by the Russian Revolution, led to a fear of communist insurrection. Skilfully playing on these fears – one poster depicted a revolutionary with a knife between his teeth – as well as on his personal prestige as the father of victory, Clémenceau led the *bloc national* to a landslide victory in November 1919. With the centre-right winning 450 of the 616 seats, this was now the most right-wing parliament since 1876, known popularly as the *chambre bleu-horizon* because so many of the deputies were ex-

new woman

In 1918 Coco Chanel's models wore short 'bobbed' hair. This image of the new, assertive woman, boyish in her appearance and independent in her outlook, shocked bourgeois society. The book which did the most to spread this notion of the new woman was Victor Margueritte's 1922 novel, *La Garçonne*. In it the heroine chooses her freedom and breaks away from her fiancé. Experimenting with lovers and lesbians she eventually bears an illegitimate child. Not surprisingly the book was condemned by the church and banned from the bookstalls. Margueritte himself was stripped of his Légion d'honneur.

servicemen wearing their sky-blue dress uniforms. True to its word, the *bloc national* ruthlessly repressed any challenges to the status quo. The way in which the government broke the railwaymen's strike of 1920 – arresting the ringleaders and then sacking 18,000 men – was intended as a stark lesson to the left. There would be no Bolshevik Revolution in France.

Electoral defeat, combined with the defeat of the strikes, intensified the internal divisions of the SFIO and led to a schism at the Congress of Tours in December 1920. Inspired by anti-war sentiment, by enthusiasm for the Russian Revolution and by disillusionment with the parliamentary process, two-thirds of the delegates voted to adhere to the Communist International. The French left was now irrevocably split between those who formed the *Parti communiste français* (PCF) and those who remained within the SFIO, and the following 15 years were marked by debilitating internecine strife. The SFIO denounced the authoritarian nature of the Soviet Union, whilst the PCF attacked their socialist counterparts as 'social traitors'.

Surprisingly in January 1920 the National Assembly elected Deschanel rather than Clémenceau to the presidency. In a fit of pique Clémenceau retired from politics. Henceforth politics in the 1920s would be dominated by two politicians, Briand and Poincaré, and by two interconnected questions – what to do about the financial crisis and what to do about reparations?

Reparations

When in 1921 the reparations commission fixed the sum owed by Germany at 132 billion gold marks, the Germans immediately claimed that such huge sums would cripple the economy. The dilemma for the French was what to do next. The refusal of the American Senate to ratify the Versailles Treaty meant that the French were isolated internationally and this effectively left them with two choices – reconciliation or strict enforcement of the peace settlement. As prime minister from January 1921 to January 1922 Briand tried to follow the first course, accepting an adjustment of reparations in return for British guarantees on security. However, when Briand was forced to resign and replaced by Poincaré, the French took a more belligerent approach. With the Americans putting pressure on the French to repay war debts, Poincaré grew all the more determined to make Germany pay up. He accused Germany of deliberately withholding payments and rejected pleas for a moratorium so that the mark could be stabilised. When the German government called on miners of the Ruhr to stop work in protest, Poincaré was incensed, sending in troops to occupy the Rhineland in January 1923. A grim, protracted standoff ensued, which triggered the collapse of the franc. Eventually Germany climbed down and the new chancellor, Gustav Stresemann, tried very hard to meet Allied demands, paving the way for the League of Nations Commission, headed by the American banker Charles Dawes, in 1924. On the face of it the Dawes Plan could be construed as a victory for the Poincaré approach. After all, it did provide for the resumption of reparations. In reality the schedule for repayment was extended and this left the Poincaré policy in tatters. Desperately needing a loan from the American banks, the French had no alternative but to accept. More than anything the Ruhr débâcle demonstrated that in the absence of backing from America and Britain, France could not impose the Versailles settlement by force.

The economic consequences of Poincaré's belligerency alarmed public opinion and led in 1924 to the victory of the centre-left alliance, the *cartel des gauches*, which won 353 out of 610 seats. The radical Edouard Herriot formed the new administration with the support, but not the participation, of socialists. Abroad Herriot laid the basis for a more conciliatory approach. The architect of this new policy was Briand, who occupied the post of foreign minister almost continually from 1925 to 1932. Briand's first success was the signing of the 1925 Locarno Treaty, whereby France and Germany agreed to respect each other's frontiers. Thereafter he was a tireless advocate of European peace and cooperation, smoothing the way for German membership of the League of Nations in 1926 and forging a proposal with the American secretary of state, Frank B. Kellog, renouncing war as an instrument of national policy and calling for the peaceful settlement of disputes. The Kellog–Briand Pact of 27 August 1928 was eventually signed by 64 states, including the Soviet Union. Significantly too in 1930 Briand outlined proposals for Franco-German economic cooperation that would form the framework for greater European unity, planting the seed of an idea which would eventually find fruition in June 1950 with the European Coal and Steel Community (ECSC).

At home Herriot tried to resuscitate anti-Catholic feeling but his threat to break off diplomatic relations with the Vatican, re-established in 1921, provoked widespread opposition, underlining how far anti-clericalism had declined as a mobilising issue. On the economic front Herriot's policies lacked conviction. He offered no alternative to deflation and as the debt got larger and the franc fell, the confidence of investors was steadily eroded. As the flight of capital abroad intensified, many on the left talked of a 'wall of money', a conspiracy of capitalist interests that was deliberately sabotaging reform. But when the SFIO proposed a tax on capital as a solution, the socialist–radical alliance floundered, leading to the Herriot government's fall in April 1925, in effect the only interlude in a prolonged period of conservative domination which lasted until 1932.

The severity of the economic crisis led Poincaré to form a government of national unity in July 1926. Supported by radicals and right-wing deputies he followed a policy of rigorous financial orthodoxy. By tackling inflation – prices had doubled between 1922 and 1928 – he wanted to stabilise the economy and restore business confidence which had been so frightened by the *cartel des gauches*. Triumph in the 1928 election gave Poincaré the courage to return the franc to the gold standard at a fifth of the 1914 value. Revaluation was a bold move and, by making exports cheaper and attracting capital back into France, it seemed that Poincaré had laid the basis for a durable economy. In the domain of foreign policy he wisely kept Briand as foreign minister, who continued with the twin policy of support for the League of Nations allied with reconciliation with Germany. Worryingly, however, this reconciliation was increasingly clouded by bitterness and mistrust. When in 1930 the American banker Owen D. Young drew up a new plan which reduced German repayments to a third of the original figure, the French only agreed with great reluctance.

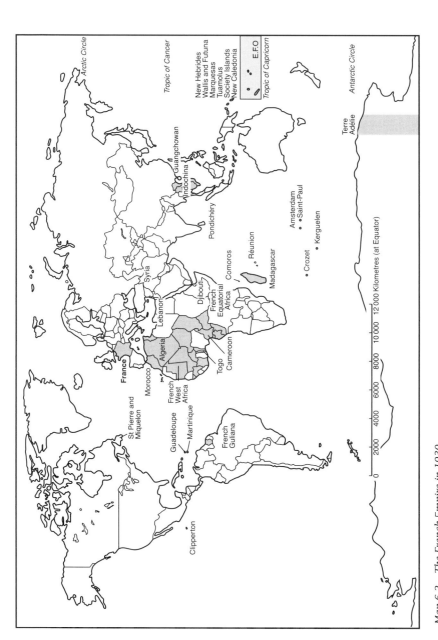

Map 6.2   The French Empire in 1930
Source: M. Alexander, French History since Napoleon, Edward Arnold, 1999.

Arctic Circle

Tropic of Cancer

New Hebrides
Wallis and Futuna
Marquesas
Tuamolus
Society Islands
New Caledonia

E.F.O.

Tropic of Capricorn

Guangchowan
Indochina

Pondichéry

Antarctic Circle

Terre
Adélie

Amsterdam
Saint-Paul

Kerguelen

Réunion

Crozet

Madagascar

12 000 Kilometres (at Equator)

Comoros

Djibouti

French
Equatorial
Africa

Syria

Lebanon

France

Algeria

Morocco

Togo
Cameroon

French
West
Africa

0   2000   4000   6000   8000   10 000   12 000

St Pierre and
Miquelon

Guadeloupe

Martinique

French
Guiana

Clipperton

The Colonial Exhibition, May 1931

During World War I the empire supplied 500,000 soldiers and 200,000 industrial workers. In this way empire took on a tangible form and the image of a close bond, uniting metropolitan and colonial France, now took hold within the popular imagination. Furthermore, it was in 1919, through the gain at Versailles of the ex-German colonies of Togo and the Cameroons and the Ottoman possessions of Syria and the Lebanon, that the empire reached its height territorially. For the Third Republic possession of this empire was seen as a statement of Great-Power status. This explains why France repressed anti-colonial rebellions in Morocco in 1925 and in Indo-China in 1930, and it also explains why the Third Republic did so much to promote empire at home through the Colonial Exhibition in Paris in May 1931. Organised by Marshal Louis-Hubert Lyautey, the hero of colonial expansion in Morocco, the exhibition was a lavish affair. Visitors, of which there were 8 million, were treated to a tour of the empire in miniature. Individual pavilions offered up glimpses of colonial life, climaxing with the central attraction, a full-scale reconstruction of the Cambodian temple Angkor Wat. The central message of the exhibition, that France was a universal culture engaged in a huge civilising mission across the globe, was carefully marketed through **postcards**, photographs and popular prints. When added to the fact that France still had the largest army, along with a seemingly robust economy (in 1930 France was basking in the third year of economic growth), this message was immensely reassuring. It confirmed French people in the belief that France had emerged from the tribulations of 1914–18 as the dominant power in Europe.

colonial postcards

In the 1920s and 1930s images depicting native women in harems were amongst the popular postcards sent from Algeria to France. In practice these posed photographs said nothing about the lives of these women but everything about French fantasies. Invariably the women were portrayed as submissive, exotic and sexually available. Indeed, the way in which the photographs objectified these women – reducing them to types such as Bedouin woman or Berber woman – was symbolic of the colonial domination in Algeria.

Figure 6.1   Colonial postcard: exoticism and eroticism
Reproduced with permission from Malek Alloula, The Colonial Harem, *University of Minnesota Press, 1986.*

Document 6a: La guerre vue par un paysan auvergnat décembre 1914

Oise, le 1 Desanbre 1914

MES TRES CHER PARENT,

. . . Cher parent, j'est reguardé la flanelle que vous m'avée renvoyée qui était sur moi; depuis un moi que je l'avet elle commençait âme devorée, elle était couvertte de pou, les plus louin se touche; sa fesé peur de tan voir de la vermine: s'est touse qui en son guarnie; on cuche dans des trou, on diret un four; la paile qui est dedan y est depuie un moi, s'est la que ont prant la vermine; met le linge ne manque pas, je change souvent.

Le froit en n'a gelée beaucoup la pouinte des pié; au tranché il ne faut pas bougé dutou de endroit que reste imobile. Moi je avet mi du papier de journale dans mé soullier, je n'est pas bien eu froit. Cher parent 'hiver s'est pénible de rever à l'été.

Ses jour si je est aprie de triste nouvelle: deux camarades qui sont été blessée acoté de moi, le 23 septenbre, sont mor à l'hàpital se jour si.

Cher parent je suis fier de pouvoir vous faire savoir ses deux ou trot mots aprait avoir passé ou je est passé: voir de pauvre cuamarade, coupé les bra, coupé les guanbe, perssé les côte, dotre coupé les main, des autres anlevée la moitier de la têt. Cher parent je remerssi Dieu qui m'a bien guardé jusque mintenant.

AD Puy de Dôme, J 966, cité par Chaulanges, Manry et Sève, *Textes historiques, 1914–1945*, ed. Delagrave 1970, p. 10. (Original spelling retained.)

Document 6b: Georges Clémenceau, 'Rien que la guerre'

Déclaration du gouvernement, à l'occasion de son investiture: 20 novembre 1917

M. Clémenceau (Président du conseil, ministre de la guerre):
'Messieurs, nous avons accepté d'être au Gouvernement pour conduire la guerre avec un redoublement d'efforts en vue du meilleur rendement de toutes les énergies. Nous nous présentons devant vous dans l'unique pensée d'une guerre intégrale [. . .]. Jamais la France ne sentit si clairement le besoin de vivre et de grandir dans l'idéal d'une force mise au service de la conscience humaine dans la résolution de fixer toujours plus de droit entre les citoyens comme entre les peuples capables de se libérer. Vaincre pour être justes, voilà le mot d'ordre de tous nos gouvernements depuis le début de la guerre. Ce programme à ciel ouvert, nous le maintiendrons.

Nous avons de grands soldats d'une grande histoire, sous des chefs trempés dans les épreuves, animés aux suprêmes dévouements qui firent le beau renom de leurs aînés. Par eux, par nous tous, l'immortelle patrie des hommes, maîtresse de l'orgueil des victoires, poursuivra dans les plus nobles ambitions de la paix le cours de ses destinées. Ces Français que nous fûmes contraints de jeter dans la bataille, ils ont des droits sur nous. Ils veulent qu'aucune de nos pensées ne se détourne d'eux, qu'aucun de nos actes ne leur soit étranger. Nous leur devons tout, sans aucune réserve. Tout pour la France saignante dans sa gloire, tout pour l'apothéose du droit triomphant.

Droits du front et devoirs de l'arrière, qu'aujourd'hui tout soit donc confondu. Que toute zone soit de l'armée. S'il doit y avoir des hommes pour retrouver dans leurs âmes de vieilles semences de haines, écartons-les. Toutes les nations civilisées sont engagées dans la même bataille contre les formations modernes des vieilles barbaries. Avec tous nos bons alliés, nous sommes le roc inébranlable d'une barrière qui ne sera pas franchie. Au front de l'alliance, à toute heure et partout, rien que la solidarité fraternelle, le plus sûr fondement du monde à venir.

continued

Champ clos des idéals, notre France a souffert pour tout ce qui est de l'homme. Ferme dans les espérances puisées aux sources de l'humanité la plus pure, elle accepte de souffrir encore, pour la défense du sol des grands ancêtres, avec l'espoir d'ouvrir, toujours plus grandes aux hommes comme aux peuples, toutes les portes de la vie. La force de l'âme française est là. C'est ce qui meut notre peuple au travail comme à l'action de guerre. Ces silencieux soldats de l'usine, sourds aux suggestions mauvaises, ces vieux paysans courbés sur leurs terres, ces robustes femmes au labour, ces enfants qui leur apportent l'aide d'une faiblesse grave: voilà de nos poilus. De nos poilus qui, plus tard, songeant à la grande œuvre, pourront dire, comme ceux des tranchées: J'en étais. Avec ceux-là aussi, nous devons demeurer, faire que, pour la Patrie, dépouillant nos misères, un jour, nous nous soyons aimés. S'aimer, ce n'est pas se le dire, c'est se le prouver. Cette preuve, nous voulons essayer de la faire. Pour cette preuve, nous vous demandons de nous aider. Peut-il être un plus beau programme de Gouvernement?

Il y a eu des fautes. N'y songeons plus que pour les réparer.

Hélas, il y a eu aussi des crimes, des crimes contre la France, qui appellent un prompt châtiment. Nous prenons devant vous, devant le pays qui demande justice, l'engagement que justice sera faite selon la rigueur des lois. Ni considérations de personnes, ni entraînements de passions politiques ne nous détourneront du devoir ni ne nous le feront dépasser. Trop d'attentats se sont déjà soldés sur notre front de bataille, par un surplus de sang français. Faiblesse serait complicité. Nous serons sans faiblesse, comme sans violence. Tous les inculpés en conseil de guerre. Le soldat au prétoire, solidaire du soldat au combat. Plus de campagnes pacifistes, plus de menées allemandes. Ni trahison, ni demi-trahison: la guerre. Rien que la guerre. Nos armées ne seront pas prises entre deux feux, la justice passe. Le pays connaîtra qu'il est défendu. Et cela, dans la France libre, toujours. Nous avons payé nos libertés d'un trop grand prix pour en céder quelques chose au-delà du soin de prévenir les divulgations, les excitations dont pourrait profiter l'ennemi. Une censure sera maintenue des informations diplomatiques et militaires, aussi bien que de celles qui seraient susceptibles de troubler la paix civile. Cela jusqu'aux limites du respect des opinions. Un bureau de presse fournira des avis – rien que des avis – à qui les sollicitera. En temps de guerre, comme en temps de paix, la liberté s'exerce sous la responsabilité personnelle de l'écrivain. En dehors de cette règle, il n'y a qu'arbitraire, anarchie. [. . .]

Un jour, de Paris au plus humble village, des rafales d'acclamations accueilleront nos étendards, vainqueurs, tordus dans le sang, dans les larmes, déchirés des obus, magnifique apparition de nos grands morts. Ce jour, le plus beau de notre race, après tant d'autres, il est en notre pouvoir de le faire. Pour les résolutions sans retour, nous vous demandons, messieurs, le sceau de votre volonté.

Topics
FOR DISCUSSION

1   Why did France go to war in 1914?
2   What does Document 6a tell us about life at the front?
3   Why did Verdun come to symbolise World War I in French consciousness?
4   What does Document 6b reveal about Clémenceau's war leadership?
5   Why did reparations become such a dominant issue in French politics?
6   What was the significance of the Colonial Exhibition in 1931? How does Figure 6.1 help us to understand the impact of colonialism?

CHAPTER 7

Timeline

1929
24 October   Wall Street Crash

1932
May   Victory of the cartel des gauches
14 December   Fall of the Herriot government

1933
30 January   Hitler comes to power and takes Germany out of the League of Nations

1934
6 February   Right-wing riots outside the National Assembly
27 July   Pact between the SFIO and PCF

1935
14 July   Popular Front demonstration in Paris

1936
7 March   Hitler remilitarises the Rhineland
26 April–3 May   Electoral victory of the Popular Front
May–June   Factory sit-ins
6 June   Formation of the Blum government
7 June   Matignon Agreements between employers and employees
17 July   Spanish Civil War begins
26 September   Devaluation of the franc

1937
February   Blum announces temporary halt to reforms – the pause
21 June   Fall of Blum government

1938
12 March   Unification of Germany and Austria
12 April   Formation of the Daladier government
29 September   Munich Agreement

France, 1931–39

By the late 1920s America was already the motor of the global economy and the supreme creditor nation of the post-war world. For Americans this dominance produced a boom period, the roaring twenties, and many investors became caught up in a wave of optimism. Hoping for quick gains, speculators feverishly bought stocks in new industries such as cars and electrical goods. In 1928 alone the average price of stocks and shares on Wall Street rose by 25 per cent. Yet these increases bore no relation to the supply of real goods or trends in world trade. Indeed, industrial production expanded little between 1926 and 1929. The price rises were just manipulations of the stock market and when the bubble of speculation burst dramatically on 24 October 1929, Black Thursday, the result was mass hysteria. As stockholders furiously unloaded shares, the New York Stock Exchange collapsed. The figures were truly staggering – in the space of seven days American investors lost $40,000 million – and with them went the economic self-confidence of the 1920s. Across America businesses went bankrupt and factories slowed down production. By 1932 there were 13 million people out of work in America. The Great Depression had begun.

The consequences of the Wall Street Crash were catastrophic for Europe. When the American

> 12 November   Daladier government ends the 40-hour week
> 30 November   Repression of general strike
>
> **1939**
> 15 March   Nazi occupation of Czechoslovakia
> 23 August   Nazi–Soviet pact
> 1 September   Nazi Germany invades Poland
> 3 September   Britain and France declare war on Germany

government suspended all loans to Europe the foundation stone of post-war recovery was destroyed in one fell swoop. Germany, given its dependency on America, was particularly vulnerable and by May 1931 it was virtually insolvent. Much to the consternation of the French, America, in an effort to aid the failing German economy, suspended reparations in June. In practice this only created a vicious cycle of mistrust. The French retaliated by immediately reneging on loans to America, which ended any commitment to mutual cooperation. Nor did it help the Germans. Instead, as industrial production halved, unemployment mushroomed from 2 million to 6 million, creating misery and suffering on a huge scale. It was the economic equivalent of World War I and the major factor in Adolf Hitler coming to power on 30 January 1933. Across Europe the incapacity of democracy to cope with the crisis was only too evident. In 1919 Europeans had been buoyed up by a belief in the ability of liberal values to deliver a better world. By 1934 such faith was badly shaken and, as capitalism broke down, large numbers of people turned towards authoritarian solutions.

The impact of the Depression in France

Unlike in other European countries, the Depression in France did not begin to bite until late 1931. Partly because of the undervaluation of the franc, which made exports cheaper, partly because of the colonies, which represented a protected market for French goods, and partly because of the small-scale nature of French industry and agriculture, which allowed businesses to slow down production rather than lay off workers, France was initially insulated from the downturn. Moreover, the fact that French producers studiously avoided indebtedness and overproduction meant that France had been spared the artificial levels of prosperity in America, with the result that France suffered much lower levels of unemployment, less than 900,000 at the height of the crisis as opposed to 6 million in Britain.

None the less, once France was hit, the Depression was more protracted there than elsewhere. Whilst most developed countries were on the road to recovery by 1932 and had surpassed 1929 levels of production by the late 1930s, in France the economy slumped from 1933 to 1935 and did not regain its 1929 level of industrial production until 1950. Across the country agricultural prices plummeted, investments fell and industrial production went into sharp decline. The colonies were particularly badly hit. In North Africa an immense rural exodus to the major coastal cities climaxed tragically with the 1937 famine, remembered amongst the native populations as the terrible year of hunger. Inevitably too the Depression fuelled a climate of racism as foreign workers recruited in the 1920s, drawn principally from Poland and Italy, were the first to be put out of work.

Haunted by the memory of inflation and currency instability, successive governments from 1931 to 1936 adopted an inflexible position and steadfastly refused to devalue the franc. Thus, whilst the devaluation of the pound in 1931 and the dollar in 1933 kick-started the British and American economies, the franc remained overvalued and this had a crippling effect on the French economy. By 1933 the value of French exports had fallen by two-thirds of the 1928 figure. As the situation worsened, the government resorted to draconian measures to balance the budget, drastically reducing armament production and cutting pensions. In practice these policies merely dampened demand and created further stagnation, and, as the incapacity of government became more self-evident, what was an economic crisis transformed itself into an institutional crisis.

> **stalemate society**
>
> According to the 1931 census figure 9 million people (43 per cent of the working population) derived their income, not from a wage, but from independent means. For the American historian Stanley Hoffmann this pattern of *petit bourgeois* ownership produced what he termed the stalemate society of the Third Republic. The stalemate society was a stabilising factor because it produced a wide consensus in favour of capitalist property relations and marginalised the working class. However, during the 1930s this republican consensus disintegrated in the face of intense social conflict and extra-parliamentary activity.

The institutional crisis

Legislative elections in May 1932 witnessed a second victory of the *cartel des gauches* with 334 deputies including 157 radicals and 129 socialists. Initially the SFIO supported the government without participating in it, but when Herriot continued to follow an economic policy of deflation, the socialists rapidly became disgruntled. Herriot's commitment to individualism and private ownership was completely at odds with the collectivist and interventionist policies of the SFIO and for this reason his government fell in December 1932. Thereafter the next 3 years witnessed 11 governments and the longer this instability lasted, the more people came to the conclusion that democracy had failed.

Inevitably, this instability fuelled support for right-wing movements, known collectively as the Leagues. Some groups had a long tradition of extra-parliamentary agitation. Charles Maurras's *Action française* had shot to prominence during the Dreyfus Affair and, although it had been condemned for extremism by the Vatican in 1926, the pungent blend of anti-Semitism, royalism and nationalism continued to attract support, especially amongst writers and intellectuals such as Robert Brasillach and Lucien Rebatet. Some groups, notably the *Jeunesses patriotes* founded by the champagne baron Pierre de Tattinger, emerged during the 1920s. Others, like *Solidarité française*, established by the perfume maker François Coty, were a direct response to the institutional crisis. However, of all these, by far and away the most important was the *Croix-de-Feu*, founded as a war veterans' organisation in 1928. Led by François de la Rocque de Severac, a retired lieutenant-colonel who styled himself as a charismatic leader, by 1935 the *Croix-de-Feu* had become a genuine mass movement, with 300,000 members drawn principally from the urban lower middle class. Populist, authoritarian, militaristic, the *Croix-de-Feu* denounced parliamentary democracy as a sham, blaming the country's accumulated ills on communists, socialists, freemasons, foreigners and Jews. But although much of the rhetoric and style echoed fascism in Italy and Nazism in Germany, it is important not to consider the *Croix* as an imitation of them. In truth the movement was the heir of the nationalist organisations of the 1880s and this in turn explains the *Croix-de-Feu*'s ideological appeal.

For the Leagues the denunciation of the Third Republic took on a concrete form with the Stavisky Affair. Alexandre Stavisky had been under investigation for financial forgery since 1927 but had escaped justice largely due to a network of influential friends in the Radical Party. The scandal became sensational when Stavisky, facing imminent arrest, committed suicide on 8 January 1934. The fact that Stavisky was Ukrainian, from a family that had converted from Judaism to Catholicism, fuelled the Leagues' belief that the Third Republic was controlled by Jews and foreigners. Immediately they organised demonstrations on the streets, claiming that Stavisky had been murdered in order to prevent damaging revelations at his trial. This show of strength climaxed with widespread rioting outside the National Assembly on the night of 6 February. During the violence the police fired into the crowd, killing 14, and in the ensuing frenzy many feared a *coup d'état*. In reality, though, the Leagues lacked unity and coordination. Whilst other right-wing groups tried to storm government buildings, de la Rocque, convinced of the need to remain within the letter of the law, held his own supporters back. De la Rocque did not want to take power, but to provoke a change of government and to this end he succeeded. The following day Edouard Daladier, a radical, resigned as prime minister, and President Albert Lebrun called on the former president, Gaston Doumergue, to come out of retirement. Doumergue immediately formed a government of *union nationale*, stretching from the radicals to the right and including several men from outside formal politics, notably Marshal Pétain, who became defence minister. Doumergue combined deflationary policies with attempts at constitutional reform. Above all he wanted to strengthen the powers of the presidency, but on this point he was fiercely opposed by the radicals, who withdrew their support in November, thus causing the Doumergue government to fall. From then on right-wing coalitions relied upon special decree powers to force through stringent deflationary policies. In this way the Pierre Laval government controversially cut all expenditure by 10 per cent, including war pensions and incomes on bonds.

The Popular Front

On the left, 6 February had far-reaching consequences. Confronted with what they saw as an imminent fascist threat, the left parties came together to form the Popular Front. Initially the impetus came from the grassroots members, who organised a general strike in defence of the Third Republic on 12 February 1934. After this it was the PCF which took the lead in trying to convince the SFIO and the Radical Party of the need for united action. At first both the SFIO and the Radical Party were extremely suspicious.

Until then the PCF had pursued a so-called class against class policy, whereby the Third Republic was denounced as a bourgeois regime and the SFIO was attacked as the main political enemy on the grounds that the socialists were diverting the working class away from revolution. Now, partly because of Hitler's rise to power, facilitated to a large degree by the disunity of German communists and socialists, and partly because of the Soviet Union's need for international allies, the International Communist Movement (Comintern) had discarded the class against class strategy in favour of a popular front policy that aimed to build the broadest possible coalition of democrats against fascism.

The impact of the new popular front policy was immediately obvious in France, where the PCF tried to unite the left around the themes of anti-fascism, patriotism and national defence, as well as strident opposition to the economic policies of the Doumergue government. The communist language now changed dramatically and henceforth the PCF assiduously cultivated patriotism, casting the workers as the heirs of 1789 and the true guardians of the Republic. As *L'Humanité* loudly proclaimed in its editorial of 11 July 1936, communists were not the enemies of the nation. On the contrary, the PCF was steeped in French history: 'Our party did not fall from the sky. We have deep roots in the soil of France. The names of our leaders have a strong, honest, native tang. Our party is a moment in the history of eternal France.'

On this basis the PCF leader, Maurice Thorez, sought to construct a broad anti-fascist alliance. The policy of the outstretched hand (*main tendue*) reached out to Catholics and small businesses. It was a strategy that led to a pact not only with the SFIO but also with the Radical Party, where younger activists, disenchanted with the old guard and led by the likes of Pierre Mendès-France, pushed for cooperation. Symbolically the three parties cemented this alliance through a mass demonstration in Paris on 14 July 1935. Led by Blum, Thorez and Daladier, the demonstration called for a new government that would defend democracy and give bread to the people and work to young people.

The formation of the Popular Front pointed towards a polarisation of politics and many on the right immediately took fright. For them the Popular Front conjured up the spectre of communist revolution in France. Yet, for all the fear of communism, the Popular Front programme of January 1936 was in actual fact very moderate, ironically because the PCF did not want to frighten off middle-class support. This was not a blueprint for fundamental change. Aside from the creation of the Bank of France and the nationalisation of the armaments industry, no major reforms were envisaged. Its economic policy was inspired by the New Deal in America, rather than by the Soviet Union. Like the Roosevelt government the Popular Front pro-

cinema

During the 1930s the film industry took off in France. Now millions went to the cinema each week and several directors, such as René Clair and Marcel Carné, achieved worldwide fame. The most famous actor was Jean Gabin, who became famous for his depiction of working-class outsiders. Many of the films were explicitly political. By depicting women workers taking control of a publishing company, Jean Renoir's 1935 film *Le Crime de Monsieur Lange* anticipated the mood of the Popular Front victory a year later.

gramme aimed to kickstart the economy through a programme of massive public works that would stimulate demand and reduce unemployment.

The emergence of the Popular Front was intimately connected to developments in international politics. As we have already noted, the rise to power of Hitler, which in effect represented the failure of French foreign policy, provoked a change in communist policy, and henceforth the belligerency of Nazi foreign policy was to dominate domestic politics. In October 1933 Germany left the League of Nations and the disarmament conference. Then in March 1935, in open defiance of the Versailles Treaty, Hitler announced that the German air force had already been rebuilt and that the army would be increased to half a million men and conscription would be reintroduced. In response the French sought new alliances. In April French, British and Italian representatives met to denounce Nazi Germany's violation of Versailles; in May the Pierre Laval government signed a pact with the Soviet Union. However, these diplomatic initiatives produced clear tensions. Thus, when Italy invaded Ethiopia in October 1935, the right, out of political sympathy for Mussolini, was hostile to any sanctions against the fascist regime. Likewise the right was suspicious of the Soviet pact, firstly because it would antagonise Hitler and, secondly, because it was supported by the PCF. Whilst large sections of the right saw communism as the principal threat and wanted to appease the dictators, the Popular Front parties called for harsh measures against Hitler and Mussolini. For this reason the PCF and SFIO were disgusted by the way in which the Sarraut government feebly caved in to Hitler's remilitarisation of the Rhineland on 7 March 1936, a further flagrant violation of the Versailles settlement.

The threat of fascism at home and abroad fostered unity and led to the unification of the trade union movement in March 1936. With the merging of the CGT and CGTU membership dramatically increased from 750,000 to 4 million during 1936. More than anything the CGT/CGTU merger symbolised the recovery of the past unity of the left, producing a new mood of optimism. The image of a regenerated left laid the ground for a particularly vicious campaign in the run-up to the April 1936 general election. On the right anti-Semitism reached new levels of hysteria and Blum himself was subjected to a vitriolic hate campaign. For the nationalist right Blum was the personification of the Jewish invasion which, it claimed, threatened the very life-blood of the true France. Maurras stated publicly that Blum was a man to be shot, but in the back – sentiments that led an *Action française* mob to brutally attack Blum on 13 February. Shouting 'Death to the Jew!' the mob left Blum so badly beaten that he had to be hospitalised for one month.

In preparation for the elections in April 1936 the Popular Front parties agreed to rally their voters to the best-placed candidate at the second round, and this electoral discipline was the basis for the famous Popular Front victory. Although the Popular Front parties won a moderate swing overall, what was striking was its electoral make-up. In the first ballot, on 26 April, the communists doubled their vote; the socialists lost 2 per cent, whilst the radicals, undoubtedly being punished for their participation in power, lost 15 per cent. In the second round this translated into 72 seats for the PCF, 146 for the SFIO and 116 for the radicals. For the first time the SFIO had overtaken the radicals as the largest party and for this reason it fell to Blum to form the Popular Front government. The PCF, worried that communist ministers would frighten off middle-class voters, announced that it would support the government from the back benches. This left Blum free to compose a radical–socialist cabinet.

Not surprisingly Blum's assumption of office was greeted with revulsion by large numbers of right-wing deputies. Xavier Vallat, the conservative deputy for the Ardèche who would serve as the Vichy regime's first commissioner general for Jewish affairs, vilified Blum in racial terms. Speaking directly to Blum in the National Assembly he declared: 'There is another reason that prevents me from voting in favour of the ministry of M. Blum: Blum himself. Your ascendance to power is incontestably a historic date. For the first time this Gallo-Roman country will be governed by a Jew.'

The Popular Front in power

The victory of the Popular Front was immediately followed in June 1936 by an unprecedented wave of strikes and factory occupations by 2 million employees, the largest uprising since the Paris Commune. Suddenly everything seemed possible and the images from the period reveal a carnival atmosphere, a world turned upside down, where singing and dancing went hand in hand with mock trials of employers. This upsurge in militancy petrified employers, who met CGT representatives in the presence of Blum and signed the Matignon Agreements on the night of 7–8 June. The agreements gave the workers major concessions, including a 40-hour week, 2 weeks' paid holidays, wage increases ranging from 7 to 15 per cent and the recognition of trade union rights. Significantly too, there were to be workers' delegates for factories with more than 10 workers. Despite the sense of victory, many workers refused to return to work, at which point Blum won communist support for an end to the strikes. Now Thorez intervened personally, famously telling workers that one has to know when to end a strike once satisfaction has been obtained.

What followed was a spectacular burst of reform. The school-leaving age was raised to 14; the organisation of the Bank of France was made more democratic; the arms industry was nationalised; and the price of wheat was stabilised through the creation of a Grain Board. Significantly too the Leagues were dissolved. In the empire the Popular Front appointed a commission to investigate living conditions in the colonies, and introduced proposals to extend voting rights to 25,000 Algerians from a population of 6 million. Finally, the Popular Front also launched an ambitious rearmament programme, aiming to produce 3,200 tanks.

The Popular Front reforms were greeted with euphoria and by the end of June the

women and the Popular Front

Even though women did not have the vote, Blum named three women as junior ministers: Irène Joliot-Curie for scientific research, Suzanne Lacore for child welfare and Cécile Brunschvicg for education. For him the move was symbolic and in this sense they were undoubtedly important in breaking the male monopoly of politics. Along with women pilots, such as Adrienne Bolland, it was another example of how women were redefining traditional gender stereotypes.

factory sit-ins had ended. However, once the strikes were over an uneasy peace reigned within the factories. Employers were determined to reassert their authority at the earliest opportunity and soon they were flouting the Matignon Agreements with impunity. The sense of class conflict was clear and unmistakable, something that was underlined by the flight of capital abroad, which in turn provoked a devaluation of the franc. As in 1926, the so-called wall of money was sabotaging reform and in this polarised climate the economy continued to falter. Blum had hoped that wage increases, allied with the strict adherence to the 40-hour week, would force businesses to take on more workers, leading quickly to increased demand and a re-launching of the economy. Instead production did not take off, firstly because the employers had no desire to renew the outdated industrial infrastructure, and secondly because the doctrinaire application of the 40-hour week had in fact stifled any revival, increasing wages and boosting inflation. By September 1936, as the budget deficit continued to mount, Blum had no option but to devalue the franc by 30 per cent. None the less the franc remained under pressure and in February 1937 Blum was forced, humiliatingly, to announce a pause in the reform programme of the Popular Front.

The pause was a desperate effort to restore business confidence and encourage French investors to repatriate their funds. In this sense it exemplified Blum's fatal predicament. The intention might have been to win over business, but in practice the pause pushed tensions within the Popular Front to breaking point. The radicals, many of whom had always been nervous about the alliance with the communists and socialists, began to distance themselves, whilst the PCF and the far left of the SFIO attacked the retreat from reform as an unforgivable capitulation to the wall of money. Moreover, there was the palpable disenchantment of the working classes. As the cost of living continued to rise dramatically, and as the employers attempted to sabotage the Matignon Agreements, enthusiasm for the Blum government began to dissipate, provoking a fresh wave of strikes in the autumn. The pause merely reinforced the growing sense of separation between labour and the Popular Front, something which deepened still further when six people, mostly socialists, were killed by the police during an anti-de la Rocque demonstration in the Paris suburbs on 16 March 1937. The reputation of the Blum government was now sullied and, as the financial crisis continued, it was only a matter of time before the administration fell. When the Senate refused to grant him decree powers, Blum resigned on 22 June 1937. To all intents and purposes the Popular Front experiment was over.

The Blum government was also fatally undermined by the Spanish Civil War. On 17 July 1936 the Spanish military, led by General Franco, revolted against the newly elected

paid holidays

When the Popular Front government introduced paid leave, many families took their first holidays and saw the sea for the first time. Because they were so near to Paris, the beaches of the north and west were the most popular destinations for the working classes. The arrival of the workers terrified the middle classes, who immediately decamped in disgust to more select resorts in the south. For them it was just another example of how, under Blum, no social space was sacrosanct.

Spanish Popular Front. Immediately Nazi Germany and fascist Italy intervened militarily to support the rebels, but, although Blum wished to give aid to his colleagues in Spain, divisions within his government (the Radical party was hostile to any involvement on the grounds that it would spark off another European war) prevented him from doing so. For Blum it was a painful dilemma compounded by two more factors. Firstly, Blum was told in no uncertain terms by the British government that, in the event of arms sales to the Spanish Republic, they would not support him; and secondly, Blum feared that, given the massive amount of Catholic and conservative sympathy for Franco, support for the Spanish Republic would bring about civil war in France. Blum therefore followed a policy of non-intervention and was, along with Britain, the principal architect of the Non-Intervention Pact of August 1936, signed by 27 nations, including Germany, Italy and the Soviet Union. On 21 January 1937 the Blum government formally inscribed this Non-Intervention Pact in law with the prohibition of volunteers and arms to Spain.

Not surprisingly Blum's policy outraged the PCF. For them it was a betrayal of the Popular Front's anti-fascist platform. Likewise many grassroots supporters felt increasingly ill at ease with the non-intervention stance. The more that Germany and Italy cheerfully supplied arms and soldiers to Franco, the more non-intervention looked like a farce, if not an act of malevolent neutrality. By refusing to arm the beleaguered Republic, the French and British governments were in effect aiding and abetting Franco's final victory.

The Popular Front in power and the Spanish Civil War radicalised the nationalist right. Conservatives felt that they were experiencing the Bolshevik Revolution at first hand and in response their rhetoric and action became more extreme. 'Rather Hitler than Blum' became a familiar phrase in wealthy right-wing circles. The right-wing press played on atrocity stories from the Spanish Civil War, warning readers that the burning of churches provided an ominous glimpse of what the future might hold for them. On the face of it, de la Rocque, who responded to the dissolution of the *Croix* by transforming it into a conventional political party, the *Parti social français* (PSF), moderated his tone. By 1937–38 the PSF had 1 million members, making it

The 1937 International Exhibition

Although conceived long before, the International Exhibition opened in Paris in May 1937 under the Popular Front government. Since 1855 successive international exhibitions had transformed the capital, above all with the construction of the Trocadero and its museums in 1878 and the Eiffel Tower in 1889. The 1937 Exhibition was largely built on the same site and within it two features were to stand out: the notorious confrontation between the Nazi and Soviet Pavilions, squaring up to each other on the right bank of the Seine, and the Modernist Pavilion, housing Pablo Picasso's *Guernica*, a portrayal of the near total destruction of the undefended Basque town by fascist planes, the first example of aerial bombardment. For Blum the exhibition epitomised the cultural goals of the Popular Front. As he stated in his preface to the exhibition celebrating French art, this was to be a people's festival that would open up culture for the masses.

briefly the most successful political movement in French history, but although de la Rocque abandoned violence, the PSF remained highly authoritarian. Indeed, even if the PSF could not be accurately called fascist, and even if the PSF remained at best ambivalent about the Third Republic, its membership still displayed considerable sympathy for Mussolini and Hitler.

To the right of de la Rocque, Jacques Doriot's *Parti populaire français* (PPF) was the most authentically fascist of all the right-wing movements between the wars. A former PCF deputy and mayor of Saint-Denis, Doriot was expelled from the party in 1934, ironically for advocating a popular front strategy before this had become Comintern policy. At this point Doriot made the switch from the extreme left to the extreme right, launching the PPF in June 1936. Modelling his paramilitary style on Hitler and Mussolini, Doriot cast himself as a saviour figure. Fiercely anti-parliamentary, fiercely anti-Semitic, fiercely anti-communist, he wanted to regenerate France. Drawing on the *sans-culottes* and the Paris Commune, as well as Joan of Arc, as symbols of vitality, Doriot was obsessed with the supposed war between the French race and international Jewry. He wanted a racial revolution that would purge the country of impure elements. The way in which the PPF not only aspired to be a radical mass movement, but also wanted to create a new type of society rather than defend the status quo, marks this out as a fascist movement. At the outset the PPF received money from Mussolini and powerful industrialists, including Pierre Pucheu, steel executive and future Vichy minister of the interior, and by 1938 the PPF had a membership of 100,000, drawn largely from the lower middle classes and including intellectuals such as Pierre Drieu la Rochelle and Alfred Fabre-Luce. The PPF was the most visible expression of a new extremism that was also to be found in the shadowy *cagoulards*, a group of high-ranking army officers who were so called because they wore hoods. Convinced that Blum was the dupe of Moscow, they tried to carry out a coup on 15 November 1937. The coup failed but the violent language of the PPF and the *cagoulards* did have an impact on mainstream conservatives, pulling many leaders such as Laval further to the right.

Path to war, 1937–39

Blum, who remained in government as deputy prime minister, was replaced by the radical Chautemps, who presided over a steadily deteriorating situation. Fresh waves of strikes combined with the growth of budget deficits paralysed the government. The SFIO refused to support his demand for decree powers and on 9 March 1938 Chautemps resigned. In foreign policy terms this paralysis could not have been more badly timed. On 13 March Hitler, after a period of political manoeuvring, completed the unification of Germany and Austria. With the *Anschluss*, a France of 41 million people now ominously confronted a Reich of 71 million.

In the wake of the *Anschluss* Blum momentarily returned as prime minister. His proposal was for a government of national unity for a war which many now saw as inevitable. It lasted just one month. Again when the Senate opposed his financial policies Blum resigned, whereupon President Lebrun turned to Edouard Daladier, veteran of

15 cabinets and three times prime minister, to take up the post. On 12 April 1938 Daladier's government was endorsed by all but a handful of deputies. Significantly the new administration contained no socialists.

Immediately Daladier had to face up to Hitler's relentless expansionism. Flushed with the success of the *Anschluss*, Hitler now turned to Czechoslovakia, where the pretext for aggression was the situation of the German minority in the Sudetenland. Of a total Czech population of 15 million, ethnic Germans accounted for 3 million and Hitler claimed that they were being subjected to terrible oppression. During the spring and summer of 1938 Hitler egged on the Sudeten Germans, who began to demand autonomy. In theory, given that Czechoslovakia was a democracy formally allied to France since 1925 and the linchpin of the French alliance system in Eastern Europe, the obligations of the Daladier government were clear and unambiguous. In practice, Foreign Minister Georges Bonnet had no qualms about abandoning the Czechs. By giving Hitler a free hand in Eastern Europe, Bonnet, along with the British prime minister Neville Chamberlain, hoped to avoid another general European war. On 29 September Hitler, Mussolini, Chamberlain and Daladier signed the Munich Agreement whereby the Czechs were forced to make concessions. In exchange for Hitler's guarantee of the redrawn borders, the Sudetenland was annexed to Germany, whilst Polish and Hungarian claims on Czech territory were also met.

On 2 October the Munich Agreement was endorsed by a massive majority – 515 for and 75 against – in the National Assembly. Only the communists, along with one socialist and one conservative, opposed it. On the right Munich received overwhelming support. Maurras proclaimed loudly that 'the French do not want to fight – neither for the Jews, the Russians, nor the freemasons of Prague'. He accused the Jews of warmongering and this climate of intolerance led to attacks on Jewish shops and businesses. When a 17-year-old illegal Jewish refugee, Herschel Grynszpan, assassinated a leading German diplomat, Ernst vom Rath, the intolerance reached unprecedented levels. As the Nazis used vom Rath's death as the excuse for the *Kristallnacht* pogrom of 9–10 November that killed 91 German Jews and destroyed 267 synagogues, Maurras was unrepentant: 'The prestige of France is not threatened when one burns down a synagogue somewhere. One can burn them all. It is not our business and it has no impact whatsoever on us. No diplomatic intervention, no war for the Jews.'

Daladier himself had few illusions about Munich. He knew that it was a betrayal and when, on his return to Paris, the crowds fêted him as a hero he famously muttered: 'the cretins'. He was convinced that war was inevitable and this led him to take determined action. From now on he by-passed parliament, repeatedly using emergency powers (from October 1938 to September 1939 he ruled by decree for over 7 months) as well as proroguing parliament on 27 July 1939 and suspending by-elections until June 1942, something without precedent in peacetime. Daladier also moved the Radical Party sharply to the right. Daladier was strongly anti-communist and he now set out to destroy the organised labour movement. In Daladier's eyes the Popular Front legislation was holding back arms production and through a series of decrees on 12 November 1938 he did away with the 40-hour week. For the workers this was an attack on their newly won rights and on 30 November the CGT called for a general strike. In response Daladier sent in troops and police, rooting out ringleaders and sacking some 800,000 workers. It was a show of force that decimated union membership. By the start of 1939 it had plummeted to 1.5 million, as against 4 million 2 years earlier. For employers November 1938 was a huge turning point. It firmly re-established traditional labour relations and in effect it gave employers *carte blanche* to take revenge on troublesome workers.

As well as organised labour, Daladier also singled out aliens and immigrants. Through the anti-immigrant decree laws of 2 May 1938 and 12 November 1938 internment camps were established and strict prison sentences for illegal aliens introduced. The laws may not have explicitly mentioned Jews, but they were clearly aimed at the new influx of Jewish refugees from Austria and Czechoslovakia and in this sense were emblematic of the new climate of intolerance. Likewise Daladier tried to arrest the demographic decline through a robust natalist policy. The Family Code of 30 July 1939 introduced a nationwide scale of family allowances, in addition to harsh penalties for birth control and abortion. Finally, Daladier underlined the renewed significance of the empire. In North Africa there was a crackdown on nationalist organisations, stigmatised as fanatical minorities in the pay of fascist agents. Such a brutal assertion of sovereignty underlined just how important the empire had become by the late 1930s. It would be no exaggeration to say that as France felt increasingly isolated on the international scene, the empire – emotionally, economically and politically – became a source of hope which had to be defended. In numerous speeches and radio addresses during December 1938 and January 1939, Daladier tried to stiffen the national resolve by reminding French people that they were not alone. Again and again he argued that the empire – transforming the nation from a 42-million weakling into a 110-million colossus – would save France.

The Daladier government, therefore, blended anti-communism, authoritarianism, imperialism and rearmament. His persecution of the PCF took the bite out of the PSF and the PPF, and during the winter of 1938–39 Daladier became the most popular leader since Clémenceau. Large numbers of people warmed to his tough, no-nonsense style. As, during spring 1939, war became inevitable, here was a man who could take decisive action and stand up to Nazi Germany.

The Nazi occupation of the rest of Czechoslovakia on 15 March 1939 produced a major shift in public opinion. This, along with Franco's victory in Spain in April, demonstrated that appeasement had failed. Now most people recognised that France had no alternative but to stand up to Germany. On 23 March Britain and France quickly promised to defend Belgium, the Netherlands and Switzerland, and over the next 3 weeks the same undertaking was given to Poland, Greece and Romania. Diplomatic overtures were also made to the Soviet Union. However, both sides were very wary. After his exclusion from Munich, Stalin was suspicious of British and French intentions and the negotiations dragged on for months. Then suddenly, to the astonishment of the world, Stalin and Hitler signed the Nazi–Soviet Pact on 23 August. The non-aggression pact freed Hitler from the prospect of war on two front and on 1 September Nazi Germany invaded Poland. Two days later Britain and France declared war on Germany.

Document 7a: Témoignages: Raymond Bressy, né le 16 mars 1914 dans la Creuse

De mars 1935 jusqu'à la fin 1936, j'étais au régiment. Lorsque je suis rentré, j'étais bien content des suites du Front Populaire car cela correspondait à mes idées. Je suis rentré au chemin de fer où j'ai débuté comme facteur aux écritures à Tolbiac. Puis je fus affecté à Etampes et c'est là que je me suis rendu compte qu'il y avait quelque chose de changé dans ma vie. En allant voir le docteur, l'un de mes collègues a su qu'il était maintenant possible de se faire rembourser les frais grâce aux assurances sociales. Là j'ai trouvé que le Front Populaire avait véritablement fait avancer les choses. Puis j'ai rencontré des jeunes qui partaient pour la guerre d'Espagne. Sur le coup, je ne les ai pas compris; cette idée qu'ils défendaient, la guerre contre le gouvernement espagnol.

Vint ensuite la période où je travaillais dans un bureau de ville. On fabriquait des billets de transport pour les gens qui n'avaient alors plus besoin de passer dans les gares. Tellement de gens n'étaient jamais partis en vacances et là, c'était l'explosion des voyages. Ces gens avaient travaillé pendant des années sans jamais pouvoir s'offrir des congés. Et d'un coup, on leur disait 'tu vas être payé pendant quinze jours pour être en vacances'. C'était vraiment une révolution. Je suis content de l'avoir vécu parce que cela me restera jusqu'au bout.

Témoignages sur www.mairie-athis-mons.fr/histoire/front.htm#temoins

Document 7b: Mai 1936: Pivert, 'Tout est possible'

Qu'on ne vienne pas nous chanter des airs de berceuse: tout un peuple est désormais en marche, d'un pas assuré, vers un magnifique destin.

Dans l'atmosphère de victoire, de confiance et de discipline qui s'étend sur le pays, oui, tout est possible aux audacieux. Tout est possible et notre Parti a ce privilège et cette responsabilité tout à la fois, d'être porté à la pointe du mouvement. Qu'il marche! Qu'il entraîne! Qu'il tranche! Qu'il exécute! Et aucun obstacle ne lui résistera!

Ce qu'ils appellent du fond de leur conscience collective, des millions et des millions d'hommes et de femmes, c'est un changement radical, à brève échéance, de la situation politique et économique. On ne pourrait pas impunément remettre à plus tard sous prétexte que le programme du Front populaire ne l'a pas explicitement définie, l'offensive anticapitaliste la plus vigoureuse.

continued

Les masses sont beaucoup plus avancées qu'on ne l'imagine; elles ne s'embarrassent pas de considérations doctrinales compliquées, mais d'un instinct sûr, elles appellent les solutions les plus substantielles, elles attendent beaucoup. Elles ne se contenteront pas d'une modeste tisane de guimauve portée à pas feutrés au chevet de la mère malade. Au contraire, les opérations chirurgicales les plus risquées entraîneront son consentement; car elles savent que le monde capitaliste agonise et qu'il faut construire un monde nouveau si l'on veut en finir avec la crise, le fascisme et la guerre.

[. . .] Tout est possible, et à toute vitesse. Nous sommes à une heure qui ne repassera sans doute pas de sitôt au cadran de l'histoire. Alors, puisque tout est possible, droit devant nous, camarades!

Marceau Pivert, *Le Populaire*, 27 mai 1936

Document 7c: Paul-Boncour, Les grèves expliquées par un ministre

Sans nier le rôle des meneurs dans les mouvements sociaux, bons ou mauvais, il faut tenir compte de ce qu'ils comportent de spontané, réactions instinctives de la classe ouvrière devant certains événements. La victoire du Front populaire, en même temps que l'enivrement de revanche contre le 6 février 1934, dont le souvenir était resté mordant, avaient fait concevoir des espoirs d'autant plus impatients que, depuis la loi des retraites, les huit heures de Clémenceau, et la loi des assurances sociales, les gouvernements, aux prises avec les difficultés financières, l'instabilité qui en était la conséquence et qui les obligeait à vivre au jour le jour, n'avaient pu réaliser certaines des grandes améliorations sociales installées de longue date dans tant d'autres pays, y compris les pays totalitaires.

Par ailleurs, le grand patronat, qui se montra alors plutôt faible et pusillanime, avait été longtemps assez égoïste et fermé pour que des modérés, des gens de droite, sans parler bien entendu de ces courageux démocrates-chrétiens, dont l'action se confondait de plus en plus avec la nôtre, le lui aient maintes fois reproché. Les revendications grondaient au lendemain de ce 13 mai 1936 [. . .] La grève pouvait servir aussi bien à soutenir une affirmation politique qu'à défendre une question de salaires ou d'heures de travail. Rien d'étonnant à ce que l'idée surgit d'en déclencher de multiples pour forcer la main à la fois au gouvernement et au patronat. Et comme, en période de chômage, les grèves sont vouées à l'échec si l'embauche subsiste, celles-ci se transformèrent vite en 'grèves sur le tas'. On occupa l'usine pour être sûr que les chômeurs ne viendraient pas prendre la place.

J. Paul-Boncour (1950) *Entre deux guerres*, Paris: Plon, p. 329

Topics
FOR DISCUSSION

1   What impact did the Great Depression have on France?
2   Account for the formation of the Popular Front.
3   What were the Popular Front reforms? What does Document 7a tell us about the hopes inspired by the Popular Front? Why did they provoke so much fear on the right? Contrast the views developed by Pivert (Document 7b) and Paul-Boncour (Document 7c).
4   Why was Blum forced to announce a 'pause' in reform?
5   What impact did the Spanish Civil War have on France?
6   What was French policy towards Nazi Germany?
7   Why did France go to war in September 1939?

CHAPTER 8

Occupied France, 1940–44

Timeline

1940
13 May   German army breaks through the Ardennes
18 June   De Gaulle's call to Resistance from London
22 June   Armistice signed
10 July   Full powers voted to Pétain
3 October   Jewish Statute
24 October   Pétain meets Hitler at Montoire

1941
22 June   Germany invades the Soviet Union
4 October   Vichy Labour Charter

1942
18 April   Laval becomes prime minister
16–17 July   Round-up of Jews in Paris
8–11 November   Germans occupy the southern zone

1943
16 February   Introduction of service du travail obligatoire
27 May   Meeting of the Conseil national de la résistance

1944
6 June   Allied landings in Normandy
25 August   Liberation of Paris

1945
8 May   Germany surrenders Throughout May savage repression of nationalist uprising in Algeria

As the historian Norman Davies had underlined, although France and Britain declared war on Nazi Germany on 3 September 1939, it is important to understand that this date did not mark the outbreak of World War II. Japan had invaded Manchuria 8 years earlier, and had been embroiled in war in central China since 1937. From August 1938 Japan was also involved in fighting against the Soviet Union on the Mongolian border, a conflict that had prompted Japan to enter into an alliance with Germany and Italy. In Spain the Civil War had begun in July 1936. Likewise March 1939 saw Germany occupy Czechoslovakia and attack Lithuania, whilst one month later Italy invaded Albania. In this sense September 1939 was but a new stage in the relentless march of war since 1931. However, because it brought Poland, the Soviet Union, Japan, Italy, France, Britain and America into conflict or potential conflict, September 1939 represents the extension of the essentially local theatres of war into a global conflict.

The Phoney War

Poland was rapidly overrun by Nazi Germany and the Soviet Union and after that the war had an unreal quality about it. Convinced that this new conflict would be a static war like 1914–18, the Allies put their faith in the Maginot Line, a series of heavy fortifications built between 1936 and 1939 along the Franco-German border. For French strategists the Maginot Line was impregnable from attack and during the winter of 1939–40 the Allies simply sat tight waiting for the Nazi invasion. However, the longer this state of affairs dragged on, the more soldiers and civilians began to talk about a phoney war, and during the winter, which was exceptionally cold, morale declined sharply. The combination of boredom, inactivity and poor logistics – the army failed to provide enough socks for the front-line troops – led some people to question the sense of the conflict, especially now that Poland had been defeated. Exploiting this mood of disquiet, Pierre Laval, along with some radicals and socialist pacifists, pushed forward the idea of a compromise peace.

The one area where the Daladier government did take decisive action was in anti-communist repression. The Nazi–Soviet Pact produced a bitter backlash against the PCF, leading Daladier to dissolve the party, ban *L'Humanité* and arrest 3,400 activists. Arguably Daladier displayed more *élan* in persecuting the PCF than in waging the war against Germany and this anti-communism reached fever pitch when the Soviet Union invaded Finland on 30 November. In the following months Daladier's witch hunt gave his government some sort of purpose and direction. By denouncing the PCF as traitors Daladier made it difficult for those conservatives who were ambivalent about the war to push for a positive response to Nazi peace proposals.

Supporters of firm action brought about the fall of Daladier on 19 March 1940. They were dismayed by his dithering and indecision and the final straw was the failure to support the Finns who had capitulated to the Red Army a few days beforehand. Reynaud now became prime minister, but, although he put together a broad coalition, Daladier remained as minister of defence, and any confidence in the new government was severely dented by the successful Nazi invasion of Norway and Denmark on 9 April.

Four weeks later, on 10 May, the German army launched a huge offensive against Western Europe. The French commander-in-chief, Gamelin, believing that this offensive would be a re-run of the 1914 German attack on northern Belgium, immediately moved the bulk of the British and French troops into the Low Countries. It was a fatal error. Instead the main Nazi attack was concentrated on the heavily wooded Ardennes which the Allies had believed would be too hilly for tanks and which was thus defended by ill-equipped reservists. Fatally too, the Maginot Line did not stretch to the Ardennes and in the face of the German onslaught, these reservists had no chance. Within just three days the tanks of General Heinz Guderian had broken through and by-passed the Maginot Line. Thereafter, the German army made a dash for the Channel, cutting off the British and French forces in Belgium. The British troops were hastily evacuated from Dunkirk. To all intents and purposes the Battle of France was now lost and on 10 June the government evacuated the capital. On 11 June Italy entered the war on the side of the Nazis and three days later the German army marched into Paris. Later on 16 June Reynaud handed over power to Marshal Pétain, the 84-year-old victor of Verdun, and on 17 June Pétain announced his desire to seek an armistice. The world was astonished. Germany had overrun France in just 6 weeks, something that it had not achieved in four years of bloodshed during World War I. Nobody could have predicted such a total defeat.

Why did France fall so easily? First and foremost this was a military catastrophe. Poor tactics and poor leadership were the reasons why France was defeated. On the face of it the German army possessed no overall numerical superiority. Tank numbers on both sides were fairly even. The French had 1,900 light tanks and 531 heavy tanks; the Germans 1,861 and 822. However, Nazi strategy was based upon the bold deployment of tank concentrations backed up by motorised infantry. Decisively, this meant that the Germans had 10 tank divisions whilst the French only had 3. Moreover, the Germans had overwhelming superiority in the air. The *Luftwaffe* had 1,600 heavy bombers, as opposed to a mere 200 in the French air force, and these were used to pulverise military targets and pave the way for the tank attacks. The wailing sirens of the German dive bombers were used to instil fear and terror and in this way *Blitzkrieg* (lightning war), finely tuned in the Spanish Civil War and the Polish campaign, simply overwhelmed the Allied forces. In contrast, the military strategy of the French high command was abysmal. Their thinking was still dominated by the memory of the trenches with the result that tanks were dispersed within the infantry units. Significantly too, with the French army relying on telephones rather than radio, communications were appalling. Thus, once the Nazi Panzer divisions had outflanked the Maginot Line, the French high command had no solutions left to offer.

Yet, even if 1940 was essentially a military defeat, the political and historical significance of this defeat cannot be overstated. 1940 was such a catastrophe because it represented the end of Great-Power status for France. Henceforth no feature of French history would be more insistent than the desire to recover rank. It explains Laval's obsessive quest for collaboration; it explains why the Fourth Republic tried so hard to hang on to the empire; and finally it explains why de Gaulle became infatuated with possessing the nuclear bomb.

The Vichy regime

The armistice, signed on 22 June in the same forest clearing in Compiègne where the French high command had presided over the German surrender in 1918, was greeted with widespread relief. By the end of June the French army had lost 100,000 men, whilst 1,850,000 had been taken prisoner. The speed of this military collapse quickly awoke fears of another Commune. The belief that, given the Nazi–Soviet Pact, the German army would stand aside and let the PCF take power convinced many in the higher echelons of the army of the absolute necessity of an armistice. For the likes of General Weygand the army had to remain intact to stave off insurrection and what compounded this fear of revolution still further was chaos caused by the huge refugee crisis. Six to 10 million people – mostly women, children and old people – had fled the Nazi advance in what was termed collectively as the *exode*. Mostly on foot, with little or no food, this immense wave of human misery quickly choked up the roads. For those involved it was a truly degrading experience – 140 people a day were dying of dysentery by the end of June and the sense of psychological disorientation was acute. Literally their lives had fallen apart and with this level of suffering it is not surprising that most people saw no alternative to the armistice.

All the same the armistice was very harsh. Germany alone decided the terms and under them France was divided into two by a demarcation line. The occupied zone comprised the whole of the north and west, including Paris and the Atlantic coast, whilst the unoccupied zone was made up of central and southern France, the poorest and least populated part of the country. Meanwhile the army was reduced to 100,000; the prisoners were to remain in Germany until the final conclusion of a peace treaty, in effect a bargaining counter for future negotiations; and the cost of the occupation was set at 400 million FF a day, a colossal sum. Thus, even though the empire was left untouched and the fleet was not disarmed, France's subordinate position in the new Nazi Europe was self-evident, a point that was rammed home by the annexation of Alsace-Lorraine by Germany in August.

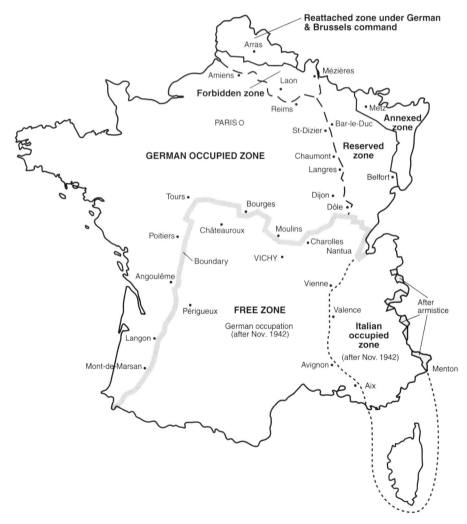

Map 8.1   Occupied France, 1940–44
Reproduced with permission from Antoine Prost, Petite Histoire de la France du XXe siècle.

Shortly after the armistice, military defeat was transformed formally into the end of the Third Republic. On 10 July the National Assembly, now camped in the spa town of Vichy, voted overwhelmingly (569 for, 80 against and 20 abstentions) to give full legislative and constitutional powers to Pétain. In this way Pétain was given a free rein to establish an unregulated authoritarian regime. For the right-wing ideologue Charles Maurras this was nothing less than a divine surprise – an act of God sent to finally punish the decadent Third Republic.

During the summer of 1940 it is possible to talk of a collective trauma. People who lived through the period remember an overwhelming sense of paralysis. The question was how to piece together their shattered lives and they understandably became preoccupied with the minutiae of everyday life: finding food, returning home, contacting prisoners of war. In this sense they turned away from politics and in on themselves, and what magnified this despair still further was the belief that the Third Republic had abandoned them. The unsavoury sight of politicians and officials fleeing their posts left them vulnerable and unprotected and in this atmosphere people instinctively looked towards Pétain as a father figure. He was a voice of paternal calm, an immediate point of reference as the world disintegrated around them. As such, the popular appeal of Pétain must not be divorced from the *exode*. In the eyes of millions of French people he assumed the status of a Christlike hero figure who, as in 1916, had come forward to save France. They knew that *he* would not desert them; they knew that *he* would not forget them in their hour of need. During the summer of 1940 Pétain's radio addresses carefully drew upon this language of sacrifice and suffering and in the tours of towns and cities of the unoccupied zone in autumn he was greeted with a religious fervour. Indeed, people suffering from scrofula, a disease that wastes the skin, actually believed that if they touched him they would be cured. These tours, underlining the unique bond between Pétain and the people, were testament to the personality cult which now surrounded the octogenarian Marshal. As the victor of Verdun he understood ordinary French people in a way that self-serving politicians never could. Like Hitler in Germany, Stalin in the Soviet Union and Franco in Spain, he was a great leader whose authority was beyond question and through books, poems and songs – most famously the song 'Maréchal nous voilà' – Vichy propaganda assiduously cultivated the image of a people united in their devotion to the Marshal.

The French historian Henri Amouroux has talked about 40 million Pétainists in the summer and autumn of 1940 and in part this was because, initially at least, Pétain seemed to transcend politics. Above all his arguments were based upon common sense: there was no alternative to the armistice because the war was over. Yet, during the autumn of 1940 the image of Pétain as being above the mêlée of politics or perhaps involved in a subtle double game with the British became increasingly difficult to sustain. As Pétain made choices, the particular politics of the Vichy regime became more and more obvious. Firstly, he launched the National Revolution. Eager to divert blame away from the army, Pétain put the defeat down to a degenerate society. Permissiveness, secularism, individualism: these were the ills of French society and what was needed to remedy them was a spiritual renewal of France. Through Vichy's moral and political crusade people now had to rediscover true French values. Secondly, Vichy was marked by a strong strain of Anglophobia, especially after Mers-el-Kebir on 3 July when the British navy, fearful that the French fleet was about to fall into Nazi hands, shot at the French navy, killing 1,300 sailors. Indeed, in 1941 Vichy almost entered the war on the Axis side. Thirdly, Pétain met Hitler at Montoire near Tours on 24 October. Here, although no details were discussed and nothing was signed, Pétain accepted the principle of Franco-German coop-eration. Symbolically too Pétain was photographed shaking Hitler's hand and in the fol-lowing days there was some consternation in France. In a radio speech on 30 October Pétain defended his decision in forthright terms. Using an explicitly Nazi phrase (*le nou-vel ordre*) Pétain explained that he had been subjected to no diktat and was entering into a policy of collaboration. For him this was essential because a favourable peace would consolidate the National Revolution.

What, then, was the National Revolution? Vichy ideology was heavily influenced by the ideas of *Action française* and in this way the National Revolution must be under-stood as the latest drama in the French civil war that had been unfolding since the French Revolution. First and foremost Vichy wanted to return to a pre-1789 hierarchical society. To this end the Republic was abolished and the revolutionary triptych of liberty, equality, fraternity was replaced by the true French values of work, family, nation (*travail, famille, patrie*). According to the National Revolution, anti-republi-canism went hand in hand with anti-capitalism. Vichy anti-capitalism took the form of a moral condemnation of the free-market system. As the expression of the excessive indi-vidualism and the Jewish spirit, capitalism had fatally undermined the moral fibre of the national community. Thus the Labour Charter of 4 October 1941 was trumpeted as a third way between capitalism and communism. By bringing together employers and employees into a corporate economy the new legislation would, it was claimed, end class conflict and stave off revolution.

The National Revolution was also anti-communist, anti-socialist and anti-radical. The desire for revenge against the Popular Front parties was a primary dynamic of Vichy ideology. In Vichy eyes it was these three parties that were responsible for the defeat. They had to be punished and for this reason the freemasons, closely linked with the Radical Party, were dissolved, the persecution of the PCF intensified and Blum even-tually was put on trial at Riom. In holding up communists and socialists as pariahs, the language of disease was never far from Vichy lips. These people, it was claimed, had infected the true France; they poisoned the nation from within. The other group to be scapegoated by Vichy in this way were the Jews. The National Revolution set out to exclude Jews from French life and turn them into second-class citizens. Therefore the Crémieux Decrees, which had given citizenship to Algerian Jews on 24 October 1870, were revoked; the 1938 Marchandeau law outlawing racism in the press was repealed, thus giving licence to print all kinds of anti-Semitic diatribe; and all naturalisations conducted since 1927 were subjected to a review. The *Statut des Juifs* of 3 October 1940 defined Jewishness in racial terms (anyone with two Jewish grandparents) and barred French Jews from elected office, the civil service, journalism and teaching. The preamble to the *Statut* made it absolutely clear that this was a punishment for suppos-edly destroying the moral fibre of the nation and thereby bringing about defeat. In June 1941 a second *Statut* was even harsher, imposing quotas of 3 per cent on the number of

Jewish students allowed to attend university and 2 per cent on the number of Jews allowed to practise law and medicine. Moreover, the Commission on Jewish Matters (*Commissariat général aux questions juives*) was established in March 1941 to coordinate anti-Semitic policy. Importantly it must be understood that this anti-Semitism was not a result of Nazi pressure. It was the outcome of a long-established racist tradition.

By proclaiming France for French people the National Revolution was feeding off the climate of intolerance that had been fostered by the influx of both Jewish refugees from Austria and Germany, some 60,000 in 1939, and Spanish republicans fleeing Franco's Spain. For many ordinary French people these groups were a threat because they were seen either as dangerous revolutionaries or as competition for jobs. However, the National Revolution was not just negative, it did offer an alternative blueprint. Building on the 1939 legislation, the National Revolution endeavoured to put women back into the home (*femme au foyer*). Women were seen as the backbone of family life and they received subsidies for staying at home and having children. The image of the woman in the home was closely linked to the other perennial theme of the National Revolution: the need to return to the countryside (*retour à la terre*). 'The earth does not lie,' Pétain famously proclaimed, and the peasant family was held up as the cornerstone of the French nation. Urbanisation, Vichy argued, had alienated French people from their roots. Young people in particular needed to rediscover rural values and they were sent off to open-air camps. Through a hardy outdoor existence Vichy tried to instil in them self-discipline, public spirit and national loyalty. Vichy also promoted Catholic values as an integral part of French identity. The regime enjoyed very close relations

Figure 8.1   Vichy propaganda: the révolution nationale *and the two Frances*

with the Roman Catholic clergy and the church remained one of its pillars to the end. Poignantly in November 1940 Cardinal Gerlier, the Archbishop of Lyons, welcomed Pétain to the city with the words 'Pétain is France, and France, today, is Pétain'. The National Revolution, therefore, was authoritarian, nationalistic, anti-Semitic and Catholic. But in characterising Vichy thus it is vital not to see the regime as an aberration. In terms of family policy, for example, there are clear continuities with the pre- and post-war regimes.

Vichy was a sovereign state recognised by America and the Soviet Union. Nazi Germany itself had little interest in Vichy's domestic agenda and, until November 1942 at least, the regime had a considerable freedom of action. In this respect it is vital to understand that Vichy was not a bloc. It was a fissiparous phenomenon made up of a variety of competing visions ranging from royalism to fascism through to technocracy and corporatism. Vichy might have espoused the ideal of a united regime, but in reality it was chaotic and faction-ridden. As such, Vichy went through a number of stages, the first of which was the Laval phase. The archetypal wheeler-dealer politician, Pierre Laval had moved from socialism to the right. It was he who engineered the vote to give Pétain full powers and thereafter he was appointed as Pétain's deputy prime minister. Laval was not interested in the National Revolution. His primary interest was how to carve out a privileged position for France in the new German order. He opened the channels of communication with Otto Abetz, the Nazi ambassador in Paris, and was the moving force behind the Montoire meeting. In contrast Pétain was more cautious and this, along with a good deal of personal animosity, led to Laval's dismissal on 13 December. Ironically, therefore, Laval's successor Admiral Darlan, with Pétain's support, went much further down the collaborationist path. In this second phase Darlan, who met Hitler in May 1941, vainly tried to arouse Nazi interest in a special naval and imperial role for France. He offered air bases to the Germans in Syria and at one point almost took France back into the war on the Axis side. The failure of Darlan's overtures led Pétain to reluctantly take back Laval in April 1942. This was the beginning of the third phase, typified by Laval's radio announcement on 22 June 1942 that he wanted a Nazi victory, or else communism would submerge Europe. France, he argued, had a moral duty to support the German war effort. Now, as Laval procured workers for German factories, only lip service was paid to the National Revolution. This in turn paved the way for the final phase in 1943–44 as Vichy changed into a police state dedicated to the repression of Resistance.

Was Vichy fascist? Of course this depends on how one defines fascism. In the way that the prefix *anti-* was a consistent theme of Vichy propaganda – anti-communist, anti-capitalist, anti-Jewish – the regime evoked much of the ideology of fascist Italy and Nazi Germany. Yet Vichy lacked the totalitarian theatrics of Nazi Germany. There was never any sense of the mass radicalism of Nazism. Vichy ceremonies looked amateurish and Pétain blocked attempts to create a single party. In the same fashion the Pétain cult was very different to that of Hitler. Pétain was never mythologised as a superman. At the age of 84, how could he be? Instead the Pétainist propaganda underlined paternal imagery. Continually he was cast as a father suffering with the people.

In comparing Vichy with other fascist regimes the American historian Robert Paxton has emphasised that no pure fascist movement ever took power. They were always an alliance between conservatives and revolutionaries. This, Paxton argues, puts Vichy very much on the conservative end of the spectrum, even if thoroughgoing fascists like Déat eventually found themselves in government.

Vichy and the Holocaust

On 22 June 1941 Nazi Germany invaded the Soviet Union. This brought millions of Jews under Nazi control and led to the first attempts at systematic extermination. Special units followed behind the German army charged with the elimination of Jews and Communist Party cadres. At first these units machine-gunned their victims and dumped them into mass graves; then they began to experiment with gas, filling specially designed vans with carbon monoxide. Within 4 months some 600,000 Jews had perished. However, the desire for greater efficiency led Nazi officials to explore unprecedented methods of mass murder. Here coordination was seen to be essential and in July 1941 Reinhard Heydrich, head of the Nazi security services, was called upon to draw up plans for the final solution to the Jewish question. Experiments using poison gas were carried out on Soviet prisoners in the autumn and the first extermination camps were built in occupied Poland by early 1942. A secret meeting bringing together all the various agencies involved in the mass deportation of Jews to the east was held on the shore of Lake Wannsee just outside Berlin on 20 January 1942. Presided over by Heydrich, it was this meeting that formalised the extermination of all European Jewry. The scale of the crime was truly staggering and to preserve secrecy, the minutes of the meeting simply referred to the Jewish question.

The Holocaust led to the death of some 6 million Jews and throughout Europe the Nazis were aided and abetted by collaboration. Vichy saw the issue of the deportation of the Jews as one of sovereignty. Laval believed that the civil authority of the Vichy state had to be upheld at all costs and it was therefore better if round-ups were carried out by French officials rather than German ones. This logic fitted Nazi needs perfectly because in July 1942 the German authorities had only 3,000 police in France. Few spoke French; fewer still possessed any extensive knowledge of where Jews might hide. Given this dearth of resources, the Nazi police commanders would be wholly reliant upon the French police who totalled close to 100,000 men. Under the agreement concluded between General Oberg and René Bousquet, the Vichy head of police, on 8 August the *gendarmerie* agreed to act vigorously against all the enemies of the Reich. In return the Germans promised to respect Vichy's autonomy over policing.

This spirit of cooperation had already been put into practice 3 weeks earlier in Paris. For Vichy a distinction was to be made between French Jews and foreign Jews. Under this distinction the former were to be made into second-class citizens, whilst the latter were an unacceptable burden, to be expelled at the earliest opportunity. For this reason Laval was more than happy to hand over foreign Jews to the Nazis and the Vel d'hiver round-up on 16 and 17 July led to the arrest of 12,884 Jews, including 4,000 children. Involving 9,000 police and several hundred PPF volunteers, the operation was planned with military precision. Seven thousand people were crammed into the Vel d'hiver sports stadium with little food or water before being taken to Drancy, an unfinished municipal housing estate just north of Paris which had been transformed into a transit camp, pending their eventual deportation to Auschwitz. It was a level of collaboration unparalleled in occupied Europe. As a result 75,721 Jews, mostly foreign born, were deported. Of these, only 3 per cent returned at the end of the war.

To understand these shocking statistics one further factor must be borne in mind: the specific contribution of the Vichy bureaucracy. In July 1941 Vichy ordered a census of the entire Jewish population in the unoccupied zone. In December 1942 Vichy forced all Jews, foreign and French, to have their identity cards stamped 'Jew'. Without doubt this statistical information made subsequent deportations all the easier.

Survival

Vichy thinking was based upon the assumption that Nazi Germany had won the war and that Britain was defeated. Given this reasoning the relentless extension of the war during 1941 was viewed with trepidation by Vichy ministers. On 22 June 1941 Germany invaded the Soviet Union. On 7 December the Japanese attacked Pearl Harbor, the main American naval base in the Pacific at Hawaii, and four days later Germany and Italy supported their ally and declared war on the USA. Then during 1942 and 1943 the war turned against Germany. On the Eastern Front defeat at Stalingrad in February 1943 meant that the offensive now passed to the Red Army. Likewise by May 1943 the German and Italian forces in North Africa had surrendered.

In the face of these events the vast majority of the French people were preoccupied with survival. Life during the Occupation was very hard. By September 1940 most essential goods were rationed and during the following 4 years these rations came to stand at 1,327 calories per day for most of the population, less than half the pre-war average. By 1944 per-capita consumption of meat, vegetables and sugar had fallen by half since 1938, whilst real wages had fallen by more than 40 per cent. Fuel too became very scarce and power cuts were a regular occurrence. Thinking about how to feed hungry mouths was very stressful and, with so many prisoners in Germany, this burden fell on women. 1.6 million prisoners left behind 790,000 wives, 616,200 with children, and for them coping with the shortage of food was to be their dominant memory of the Occupation. In the struggle for survival, many were forced to look to the black market. There, however, the fact that the price of butter was over ten times the official one fuelled resentment towards the countryside and the accusation that the peasantry were profiteering became a familiar one.

Of course everyday life went on. People went to films and dances. The birth rate went up and there was a revival of Catholicism. However, the winter of 1941–42 was very harsh and as the situation deteriorated there was growing disenchantment with Vichy. Further, German defeats in 1942–43 meant that a Nazi victory was no longer seen as inevitable. Even so, as the context of the war changed dramatically, the majority opted for self-preservation. They were cautious and passive, waiting on events. In contrast a small minority made explicit choices between collaboration and resistance.

Collaboration

Collaboration took many forms, the most obvious of which was state collaboration. We have already noted the scale of Vichy collaboration in respect to the Holocaust, but there was equal collaboration in providing workers for the Nazi war effort. In May 1942 Germany asked for 250,000 French volunteers for German industry. In response Laval negotiated an exchange system (*relève*) under which he tried to buy the freedom of a prisoner of war for every three skilled workers sent to Germany. Six months later, following the Allied landings in North Africa, the whole of France was occupied. Now, with the armistice army disbanded, the empire lost and the navy scuttled, the independence of Vichy became a fiction. Yet, at this point Laval did not trim his sails. Instead he chose to intensify collaboration. To meet the Nazi demands for more workers, on 16 February 1943 he introduced compulsory labour service (*service du travail obligatoire*) (STO) which conscripted all young men born between 1920 and 1922. Under STO 650,000 workers were sent to Germany, the largest male foreign-worker group there by the end of 1943. Laval also created the *Milice* in January 1943, a special paramilitary force dedicated to the repression of the Resistance. Led by Joseph Darnand, and working closely with the Germans, the *Milice* was to develop a fearsome reputation for violence and brutality.

There was also economic collaboration. By 1943 the French economy was firmly locked into the Nazi war effort. The fact that 4 million French workers were producing, amongst other things, 42 per cent of German transport planes, underlines how important the French economy was. Indeed, as regards production, Germany took more from France than any other occupied country. But this was not a one-way street. French business too profited from collaboration with Germany. It was for this reason that Renault was nationalised at the Liberation.

Hard-line collaborators, who explicitly identified with Nazism, gravitated to Paris and traditionally a distinction has been made between state collaboration and the ideological collaboration of the Paris-based parties, such as Jacques Doriot's PPF and Marcel Déat's *Rassemblement national populaire* (RNP). In general these parties saw themselves as more revolutionary than Vichy, even if all proclaimed allegiance to Marshal Pétain. For them the National Revolution was too archaic, too conservative, too timid. Instead they saw themselves as visionaries, the pioneers of a new age of European fascism. However, it is important not to overplay the distinction. Laval cultivated links with Abetz and in 1940 appointed as French Ambassador to the German Reich in Paris Fernand de Brinon, an open admirer of Nazism who had worked for the close partnership of France and Nazi Germany during the 1930s. The Vichy head of police, René Bousquet, was a frequent visitor to Paris. One of Darlan's ministers, the minister of the interior, Pierre Pucheu, had been a member of the PPF. In November 1941 Pétain sent a letter of support to the Legion of French Volunteers against Bolshevism (LVF) before it departed for the Russian Front. Finally, although Doriot had always been excluded from Vichy, Déat entered government in January 1944. In this sense the ideology of Vichy and Paris did converge at key points. Both wanted a Nazi victory; both hated Britain; both feared communism; and both despised Jews.

How much support did these collaborationist parties enjoy? There was no more enthusiastic supporter of the Nazi order than Robert Brasillach, and his paper *Je suis partout* had a circulation of 300,000. But how far this was a measure of genuine support is difficult to tell. Certainly Parisians joked that people bought *Je suis partout* because it was printed on better-quality paper and thus burned better in the fireplace. The LVF, despite the propaganda and despite the high pay, never procured more than 6,000 volunteers. Likewise the *Milice* was made up of 45,000 recruits. Overall, therefore, these parties were a minority phenomenon – 250,000 at most.

In large part the failure of the various parties to unite was because Hitler operated a divide and rule policy. He did not want to encourage potentially popular movements that might eventually threaten Germany. Thus, although Doriot and his Parisian brethren embraced the idea of a New Fascist Europe, in reality this was fantasy politics. Hitler wanted a vassal state, not partnership.

Resistance

Like collaboration the Resistance was a minority phenomenon, comprising 2 per cent of the population or approximately 400,000 individuals. In the beginning it was composed of like-minded people coming together to make a stand. In this sense early resistance was not about military action. It was about the formation and articulation of dissident opinions which were then expressed through a clandestine press. Gradually through papers like Henry Frenay's *Combat*, launched at the end of 1940, these underground groups challenged Vichy's monopoly of truth.

Combat was based in the Lyons area and drew recruits from professionals and intellectuals. Elsewhere in the southern zone, *Libération* was led by the radical ex-naval officer Emmanuel d'Astier de la Vigerie; *Franc-Tireur* was organised by a group of Parisian exiles, including the historian Marc Bloch; and *Témoignage chrétien* brought together radical Catholics, including Renée and François Bedarida and André Mandouze. Given the continuing German presence in the northern zone the military rationale for resistance was more obvious and networks like *Alliance* developed links with the Free French in London and the Special Operations Executive, the special unit set up by Churchill to encourage military resistance across occupied Europe. Similarly, the *Organisation civile et militaire* recruited amongst soldiers and civil servants, although Jean Texcier's *Libération-Nord* brought together socialist and Catholic trade unionists.

diaries

In the summer of 1940 in Lyons Auguste Pinton, a future member of *Témoignage chrétien*, began keeping a diary. Through the diary he expresses his anti-Vichy and anti-Nazi feelings. He writes about his sense of alienation from other French people, his depression at the strength of support for Pétain, his disgust at the National Revolution. Clearly the diary was a therapeutic exercise. By confiding his thoughts to it Pinton was overcoming isolation and clarifying his ideas. It is an example of how everyday objects, such as writing a diary, could take on new, subversive meanings in the context of the Occupation.

Each of these groups had its own history and each had developed independently of the rest. They were also to become involved in diverse activities. Some were to organise escape lines; some were to shelter Jews; others still were to carry out military action. Essentially this early resistance was urban based and although large numbers were on the left – republicans who were instinctively hostile to Vichy ideology – it also contained nationalist right-wingers whose anti-German perspective did not allow them to accept the defeat. Some of the latter even believed that Pétain was involved in a subtle double game, entering into secret negotiations with the British.

The one movement that straddled both zones was the *Front national*, established by the PCF in May 1941 but open to communist and non-communist alike. The shock of the Nazi–Soviet pact had thrown the PCF into confusion. Wishing to remain faithful to anti-fascism, some members in Brittany and Limoges did take a stand against the Germans. However, this was without the authorisation of the party leadership which, although it denounced Vichy and did organise strikes in May 1941, was silent about the Nazi occupation. This silence was transformed with the Nazi invasion of the Soviet Union on 22 June 1941. At this point the PCF threw itself into resistance and by the end of 1941 communists had carried out 107 acts of sabotage. However, distrust was to remain until the end of the war. The British and the Free French in particular always feared that the PCF was using resistance as a cover for revolution.

Outside of France the starting point for resistance was General Charles de Gaulle. Aged 50, de Gaulle was an unknown junior general who had advocated mobile warfare during the 1930s. Yet, on 17 June 1940 de Gaulle, by then undersecretary for war in the Reynaud government, was flown by the British to London. The following day he made a broadcast on the BBC calling on French people to continue the war. Although the 18 June speech was to become the foundation stone of Gaullist ideology, proof of the way in which he incarnated the destiny of the French nation, few people heard the broadcast and fewer still rallied to his cause. The one note of optimism was provided by the empire in August 1940 when AEF, Cameroun, New Caledonia and the Pacific Islands came out in support of de Gaulle.

From the beginning de Gaulle was heavily dependent on British and American patronage. Breaking free of this dependency and asserting French independence became a fundamental *raison d'être* and caused great friction with the Allies. Churchill famously remarked that the Cross of Lorraine, the Gaullist symbol, was the heaviest cross he had to bear, whilst Roosevelt was especially suspicious of de Gaulle's authoritarian tendencies and did everything to sideline him.

One way in which de Gaulle tried to increase his legitimacy was through the unification of resistance under his leadership. This was a difficult undertaking. Many resisters saw him as a military man whose ideas and upper-class background marked him out as a right-winger close to Maurras. The task of winning over the Resistance was entrusted to Jean Moulin, who was parachuted into France on 1 January 1942. In the following weeks Moulin successfully brought together the three main movements in the southern zone into *Mouvements unis de la Résistance* which then immediately acknowledged de Gaulle as the leader. It was a spectacular coup, followed by the establishment of a coordinating committee in the northern zone. Throughout Moulin was insistent that any unification had to involve the PCF. For its part the PCF too began to talk about the need to build alliances with the other resistance movements and this smoothed the way for communist participation in the *Conseil national de la résistance* (CNR). Meeting for the first time on 27 May 1943 in rue du Four in Paris, the CNR united all the resistance groups under de Gaulle and called on him to form a provisional government. It was to be Moulin's final achievement before his death at the hands of Nazi captors in Lyons 6 weeks later.

The CNR transformed de Gaulle's standing at a vital moment. In the wake of the Allied landings in North Africa, conducted without de Gaulle's knowledge, the Americans tried to sideline him. They opened negotiations with Admiral Darlan, now minister of defence at Vichy, who agreed a ceasefire with the Allies. Moreover, when Darlan was assassinated in mysterious circumstances, the Americans continued to ignore de Gaulle and looked instead towards General Giraud, a Pétainist officer who had escaped from a German prisoner of war camp. Momentarily de Gaulle seemed to have been eclipsed. However, neither the Americans nor Giraud were a match for de Gaulle's razor-sharp political instincts. Firstly, de Gaulle admonished Giraud for not re-establishing the laws of the Republic. The fact that Pétain's picture still hung in all the government offices and that Vichy's anti-Semitic laws had not been revoked in Algeria were symptomatic of the way in which the spirit of the National Revolution had been allowed to continue. Secondly, de Gaulle rejected the notion, floated by the British, of a joint leadership.

The CNR, therefore, was important because it confirmed de Gaulle's legitimacy in the eyes of the Resistance and at this point Giraud lost all authority. Algiers now became the capital of Free France. To underline this point, November 1943 witnessed the creation of the Consultative Assembly which, looking ahead to liberation, began to rethink metropolitan France. Its ambitious plans became the basis of the Resistance Charter on 15 March 1944.

During 1943 in France the Resistance grew as support for Vichy began to seep away and the tide of the war turned against Germany. The major fillip for the Resistance was the introduction of STO on 16 February 1943. To evade the call-up 150,000 young men took to the hills and in the remote rural countryside they formed what became known as the *maquis*, derived from the Corsican word for scrub. These *maquis* units then began to look for arms and supplies from parachute

women and the Resistance

In 1944 the communist Fernand Grenier presented his amendment in support of women's suffrage to the Provisional Assembly in Algiers. He argued that through their participation in the Resistance women had won their citizenship, and the vote was passed by 51 to 16. Many women, such as Lucie Aubrac and Marie-Madeleine Fourcade, did become household names after 1945. Yet only six women, out of a total of 1,057, were granted the honour of *Compagnon de la Libération*. In large part this was because the Resistance was defined in terms of armed combat, something traditionally associated with men. Thus, the recognition due to other forms of participation, in particular the role of women in housing and feeding the Resistance, was denied.

drops and during the spring of 1944 they became involved in pitched battles with the *Milice* and the German army. One such battle, on the Glières plateau south of Geneva, brought about terrible reprisals and left 400 *maquisards* dead.

Liberation and the purge

On 6 June 1944 the Allies landed in Normandy and what followed was a spectacular military victory. By September large parts of the country had been liberated and in the face of the Allied advance the Vichy regime disintegrated, at which point Pétain was humiliatingly whisked off to Germany to form a government in exile there. The Allies, however, still did not trust de Gaulle and at first entertained the idea of running France like an occupied country. Once again, therefore, de Gaulle had to impose himself through sheer will power. He made sure that it was French troops who first entered Paris and, when the Germans surrendered the capital on 25 August, de Gaulle arrived that afternoon proclaiming that Parisians had liberated themselves. The following day he led a procession down the Champs-Elysées to symbolise the victory of France. Marginalising the CNR, de Gaulle formed a new government of unity. On 23 October this government was officially recognised by the Allies and France treated as a co-belligerent.

De Gaulle was absolutely determined to ensure a smooth transfer of power between Vichy and himself. He wanted to prevent any revolution and quickly restore law and order. Thus, he cracked down on the purge, the rough justice that accompanied the Liberation and led to about 10,000 summary executions. He also integrated the Free French into the regular army on 27 September and disbanded the patriotic militias on 28 October. Despite protests the PCF stood down because it did not want to be accused of sabotaging the war effort.

femmes tondues

At the Liberation women accused of collaborating with Germans had their heads shaved. There was a strong ritualistic aspect to the violence and these women were paraded in the streets and in some cases put in cages. Given that so few women held positions of power in Vichy, why they were targeted is a complex psychological problem. For example, for some latecomers to the Resistance, humiliating women collaborators was often a way of publicly demonstrating their anti-Nazi credentials.

Vichy syndrome

In the interest of national unity de Gaulle quickly drew a veil over the divisions of the Vichy years. The purges did not go deep and the police, army and civil service were left largely untouched. By limiting the trials to leading figures, notably Laval, Darnand, Pétain and Maurras, de Gaulle wished to project an image of France united behind Gaullist Resistance. Of course this was an interpretation of the immediate past conditioned by the political needs of the present and the French historian Henry Rousso has diagnosed this act of psychological and political repression as the beginning of the Vichy syndrome. In his opinion, it explains why, once the Gaullist mythology fell apart in the late 1960s, the French public and media were to return again and again to the complexities of the Vichy years.

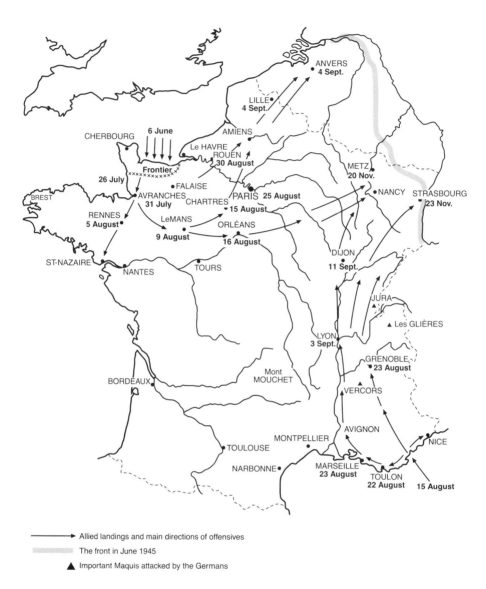

Map 8.2   The liberation of France
Reproduced with permission from Antoine Prost, Petite Histoire de la France du XXe siècle.

At the same time de Gaulle did everything to underline the recovery of national greatness. French soldiers fought on the Western Front and in Algeria there was a brutal reassertion of national sovereignty on 8 May 1945 when independence demonstrations were violently repressed, leading to up to 45,000 deaths. However, such action could not disguise the fact that France was not treated as an equal by Britain, America and the Soviet Union. The big three excluded de Gaulle from decision-making about the shape of the post-war world and this wounded him deeply.

Document 8a: 'Maréchal Nous Voilà'

Une flamme sacrée
Monte du sol natal
Et la France enivrée
Te salue Maréchal!
Tous tes enfants qui t'aiment
Et vénèrent tes ans
A ton appel suprême
Ont répondu 'Présent'

{Refrain:}
Maréchal nous voilà!
Devant toi, le sauveur de la France
Nous jurons, nous, tes gars
De servir et de suivre tes pas
Maréchal nous voilà!
Tu nous as redonné l'espérance
La Patrie renaîtra!
Maréchal, Maréchal, nous voilà!

Tu as lutté sans cesse
Pour le salut commun
On parle avec tendresse
Du héros de Verdun
En nous donnant ta vie
Ton génie et ta foi
Tu sauves la Patrie
Une seconde fois:
{au Refrain}

[. . .]
La guerre est inhumaine
Quel triste épouvantail!
N'écoutons plus la haine
Exaltons le travail
Et gardons confiance
Dans un nouveau destin
Car Pétain, c'est la France,
La France, c'est Pétain!
{au Refrain}

Document 8b: Extract from Auguste Pinton's diary

31 octobre 1940
Je songe à l'isolement qui nous accable, à l'impossibilité où nous sommes de rien faire d'utile. Il faudrait pourtant se voir, parler, comparer nos pensées, essayer de bâtir des règles d'action.

25 décembre 1940
Aujourd'hui, amertume, angoisse rancœur contre la présence et les exigences du vainqueur et surtout cette honte infinie qui nous resentons à l'attitude de Français devant cette insanité que l'on appelle collaboration. Irritation devant la sordide réaction qui s'est baptisée révolution nationale.

Document 8c: 'L' héroïsme et le courage des femmes français-es', anonymous letter to the clandestine paper *Le Populaire*, 15 July 1944

D'autres femmes prennent part elles-mêmes à la lutte dans les mouvements de résistance: elles portent les courriers, assurent les liaisons, travaillent aux services des renseignements, parrainent les FTP, secourent les victimes de la répression, organisent parmi les femmes la résistance sous toutes ses formes. Elles sont traquées par la police comme leurs compagnons. Au moment où l'Assemblée Consultative d'Alger propose de donner aux femmes françaises le droit de vote, il faut que le pays tout entier sache combien cet honneur est mérité.

Topics FOR DISCUSSION

1 Why did France fall in 1940?
2 Explain the popular appeal of Pétain in 1940. What does Document 8a reveal about the nature of Pétainism?
3 What was the National Revolution? How does Figure 8.1 help us to understand Vichy ideology?
4 What role did Vichy play in the Holocaust?
5 What different forms did collaboration take?
6 What was the Resistance? How does Document 8b help us to understand the origins of the Resistance?
7 How does Document 8c help us to understand the role of women in the Resistance?

CHAPTER 9

Timeline

1946
20 January   Resignation of de Gaulle
24 January   Tri-partite alliance of Mouvement républicain populaire *(MRP)*, *SFIO* and *PCF*

1947
28 January   Formation of Ramadier government
7 April   Formation of RPF
4 May   Communist ministers dismissed from Ramadier government
5 June   Launch of Marshall Aid
18 November–9 December General Strike

1948
24 June   Berlin blockade

1949
4 April   Foundation of North Atlantic Treaty Organisation *(NATO)*

1951
9 May   Launch of the European Coal and Steel Community *(ECSC)*

1952
6 March   Formation of the Pinay government

1954
7 May   Fall of Dien-Bien-Phu
18 June   Formation of Mendès-France government
1 November   Beginning of the Algerian insurrection

1956
2 January   Victory of the Republican Front in national elections
12 March   Vote of special powers
5–6 November   Suez expedition

The Fourth Republic, 1944–58

Although America, Britain and the Soviet Union were allies during World War II, below the surface there was much distrust between them. The Soviet Union suspected that the Americans and British delayed opening the second front because they wanted the Germans to bleed the Red Army dry, whilst the British and Americans feared that the Soviet strategy aimed not just to defeat Germany, but to install communist regimes in Eastern Europe.

Given that the Red Army was the first to reach Berlin in May 1945, the division of Europe into East and West was already implicit in the state of affairs at the end of the war. However, it was Winston Churchill who publicly acknowledged this new international reality in a speech on 5 March 1946 at Fulton, Missouri, in America. The fact that the capitals of Central and Eastern Europe now lay trapped behind an 'iron curtain' demonstrated, in Churchill's view, that the Soviets were intent on expansion. With President Truman at his side, Churchill warned his audience not to repeat the mistakes of appeasement. What was needed was strong action to stand up against communist aggression.

Yet, as Churchill well knew, when it came to taking the lead in any anti-Soviet stance, Britain was a spent force. Confronted with major crises in India, Egypt and Palestine, Britain was in no

1957
7 January   French army given police powers in Algiers
25 March   Signing of the Treaty of Rome, establishing the European Economic Community (EEC)

1958
2 June   De Gaulle voted full powers to establish new regime

position to prop up the Greek government in its war against communist insurgents, and the Labour government appealed directly to Washington for financial aid. It was a pivotal moment in twentieth-century history. America was being asked to shoulder the burden of anti-communist resistance and on 12 March 1947 President Truman obliged by declaring that it 'must be the policy of the United States to help free peoples who are resisting subjugation by armed minorities or outside pressure'. The Truman Doctrine sought to check further Soviet expansion in Europe by giving military aid to governments threatened by communist subversion. Three months later, Truman's secretary of state, George Marshall, backed this up with plans for the economic recovery of Europe. The purpose of this economic aid, Marshall explained, was to 'assist in the return of normal economic health in the world, without which there can be no political stability or assured peace'. He recognised that economic stability was the basis of political stability and the Marshall Plan ran from 1948 until the end of 1951, dispensing $12,500 million to 16 participating countries. Stalin immediately condemned Marshall Aid as a plot to extend American influence. He forbade any country under Soviet influence from participating and called on communist parties in the West to resist. In this way the Marshall Plan effectively separated the continent into two economic systems.

The 'iron curtain' was now the defining feature of post-1945 Europe. Consequently when the communists took power in Czechoslovakia on 25 February 1948, Britain, France and the Benelux countries immediately formed a 50-year alliance providing for economic and military cooperation. Predictably it was Germany that was to be the major flashpoint of East–West tensions. In 1945 the country had been divided into four zones – the Soviet, American, British and French – a division that was mirrored in Berlin. When America, Britain and France introduced a new currency into the three allied zones, the Soviets saw this move as an act of aggression and refused to accept it. On 30 March 1948 the Soviets imposed restrictions on rail traffic in the corridor between Berlin and the Western zones, expanding this to a complete blockade 3 months later. In response, the Americans and British organised an airlift of essential supplies that lasted 11 months. However, by the time the Soviets lifted the blockade in May 1949, a separate West German state had come into being. Not to be outdone, Stalin replied by creating the German Democratic Republic in October 1949. The division of Europe into East and West was now an established fact, something that was formally completed by formation of the North

The Cold War

The Cold War was so called because it never developed into a full-blown confrontation or hot war in Europe. In terms of armed conflict the Cold War was fought out in Asia, Africa and Latin America. The Cold War ended in autumn 1989 with the fall of the communist regimes in Eastern Europe.

Atlantic Treaty Organisation (NATO) on 4 April 1949 and the Soviet-dominated Warsaw Pact on 14 May 1955.

Given the strength of the PCF in the immediate post-Liberation period, it is not surprising that France became a key battleground in the Cold War.

Fourth Republic politics

Amongst many rank and file resisters, there was considerable disappointment that the solidarities of the war years had not translated into a single united Resistance Party committed to democratic socialism. Instead between autumn 1944 and summer 1945 three parties came to dominate French politics – the PCF, the SFIO and a new grouping, the *Mouvement républicain populaire* (MRP). These parties were closely identified with the Liberation and they were supported by three-quarters of the electorate. In contrast the pre-war parliamentary right was tainted by its support of Vichy, whilst the Radical Party was damaged from its association with the discredited Third Republic. Given the prestige of the USSR in defeating Nazism, and the role of communists in the Resistance, it is not surprising that the PCF enjoyed a surge of support at the Liberation. The way in which famous figures like the painters Pablo Picasso and Fernand Léger emphatically announced their adherence to the PCF underlined the intellectual and political ascendancy of the communist idea. Yet, although the party could count on a quarter of the electorate, the leadership adopted a prudent strategy. Under orders from Moscow not to carry out a revolution that would divide the Allies, the PCF called on workers to fulfil their patriotic duty and rebuild France. In this way the 'battle for production' ensured that virtually no strikes occurred in the 2 years after the Liberation. The strength of the PCF left the SFIO feeling threatened. Although the SFIO defined itself as Marxist, it rejected the Soviet model. Blum, who was only too aware of the way in which communist parties in Eastern Europe had used alliances to devour their socialist partners, was absolutely determined to preserve the independence of the SFIO. For Blum the PCF was controlled by Moscow, a view that was reinforced by Mollet's famous quip that the PCF is 'not on the Left, but in the East'. For this reason Blum made sure that the two parties submitted separate lists for elections.

The MRP was France's first large-scale Christian Democrat party. An intriguing synthesis, it could be seen as conservative, reformist or even revolutionary. Certainly the MRP saw itself as the embodiment of the spirit of the Resistance. It was emphatically republican and was opposed to capitalism, although this could be seen as the defence of economically backward regions threatened by big business. It wanted to bring together the working classes and the church, and its style and rhetoric drew on the pre-war youth organisations, JEC, JAC and JOC, which had been trying to rethink the relationship between politics and faith. Yet, it was progressively pulled to the right after 1945 by its increasingly conservative, Catholic electorate. They found refuge in MRP as a barrier to communism and areas that had traditionally voted for the right, like Brittany, Haute-Savoie, Alsace-Lorraine, now voted for the MRP. Furthermore, many leading MRP politicians, such as Robert Schuman who voted full powers to Pétain, were reassuring to a conservative electorate.

Each of these parties was committed to reform and as members of de Gaulle's provisional regime they undoubtedly coloured the programme of structural reforms carried out between the Liberation and the re-establishment of full parliamentary institutions in July 1946. These led to widespread nationalisations in the fields of energy, transport, banking and insurance, the establishment of the welfare state, and the first steps towards a planned economy. But although these reforms were infused with the language of socialism, in practice, they did not mark a break with capitalism. In the main, industry remained in private hands. Moreover, the promised worker participation was inconsequential, and the state sector was run on *dirigiste* rather than socialist lines.

These reforms seemed to point to a spirit of cooperation. In reality there was tension not just between the three parties, each of which was jockeying for power, but between the parties and de Gaulle. Here the major bone of contention was the new constitution. Under the referendum on 21 October 1945, 96 per cent rejected the proposal to restore the Third Republic. The PCF wanted the Constituent Assembly to have full powers, whilst de Gaulle argued that the Assembly should not be sovereign but strictly limited in duration and that any constitution should be put to the vote. The result was that although the PCF emerged as the largest party with 160 seats, whilst the SFIO had 146 and the MRP 152, 66 per cent followed de Gaulle's line of argument. On 13 November de Gaulle was voted unanimously as head of government but he was quickly brought into conflict with the communists to whom he refused to give any of the key ministerial posts, in particular the home office, war or foreign affairs. Their relationship was increasingly poisoned, especially on the question of the constitution. For de Gaulle the communist preference for a unicameral parliament with strict control over the government represented a return to the divisions of the Third Republic, and on 20 January 1946 he resigned. This immediately raised the prospect of a communist-led coalition with the SFIO, but the latter held back because they were fearful of doing anything that would strengthen the PCF. Instead they succeeded in persuading the MRP to enter into an alliance as a counter-weight under the premiership of the socialist Félix Gouin.

Both the PCF and the SFIO campaigned vigorously for a single chamber but this was rejected by 53 per cent on 5 May 1946, largely because of the fear of communist domination of such an assembly. A new Constituent Assembly was now required, and elections on 2 June saw the MRP emerge as the largest party with 169 seats, as opposed to 153 for the PCF and 127 for the SFIO. The MRP leader Georges Bidault formed the new government and a revised constitution, which included a second chamber, the Council of the Republic, and a stronger executive, was approved on 13 October, albeit by just over a third of the electorate (8 million in favour, 8 million against and 8 million abstentions). In terms of popular legitimacy it was hardly an auspicious start for the new regime. Even so, on 10 November national elections saw the PCF win 182 seats, the MRP 164 and the SFIO 101. On 16 January 1947 the new National Assembly voted in as president Vincent Auriol, who then asked the socialist Paul Ramadier to form another tripartite government.

The Ramadier administration was quickly faced with a deepening economic crisis. The Liberation had created the hope that life would be immediately transformed for the better. In reality conditions got much harder. By 1946 inflation had spiralled out of control to 63 per cent; between April 1945 and April 1947 the purchasing power of the average hourly wage actually declined by over a quarter; whilst 3 years after the Liberation bread rationing was even more stringent than under Vichy. Indeed, when Ramadier lowered the bread ration to 250g a day on 1 May 1947 he immediately earned himself the nickname 'Ramadan Ramadier'. Not surprisingly there was a growing mood of anger, particularly with the PCF and CGT, as many workers began to question the point of their sacrifices.

If the dire economic situation deepened divisions within the tripartite alliance, the intensification of the Cold War brought them to breaking point. Negotiations in Washington in May 1946, whereby wartime debts were converted into interest-free reconstruction loans, demonstrated just how far the French were reliant upon the Americans. However, the Americans were unhappy about the presence of communists in government and Ramadier, worried that PCF ministers might jeopardise badly needed aid, began to look for a pretext for dismissing them. Here the specific issue was to be Ramadier's harsh policy of wage and price controls. Afraid of losing control of its working-class base, who were frustrated at the failure to improve living standards, PCF ministers voted against the government over deflationary policies on 4 May. The following day Ramadier sacked them. Tripartism was at an end and the reward was Marshall Aid, of which France received $2,629 million between April 1948 and January 1952.

Initially the PCF expected to return to government, but once these hopes had dissipated the party entered into a period of entrenched militancy, denouncing American imperialism and opposing the colonial war that the French army waged in Indo-China. Moreover, when Ramadier abolished the coal subsidy, thereby causing coal prices to rise by 40 per cent, the PCF and CGT launched a series of violent strikes in the winter of 1947–48. As the conflict deepened, soon 3 million people were out on strike, and many began to fear a communist-inspired revolution. On 4 December the National Assembly granted the new government, led by the MRP's Robert Schuman, the right to call up reservists. In the face of this show of force the PCF and CGT were forced to stand down and henceforth anti-communism was to be a permanent fixture in French politics. Not only was all hope of cooperation between the PCF and the SFIO now at an end, but the CGT split with the creation of an anti-communist trade union, *Force ouvrière*, which received financial aid from **America**.

Anti-communism was also a fundamental aspect of the *Rassemblement du peuple français* (RPF) launched by de Gaulle in Strasbourg on 7 April 1947. De Gaulle stressed that this was not a party but a movement, an

America

America provoked sharp conflicts among French people. On the one hand the PCF called for resistance to Americanisation. In their eyes American consumerism was destroying the French way of life, a view echoed by Gaullists, and for this reason they organised opposition to NATO and to the introduction of Coca-Cola. Yet many were also attracted to American culture. In the cafés and clubs of St-Germain-des-Prés jazz was hugely popular. The trumpeter Miles Davis and the hard bop drummer Art Blakey were just two of the jazz musicians who regularly performed there during the 1950s.

extension of Gaullist resistance. Marked by doctrinal vagueness, the RPF mixed anti-Soviet rhetoric with opposition to the Fourth Republic, derided as a fatally weak regime, and calls for national renewal. Huge torchlight rallies focused upon de Gaulle as the great leader, leading to the accusation from opponents that the RPF had fascist over-tones. None the less the movement soon had 1 million members, many of them drawn from the MRP, and in municipal elections in October 1947 it won 40 per cent of the vote, taking control of Bordeaux, Paris, Rennes, Lille, Nancy, Strasbourg and Marseilles.

In the face of the twin threat of communism and Gaullism the other parties came to together to form the Third Force. Stretching from the SFIO to the moderate right, the Third Force stabilised the Fourth Republic. Beyond the common desire to exclude the Gaullists and the communists, what united the Third Force was support both for the Atlantic Alliance against the Soviet Union and the construction of a united Europe. So, as the Cold War gathered pace, the Third Force brought France under the American umbrella through participation in the Bretton Woods monetary system, Marshall Aid, the GATT trade agreements and finally, in the realm of defence, the establishment of NATO in 1949. Likewise, from the founding of the Organisation for European Economic Cooperation in 1948 through to the establishment of the Council of Europe in 1949 and the European Coal and Steel Community in 1951, the Fourth Republic leaders were the pioneers of European integration. Here the hope was that these European institutions would not only save liberal democracy from communism, but also neutralise the threat of West Germany and lay the basis of Franco-German rapprochement. For this specific reason the René Pleven government launched the idea of the European Defence Community on 24 October 1950. Under this framework a Western European army, including German troops, would operate under a multi-national command. The proposal provoked immediate opposition from communists and Gaullists. Playing on the memory of the Occupation, as well as that of World War I and the Franco-Prussian War, the PCF claimed that the EDC was a cloak for a resurgent German militarism which the Americans were planning to unleash on the Soviet Union at the earliest opportunity. For the Gaullists the EDC was symptomatic of the way in which the process of integration into the western bloc was destroying French sovereignty.

intellectuals

Paris was the centre of the existentialist movement in the late 1940s and 1950s. The two main leaders were Jean-Paul Sartre and Simone de Beauvoir, who founded the influential monthly review *Les Temps modernes* in 1945. Both saw themselves as committed intellectuals who had a moral duty to intervene in politics. In 1953 they opposed the electrocution of Julius and Ethel Rosenberg by the Americans for supposedly betraying scientific secrets to the Soviet Union. In September 1960 both signed the Manifesto of 121 calling for illegal opposition to the Algerian War.

With the PCF and the RPF, which represented over 40 per cent of the popular vote, excluded from government, instability became a permanent feature of the political landscape. Now coalition governments had to be fashioned out of various combinations of socialists, MRP, radicals and independents and this condemned the regime to a succession of ineffective ministries whose average life span was six and a half months. In large part the problem was that although the Third Force could find common ground in pro-American and pro-European policies, there were tensions over subsidies to Catholic schools, economic strategy and the management of the empire. Thus, the radicals might side with the SFIO over opposition to state aid to Catholic schools, but they saw the SFIO as too interventionist over the economy and certainly too conciliatory to anti-colonial nationalist movements. The upshot of these tensions was that the Third Force governments fell apart on a regular basis, but with each new administration the same faces appeared time after time, albeit in different ministerial positions. In the eyes of public opinion this sapped the legitimacy of the regime, giving the impression that the Fourth Republic was little more than a farcical game of musical chairs played out for personal advancement.

If the first phase of the Fourth Republic was tripartism and the second phase was Third Force politics, the next phase was the re-emergence of the right brought on by 17 June 1951 elections. To shore up the Fourth Republic, in a cynical move which further undermined the regime, electoral reforms were introduced with the explicit intent of preventing the PCF and the RPF from making widely predicted gains. Under this new system joint lists of parties would take all the seats in a department if they secured an absolute majority. In view of the fact that nobody wanted to enter into an alliance either with the PCF or the RPF, the victory of the Third Force was built into the system. Consequently the socialists won 106 seats, the MRP 88, the radicals 99 and assorted moderates 99, whilst the PCF gained 101 and the RPF 117 despite the fact that they had gained 25.9 and 20.4 per cent of the votes. Although the communists and Gaullists had been successfully barred, it proved impossible to construct a durable majority from the Third Force, principally because the MRP and the SFIO in particular were at loggerheads over the question of subsidies for Catholic schools. Confronted with this impasse the way was now open for a right-wing government and on 6 March 1952 Antoine Pinay formed a new government. A member of the conservative *Conseil national des indépendants et paysans* (CNIP), Pinay had voted for Pétain in 1940 and had sat on Vichy's *Conseil national*. In this respect the Pinay administration represented an important stage in the rehabilitation of former Vichyites. Light years away from the ambitious reforms of the post-Liberation era, the basis for Pinay's government was right-wing radicals, the MRP and, to the disgust of de Gaulle, who subsequently dissolved the RPF parliamentary wing and retired from politics, some 27 RPF deputies. Pinay used the radio to good effect and his financial orthodoxy, which underlined the importance of limiting state expenditure and reducing taxation, struck a popular chord. In fact when his government fell at the end of 1952, because the MRP felt that it was too conservative, Pinay's approval ratings were at a level rarely equalled by a Fourth Republic politician. Thereafter the Fourth Republic was marked by bewildering instability as a succession of centre-right coalitions came and went until June 1954. Such weakness only fuelled popular disaffection and in November 1953 the leading radical politician Pierre Mendès-France, speaking to his own party conference, warned that the country was on the cusp of a new French Revolution. 'Listen to the murmurs of discontent rising,' he told his audience. 'We are in 1788!'

Economic and social change

The political instability of the regime has meant that the Fourth Republic has traditionally received a bad press. Yet, in economic terms it laid the basis for the economic
miracle, the so-called **trente glorieuses**, that lasted from 1944 until 1974. The
Liberation reforms, above all the nationalisation of key sectors of the economy, the
establishment of the welfare state and the introduction of planning, provided the
impetus for economic modernisation and what followed was an unprecedented
economic and social revolution, arguably bringing about the greatest changes in French
society since 1789. Certainly the figures are astounding. Between 1949 and 1959
annual growth was 4.5 per cent, increasing to 5.8 per cent during the 1960s, rates only
surpassed by the Germans and Japanese. Likewise, once the economy had been rebuilt,
industrial production tripled between 1946 and 1966.

The end result was the transformation of France into a modern consumer society.
Why then did this transformation happen and, more precisely, why did it take place in
such a short space of time? The first factor was the opening up of the economy to the
rest of the world. Participation in the world free-trade system as well as the move
towards European integration forced French businesses to be much more competitive.
Gone was the insular mentality of the 1930s. Now businesses had to be dynamic,
forward-looking and open to innovation. In particular, exports were re-orientated
towards technologically advanced goods for the Western European market. The second
factor was Marshall Aid. France was one of the largest recipients, receiving one-fifth of all
the credit made available to Europe, and this allowed economic planners to import the
raw materials vital for recovery. The third factor was the end of empire. France could no
longer rely upon the imperial bloc as a trading partner and this was another incentive for
businesses to break with protectionism and become more adventurous in the search for
new markets. The fourth factor was the demographic boom of the 1940s and 1950s.
Between 1940 and 1962 the population surged from 40.3 million to 47 million, an
increase that was due to the burgeoning birth rate, the influx of workers from North
Africa and, in 1962, the 'return' of 1 million settlers from Algeria. The final factor was a
new system of planning, introduced by Jean Monnet, which brought together the most
dynamic elements in public administration
and private enterprise. Through this partnership the state defined broad goals and the aim
of the first plan (1946–52) was the modernisation of the infrastructure, in particular coal,
steel, electricity, transport and agriculture. The
next plan (1952–57) put the emphasis on the
renewal of capital equipment and increases in
productivity and within this process government spending was seen as the motor of the
economy. Indeed, between 1947 and 1958 this
spending rose from 40.8 per cent of gross
domestic product (GDP) in 1947 to 50 per cent.

les trente glorieuses

Expression coined by Jean
Fourastié in 1979 to describe the
30 years of economic growth
1944-74. In 1973, in retaliation for
Western support for Israel, Arab
countries dramatically increased
oil prices. The cost of oil imports
multiplied by four, leading to high
inflation, unemployment and
reduced growth and putting an
end to 30 years of prosperity.

The combination of the above factors did away with the 'stalemate society' and completely redrew French social structures. The modernisation of agriculture, epitomised by the spread of the tractor, led to the disappearance of small farms and provoked a huge rural exodus. The result was that, as the farming community shrank from 36 per cent of the working population in 1945 to 16 per cent in 1968, the urban population grew from 50 per cent in 1945 to 70 per cent in 1968. By the late 1950s the working class assumed its greatest social weight before or since. However, this was a new working class, no longer based on the railways or in coal but in the new engineering, chemical, electrical and car industries. Importantly too this was a working class bolstered by immigration from Portugal and the former North African colonies.

The structures of the middle classes were also profoundly changed as small businesses were squeezed out in favour of large-scale firms. The need to run such complex operations led to the recruitment of technical managerial personnel and the emergence of the new middle classes, the *cadres*, who believed in scientific organisation of the economy. The rise of the new middle class was accelerated still further by the rapid expansion of private and public services in the tertiary sector and between 1954 and 1968 the category of *cadres* doubled in importance to over 15 per cent of the working population. If the *cadres* were the winners in the French economic miracle, the losers were small shopkeepers and artisans. Ill at ease in the new technocratic society, these were the people whose working practices were most threatened by modernisation, a trend which intensified in the 1960s when some 108,000 small businesses and artisans disappeared. The economic miracle was also unequal in terms of region. In the main, growth was concentrated in the Paris basin and the big cities.

Clearly the French economic miracle transformed class structures, but what impact did it have upon women? Within the Fourth Republic Constitution contradictory discourses shaped the situation of women. On the one hand, they were granted the right to vote and to run for public office. Furthermore, the constitution explicitly stated that women had equal access to the right to work. On the other hand, post-war social reforms underlined their traditional role. First and foremost women were seen as mothers and told that they had a duty to provide a home and increase the birth rate. Continuing in the vein of the 1939 Family Code and Vichy policy, the goal of social legislation was to increase the population by 12 million. Moreover, the return of 1.5 million prisoners meant that there was an overriding expectation that women should concentrate on the home, making family life their first priority.

The political parties made no attempt to adapt themselves to women. Political life was still seen as a male preserve, indeed even more so because male party politicians were anxious to reassert the influence they had lost since 1940. Thirty-three female deputies were elected in 1945 but after that their numbers saw a steady decline. In this sense many women felt estranged from formal party politics. They were also largely excluded from trade unions, which were still based on an idea of the proletariat as being essentially masculine. In specific terms, women, by and large, supported right-wing parties. In the 1951 election the three parties with the highest proportion of female voters were the MRP (61 per cent), the RPF (52 per cent) and the CNIP (53 per cent), whilst those with the lowest proportion were the SFIO (40 per cent), the PCF (39 per cent) and the radicals (49 per cent).

During the Fourth Republic family life was still based on the idea that the man was the breadwinner and women did the housework. Allied to this the 1950s witnessed a new focus on the private home. Housing construction took off in the 1950s in a dramatic fashion, 100,000 new homes being built in 1953, rising to 300,000 in 1959, and this meant that the division between the world of work and the world of the home became much more sharply defined. This division was deepened still further by the decline of working at home; the rise of families watching television in the evening; and the emergence of women's magazines that underlined the new-found importance of the domestic sphere. *Elle*, for example, was launched in November 1945 and by 1950 it was selling 500,000 copies a month. Articles in *Elle* told women not only how to get a husband, but how to hold on to him by organising the home efficiently. Women were supposed to be domestic goddesses and endless adverts celebrated the importance of domestic technology, washing machines, fridges and food mixers in making housework and cooking not just easy, but enjoyable. In this way those women who had jobs could do a double shift: go out to work *and* look after the house. Even so, on the birth of a child, women usually gave up work. When they returned to employment, it was normally to the tertiary sector, where work was characterised by low status and low pay: 42.3 per cent of working women were office workers or shop employees in 1946 and this rose to 59.6 by 1968. Moreover, until the late 1950s women were excluded from the most prestigious *grandes écoles*. The cumulative effect of all these pressures was to turn women away from party politics, reinforcing the notion that the private was still female and the public still male.

But the status of women did change. Women led the rural exodus and more and more middle-class and lower middle-class women were going to university. Education instilled in them a determination to participate fully in society and many were influenced by Simone de Beauvoir, whose analysis of the female predicament, *Le Deuxième Sexe*, was published in 1949. For the likes of Hélène Cuénat, who began a degree at the Sorbonne in 1954 and joined the PCF, de Beauvoir was a role model of a liberated woman.

Decolonisation and the end of the Fourth Republic

At the Liberation no issue produced a broader consensus than the need to retain the empire. For de Gaulle the empire, even if he recognised that the relationship had to evolve, proved that France was still a Great Power; for the SFIO the empire was the embodiment of France's universal civilising mission; whilst the PCF held up the empire as a bulwark to American imperialism, arguing that it could be transformed into an equal association of countries much as the Soviet Union had supposedly transformed the Russian Empire into a union of fraternal republics.

The Fourth Republic Constitution replaced the empire with a new concept: that of the French Union, which consisted of territories and states associated with the indivisible French Republic. However, from the beginning, ambiguities were present. It was not clear whether the new Constitution was offering full citizenship to those in the colonies

Figure 9.1   Advertisement from Paris-Match, *1959*

or a federation of equal peoples. Similarly, it was difficult to disguise the tension between the idea of equality of rights and the notion of the traditional civilising mission, reiterated at the beginning of the Constitution without apology. The image of a rejuvenated empire was, therefore, central to the Fourth Republic's political self-identity and this importance was also reflected in the economic sphere. In 1952 the French Union accounted for 52 per cent of exports; between 1947 and 1957 France invested $542 million in West Africa; and, until 1960, the empire was France's most important trading partner. Thus, emotionally, politically and economically the empire was a key platform of the Fourth Republic. Yet, paradoxically this was just at the moment when anti-colonial nationalisms were beginning to push for independence. This clash explains why decolonisation was so protracted and why ultimately the whole process was the crucial factor in ending the Fourth Republic. Decolonisation cruelly exposed the fundamental weaknesses of the regime because successive governments were just too shortlived to assert their authority. All they could do was deal with the colonies on a piecemeal basis.

The first major colonial war was in Indo-China. Initially the situation seemed to be heading towards a negotiated settlement. In September 1945 the communist Vietminh led by Ho Chi Minh declared an independent Vietnam and 6 months later General Leclerc and Admiral Thierry d'Argenlieu recognised this independence *within* the context of the Indo-Chinese federation and the French Union. However, in truth d'Argenlieu was never reconciled to the agreement and when Ho Chi Minh flew for talks in Paris at the end of May 1946, he seized the opportunity to proclaim a separate Cochin-Chinese republic at Saigon which would be subservient to France. D'Argenlieu knew that this was a provocative act which would sabotage all negotiations and on 23 November he followed this up with the bombardment of Haiphong, which left 6,000 dead. When Ho Chi Minh tried to reopen negotiations with the Blum government, d'Argenlieu intervened to deliberately hold up the telegram. At this point Ho Chi Minh was overtaken by hardliners who attacked French forces on 19 December 1946. It was the beginning of a war that lasted seven and a half years.

In June 1949, in an attempt to separate communists from other nationalists and shore up French influence in the region, the Fourth Republic recognised the new state of Vietnam in return for acceptance that the country, along with Laos and Cambodia, should remain within the French Union. But, although the Annamite emperor Bao-Dai was installed as head of state, the war continued unabated. By January 1950, at which point the Democratic Republic of Vietnam was recognised by the Soviet Union and the newly communist China, Indo-China was on the front line of the Cold War. Inevitably, therefore, France now looked towards America to shoulder the cost of anti-communism. Indeed, by 1954 the US government was bearing 80 per cent of the military budget.

Slowly but surely the Indo-China war poisoned civil–military relations. The war was fought by professional soldiers and in their eyes it was an international war against communism. For this reason they had nothing but contempt for the Fourth Republic which they dubbed as weak and effeminate, lacking the necessary will power to win. The war was also a further polarising factor as regards domestic politics. The PCF, along with intellectuals like Jean-Paul Sartre, organised vigorous opposition to what they called the 'dirty war'. Equally Pierre Mendès-France increasingly saw the war as a drain on resources, blocking all hopes of renewal. Not surprisingly all such opponents were denounced as traitors by the army and the right.

Indo-China was an expression of the determination to hang on to empire, a determination that was also mirrored in Madagascar, Morocco and Tunisia. In Madagascar the March 1947 uprising, which saw the killing of 200 French settlers, brought a fierce response. The main Malgache nationalist party was dissolved and the insurgents starved into submission with the loss of 89,000 lives. In Morocco *Istiqlal*, the independence party formed in 1943, had developed into a mass party of some 100,000 members by 1951. Rioting in Casablanca in December 1952 led the French to ban *Istiqlal*. Further, the settlers, who numbered 200,000 of a population of 9 million, were alarmed by the nationalist sentiments of Sultan Mohammed Ben Youssef and on 20 August 1953 he was sent into exile to be replaced by the more compliant Ben Arafa. However, it quickly became apparent that Ben Arafa had no popular legitimacy and Morocco became locked into a spiral of violence and counter-violence. The same pattern of repression also existed in Tunisia, where in June 1950 the Robert Schuman government had opened negotiations with the nationalist leader Habib Bourguiba. Yet, under pressure from the settler population, who amounted to 150,000 out of a total of 3 million, the government capitulated, arresting Bourguiba and cracking down on the nationalist *Neo-Destour*. The situation rapidly deteriorated and in December 1952 Ferhat Hached, a leading pro-independence trade unionist, was gunned down in Tunis by the Red Hand, a shadowy group of settler terrorists.

On the face of it the only solace was West Africa, but even there large-scale strikes had erupted in 1949 followed by rioting in the Ivory Coast the year after. So, by 1954, despite the use of force, the Fourth Republic was under pressure from all sides over the colonial issue. As such, the break-up of the French Union cannot be divorced from the wider international context. Decolonisation was a dominant feature of the post-1945 world, a global phenomenon that happened suddenly and with extraordinary speed. Once Britain had conceded independence to India in 1947, and once the newly independent countries of Africa and Asia came together for the Bandung conference in Indonesia in April 1955, anti-colonialism had an unstoppable logic. In this way the colonial crisis encapsulated the incapacity of the Fourth Republic to renew France.

With defeat at Dien-Bien-Phu on 7 May 1954 the war in Indo-China was lost. Humiliation at the hands of the communist insurgents precipitated the downfall of yet another administration and paved the way for Pierre Mendès-France. Because he was a Jew, a freemason and a former resister, Mendès-France was a hate figure for the right. However, his tenure in office was characterised by a sudden burst of energy and reform as his government set out to reconfigure politics. Supported by the SFIO, USDR, RPF and half the radicals, Mendès-France took decisive action to resolve the colonial problem, modernise the economy and reduce social inequalities. Presiding over a youthful cabinet, Mendès-France was invested as prime minister on 18 June with a majority of 149. Immediately he took over the Indo-China negotiations, ending the war with the signing of an armistice on 21 July which divided the country along the 17th parallel. Ten days later his declaration at Carthage in Tunisia opened the way for the return of Bourguiba and independence. The following year his successor Edgar Faure completed these negotiations and then used the Tunisian blueprint as way to resolve the Moroccan Crisis. In March 1956 both countries became officially independent.

Mendès-France also adopted a new approach over German rearmament. The final treaty for the European Defence Community had been signed in Paris on 27 May 1952, but, given the implacable hostility of the communists and the Gaullists, successive governments knew that ratification of the treaty would be divisive and had studiously avoided any vote. In contrast, Mendès-France seized the initiative and submitted the treaty for debate on the proviso that ratification was not an issue of government confidence. Unsurprisingly the treaty was rejected on 30 August but Mendès-France immediately countered, signing a treaty that recognised West Germany and integrated the West German army into NATO. In this way he ingeniously diffused an issue that had paralysed the Fourth Republic.

Beyond parliament, opposition to Mendès-France came from the *Union de défense des commerçants et artisans* (UDCA) led by Pierre Poujade, a stationer from the Lot in south-west France. Strongly anti-Semitic and anti-communist, Poujade garnered support from the groups most threatened by Mendès-France's modernisation, namely peasants, shopkeepers and the lower middle classes. Poujade was particularly incensed by the campaign against alcoholism, which he saw as a direct attack on the livelihoods of café owners, and he gave vent to this anger through strikes, boycotts and direct action.

Within parliament there was growing opposition over Mendès-France's Algeria policy. On 1 November the *Front de libération nationale* (FLN) launched attacks across Algeria. In essence the FLN was composed of a younger generation of nationalists, such as Ahmed Ben Bella and Mohamed Boudiaf, who, since the repression of May 1945, saw violence as the only way of achieving independence. But, given that Algeria was constitutionally part of the Republic and given that the ties of kith and kin were so strong – 1 million settlers out of a total population of 10 million – Mendès-France and the interior minister, François Mitterrand, both took an uncompromising stance. In a fighting speech to the Assembly on 12 November Mendès-France made it clear that the unity of the Republic would be defended to the hilt. In the same debate he was backed up by Mitterrand, who refuted any parallel with policy in Morocco and Tunisia by reaffirming that Algeria was France. Nevertheless both saw the importance of applying the 1947 reforms, notably the enfranchisement of Muslim women and the expansion of education for the native population, which until then had been blocked by the settlers. With this aim in mind Mendès-France appointed Jacques Soustelle, former resister and left-wing Gaullist deputy for Lyons, as governor-general in Algiers. Soustelle instantly aroused the suspicion of the settlers, who saw him as somebody who could sell out French Algeria. René Mayer, the radical deputy for Constantine in Algeria and leader of the *Algérie française* in parliament, led the attack and on 5 February 1955 the Mendès-France government was overturned.

Mendès-France's successor was another radical, Edgar Faure, who formed a centre-right government on 23 February. Henceforth government policy became dominated by the worsening situation in Algeria and on 3 April Faure declared a state of emergency. In Philippeville, in the east of Algeria, an FLN uprising on 20 August led to terrible reprisals with settler vigilante committees summarily executing Muslims. Looking for a fresh mandate to strengthen his position over Algeria, Faure brought the legislative elections forward to 2 January 1956. The campaign took place in a highly charged atmosphere, the biggest shock being the success of the pro-French Algeria Poujadists who won 11.6 per cent of the vote and 51 seats. Initially the electoral arithmetic was somewhat confused, with the PCF winning 25.8 per cent of the vote, the SFIO 14.9 per cent, the radicals 14.3 per cent and the MRP 11.3 per cent. However, it soon became clear that the only group capable of forming a government was the Republican Front, a coalition of the SFIO, Mendès-France supporters, François Mitterrand's *Union démocratique et socialiste de la résistance* (UDSR) and a faction of the Gaullist groups led by Jacques Chaban-Delmas, and on 26 January President Coty entrusted Guy Mollet, the SFIO leader, with the premiership.

Mollet's administration was to be the longest-lasting government of the Fourth Republic. It was initially supported by the PCF, who hoped to replicate the Popular Front.

It introduced universal pensions, medical benefits and the extension of the annual holiday and completed the decolonisation process in Morocco and Tunisia. In June 1956 the minister for overseas France, Gaston Defferre, introduced a package of reforms which, by accepting that territorial assemblies had the right to vote on local budgets, paved the way for self-government in West Africa. On 25 March 1957 the Mollet government ratified the Treaty of Rome which established the European Economic Community (EEC).

However, it was the Algerian question that was to dominate the Republican Front government. Mollet had campaigned on a platform of peace in Algeria and for this reason, when he visited Algiers on 6 February, the prime minister got a rough reception from the settlers. They bombarded him with tomatoes and rotten eggs and he was left badly shaken. Hitherto ignorant of Algerian life, Mollet was shocked to discover that the majority of settlers were not rich colonialists but ordinary workers. Suddenly Mollet saw Algeria through the prism of the appeasement era. He was adamant that the settlers must not be betrayed like the Czechs in 1938. For him it was a battle between the universal civilising mission of the Fourth Republic and an Arab nationalism that was feudal and religiously fanatical in character. There would be no negotiations with terrorists who threatened the Republic, and to reassure the settlers Mollet passed a series of measures, the first of which was to name a notorious hardliner, the socialist deputy Robert Lacoste, as governor-general. Then on 12 March 1956 the National Assembly, including the PCF deputies, voted the special powers, giving the army dictatorial power to break the FLN rebellion; 400,000 reservists were recalled in May and the Algerian Assembly was dissolved. The intention of this strategy, Mollet explained, was to 'pacify' the country and prepare the way for elections.

In the eyes of many people Mollet's volte-face was the real beginning of the Algerian War and in May Mendès-France resigned in protest. All the same the Republican Front continued to intensify the conflict. Anti-war riots by some 20,000 reservists were quashed and in June President Coty invoked the memory of Verdun as a rallying call for victory in Algeria. Furthermore, convinced that Egypt was the real force behind the FLN, France joined with Britain in a military expedition against President Nasser ostensibly provoked by the latter's nationalisation of the Suez Canal. When in November 1956 the expedition ended in a humiliating withdrawal, under pressure from the two superpowers, this merely redoubled the government's resolve to crush the rebellion. The Republican Front cravenly caved in to the military. In light of what had happened in Indo-China the army was determined not to lose in Algeria and, fearing that the government was involved in secret negotiations with the FLN, on 22 October it hijacked an aeroplane taking Algerian leaders Ben Bella, Boudiaf, Khider and Aït Ahmed to Tunis. Mollet had no choice but to sanction the army's actions, a blurring of civil–military relations that was ultimately to be fateful for the Fourth Republic.

The Algerian War?

Three million Frenchmen fought in Algeria. Yet, at the time, in an explicit effort to minimise what was happening, the conflict was not referred to as a war but as a law and order problem (*maintien de l'ordre*). Only in June 1999 did the French government officially recognise what took place in Algeria as a war.

torture

In February 1958 the Éditions de Minuit published Henri Alleg's *La Question*. In this book Alleg, a member of the Algerian Communist Party, had written a harrowing account of tortures suffered at the hands of parachutists during the Battle of Algiers. In 2001 General Paul Aussaresses, who in 1956–57 was on the intelligence staff of Massu's 10th Parachute Division, admitted in his memoirs, *Services spéciaux: Algérie 1955–57*, that torture was routine.

In August 1956 FLN leaders met in the valley of the Soummam in the Kabyle mountains. There the decision was made, in an effort to relieve hard-pressed rural guerrilla units, to launch a campaign of indiscriminate terrorism in Algiers. Responding to settler outrages, the first FLN bomb exploded on 30 September 1956 in two fashionable cafés frequented by students. The Battle of Algiers had begun and, as law and order broke down, Lacoste handed over police powers to General Massu's paratroopers on 7 January 1957. In the sinewy alleyways of the Algiers Kasbah the paratroopers and the FLN fighters fought out a deadly game of cat and mouse. Controversially the army used **torture** to extract information and during the next 10 months 3,000 prisoners disappeared. By October the FLN networks had been dismantled but the outcry over the methods left France isolated on the international scene.

On 21 May 1957 the Mollet government fell and thereafter successive governments were overwhelmed by Algeria. On 8 January 1958 the air force pursued an FLN unit across the Tunisian frontier and bombed the village of Sakhiet, killing 69 people. In the face of international condemnation, the military and settlers were disgusted by the lack of political will power in Paris. Now the regime entered a protracted crisis where governments were little more than a reshuffling of ministries between socialists, MRP and radicals, each of which was unable to produce a solution to Algeria. At one point no one could form a government for 38 days.

Eventually, in May 1958 Coty called upon Pierre Pflimlin of the MRP to form a government. But Pflimlin had called for negotiations and his appointment on 13 May 1958 provoked demonstrations in Algiers. There the governor-general's office was sacked and a Committee of Public Safety was established by General Massu. What followed was a tense standoff between Paris and Algiers which took on a new direction when General Salan, the commander-in-chief in Algiers, shouted 'Vive de Gaulle' from the balcony of the governor-general's building on 15 May. De Gaulle replied by declaring that he would be ready to assume the powers of the Republic. He then played a very skilful game. To the army and the settlers he presented himself as the man to save French Algeria, whilst to the politicians and the public at large he cast himself as the only bulwark against a military takeover. With the threat of an army invasion from Algeria becoming ever more real by the day, the PCF organised a demonstration in Paris of 200,000 people on 28 May. In this civil-war atmosphere the likes of Mollet and Pinay deserted Pflimlin and flocked to de Gaulle as the saviour of the nation. Pflimlin now resigned and on 29 May Coty invited de Gaulle to form a new government. On 1 June, by 329 votes to 224, de Gaulle was given emergency powers to restore order and draft a new constitution. The Fourth Republic was over.

Document 9a: The representation of women in elected assemblies, 1945–83

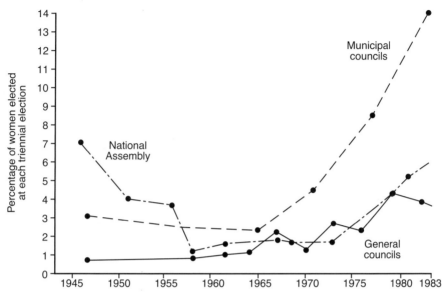

Figure 9.2   The representation of women in elected assemblies, 1945–83

Document 9b: Boris Vian

Vian was a writer, jazz musician and existentialist philosopher. In 1955 he released the song, 'Complainte du progrès', satirising the rise of consumer society.

Autrefois pour faire sa cour
On parlait d'amour.
Pour mieux prouver son ardeur
On offrait son cœur.
Aujourd'hui, c'est plus pareil
Ça change, ça change.
Pour séduire le cher ange
On lui glisse à l'oreille.
(Ah? Gudule!)

{Refrain:}
Viens m'embrasser
Et je te donnerai;

Un frigidaire,
Un joli scooter,
Un atomixer,
Et du Dunlopillo,
Une cuisinière,
Avec un four en verre,
Des tas de couverts,
Et des pell' à gâteaux.

Une tourniquette,
Pour fair' la vinaigrette,
Un bel aérateur,
Pour bouffer les odeurs.

Des draps qui chauffent,
Un pistolet à gauffres,
Un avion pour deux,
Et nous serons heureux.

Document 9c: Extract from Henri Alleg, *La Question*, Paris: Éditions de Minuit, 1958

Cha . . ., toujours souriant, agita d'abord devant mes yeux les pinces que terminaient des éléctrodes. Des petites pinces d'acier brillant, allongées et dentelées. Des pinces 'crocodiles', disent les ouvriers des lignes téléphoniques qui les utilisent. Il m'en fixa une au lobe de l'oreille droite, l'autre au doigt du même coté

D'un seul coup, je bondissai de mes liens et hurlai de toute ma voix. Cha.-
. . . . .venait de m'envoyer dans le corps la première décharge électrique. Près de mon oreille avait jailli une longue étincelle et je sentis dans ma poitrine mon cœur s'emballer. Je me tordais en hurlant et me raidissais à me blesser, tandis que les secousses commandées par Cha. . . . .magnéto en mains, se succèdaient sans arrêt. Sur le même rythme, Cha. . . . .scandait une seule question en martelant les syllables: 'Où es-tu hebergé?'

Topics FOR DISCUSSION

1   Why did de Gaulle resign in January 1946?
2   What was the Cold War? What impact did it have upon France?
3   Why was the Fourth Republic so unstable?
4   How did French society change between 1944 and 1958?
5   How was the position of women transformed during this period? What do Document 9a, Figure 9.1 and Document 9b tell us about this transformation?
6   How did the Fourth Republic approach decolonisation?
7   Why did the Republican Front intensify the Algerian War in spring 1956? What does Document 9c reveal about French army tactics?
8   Why did the Fourth Republic fall?

CHAPTER 10

Timeline

1958
4–7 June   De Gaulle visits Algiers
28 September   De Gaulle wins referendum on the constitution
28 December   Creation of new franc

1959
8 January   De Gaulle assumes presidency
16 September   De Gaulle's speech on self-determination in Algeria

1960
24 January–1 February Barricades week

1961
22–5 April   Generals' putsch in Algiers
17 October   Violent repression of Algerians in Paris

1962
1 July   Algeria wins independence

1963
14 January   De Gaulle vetoes Britain's candidature for the EEC

1965
5–19 December   Presidential election

1966
7 March   France withdraws from the command structure of NATO

1967
5–12 March   Legislative elections

1968
22 March   Student occupation at Nanterre
3 May   Clashes between students and police in the Latin Quarter

The Gaullist Revolution, 1958–69

De Gaulle had ambitious plans for renewal. He wanted a France that was modern, dynamic and forward-looking. To realise this vision de Gaulle drew up a new constitution that was based on the principle of strong government. Thus the basic and most fundamental difference of the new Fifth Republic was to be the shift of power from the parliament to the president. Elected by a college of 80,000 *notables*, the president could now appoint the prime minister, dissolve the National Assembly, submit important issues to a popular referendum, and exercise supreme power in a time of crisis. Parallel to this the ability of parliament to censure a prime minister and amend legislation was drastically curtailed. Armed with these powers, therefore, the presidency would be the motor of fundamental change, giving the country leadership and direction.

Sensitive to criticism that he was installing a presidential dictatorship, de Gaulle outlined the constitution in the Place de la République on 4 September 1958, the anniversary of the declaration of the Third Republic in 1870. Just over 3 weeks later, on 28 September, the new constitution was endorsed by an emphatic 79 per cent of the vote with opposition coming from the PCF, Pierre Mendès-France and François Mitterrand. Voters in

10–11 May   Night of the
barricades
20 May   10 million on strike
23–30 June   Legislative
elections
1969
27 April   Victory for the no
campaign in the referendum
28 April   De Gaulle resigns

Algeria and in 12 out of 13 of the overseas territories also gave de Gaulle a resounding vote of confidence.

Thereafter the parliamentary elections of 23 and 30 November represented another comprehensive rejection of the Fourth Republic. Only 131 out of 537 sitting deputies were returned, as votes for the PCF, SFIO, radicals and Poujadists all collapsed. There were massive gains for the new Gaullist party, *Union pour la nouvelle république* (UNR), and other conservatives and some 70 per cent of those elected were supporters of de Gaulle. De Gaulle himself was voted in as president by a college system on 21 December and on 8 January 1959 he took office, naming the veteran Michel Debré as prime minister.

Decolonisation and the end of the Algerian War

The Defferre reforms of June 1956 had conceded greater powers to the colonies. Momentarily de Gaulle tried to claw back some power with a new concept of community, but in reality the way was open for the transition to independence. In September 1959 African leaders asked for complete authority to be transferred to them and by mid-1960 decolonisation in sub-Saharan Africa was complete. The fact that this was a largely peaceful process was in marked contrast to the ongoing crisis in Algeria.

It was Algeria that had brought de Gaulle back to power and for the first 4 years this issue dominated his presidency. The army hardliners and the settlers believed that the new constitution was a statement about the integration of Algeria into France. But, although he received a triumphant reception in Algiers on 4 June, he hung back from a ringing endorsement of the status quo, uttering '*Vive Algérie française*' only once, in Mostaganem. He had absolutely no intention of being a tool of either the army or the settlers. With this explicit aim in mind he quickly set out to re-establish the separation of civil and military powers, something that had been so gravely undermined during the end of the Fourth Republic. Thus, in October 1958 Massu was told to stand down from the Committee of Public Safety, which was then disbanded altogether, whilst Salan was replaced by General Maurice Challe. In tandem with this reassertion of civil power de Gaulle announced in Constantine a plan to spend 100,000 FF per annum over 5 years on a programme of economic and social reform aimed specifically at Muslims, and made a direct appeal to the FLN for an honourable ceasefire. However, when in 1959 this initiative was rejected by the provisional Algerian government in Tunis, de Gaulle gave the army the go-ahead for a series of huge operations to destroy the FLN in Algeria. Organised by General Challe, these sweeps were a huge success, in large part due to the use of Muslim auxiliaries, the *harkis*, whose numbers were expanded from 26,000 to 60,000. The eyes and ears of the army, the *harkis* were briefed to locate and pin down FLN units. Once this had been done, paratroopers would be quickly helicoptered in to finish off the job, hitting the guerrillas again and again until they had finally been broken.

Whatever the success of the Challe offensive, de Gaulle knew that ultimately the way ahead over Algeria was to be found in a political, rather than a military, solution. During 1959 his stance over Algeria was constantly evolving as he felt his way towards a policy. At times he seemed highly ambivalent, giving differing responses to different people. Nevertheless two things were always at the forefront of his mind. Firstly, he wanted to be in a position of strength with a free hand to do what he judged best: this was the rationale behind the Challe offensive. Secondly, he always subordinated the interests of Algeria to those of metropolitan France. This meant that he came to see the war as a drain on resources, blocking his wider plans for renewal. As such, it is impossible to overestimate the significance of de Gaulle's nationwide radio and television address on 16 September 1959. De Gaulle outlined three possible solutions, the first of which was secession, which de Gaulle warned would open the way to chaos and communist dictatorship, the second full integration, whereby Algerians would become part and parcel of the French people, whilst the third, implicitly de Gaulle's preferred choice, was self-government by Algerians in close association with France. Undoubtedly the speech, the longest he devoted to the Algerian issue, was a major turning point during the war because de Gaulle recognised the right of all Algerians to self-determination, even conceding that those taking part in the rebellion would not be excluded from playing a part in a future Algerian policy. Such an offer put paid, once and for all, to *Algérie française.*

Not surprisingly, amongst the army and the settlers the speech produced a flood of anger. In an interview with a German newspaper in January 1960 Massu voiced his disquiet with de Gaulle's Algeria policy. At once Massu was recalled to Paris, a move which immediately provoked the settlers, with the aid of some army officers, to mount a fresh revolt, known as *la semaine des barricades.* The stage was set for another stand-off between the government and Algiers, but here, unlike Mollet or Pflimlin, de Gaulle stood up to the rebels. In a televised speech on 29 January de Gaulle, dressed in his general's uniform to underline his personal legitimacy as the man who had saved the honour of France in June 1940, called for army loyalty and in the face of his resolve the rebellion simply collapsed. For the present de Gaulle had restored his political authority but in the following month he was confronted with pressure from another quarter, this time the extreme left, when it was discovered that a small minority of French people had been illegally aiding the FLN in France. Motivated by what they saw as the failure of the mainstream left, above all the PCF, to oppose the war, 18 of the activists were arrested and put on trial in September 1960. Seizing this moment, 121 intellectuals demonstrated their solidarity with the accused by signing a manifesto calling on conscripts to refuse to fight in Algeria. The fact that some of the most prominent people in France, including the actress Simone Signoret, the novelist Françoise Sagan, the Resistance hero Vercors and the philosophers Jean-Paul Sartre and Simone de Beauvoir, were willing to incite soldiers to desert shocked mainstream society. Like the actions of those on trial, the signatories' motivations polarised public opinion.

In 1960, therefore, the debate about the war was more strident than ever, and as the Algerian crisis worsened, de Gaulle opened secret talks with the FLN in June. Although the negotiations broke down, they still convinced de Gaulle of the necessity

the media

By the early 1960s French people possessed 3 million televisions and 10 million radios. De Gaulle understood the importance of the mass media and was to use television and radio to decisive effect during the Algerian War. Furthermore, the late 1950s witnessed the introduction of cheap portable radios as the transistor replaced the vacuum tube. On 23 April 1961 thousands of conscripts in Algeria huddled around their transistor radios to hear de Gaulle's impassioned plea to disobey the putsch. Thereafter, the transistor radio, allowing the media to specifically target young people, would become the vehicle for the development of youth culture.

17 October 1961

On the night of 17 October 1961 in Paris the FLN organised a peaceful protest of 30,000 people against the curfew that had been imposed by the French police on Algerians. The resulting police violence, openly sanctioned by the head of police, Maurice Papon, was ferocious and led to the death of 200 Algerians. Since the 1980s there has been a campaign for the state to officially recognise what happened. In October 2001 the mayor of Paris, Bertrand Delanoë, unveiled a plaque on the Pont St Michel bridge. The inscription reads: 'A la mémoire des nombreux Algériens tués lors de la sanglante répression de la manifestation pacifique du 17 octobre 1961.'

to put his plan for the preparation of Algerian self-determination before the French people and on 8 January 1961 a referendum on independence was won by 75 per cent. On 7 April further negotiations opened with the FLN but the prospect of independence provoked another revolt in Algeria. This time four generals, Challe, Jouhaud, Zeller and Salan, seized power in Algiers on 22 April 1961. Yet again de Gaulle did not capitulate and in another dramatic television speech he forbade all soldiers to follow the putsch. Soon the four generals were isolated and by 25 April the rebellion had fallen apart. The way was open for further negotiations but this proved to be a long-drawn-out process, largely because de Gaulle wanted to hold onto the oil reserves in the Sahara. Eventually the talking ended with a ceasefire agreement on 18 March 1962, signed at Evian, a French spa town on Lake Geneva which was subsequently approved by 91 per cent of French voters in a referendum on 8 April and by almost 100 per cent of Algerians on 1 July. On 3 July Algeria became formally independent.

All of these talks took place in a climate of uncontrolled violence. Army dissidents and settlers formed the *Organisation de l'armée secrète* (OAS) which carried out bombing campaigns in France and Algeria, including several attempts to assassinate de Gaulle. Then, once independence was inevitable, the OAS operated a scorched-earth policy. Nothing was to be left to the Algerians as roads and buildings were destroyed. Inevitably such violence drove a wedge between the two communities and made it impossible for the million settlers to remain in the new independent Algeria. Virtually all 'returned' to France. In contrast de Gaulle was adamant that the *harkis* could not be repatriated. For him they belonged to a separate culture and religion and they were left to face pitiless FLN retribution. It has been estimated that as many as 70,000 were slaughtered in the massacres carried out after independence.

For France the end of French Algeria was enormously significant. Firstly, it put a stop to 23 years of continuous war and meant that the country was at last at peace. Secondly, the purge of the military carried out after the 1961 putsch meant that the army was removed from politics and thoroughly republicanised. Thirdly, there was the 'return' of the million settlers, many of whom, like the fashion designer Yves St-Laurent, proved to be a very dynamic element in the economy, largely because they had lost everything and were thus more willing to take entrepreneurial risks. Fourthly, there was the dramatic increase in the Algerian population in France, which shot up from 211,000 in 1954 to 436,000 in 1962. Ironically they were brought in to make up for the chronic labour shortage caused by conscripts fighting in the war, but their presence led to a steady rise in anti-Algerian racism, something that has become a permanent feature of French society. Finally, there were the returning French soldiers. Many retreated into silence, angry at the way in which politicians had not only condemned their generation to waste the best years of their lives in a pointless conflict but also, by refusing to face up to the legacy of the war, left the same generation to carry an intolerable burden of guilt at what they had done in Algeria.

De Gaulle himself cast the Algerian War as a victory for modernisation. Having shaken off the burden of colonisation, the new France had to turn the page in a bold and assertive manner, embracing the challenges of economic modernisation. At an official level the Algerian War had to be forgotten and in this sense the conscripts, as well as the settlers and the *harkis*, became untidy reminders of outdated colonial values. Indeed in the case of the *harkis*, the government deliberately segregated them from the rest of society. Those that managed to escape to France were housed in makeshift villages and employed in forest clearance.

words and the Algerian War

As result of 132 years of colonisation in Algeria a number of words entered the French language:

Pied-noir was the nickname given by the native population to the French soldiers in the 1830s who were struck by the fact that they wore black shoes. The settlers, most of whom 'returned' to France in 1962, took over the name. Most now live in the south of France and large numbers vote for the *Front national*.

Harki is derived from the Arabic word for 'movement'. It is the term used to refer to Muslim auxiliaries raised by the French army between 1954 and 1962. Of the *harkis* who managed to escape to France in 1962, most were housed in shanty towns in the south. Fuelled by a deep sense of injustice, the *harki* community, which numbers some 500,000, has campaigned against its marginalisation in society. In 2001 the government established 25 September, the date when the Algerian Republic was officially proclaimed, as France's first national *harki* remembrance day. Colonisation also produced a vocabulary of racist slang. Pejorative words for North Africans, *melon*, *bougnoule* and *raton*, are now part of the everyday French language, testament to the pernicious legacy of the Algerian War.

Constitutional reform

With the Algerian War over de Gaulle was free to carry out his regeneration of France. An important aspect of this was his desire to ensure the Fifth Republic would survive him. Partly because of OAS attempts on his life, notably at Petit-Clamart on 22 August 1962, and partly because of the revival of party politics, de Gaulle was only too aware of the extent to which the regime was closely tied to his personal legitimacy as the man of June 1940. Any successor, therefore, would need to have the endorsement of universal suffrage and for this reason, 2 weeks after Petit-Clamart, de Gaulle announced a referendum to change the method of presidential election from a college system to one of popular election. The snap decision provoked immense controversy. By calling for a referendum de Gaulle was by-passing parliament, violating article 89 of the constitution which stated that any amendment could only be revised with the prior agreement of parliament. On 5 October the assembly passed a vote of censure on the Georges Pompidou government. Furious, de Gaulle countered by dissolving parliament and calling new elections for 18 November. Here de Gaulle made it clear that both the referendum and the election were a personal plebiscite. If the proposals were rejected, he would resign.

On 28 October 62 per cent of those who voted approved the change. The elections too were a crushing defeat for de Gaulle's opponents, with the UNR winning 35 per cent of the vote and 233 seats. Nevertheless the opposition did regain some confidence over the next 3 years, largely through the emergence of new forums, such as the *Club Jean Moulin* and the *Citoyens 60*, which aimed to renew opposition politics. There was also the impact of progressive left-wing weeklies *L'Express* and *Le Nouvel Observateur* and the creation in 1960 of the *Parti socialiste unifié* (PSU) which, though small, was to provide a socialist alternative to the SFIO. Old parties too began to regain confidence in advance of the presidential elections in 1965. After the death of Thorez on 11 July 1964 the PCF wanted to break out of isolation, and after much manoeuvring, embraced an alliance with François Mitterrand, allowing him to become the single candidate of the left. Mitterrand fought an impressive campaign, foregrounding women's issues and coming out in support of contraception, and in the first round on 5 December he got 32 per cent of the vote, against 45 per cent for de Gaulle, thereby forcing de Gaulle into a humiliating second round. Two weeks later de Gaulle won the run-off by 55 per cent, but his authority had been dented. Significantly too Mitterrand now established himself as the major anti-Gaullist candidate of the left.

The March 1967 parliamentary elections confirmed the recovery of the left and a further weakening of the Gaullists. Mitterrand formed the *Fédération de la gauche démocratique et socialiste* (FGDS), which united the non-communist left, and then reached an agreement with the PCF whereby each party would stand down in favour of the best-placed candidate after the first ballot. In response the prime minister, Georges Pompidou, tried to create a new modern Gaullist party, the *Union des démocrates pour la V* (UDV), whilst the MRP, radicals and some independents formed themselves into *Centre démocrate* (CD). The results, which gave the government a majority of two in the Assembly, left Pompidou in the invidious position of scrambling around for support from Valéry Giscard d'Estaing's small *Républicains indépendants* party. During the campaign Giscard made clear his critical stance towards de Gaulle with the phrase 'Oui, mais', and, although he did agree to bolster Pompidou, he tried to dissociate himself from the more authoritarian aspects of the regime, casting his own party as modern, centrist and European. Thus, near electoral defeat was another indication of the way in which de Gaulle's prestige was on the wane and between April and October 1967 Pompidou had to resort to decree rule in economic and financial matters.

Foreign policy

For de Gaulle France was nothing without international greatness (*grandeur*). Significantly, therefore, foreign policy was the privileged domain of the president and, once free of the Algerian War, he was to use this power to try and make a lasting impact upon international politics.

In formulating foreign policy de Gaulle saw the nation state as the bedrock of international relations. In his opinion, ideologies could come and go but nation states, and national interests, always remained. Thus the assertion of national independence was a fundamental principle for de Gaulle. For this reason he greeted the news of the first French atomic test, on 13 February 1960 in the Sahara, with fervent joy, declaring that henceforth France would be stronger and prouder. In de Gaulle's eyes it was the possession of the nuclear deterrent, rather than the possession of empire, that was the new measure of Great-Power status, the symbol of France's independence from the two superpowers.

De Gaulle's belief in French independence also explains his unbridled opposition to the Cold War. He wanted to break the dominance of the two superpowers in order to create a multi-polar world of nation states. Within the Western Alliance de Gaulle took a clear anti-American stance. For him, therefore, NATO was not a multi-national coalition but a military structure dictated by American Cold War interests. His fear was that America would use NATO to embroil the rest of the West in a confrontation with the Soviet Union and for this reason he progressively took the French out of the NATO command structure, climaxing with full withdrawal on 7 March 1966. Elsewhere de Gaulle denounced the Vietnam War, where the Americans were propping up South Vietnam against communist guerrillas, and tried to limit the importance of the dollar as a global currency by converting French reserves into gold. He also blocked British entry to the EEC in 1963 and 1967, on the grounds that Britain would act as a conduit for American influence in Europe, and courted the Soviet Union by visiting Moscow in June

Jean Moulin

Through the burial of the Resistance hero Jean Moulin in the Pantheon in 1964, a huge state occasion, Gaullism constructed a specific memory of the Resistance that stressed the unity of the French people behind de Gaulle, a unity, it was claimed, that was now being rediscovered under the Fifth Republic. Locating the legitimacy of the Fifth Republic in Gaullist resistance, rather than the specific events of May 1958, allowed de Gaulle to dissociate himself from the threat of the military putsch which returned him to power.

1966 in order to promote his vision of a Europe from the Atlantic to the Urals. Nevertheless, for all this sabre-rattling, in the final analysis de Gaulle understood that France had no choice but to line up with the Western Alliance. So, in October 1962 when the siting of missiles in Cuba by the Soviet Union brought the world to the brink of nuclear war, de Gaulle immediately signalled his full support for the Americans, though as an equal rather than a subordinate partner. Similarly, although de Gaulle pulled out of the NATO command structure, he never left the NATO treaty.

Given his desire to uphold French independence, de Gaulle was very suspicious of supra-national institutions. He was, therefore, very disparaging about the United Nations. In the same vein he was constantly opposed to what he saw as the federalist ambitions of the EEC. For him the EEC was an economic, not a political, union and on these grounds he blocked attempts to increase the European Commission's powers, boycotting meetings in the second half of 1965 in order to defend the right of individual states to a veto. In de Gaulle's view international relations were to be conducted through alliances between individual states and with this aim in mind he signed the Elysée Treaty on 22 January 1963 with Chancellor Konrad Adenauer. For de Gaulle there was no question that it would be this new Franco-German axis rather than the EEC Commission in Brussels that would give Western Europe clear leadership.

In his attempt to break down Cold War divisions, de Gaulle tried to extend French influence in the Third World. By his diplomatic recognition of communist China in January 1964 (the first western country to do so), his critique of American involvement in Vietnam and his assertion in 1967–8 that the French nuclear force was multi-directional and not necessarily pointed at the Soviet Union, de Gaulle set out to increase French prestige with the non-aligned movement in Africa, Asia and Latin America. This determination to pursue an independent line, which he hoped would carve out a special role for France as a leader of the Third World, also led him to seek a closer alliance with the Arab world, condemning Israel after the Six-Day Arab–Israeli War in June 1967. Likewise it was the motivation behind his support for Quebec separatism, voiced, much to the annoyance of Britain and America, during an official visit to Canada in July 1967.

How successful was de Gaulle's foreign policy? In the short term it was a failure. Despite de Gaulle's efforts the Cold War continued to be the defining factor in international relations, a fact cruelly underlined when the Soviet Union invaded Czechoslovakia in August 1968 to crush a reformist communist government. Yet, in the longer term it can be seen as prophetic, anticipating the end of the Cold War and the emergence of a multi-polar world. Significantly too in any assessment of de Gaullist foreign policy it is vital to remember that in large part it was for domestic consumption. His policy, above all his strident anti-Americanism, won huge support at home, particularly on the left. In this way it created a popular consensus and served to legitimise the Fifth Republic.

Economic and social change

As we saw in the last chapter, the Fourth Republic laid the basis for economic renewal which de Gaulle would then benefit from. Nevertheless, ever sensitive to symbolism, de Gaulle immediately introduced a programme of ambitious reforms in 1958. These reforms would underline the extent to which the Fifth Republic was a new beginning. Furthermore, by producing a strong economy and instilling a new determination and new self-confidence, these reforms would be a statement about national indepen- dence.

The brainchild of Jacques Rueff, one of France's leading economic experts, and Antoine Pinay, minister of finance, the most dramatic innovation of the Rueff–Pinay plan was the creation of the new franc, equivalent to 100 old francs. This new franc was then devalued by 17.5 per cent whilst taxation was increased, government expenditure reduced and restrictions on trade removed. The overall effect of these reforms not only made exports very competitive – foreign trade increased by 10.8 per cent between 1959 and 1974 – but also reduced the budget deficit and inflation. Together with entry to the EEC, they sustained the growth of the economy and between 1958 and 1970 exports to Europe increased from 10 per cent to 50 per cent of total exports. In turn real wages rose by two and a half times between 1954 and 1968, producing a consumer-led boom as spending on cars, electrical goods, household appliances, as well as leisure time in general, took off dramatically. Between 1959 and 1973 household expenditure rose at an average rate of 4.5 per cent, whilst during the 1960s the numbers owning a car doubled to 60 per cent of the total population.

The Gaullist revolution was based upon a belief in science and progress. Modernisation and growth were the mantras of the new technical society as France, in de Gaulle's famous phrase, at last married the twentieth century. This explains why de Gaulle attached so much importance to the announcement on 29 November 1962 of the development of Concorde, a supersonic passenger jet to be jointly built by Britain and France, the symbol *par excellence* of the brave new France. In the same way this explains why de Gaulle put so much emphasis on the development of nuclear energy (the first nuclear plant was constructed in 1967) and an independent nuclear deterrent. Gaullist economic policy also actively encouraged the merger of firms. This stemmed from the conviction that larger enterprises could be run more efficiently, thereby making France a world force in the global economy. Moreover, modern management techniques would not only rescue older industries, such as shipbuilding, but also create competitive busi- nesses in the most advanced sectors such as computers, aeronautics and space. Specific measures were introduced in August 1967 to speed up company concentration and between 1966 and 1972 an annual average of 136 com- panies merged. In part too this surge in merg- ers was a reflection of greater investment in private industry, itself fostered by the state through a lowering of indirect taxation and the encouraging of saving. Throughout the 1960s the state worked in close partnership with major financial institutions, such as Suez and Rothschild, to release the funds necessary to finance take-over and investment programmes.

hypermarkets

The growth of car ownership combined with rapid urbanisation transformed everyday lifestyles. Increasingly people did their shopping in supermarkets and hypermarkets. The first Carrefour hypermarket was opened in 1963 at Sainte Genèvieve-des-Bois, a southern suburb of Paris. By 1969 there were 253 Carrefour hypermarkets in the Paris suburbs.

What impact did the Gaullist revolution have upon society? In large part it intensified trends that we have already noted in the last chapter. Agricultural employment continued to decline, principally in the east, the south-east, Normandy and Brittany, whilst the tertiary sectors and the new industries continued to grow. Indeed these imbalances became so striking that in 1963 the government created the *Délégation à l'aménagement du térritoire et à l'action regionale* (DATAR) whose task was to renew declining regions and share out growth. There was also increased immigration not only from Spain and Portugal but from North and West Africa. Similarly, many more women had been drawn into employment. Immigrants and women were increasingly prominent in semi-skilled jobs, such as the car industry, where work was characterised by the routine of the assembly line. Indeed by 1968 immigrants accounted for 14 per cent and women 25 per cent of semi-skilled workers. Furthermore, many of the new industries, oils, electronics and space technology, were concentrated in ever larger firms where unions had little or no influence. During the 1960s the influence of the CGT declined dramatically, to such an extent that by 1968 only 25 per cent of the workforce were union members.

However, impressive as the Gaullist economic revolution was, many began to feel a sense of alienation from this new technological society. Increasingly the new France was seen as a soulless entity that had sacrificed quality of life for economic growth. There was also a feeling that the Gaullist revolution had produced a society that was bureaucratic, over-centralised and inflexible. In 1970 the French sociologist Michel Crozier talked about how France had become a 'blocked society'. On the one hand, he argued, France had undergone an unprecedented economic transformation since 1945, becoming a modern industrial power. Yet, when it came to societal attitudes, Crozier maintained, France was still stuck in the early nineteenth century. At work, in schools and universities, in the family, in respect to male–female relations, and finally in terms of de Gaulle's style of government – from top to bottom society was still characterised by authoritarian power structures. It was what the political activist and commentator Régis Debray was to call the 'two-speed society', with the economy in high gear and society in low gear. These contradictions were to provoke the student rebellion of May 1968.

The roots of May 1968

In 1965 Jean-Luc Godard's film *Alphaville* conjured up a nightmarish vision of a remote and uncaring society dominated by computers. Two years later he released *La Chinoise*, a story of young people in Paris inspired by Chinese communism. Retrospectively both films can be seen as prophetic, militant critiques of Gaullist society that anticipated the events of May 1968. Yet, at the time the scale and anger of the student rebellion, which quickly triggered off the largest strike in French history and seemingly brought France to the brink of revolution, were wholly unexpected. What then were the roots of the student revolt?

The social roots were to be found in the huge post-war demographic explosion. Between 1946 and 1968 the French population increased from 40.5 million to 49.7 million. During the 1960s these so-called baby boomers came of age and entered higher education and the world of work, and many of them came to believe that they were being held back by an authoritarian mentality, symbolised above all by de Gaulle. This meant that the generational divide of May 1968 was very strong and nowhere was this tension more apparent than in the realm of higher education. By the 1960s the student population was 10 times larger than that in the late 1930s. In the academic year 1967–68 there were 605,000 students in higher education and this massive expansion of numbers, designed to produce an educated and technical workforce for Gaullist revolution, had not been matched by increased funding. Students were confronted with overcrowded classes, a lack of access to lecturers and an unresponsive administration and this dearth of resources created a mood of anger and disaffection, fertile ground for extreme-left groups such as Alain Krivine's *Jeunesse communiste révolutionnaire* (JCR). Further, they were increasingly irritated by what they saw as the petty restrictions of university life, notably the segregation of the sexes into different dormitories. For the *Union nationale des étudiants de France* (UNEF) such bureaucracy typified the paternalism of Gaullist society and in February 1968 it organised a series of protests over the segregation issue. The combination of poor facilities and stifling administration was particularly self-evident at Nanterre, one of the new universities opened in 1963 in the Paris suburbs to relieve the overcrowded Sorbonne. Built in the middle of an immense slum (*bidonville*) where Algerian immigrants lived in appalling conditions, Nanterre was made into something of a student ghetto by poor train and bus services which cut it off from central Paris. The campus was hideous and by 1968 there was still no library building, thereby forcing students to commute to the Latin Quarter. Given these conditions it was not surprising that Nanterre became the centre of rebellion in the May events.

la nouvelle vague

This was the phrase used to describe a generation of young film-makers in the late 1950s, notably François Truffaut, Jean-Luc Godard, Claude Chabrol, Jacques Rivette and Eric Rohmer. Characterised by low budgets and small crews, many of the films had a documentary look. Inspired by Hollywood directors such as Hitchcock and Hawks, much *nouvelle vague* work was to focus upon questions of modernisation and France's ambiguous relationship with America and Americanisation.

les yé-yés

During the 1950 and 1960s the concept of the teenager, that is adolescents with their own fashions, habits and music, emerged within the western world. In France *Salut les Copains*, a radio show launched in 1959 and which broadcast British and American music, inspired the 18-year-old Françoise Hardy to record *Tous les garçons et les filles* in April 1962. By mid-1963 it had sold over 2 million copies, making Hardy the figurehead of the *yé-yé* phenomenon. Undoubtedly pop culture became a way of challenging established norms. Serge Gainsbourg in particular was to use music to test the boundaries of society. The explicit sexual references in his 1969 duet with Jane Birkin, *Je t'aime et moi non plus*, led it to be banned in 20 countries.

The political roots of the student movement are to be found in opposition to the Algerian War. As we have already seen, on 5 September 1960 18 French people went on trial accused of aiding the FLN. The muted response of the PCF led the UNEF to organise a demonstration in solidarity with the accused in Paris on 27 October. Despite PCF attempts to sabotage the UNEF initiative, the demonstration still went ahead, attracting some 20,000 people. The longer-term significance of 27 October 1960 was that it broke the PCF's monopoly of action on the left. By situating itself to the left of the PCF, which was accused of playing electoral politics, the UNEF anticipated much of May 1968, establishing a tradition of direct action which would be at the heart of the student revolt. In the intervening years, although membership did decline (in 1962 the UNEF mobilised 100,000 out of 220,000 students as opposed to a mere 45,000 out of 500,000 in 1968), the UNEF did remain very important at the level of ideas. Here the UNEF was very much influenced by the new left that arose in the wake of Soviet intervention in Hungary in November 1956. Disenchanted by the way in which the PCF had supported the invasion of Hungary, many members, such as Gerard Spitzer, left the party and began to explore revolutionary alternatives to Stalinism. Some looked to Algeria as the beginning of a general Third World revolution; some to communist China, which had split with the Soviet Union; some to the Italian Communist Party, which seemed less dogmatic than the PCF; whilst others looked to new political groupings such as the PSU and the **Situationists**. Undoubtedly the impact of these ideas explains the strong anti-Stalinist dimension of May 1968. Like de Gaulle, the PCF was seen by many of the younger generation as outdated and authoritarian.

The Gaullist revolution was based on a belief in rationalism, science and progress. Since the Enlightenment such assumptions had been deeply embedded within French culture and society, but during the 1960s a number of influential thinkers, notably Michel Foucault, Jacques Derrida and Roland Barthes, began to question these certainties in a fundamental way. Foucault in particular, through his subtle analysis of the relationship between power and the origins of the prison and the mental institution, revealed how these institutions were not about reform or humanitarianism but control. In the same way Herbert Marcuse analysed the new forms of domination that operated through the media and consumer society. Collectively these intellectual currents, opposing as they did all forms of coercion, were to have a powerful influence during May 1968. They were to be evident through such slogans as 'prohibiting is prohibited', 'demand the impossible' and 'all power to the imagination' which encapsulated a rejection of modern capitalist society.

The Situationists

Situationism was a small, but nevertheless highly influential, avant-garde international movement that was founded in 1957. The most prominent situationist writer was Guy Debord, whose 1967 book, *La Société du spectacle*, was a stinging critique of the new consumer society. Enormously influential in May 1968, the Situationists attacked the way in which the Gaullist economic miracle had produced a world of objects and spectacles that only required passive consumption. Their aim was to reintroduce imagination and creativity into everyday life.

Finally May 1968 cannot be divorced from the international context. The mass media meant that students followed closely the civil rights movement in the USA, the Cultural Revolution in China and, most important of all, the Vietnam War. Indeed the intensification of the war at the beginning of 1968 was to be the immediate trigger for the May events.

The events of May 1968

In Paris on 18 March 1968, bomb attacks were carried out on the offices of the American Express Company in protest at the Vietnam War. When students from Nanterre were arrested on suspicion of involvement, others immediately organised a campaign of support, occupying the university's administrative block on 22 March. The 22 March movement was led by Daniel Cohn-Bendit, a half-German sociology student and activist, and included far-left groups as well as the Vietnam Solidarity Committee. Their overriding aim was to use student discontent to detonate a general revolt in society and further clashes with authorities led the administration to close the campus between 28 March and 1 April. On 3 May all teaching at Nanterre was suspended.

At the Sorbonne in central Paris fears over clashes between left-wing and right-wing students led the authorities to suspend lectures and seminars there too. Police were called to restore order but when they brutally arrested a number of demonstrators they were immediately set upon by the other students. In the confrontation that followed 590 people were arrested and numerous people injured and over the next 10 days this pattern of violence and counter-violence was to become a familiar one as the riot police and students fought out a series of protracted battles. On the night of 10–11 May the students erected barricades and baited the police by hurling stones and Molotov cock-tails. In response the police resorted to baton charges and the use of water cannon, tactics which were seen to be increasingly heavy-handed. Television scenes of the riot police lashing out indiscriminately provoked a wave of sympathy for the students across France. Such brutality was seen to symbolise the authoritarianism of the Gaullist state and the trade unions called a general strike. On 13 May, the tenth anniversary of the Algiers rebellion that had brought de Gaulle to power, more than 750,000 workers and students marched through Paris.

13 May sparked off a dramatic widening of the protest movement. Workers, especially the young and unskilled, felt threatened by unemployment as the downturn of 1967 had pushed those out of work up to 500,000, a figure unprecedented since 1945. Moreover, there were the explosive issues of pay and conditions. Unlike the *cadres* the working class felt that they had been excluded from the French economic miracle and denied their fair share of increased prosperity. Moreover, they felt powerless within the workplace. Angry at the CGT, which for many workers had become part of the system and was afraid of standing up to the employers, they wanted more control and partici-pation. Many from the professional classes too joined in the protests. Journalists, for example, denounced state control of the media and went on strike. As the strike move-ment spread, the CGT and the PCF adopted a hostile stance. Fearful of losing control of the situation, the PCF did everything it could to prevent the workers from mixing with

Figure 10.1   Underground student poster, May 1968

the student movement, denouncing the latter as 'counterfeit revolutionaries'. In response Cohn-Bendit attacked the PCF as counter-revolutionary 'Stalinist filth'.

In the face of the revolt the government wavered. In an effort to defuse the situation Pompidou made conciliatory gestures and reopened the Sorbonne. In contrast de Gaulle seemed to favour a hardline response and on 11 May even considered sending in the army before departing for a state visit to Romania on 14 May. He returned on 18 May, and on 24 May he made a television broadcast in which he promised a referendum on the issue of participation in universities and industry for 13 June. It was a failure and there was widespread rioting. Pompidou meanwhile saw the need to do more to meet the workers' demands and he, along with the employment minister Jacques Chirac, now moved quickly to bring union and employer representatives together at the ministry of labour, rue de Grenelle. However, the resulting Grenelle agreements of 27 May did little to calm workers' anger. Demands for greater worker participation were dropped and when the CGT general secretary, Georges Séguy, announced to Renault car workers at Billancourt an immediate pay rise of 7 per cent, to be followed by 3 per cent in October, he was shouted down.

France seemed more polarised than ever and with de Gaulle seemingly losing control Mitterrand called a press conference on 28 May to announce that he and Mendès-France were ready to form an interim government. The PCF declared too that it would support the creation of 'popular government of democratic union'. Now Pompidou, fearing a PCF rising, put the armed forces on standby, at which point de Gaulle cancelled a cabinet meeting and disappeared. It was thought that he and his wife had gone to their country home at Colombey-les-Deux-Eglises, but in fact he had been to visit the commander-in-chief of French forces in Germany, General Massu. Assured of army support de Gaulle recovered his nerve and when he returned to France on 30 May he immediately appeared on television. Conjuring up the spectre of communist revolution he presented people with a stark choice: him or chaos. He then dissolved the National Assembly and ordered fresh elections. The right-wing backlash had begun and more than 500,000 marched through Paris to express their support for de Gaulle. With no alternative to the General, the revamped Gaullist party, now called *Union pour la défense de la république* (UDR), secured an overwhelming electoral victory on 23 and 30 June, winning 358 seats out of 485. The political atmosphere had changed dramatically and in this new context the strikers drifted back to work. By this point the extreme left was hopelessly isolated.

What were the consequences of May 1968? In the short term de Gaulle seemed more firmly entrenched than ever. Irked at the way Pompidou had handled the crisis, de Gaulle dismissed the prime minister and replaced him with Couve de Murville. He then pressed ahead with far-reaching reforms of the universities and renewed attempts at finding a 'third way' between capitalism and communism through greater worker participation in the workplace. Yet it soon became apparent that de Gaulle's authority had been fatally undermined by the student revolt. On the one hand, Pompidou had clearly established himself as a dependable successor. Thus conservatives were no longer perturbed about how the regime would survive de Gaulle. On the other hand, some of the personal legitimacy had gone forever. De Gaulle himself sensed this and when he called a referendum in April 1969, ostensibly on the issues of regional devolution and a reduction in the powers of the senate, no one was in any doubt that this was a vote of confidence. In the campaign de Gaulle was opposed not just by the left but by also significant members of the conservative majority, notably Valéry Giscard d'Estaing, who, still angered at his dismissal from the finance ministry in 1966, urged a 'no' vote late in the day. On 27 April 1969 de Gaulle's proposals were rejected by 53 per cent of French voters. He immediately resigned and returned to his private life. Eighteen months later he died, on 9 November 1970. Ever sensitive to symbolism, de Gaulle ensured that he was absent from France on both 18 June 1969 and 18 June 1970.

Was May 1968 a failed revolution? To a large extent this question misses the point. Many of the supporters of the student revolt were deeply suspicious of political power and political parties. As such they did not want to carry out an orthodox revolution and overthrow the regime. In a broader sense their aim was to change societal attitudes towards women, the family and the environment through grassroots activism. Moving away from political parties they conceived of themselves as liberation movements. This is perhaps most clearly illustrated by the emergence of gay activism in the wake of May 1968. Now a number of militant 'homosexual liberation groups' took up the cause of gay and lesbian rights. Mirroring developments in Britain and America, they celebrated an openly gay culture and in turn this was to have a lasting impact upon mainstream politics. In 1981 the first Mitterrand government reduced the age of consent to 15.

Topics
FOR DISCUSSION

1 How did de Gaulle eventually resolve the Algerian War? Why did his policy provoke so much opposition from the army and the settlers?
2 What was the nature of the Fifth Republic Constitution? Why did he introduce further changes in 1962?
3 What was de Gaulle's foreign policy?
4 What impact did Gaullist economic policy have upon society?
5 What were the origins of May 1968? How does Figure 10.1 help us to understand these origins? How did de Gaulle deal with the May crisis? What were the consequences of May 1968?

CHAPTER 11

After de Gaulle: Pompidou, 1969–74 and Giscard, 1974–81

Timeline

1969
June   Pompidou elected president

1970
9 November   Death of de Gaulle

1971
April   Manifeste des 343 in Le Nouvel Observateur in favour of legalising abortion
June   Re-unification of the socialist movement at Congrès d'Épinay

1972
June   PS and PCF sign up to a common programme
July   Chaban is sacked by Pompidou

1973
October   Huge oil price rise with grave consequences for the economy

1974
2 April   Pompidou dies
May   Valéry Giscard d'Estaing wins presidential elections
June   Jacques Chirac becomes prime minister

1975
17 January   Veil law legalises abortion
June   Law allowing divorce by consent

1976
August   Raymond Barre becomes prime minister
December   Creation of the Gaullist RPR

1977
September   PS/PCF union breaks down

Could Gaullism survive without de Gaulle? Would the institutions and the spirit of the Fifth Republic be eroded once its charismatic architect had left the political stage? The half-failure of the 1967 elections, the turmoil of May 1968 and the weariness expressed in April 1969 meant that the right had to find a way to reconcile the Gaullist legacy with new aspirations. This was made all the more urgent by the growing strength of the left under a rejuvenated Socialist Party, the rise of new social demands, such as feminism and regionalism, and the deepening of the economic crisis which put an end to the *trente glorieuses* after the 1973 oil crisis. The presidencies of Georges Pompidou (1969–74) and Valéry Giscard d'Estaing (1974–81) revealed the difficulties in reconciling a desire for reforms with a natural conservative instinct. They also illustrated the progressive erosion of traditional Gaullism, the rise of new political forces on the left and the growing polarisation of French political life. However, both

1978
February   UDF established
March   Right wins elections

1979
July   Second oil crisis

1981
May   François Mitterrand
wins presidential election

presidencies confirmed the Gaullist interpretation of the constitution and ensured that
the president remained its cornerstone.

From Gaullism to conservatism? France under Pompidou

The outcome of the 1969 presidential elections was fairly predictable. For the majority, Pompidou appeared to be de Gaulle's natural heir. Despite this, Pompidou's electoral strategy ensured that he did not become the prisoner of traditional Gaullist circles. For instance, he won the support of the moderate right, having promised to relaunch the European construction, a marked departure from Gaullist policy. His only credible opponent was the centrist president of the Senate, Alain Poher. As caretaker president since de Gaulle's departure, he had no other programme than the defence of parliamentary prerogatives against the presidentialisation of the regime. His popularity quickly floundered and with it, the hope of the centre playing a political role. In the aftermath of May 1968, the left was so divided and indecisive that none of its four candidates was able to secure enough votes to reach the second round of the presidential elections, despite the respectable score of Duclos, the communist candidate (21.5 per cent). The final battle was between two right-wing candidates, Pompidou (44.5 per cent) and Poher (23.5 per cent). The fact that together they had secured 68 per cent of the votes clearly demonstrated the disarray of the left. Refusing to choose between the 'plague and cholera' (Duclos), a large proportion of left-wing voters did not turn out (the abstention rate was 31.5 per cent) and predictably, in the second round, Pompidou secured an easy victory with 57.6 per cent.

The new president chose Jacques Chaban-Delmas as prime minister. Former resister, mayor of Bordeaux since the Liberation, president of the National Assembly since 1958, Chaban-Delmas seemed to have sufficient political credentials to reassure traditional Gaullists and enough parliamentary skills to rally the moderate right and the centre around the Gaullist party (UDR). The appointment of personal advisers, such as Pierre Nora, close to Mendès-France or Jacques Delors, a Christian trade-unionist, showed Chaban's willingness to reform and modernise French society and listen to ideas developed beyond the limits of the right. The liberal and proactive programme of government he presented to the National Assembly in September 1969 described France as *une société bloquée*, weakened by vested interests and the archaism of its social structures, such as its education system. France suffered from inefficient state intervention and irrational centralisation, both of which stifled its economic dynamism. Chaban proposed the creation of a 'new society' which would turn France into a modern and powerful industrial nation and would reconcile freedom with generosity. At the heart of his project was the promotion of new contractual relations between socio-economic actors and the state. It was argued that unilateral decisions taken at the top by an arrogant bureaucracy only favoured confrontation and resignation. Instead, private companies, public services, central and local administrations should nurture a culture of dialogue in order to become more dynamic, competitive and responsive to changes and to ensure that the resulting economic gains would be fairly distributed. The relative relaxation of state control over television, the tentative reform of higher education, the greater autonomy given to public companies (SNCF, EDF-GDF), the contracts negotiated between employers and trade unions for the development of professional training, the creation of a minimum wage indexed on economic growth (*salaire minimum indexé sur la croissance*, or SMIC), the replacement of weekly wages by monthly wages for a large number of workers and the improvement of social security benefits, all demonstrated Chaban's desire to find innovative social solutions. No less important were the initiatives aimed at strengthening the French economy and modernising its industrial potential. The pragmatic devaluation of the French franc (12.5 per cent) in July 1969, which had been rejected by de Gaulle on the ground of national prestige, boosted French exports. Measures were taken to reinforce industrial concentration in key sectors to improve the strength of French companies in the international market. The state also supported the launch of major industrial and technological projects, such as Airbus, symbols of industrial dynamism and modernity.

President Pompidou did not welcome Chaban's initiatives. First, Chaban had presented his programme to the National Assembly without consulting the president. Defending a strict Gaullist interpretation of the Fifth Republic, Pompidou reminded Chaban that it was the president, not the prime minister, who defined the general orientations of the government. The prime minister was only the executor of the president's will and his main task was to coordinate the government's policies. Even without de Gaulle's charisma, any president had enough constitutional prerogatives to dominate the executive. This was the unwritten logic of the Fifth Republic and Pompidou was quick to reassert it. Secondly, the president did not entirely agree with Chaban's progressive policies, mainly for electoral reasons, thinking that they might alienate his conservative supporters. His personal advisers (Pierre Juillet and Marie-France Garaud) mounted a corrosive campaign against the prime minister and accused him of betraying de Gaulle's legacy, displaying too much sympathy for social democracy, encouraging the development of dangerous social demands (feminism, regionalism, **autogestion**) and lacking the necessary political skills to prevent the rejuvenation of the left. In particular, they thought that the decisions made by his government to curb extreme-left violence were not tough enough to eradicate the culture of protest

> ### *autogestion* (self-management) and the Lip *affaire*
>
> In 1973 watchmaking workers from Lip in Besançon rejected the closure of their company and illegally but successfully took over its management and restarted production. '*On fabrique, on vend, on se paye.*' Police attempts to quell this experiment in *autogestion* failed, partly due to massive public support, and in January 1974 negotiations began between employers and trade unions to inject new capital into the company. By 1976 more than 600,000 watches had been produced annually. In the aftermath of 1968, the Lip affair demonstrated that alternatives to capitalist management could be successful and this raised fears among the conservative elite.

fostered by May 1968. This last criticism was unfair since *la loi anticasseurs* (1970), which increased police and judicial powers against 'troublemakers', notably Maoist groups, was wholeheartedly backed by the prime minister. However, Chaban's massive support in the National Assembly was not enough to protect him against a president who intended to show that the prime minister was responsible first to him. In July 1972 Chaban was sacked and Pierre Messmer, an orthodox Gaullist, became Pompidou's docile prime minister. His major task was to prepare the 1973 general elections and to rally the right against the new-found dynamism of the left.

In the early 1970s two major events helped the left to regain the dynamism and credibility it had lost after May 1968. In June 1971, at the Epinay congress, François Mitterrand federated under his leadership a variety of clubs and socialist factions, giving birth to a new Socialist Party. He had two clear objectives: firstly to turn the Socialist Party (PS) into an electoral machine which could match the strength of the Communist Party (PCF); secondly to achieve the union of the left, a necessary prerequisite to overcome the right's electoral potency. In June 1972, after taxing and lengthy negotiations, the PS and the PCF presented a Common programme of government, which included, among other things, the nationalisation of major industries, the abolition of private education and the reduction of presidential prerogatives (emergency powers under Article 16 would be abolished, the use of referendum would be curtailed and the presidential term of office would be reduced to 5 years). A common electoral strategy was also designed. In the second ballot, only one candidate would represent the left-wing forces. This radical strategy compelled the political centre to join forces with conservatives. Their anti-communism was far stronger than their distaste for Gaullist lack of respect for parliamentary prerogatives. By doing so, the Centrists condemned themselves to be absorbed by the right and to lose part of their distinctive appeal. As for the Gaullists, their electoral programme insisted on law and order, personal morality and state voluntarism. If Chaban had thought that the art of government rested on consensus building, negotiations and reforms, Pompidou believed that 'to govern was to constrain'. The electoral results comforted the right (268 seats out of 490) and confirmed the dominance of the Gaullists (183 seats). They also demonstrated that the PS (89 seats) had become a force to be reckoned with. The PCF (73 seats) did not seem to have benefited from the 'Common programme' and started to wonder whether it was a sound strategy.

On the domestic front, the right-wing victory allowed the president to pursue conservative policies, which gave rise to considerable protest. Anti-militarist, regionalist and environmentalist groups staged demonstrations against conscription and the use of the Larzac plateau, a region of unspoilt beauty, as a military training camp. Clashes between students and the police were often violent, giving the impression that the issues brought to the fore in May 1968 had not yet been solved. The 1973 oil crisis put an end to the *trente glorieuses* and triggered further social protests. The president's popularity collapsed and his foreign policy did not help to revive his credentials in the way he would have wished.

Pompidou's foreign policy followed de Gaulle's track. Strengthening of the French nuclear deterrent was seen as essential in maintaining a privileged and independent position between the two superpowers. However, Pompidou was more proactive than de Gaulle on European issues and lifted the veto against the accession of the United Kingdom to the EEC. To regain some prestige, he organised a referendum on the enlargement of the EEC to include the UK, Ireland and Denmark in 1972. Although 68 per cent approved the inclusion of these new countries, the question did not interest voters and 40 per cent of the electorate abstained. Pompidou thus failed to turn this referendum into a personal plebiscite. From 1973, the leukaemia from which he suffered prevented him from giving new impetus to his conservative rule. His sudden death on 2 April 1974 dramatically ended his 5-year rule.

La petite alternance under Giscard

Unlike in 1969, the 1974 presidential elections saw unity on the left and division on the right. The 'Common programme' defined in 1972 meant that Mitterrand had the support of the communists and other small left-wing parties as well as the backing of major trade unions. He became the 'common candidate' of the left. The right presented two credible candidates. Less than 48 hours after Pompidou's death, Chaban announced that he was to be the Gaullist candidate. This hasty political move appeared distasteful to many. A few days later, Valéry Giscard d'Estaing also put his name forward. Giscard came from a small right-wing family – *les républicains indépendants* – which through the 1960s had lived under the shadow of the Gaullist party. Giscard represented the liberal right and called on people to vote against de Gaulle's referendum in 1969 in the name of a 'more liberal orientation of political institutions'. *Énarque* and *polytechnicien*, he was first appointed minister of finance at the age of 36 and occupied this post for 9 years (1962–6 and 1969–74). The Gaullist party had been in power for 16 years. If Mitterrand and his communist allies represented a radical alternative, Giscard portrayed his candidacy as a 'change without risk'. Furthermore, Jacques Chirac, the 42-year-old Gaullist interior minister, prompted by Pompidou's advisers who disliked Chaban's progressive ideas, led a rebellion against the ex-prime minister. Forty-three prominent Gaullists exhorted people to vote for Giscard against the candidate of their own party. Chaban's campaign soon collapsed, leaving Mitterrand to face Giscard. The latter won the second ballot with a slim majority (50.8 per cent). For the first time since 1958, the president was not to be a Gaullist, but a liberal. He appointed Chirac as prime minister. A younger generation of political leaders, who had taken no part in the Resistance, emerged. Giscard declared that his presidency would modernise and reju-venate French politics. One of his first decisions was to reduce the voting age from 21 to 18.

Giscard's aim was to turn France into an 'advanced liberal society'. Firstly, he deplored the pervasive culture of conflict and sterile opposition which had for too long characterised French political and social life and wished to promote a pluralist and tolerant conception of democracy. The direct and often dogmatic clashes between an arrogant majority and an unreasonable opposition should give way to a more measured and reasonable debate about the definition of the common good. In

Démocratie française (1976) he defined the *décrispation* of French political life as 'an essential dimension of the modernisation of our democracy'. The search for consensus between rival political elites was intended not to sanitise political life, but to ensure that all reasonable political options were openly debated and properly selected. With this perspective in mind, Giscard strengthened the opposition's powers. He made it easier for the opposition to invoke the Constitutional Council in order to check whether a law conformed to the constitution. Other institutional reforms gave parliament more powers to scrutinise government activities, notably the right of the opposition to ask the government direct questions without prior notice. State control over broadcasting was greatly relaxed, the time allocated to opposition leaders was substantially increased and the government promised not to interfere with the content of television programmes. However, no attempt was made to authorise private broadcasting.

Second, Giscard was less inclined to defend a *dirigiste* economy than the previous Gaullist presidents had been. Although he recognised the shortcomings of *laissez-faire* and the past success of a *dirigiste* strategy, he thought that competition, innovation and risk-taking should be encouraged and rewarded because they formed the basis of economic expansion. Without regulations, however, market forces could have destructive effects. For Giscard, such forces should be channelled, for their dynamism could not be an end in itself and the common good could not be reduced to economic self-satisfaction. He was thus keen to promote a social market economy.

Third, the new president was opposed to the uniformity of mass culture and the dehumanising effects of collectivism. He claimed that the government should strive to enhance *l'épanouissement personnel*, to give each individual the freedom to fulfil his or her own objectives. For instance, efforts to increase the prestige of vocational training and the introduction of the comprehensive principle in secondary education (*loi Haby*, 1975) were supposed to give better educational opportunities to all children, regardless of their social origin.

The first 2 years of his presidency witnessed the introduction of significant social reforms. Yet the domestic and international contexts were not particularly amenable to the implementation of his liberal ideas. Political opponents usually rejected *la décrispation*. Giscard's presidency, in fact, was marked by increased polarisation between left and right and more damagingly by growing tensions between the liberal and Gaullist factions. Likewise, the international economic crisis fortified rather than undermined *dirigisme*.

Liberal reforms and their limits

May 1968 had revealed new social values which questioned the ways in which identities were constructed and gave greater priority to issues related to quality of life, rather than material satisfaction. Gender and regional identity as well as the quality of the environment became salient issues. Giscard's reforms tried to address these issues. For instance, he liked to present himself as the first president who really made an effort to improve women's rights. The creation in 1974 of a ministry for women illustrated this effort. Giscard's liberal approach was primarily concerned with formal equality between men and women, reflected, for instance, in the attempt to make equal pay a legal requirement or to encourage a greater involvement of women in local politics. However, these policies appeared patronising and trivial to many feminists. The *Mouvement de libération des femmes*, founded in 1970, cultivated more radical views and linked women's oppression to the logic of capitalism or to the prevalent patriarchal culture which kept women in a state of social, psychological and sexual subordination. In this context, abortion became a central issue. In 1971, 343 women, including the actress Catherine Deneuve and writers such as Simone de Beauvoir and Marguerite Duras, signed what became known as *le Manifeste des 343 salopes*, all admitting to having had an abortion. They asked for the abrogation of the law which made abortion illegal and called for free access to all means of contraception. In 1974, Simone Veil, Giscard's health minister, presented a law to parliament which authorised abortion in the first 10 weeks of pregnancy. Doctors, on moral grounds, could refuse the operation and the patient had to bear all the costs. Feminist movements criticised the law for its lack of radicalism and pointed out that financial costs would force poorer women to opt for lurid and unhealthy back-street solutions. Of the 314 deputies in the right-wing majority, 215 voted against the law, some hurling insults at Veil during parliamentary debates. The law was only passed with the support of the left. Other similar issues pitted the president against his own majority, such as a new divorce law (1975) which made it possible for couples to end their marriage by mutual consent rather than having to bring to court, as previously required, evidence of their spouse's misconduct or infidelity.

Giscard's concerns for quality of life were also reflected in his interests in environmental protection. His policies were in sharp contrast with Pompidou's love for motorways and skyscrapers. The development of mass tourism, encouraged by previous Gaullist governments, had already turned part of the Mediterranean coast and the Alpine ski resorts into an architectural disaster. Areas of natural beauty were submerged in brutal and impersonal buildings which did not use local materials or respect local styles. Under Giscard, a series of laws were passed to protect France's 'natural heritage', to preserve green spaces and coastlines from unscrupulous development schemes and to promote the creation of national parks. Giscard's conservationist policy, however, had its own limits. Giscard was determined to equip France with a network of nuclear power plants to reduce national dependence on expensive oil imports. Objections put forward by conservation groups were brushed aside with contempt. The full authority of the state, including the use of the police force, was employed to impose the presidential will against anti-nuclear protesters. Consultation with local groups was mainly ignored. Administrative and judicial procedures, which were normally required for such development, were often by-passed and this frequently resulted in violence, as was the case in **Plogoff**, Brittany.

The real or perceived arrogance of central authorities fortified the cause of regionalist movements. If Giscard was interested in regionalism, it was mainly to

Plogoff

Symbol of anti-nuclear resistance. The decision to build a nuclear plant in Plogoff, Brittany, as part of France's strategy to reduce its dependence on oil imports for energy production, met with the fierce resistance of the local population, supported by green, regionalist and radical activists. The legal consultation process, conducted after the deployment of police and army forces, turned into a farce and revealed the government's determination to pursue its plans, regardless of public opposition. From February 1980 violent clashes erupted, daily marches were held, often led by local women, mass demonstrations were organised, bomb attacks on public buildings were carried out. Faced with massive opposition, the government delayed its final decision, which was finally abandoned by the incoming socialist government in 1981.

improve the efficiency of local economic activities and their harmonious development throughout the territory. Although he was not opposed to the protection of regional cultures, he rejected unambiguously any form of political regionalism. Regions such as Corsica and Brittany, which had a distinctive culture but also suffered from economic underdevelopment, witnessed a surge in regionalist agitation. Some Bretons, for instance, argued that their region had become a French internal colony, whose cultural identity was constantly being denigrated as archaic by the Parisian elite and whose economic interests were never taken seriously. In Corsica strikes, demonstrations and sometimes terrorist acts gave regionalist demands increased visibility. The government made some concessions. Major industrial plants were transferred to Brittany (Thompson-CSF in Brest, Alcatel in Rennes). In Corsica, local transport was improved, the *loi Dexonne* gave a legal status to the Corsican language and two new Corsican *départements* were created to improve the island's political representation. No concession, however, was made to the idea of political autonomy.

Economic crisis and political polarisation

Giscard's liberal reforms were not readily accepted by the most conservative elements on the right. Their introduction also coincided with the most important international economic crisis since the end of the war. An upsurge in unemployment (900,000 in 1975), coupled with reduced growth (4.3 per cent in 1975 compared with 6 per cent in 1973) and high inflation (11.7 per cent in 1975) led to social discontent and a strong mobilisation of left-wing opposition. Gaullists had nothing to gain from being associated too closely with a liberal president trapped in a socio-economic crisis. Prime Minister Chirac resigned in 1976 and was replaced by Raymond Barre, a top civil servant and a professor of economics, chosen for his expertise, rather than his political skills. Rejecting the stop–go policies pursued by Chirac, Barre chose economic austerity. The *Plan Barre* (1976–80) first aimed at ending the deficit and curbing inflation. Money supply was reduced, indirect and income taxes were increased, prices were frozen for 3 months, constraints were introduced to limit pay rises, except for lower wages. Barre also tried to restore France's trade and to encourage growth, a necessary prerequisite for reducing unemployment. To increase competitiveness, especially in small and medium industries, aid for export investments and subsidised loans were introduced. Special incentives were given to companies involved in new technologies (nuclear energy, telecommunications, computing, bio-industries). French industry was encouraged to cooperate or merge with foreign companies, questioning the Gaullist ambition to promote 'national champions'. The second oil crisis in 1979 severely limited the impact of these vigorous but unpopular policies and put an end to the attempt to introduce more *laissez-faire* measures. If growth rates remained at a respectable level (3 per cent) and exports substantially increased, the inflation rate reached 13.5 per cent and unemployment grew to a critical level (1.5 million) in 1980. The left criticised the government's failure to halt the rise of unemployment and to promote an ambitious social policy to cushion the dramatic effects of the crisis. The Gaullists deplored a liberal policy which sacrificed French autonomy to international markets. Opposed to the 'bureaucratic collectivism' put forward by the left, the Gaullists called for a voluntarist and nationalist economic policy.

Politically, persistent Gaullist criticisms were probably more damaging to Giscard than the frontal opposition of the left. In 1976 Chirac became the president of a revamped Gaullist party, the *Rassemblement pour la république* (RPR), a fantastic electoral machine whose prime objective was to help its leader to win the next presidential election. Although the 'socialist–communist' threat compelled the RPR to support the government, it did so reluctantly and never missed an opportunity to undermine Giscard's ambition to become the sole leader of the right. His election as mayor of Paris in 1977 against the president's candidate provided Chirac with a prodigious platform to articulate his ideas and voice his criticisms. It became crucial for Giscard to create a party which could balance the influence of the RPR. In February 1978, the *Union pour la démocratie française* (UDF), a cartel of liberal and centrist parties, became the 'party of the president', ready to fight the 1978 general elections.

On the left, the *Union de la gauche* had created a positive electoral dynamism for the opposition. However, the PCF realised that the union mainly benefited the PS, which had become the dominant party of the left under Mitterrand's leadership. The PCF's leader, Georges Marchais, thought that voters could be wooed back if the party defended a more radical stance. Marchais put forward an economic programme proposing the nationalisation of a large number of banks and industries, which would be largely placed under trade unionists' control. The PS rejected what seemed an electorally and economically irresponsible programme, and it was accused by the PCF of right-wing deviation. The *Union* collapsed in September 1977. However, the left appeared radical enough to press Giscard into warning the nation against the dangers of a left-wing victory and its potentially fatal effects on France's economic dynamism and international standing. Giscard dramatised the issue when he confessed that the constitution did not give him enough power to prevent the implementation of such a programme if the left won the elections, a possibility which was supported by numerous opinion polls. Thus, despite tensions in each camp, two distinctive visions of France's future were proposed by the left and the right, the left agreeing on a clear rupture with the prevalent policies and the right denouncing the threat of a socialist-communist revolution. The election results confirmed the resilience of the right, the progress of the left and the bi-polarisation of French politics. The UDF (137 deputies) strengthened its ascendancy over the right-wing majority. Although the RPR remained the biggest party (154 deputies), it no longer occupied a dominant position. The PS asserted its leadership on the left (114 deputies) and the PCF increased its number of deputies from 71 to 84. Giscard, with a clear majority and a strong party behind him, had fortified his political position but had by no means put an end to left-wing dynamism or tamed its Gaullist 'allies'.

Foreign policy

When Giscard defined France as a 'medium-size power', he provoked the anger of the Gaullists. The president seemed to have traded off the *politique de grandeur* for an Atlantic and European strategy. The criticisms were partly unjustified, for Giscard's foreign policy maintained the overall objectives defined by de Gaulle. If his subdued style was different from de Gaulle's flamboyant approach, French national independence remained his prime objective. The modernisation of the French nuclear deterrent and the strengthening of conventional forces, a continuous dialogue with the USSR which should have made France the leading power in East–West relations, the belief that the Franco-German alliance should take the lead in the construction of Europe, France's interest in Third World development (*dialogue Nord–Sud*), the tendency to consider Africa as France's private possession or *chasse-gardée* – all these bore the marks of a Gaullist strategy. However, the concept of *sanctuarisation élargie*, which proposed to extend French nuclear defence to NATO's eastern borders, was perceived by orthodox Gaullists as a dangerous Atlantic move, reducing French independence through increased collaboration with NATO. Likewise, Giscard's proactive European policy attracted many criticisms from Gaullist quarters. In December 1979 Chirac, in his *discours de Cochin*, accused Giscard of belonging to '*le parti de l'étranger*', selling out French national sovereignty to a chimerical Europe. In fact, the decisive impetus Giscard gave to the creation of the European Council and the European Monetary System was supposed to allow France to shape Europe to its own convenience and to defend its national interests more efficiently. Giscard's European initiatives strengthened cooperation between nations, but they rarely promoted supra-nationalism, his support for the direct election of a weak European Parliament by European citizens in 1979 being the notable – but inoffensive – exception.

> **sanctuarisation**
>
> Asserting the independence of the French defence policy, the concept of *sanctuarisation* implied a strategy based on defence of French territory by means of a massive nuclear reply to any attack. It showed little solidarity with allies and little interest in destabilising events beyond France's borders. The concept of *sanctuarisation élargie* implied more of a commitment of France's armed forces to the defence of Western Europe, particularly West Germany, but was not implemented before the mid-1980s.

Fin de règne

In 1974 Giscard had invited road-sweepers for breakfast at the Elysée and he often visited ordinary French families to share a simple meal with them. Although these gestures made him look rather condescending, they indicated that he wished to modernise the stiffness of Gaullist protocol. By the end of his term, Giscard had developed a monarchical and haughty style. Making public the directives he issued to the government, he confirmed and reinforced the primacy of the president over the executive. By 1981 public opinion seemed to have forgotten the liberal reforms he had introduced 7 years earlier and was now appalled by a series of scandals, which tarnished the last years of Giscard's term, such as the suspicious death of three ministers in the space of one year. More damagingly, the infamous 'diamonds affair', which revealed that the president had illegally benefited from precious gifts offered by his disreputable African ally 'Emperor Bokassa', developed into a political farce. The second oil crisis in 1979, which had further eroded living standards and worsened unemployment, triggered social discontent. Giscard's efforts to contribute to the *détente* between the two superpowers were not always understood, notably his half-hearted condemnation of the Soviet invasion of Afghanistan on 25 December 1979. The public mood was gloomy. However, Giscard established himself as the most influential leader of the right against Chirac. In the first round of the 1981 presidential elections, he gathered 28.3 per cent of the vote against 18 per cent for Chirac. Yet, this time, the socialist leader Mitterrand managed to capture the imagination of the French, promising to '*changer la vie!*' The second round organised on 10 May saw the victory of Mitterrand (51.75 per cent) over Giscard, who did not receive Chirac's full support. After 23 years of uninterrupted rule, the right lost the Elysée to the left. The new president had consistently opposed de Gaulle and the institutions of the Fifth Republic. The *grande alternance* of 1981 promised to bring radical changes.

Document 11a: La 'nouvelle société'

Comment s'adresser aux Français sans évoquer le rôle que la France peut aspirer à jouer dans le monde? Le général de Gaulle l'a clairement défini: assurer l'indépendance nationale, condition du combat pour la paix du monde et pour la solidarité entre tous les peuples. Mais, il serait illusoire d'affirmer [. . .] une telle continuité pleine d'exigences, si nous ne dotions pas la France, des moyens de réaliser nos raisonnables ambitions. Or, j'affirme qu'aujourd'hui, plus encore qu'hier, l'action internationale de la France ne saurait être efficace si l'évolution de son économie ne lui permettait pas d'accéder au rang de véritable puissance industrielle. Depuis vingt ans passés, de multiples efforts ont été faits dans ce sens. La France industrielle a commencé à devenir une réalité. Mais l'ouverture toujours plus large des frontières, la compétition plus vive qui en découle, nous commandent des changements profonds d'objectifs, de structures, de moyens et même, et peut-être surtout, de mentalité. De cette société bloquée, je retiens trois éléments essentiels au demeurant liés les uns aux autres [. . .]: la fragilité de

continued

notre économie, le fonctionnement souvent défectueux de l'État, enfin l'archaïsme et le conservatisme de nos structures sociales. [. . .] Le renouveau de la France après la Libération, s'il a mobilisé les énergies, a aussi consolidé une vieille tradition colbertiste et jacobine, faisant de l'État une nouvelle providence. Il n'est presque aucune profession, il n'est aucune catégorie sociale qui n'ait, depuis vingt cinq ans, réclamé ou exigé de lui protection, subventions, détaxation ou réglementation. Nous sommes encore un pays de castes. Des écarts excessifs de revenus, une mobilité sociale insuffisante maintiennent des cloisons anachroniques entre les groupes sociaux [. . .]

Les groupes sociaux et les groupes professionnels sont, par rapport à l'étranger, peu organisés et insuffisamment représentés. Ceci ne vise aucune organisation en particulier mais les concerne toutes, qu'il s'agisse des salariés, des agriculteurs, des travailleurs indépendants, des employeurs. Le pourcentage des travailleurs syndiqués est particulièrement faible [. . .] La conséquence de cet état de choses est que chaque catégorie sociale ou professionnelle, ou plutôt ses représentants, faute de se sentir assez assurés pour pouvoir négocier directement de façon responsable, se réfugient dans la revendication vis à vis de l'État, en la compliquant souvent d'une surenchère plus ou moins voilée [. . .]

Nous [devons] construire une nouvelle société. Cette nouvelle société, je la vois comme une société prospère, jeune, généreuse et libérée [. . .] Nous devons aussi apprendre à mieux respecter la dignité de chacun, admettre les différences et les particularités, rendre vie aux communautés de base de notre société, humaniser les rapports entre administrations et administrés, en un mot transformer la vie quotidienne de chacun.

Extrait du discours de Chaban-Delmas à l'Assemblée Nationale, 16 septembre 1969

Document 11b: La loi Veil vue par un mouvement féministe

[. . .] Il y a toujours en France des femmes acculées à l'infanticide, des femmes qui meurent ou se mutilent en tentant d'avorter, des centaines de milliers de femmes qui ont toujours comme seul choix le recours aux 'faiseuses d'anges', ou si elles ont de l'argent et l'information nécessaires, au trafic des cliniques privées en Angleterre. Rien n'a changé pour la plupart des femmes qui désirent avorter, et surtout pour celles des couches ouvrières et populaires. Alors la loi Veil? Cette loi qui prétendait 'libéraliser' l'avortement, cette loi que le gouvernement dans sa phase réformiste, moderniste avait fait voter sous la pression de la lutte des femmes, était bien une loi de classe, une loi hypocrite, faite pour n'être pas appliquée. Pourtant cette loi dérisoire et non appliquée représente encore trop aux yeux de la bourgeoisie qui se sent aujourd'hui menacée par l'aiguisement de la lutte des classes. Face à la crise, dans le même temps qu'il organise le chômage, le blocage des salaires, dans le même temps qu'il attaque les acquis des travailleurs (sécurité sociale, équipements collectifs, crèches), le pouvoir prône le retour des femmes au foyer et mène une politique nataliste. Dans ces conditions, des députés [. . .] tentent d'imputer le déficit de la sécurité sociale au remboursement des contraceptifs et des interruptions de grossesse [. . .] D'où enfin la publicité faite par la presse et la télévision au récent congrès de 'laissez-les vivre', organisation soutenue par l'extrême-droite et l'ordre des médecins et qui qualifie la loi Veil de 'meutrière et perfide', reconnaissant comme seul rôle aux femmes celui de machine à reproduire des enfants. Face à cette attaque organisée de la bourgeoisie, il est urgent de reprendre le combat.

'Mouvement pour la libération de l'avortement et de la contraception', n° 4, 1976, in Claire Laubier (ed.) *The Condition of Women in France – 1945 to the Present: a documentary anthology*, London: Routledge, 1990

Topics
FOR DISCUSSION

1   Why and how did Chaban-Delmas set out to transform France? How does Document 11a help us to understand his policies?
2   What did Giscard mean by an 'advanced liberal society'? What reforms did Giscard introduce?
3   What was *la loi Veil*? How is *la loi Veil* criticised in Document 11b?
4   Why did Giscard lose the presidential elections in 1981?

CHAPTER 12

Timeline

1981
10 May   Mitterrand elected president
Pierre Mauroy is appointed prime minister
14–21 June   Victory for the PS in general elections
18 September   Death penalty abolished

1983
March   Government introduces austerity measures to combat economic crisis
4 December   March of the beurs *against racial discrimination*

1984
17 June   Front national wins over 10 per cent in the European elections
July   Laurent Fabius is appointed prime minister

1986
March   Right wins legislative elections. Chirac is appointed prime minister

1988
8 May   Mitterrrand wins second term as president. Michel Rocard is appointed prime minister

1989
9 November   Fall of the Berlin Wall
November   Three girls expelled from school in Creil for wearing Islamic headscarf

1990
2 August   Iraq invades Kuwait

1991
17 January–28 February France participates in the Gulf War
15 May   Edith Cresson is appointed prime minister

1981–2002: From *la grande alternance* to normalisation?

In 1974, during the presidential campaign, Giscard had accused Mitterrand of being *l'homme du passé*. In 1981, with a deepening of the economic crisis and a rise in unemployment, Mitterrand retorted that Giscard was *l'homme du passif*. Mitterrand had a long political career behind him. He had been a minister 11 times under the Fourth Republic, had denounced the constitution of the Fifth Republic as a *coup d'état permanent*, had become De Gaulle's major opponent, but had lost his credibility in the aftermath of May 1968. Although his personal political history certainly placed him on the left, he did not become a member of the Socialist Party until 1971. To some, he was ideologically close to the French *radical* tradition, concerned with the defence of democracy and social justice, whereas Marxism and anti-capitalism were alien to his personal outlook. To others he appeared as a brilliant strategist whose political skills turned the PS into a powerful electoral machine and made it the dominant

1992
*April   Pierre Bérégovoy
becomes prime minister
April   Eurodisney opens
outside Paris
September   French approve
the Maastricht Treaty by 51
per cent*

1993
*March   Right wins huge
majority. Edouard Balladur
becomes prime minister*

1995
*May   Chirac wins
presidential elections. Alain
Juppé becomes prime minister
June   Chirac announces new
nuclear tests in Polynesia
December Widespread strikes*

1996
*8 January   Death of
François Mitterrand*

1997
*June   Left wins elections and
Lionel Jospin becomes prime
minister*

1998
*30 June   France wins World
Cup*

1999
*December   Bill approving
35-hour week*

2000
*June   Presidential term is
reduced to 5 years*

2001
June   Conscription ended

2002
*February   Franc ceases to be
legal currency, replaced by
the euro
5 May   Chirac wins second
round of presidential
elections against Le Pen. Jean-
Pierre Raffarin is appointed
prime minister*

2003
*March   France opposes use
of force in Iraq. Major
diplomatic clash between
France and the USA*

party of the left, at the expense of the PCF. Faced with Giscard's failure to halt unemployment and reform French society, he called for a radical change of policy, illustrated by a vast programme of *110 propositions*. He encouraged the PS to develop a Marxist rhetoric and indulged in ideological incantations to galvanise left-wing voters. At the same time, Mitterrand was anxious to portray himself as a reassuring candidate and made good use of political marketing. Electoral billboards pictured him as a provincial *notable*, standing in front of a traditional French village, with its church, peaceful dwellings and green pastures. This image was aimed at wooing potential right-wing and floating voters, disillusioned with Giscard's social and economic record. Mitterrand's decisive victory (51.75 per cent) against Giscard on 10 May 1981 was followed by the immediate dissolution of the National Assembly. The June 1981 general elections gave an absolute majority to the PS (270 deputies out of 491). With the RPR, UDF and PCF all losing half of their seats, the PS became the dominant party in French politics. The poor result achieved by the PCF (16 per cent, 44 deputies) made it a weak ally and Mitterrand could, without risk, appoint 4 communist ministers to symbolise the victory of the 'people of the left' and to prepare for *la grande alternance.*

La grande alternance, 1981–86

Hopes of far-reaching changes and a willingness to make a clear break with previous governments followed the victory of the left. A left-wing deputy claimed that 'it is not enough to say that heads are going to roll, we also must say which ones', and indeed, many among the higher echelons of the civil service, suspected of right-wing allegiances, were sacked and were often replaced with party militants. A new tax on large fortunes clearly indicated that 'the rich had to pay'. However, Mitterrand chose to appoint a pragmatic prime minister, Pierre Mauroy. An active trade unionist and mayor of Lille, a city in the heart of France's northern mining region, Mauroy had good working-class credentials and a reputation for moderation. His task was to launch and coordinate the major reforms which were supposed to *changer la vie*.

A new departure

Important decisions were taken to symbolise a new departure from the old order. The death penalty was abolished, military tribunals were suppressed, homosexuality was decriminalised, private local radio stations were allowed to broadcast on the FM band and an independent body was set up to free the media from government interference. All showed a commitment to a more liberal and culturally open society. Likewise, the government undertook to transform relations between local government and the state. The 1982–83 decentralisation laws, prepared by Gaston Defferre, the mayor of Marseille and also the interior minister, became *la grande affaire du septennat*. They were partly motivated by a desire to improve local democracy and to respond positively to growing regionalist demands. They also intended to modernise an administrative system deemed too bureaucratic and remote from people's daily concerns. Finally, they were designed to boost local economic development. Consequently, the prefects acquired a new role. Rather than punctilious and forceful agents of the state at the local level, they became local coordinators of central services and power-brokers between local officials and the central administration. In the name of local democracy, they no longer vetoed decisions taken by local governments on political grounds, but could only challenge their legal basis in a local administrative court. Twenty-two regions were created and each of them was endowed with an assembly (*conseil régional*), directly elected by universal suffrage. The responsibilities of each level of local government were redefined. The regions were to promote economic development, the *départements* to manage social and health policy and the municipalities to take responsibility for urban planning. Decentralisation thus put an end to the Jacobin centralisation of power which had prevailed since the French Revolution. Gradually, it became accepted by all major political parties.

From *relance* to *rigueur*

More contentious were the policies aimed at solving the socio-economic crisis which affected all western societies. Inspired by Thatcher in Britain and Reagan in the USA, most western governments thought that neo-liberal policies offered an attractive alternative to a Keynesian model which now seemed to have run out of steam. State intervention was deemed technically inefficient, if not morally dangerous, compared to market solutions. The state should be rolled back and private initiatives encouraged. Conversely, the French socialists believed that it was the half-hearted commitment of previous French governments to Keynesianism which was responsible for the current economic turmoil. Therefore, it was time to give the state the means to play its proper role and to embark on a comprehensive *politique de relance*.

The nationalisation of major banks and industries best exemplified the idea that the state had to play a proactive role in the management of the economy. In February 1982 five major industrial groups (including Rhône-Poulenc and Saint-Gobain) were nationalised. The operation was costly, because the government insisted, as a radical gesture, that the state should own 100 per cent of their capital. Further, the state took majority holdings in innovative (computing) and strategic (armament) companies but also in ailing steel and iron companies, whose workers had formed the traditional electoral backbone of the left. Finally 39 banks and two financial companies (Suez, Paribas) were nationalised, providing the state with the necessary instruments to finance industrial growth, investment and consumption through affordable lending rates. Nationalised companies were supposed to become a model for a private sector deemed unable or unwilling to face its own economic challenges. They were to display enterprising qualities, forward thinking and an ability to develop progressive industrial relations. State planning (*le plan*) was also revived in order to organise and stimulate industrial growth, boost industrial research, support French industry against foreign competition and fight unemployment.

An ambitious social policy was put forward. The state created 180,000 jobs in the public sector to absorb part of the unemployed. Furthermore, the legal retirement age was lowered to 60, voluntary retirement at 55 was financially supported, the working week was reduced from 40 to 39 hours without pay cuts and professional training was financially encouraged. It was estimated that these measures allowed the creation of some 400,000 new jobs. In 1982 the **lois Auroux** expanded employees' rights. Paid holidays were extended from 4 to 5 weeks. Rejecting the previous government's austerity programme, the socialists introduced measures to reduce social inequalities and to boost consumption. The minimum wage was increased and welfare payments, such as familly allowance and low income payment, were substantially improved. These measures were financed through budgetary deficit and government borrowing. The government hoped that its efforts to stimulate growth would eventually offset these costs. However, it underestimated the weight of external constraints which would finally compel the socialists to dramatically review their objectives.

Lois Auroux

(October 1982): attempt to democratise labour relations and to make employees 'active citizens in their companies'. Through the *comité d'entreprise* (works council), employees acquired a greater voice in management, gained access to their companies' accounts, were encouraged to solve conflicts through negotiations and had to be consulted before important decisions were made (introduction of new technologies, reallocation of activities). New individual rights were also introduced (for instance, it became illegal to sack an employee because of his or her ethnic origin).

The 1982–83 U-turn

An adverse international context ruined the socialists' policy. The upturn in domestic consumption (+ 4 per cent) did not lead to an increase in industrial production. Indeed,

French consumers preferred to spend their accrued purchasing power on imported goods, whereas deflationary policies pursued in other Western countries made it difficult for French companies to find new export outlets. At the same time, the strength of the US dollar, aggravated by a devaluation of the national currency in November 1981, increased the cost of borrowing abroad, maintained inflation at a high level and deepened the trade deficit which grew from 50 to 94 billion FF between 1981 and 1982. In June 1982, a new devaluation of the franc under external pressure led the government to freeze wages and impose price controls. Even if Mauroy endeavoured to present the austerity package (*la politique de rigueur*) as a necessary but temporary phase of *le changement*, it soon became clear that 'socialism in one country' was a strategy doomed to failure and that 'economic realism' had to prevail. After a third devaluation in March 1983, a new austerity plan was introduced to limit budgetary deficit, deflate demand and reduce imports. Welfare benefits were lowered, tax and social security contributions were increased and purchasing power was severely cut. The declared objective of the government was to align its policy with its European partners and to give priority to profitability. Inflation started to decrease and the trade and payment deficits were markedly reduced. However, the price to pay for economic austerity was a sharp rise in unemployment, which grew from 1.8 to 2.5 million between 1981 and 1985. Policies to cushion the socially damaging consequences of unemployment were designed, but improving companies' performance now seemed more important.

A new motto: 'modernisation'

From 1983, the socialists 'discovered' some virtues in market economics, began pampering entrepreneurs and stopped scorning profit as the root of all evil. The charismatic businessman Bernard Tapie appeared on television programmes to explain that Mitterrand's France was a country where individual initiative and economic success were not only possible, but rightly rewarded. A crucial change in left-wing political culture was underway. The appointment of Laurent Fabius as prime minister in 1984 reflected this major shift. As a young *énarque*, from a wealthy background, Fabius projected the image of a modern and managerial left. The rhetoric on *le changement* was subtly replaced with one on the necessary *modernisation*. The public sector was not to provide an alternative to market forces, but had to demonstrate that it could beat the private sector at its own game and become a model of efficiency, competitiveness and profitability. The communists refused to participate in a government veering towards the right. They had no intention of supporting unpopular policies. When in August 1984 the government allowed Citroën to sack some 2,000 workers, the PCF talked of treason. When in December 1984 the government presented a budget which limited public spending growth to 5.9 per cent, the PCF voted against it. Many left-wing voters, who had hoped for a radical change in 1981, were disappointed by the Fabius government. However, the most important challenge to the government did not come from its left, but from a new combative right.

From 1981 the right had vigorously castigated the 'Marxist drift' of the left and denounced its policies as archaic, technically flawed, economically disastrous and morally dangerous as the expansion of state intervention appeared to restrict individual freedom. Whether the French right, and in particular the Gaullists who had traditionally supported state intervention, had genuinely found in neo-liberalism a new ideological creed is debatable. Nevertheless, the defence of freedom against further state infringements became an electoral banner under which the right could unite and it did so with relative success, winning many seats in the local and European elections. In 1984 the attempt by Savary, the education secretary, to absorb private schools into the public sector provided the right with a golden opportunity to denounce a further attack on freedom, in this case parents' freedom to choose a school for their children. The right successfully mobilised its troops and organised a series of demonstrations throughout the country to defend educational pluralism: 80,000 demonstrators marched in Bordeaux in January, 400,000 in Rennes in February and 800,000 in Versailles in June 1984. Mitterrand finally withdrew the project in July 1984 and Savary resigned. Under Fabius' premiership, no further attack was made on private education. The stress was put on the modernisation of the public sector. Substantial investments in computing equipment introduced modern technology into the classroom. Programmes were revised to provide pupils with a better economic and business culture. At the same time, the new education minister, Chevènement, developed a republican vision of education. Schools had to provide a solid civic culture and to offer the vast majority of pupils the possibility of improving their social and professional prospects. By 2000, Chevènement argued, 80 per cent of a given age cohort should reach the *baccalauréat.*

Rise of the *Front national*

The Fabiusian modernisation, however, was not enough to save the socialists from electoral defeat in the 1986 general elections. Profits rose, but unemployment had not been tamed and became a major preoccupation among voters. The demagogic diagnostic put forward by Le Pen, leader of the extreme-right party *Front national* (FN), seduced many voters. Le Pen claimed that immigration was the main cause for unemployment, argued that '3 million immigrants' = '3 million unemployed' and called for the repatriation of immigrants, using racist arguments and often violent tactics. The relative success of his party (11 per cent in the 1984 European elections, 9 per cent in the 1985 local elections) proved to be more than a flash in the pan. Indeed, the FN was to establish itself as an enduring protest party. In this context, Mitterrand's electoral scheming gave the FN an unexpected political boost.

Anxious to limit the defeat of the left, Mitterrand forced parliament to change electoral law and introduce proportional representation (April 1985), thus increasing the possibility for small parties to win seats in the National Assembly. Mitterrand hoped that the FN would syphon enough votes away from the right to deprive it of an absolute majority. He calculated that the right could not ally itself to the FN, which would amount to political suicide. The right would have to find support from the centre-left, and consequently it would be unable to force the most radical elements of its programme through parliament. Mitterrand's tactics failed. On 16 March 1986 the right obtained a slender but absolute majority (291 deputies out of 577) and the FN, with 35 deputies, gained a new legitimacy. Mitterrand had gambled and lost, and he had little choice but to appoint Chirac as prime minister.

La cohabitation, 1986–88

A weaker president?

The **cohabitation** between a socialist president and a Gaullist prime minister compelled both players to return to the text of the 1958 constitution. The presidential interpretation of the original text, from de Gaulle to Mitterrand, had blurred the actual powers given to the prime minister, who had always been considered the instrument of the president's will. Although the constitution granted substantial powers to the president, there was speculation that the cohabitation would allow the prime minister to gain more weight and would eventually alter the overtly presidential nature of the regime. In fact, *this* cohabitation revealed the president's ability to resist a weakening of his position. It became clear that Mitterrand and Chirac would be the two major candidates in the forthcoming 1988 presidential elections and this context favoured the president. First, Chirac was reluctant to circumscribe the powers of a presidency he intended to conquer for himself. Nothing in the constitution, for example, justified the president's supremacy over foreign and defence policy. What had been considered as the president's *domaine réservé* was the result of a practice inherited from de Gaulle, rather than a constitutional prerogative. Chirac did not challenge this. Although there was a broad consensus between the president and the prime minister on foreign affairs, the pre-eminence of the president was respected and it was he who reaped the benefits of prestigious negotiations with other world statesmen. Rather than direct confrontation with the president on foreign affairs, Chirac tried to reinforce his credentials through a tireless occupation of the domestic ground but inevitably ran the risk of getting stuck in the mud of daily business. Mitterrand, far from appearing as a brooding prisoner in his Elysée palace, assumed the enviable role of a benevolent father and never missed an opportunity to scold an overactive prime minister. Reminding voters that the constitution made him the guardian of national unity, Mitterrand sought to restrain a partisan prime minister. The way he reacted to Chirac's privatisation programme illustrated this point.

cohabitation

When results in a parliamentary general election give a majority opposed to the political orientations of the president, the latter has a choice: either resign or appoint a prime minister coming from the new majority. In the latter scenario (*cohabitation*), the president's ability to initiate policies is strongly circumscribed. He is less a player and more a referee. However, no constitutional constraint prevents him from criticising the government. As guardian of the constitution and national unity, his preeminence in foreign and defence policies is maintained.

Neo-liberalism *à la française*

Neo-liberalism had provided the right with an electoral platform which pledged to undo most of the socio-economic policies introduced by the socialists since 1981. The tax on large fortunes was ended, corporate taxes were lowered and it became easier for companies to sack employees. Deregulation and privatisation became the key words of the new government's economic policy. Nevertheless, the right's commitment to true neo-liberal ideas could be questioned. For instance, faced with a continued rise in unemployment, the government had no qualms about subsidising 'lame' industries, such as shipbuilding, to save employees' jobs. This was certainly a wise electoral move, but it bore little relation to neo-liberal principles. The government's privatisation programme showed this ambivalence between a newly found neo-liberal inspiration and an entrenched interventionist culture. Balladur, Chirac's finance minister, believed that the privatisation of more than 65 companies in 5 years would boost economic growth and provide cash to reduce the national debt. Furthermore, he hoped that the diffusion of shares among the general public, presented as a modern version of Gaullist *participation*, would foster a sort of popular capitalism. However, there was no attempt to privatise public utilities, such as electricity (EDF), and providers of public services such as the railways (SNCF) remained under state control. Moreover, the government was reluctant to abandon newly privatised companies to the uncertainties of market forces. The state kept a hard core of shares in some privatised companies or allocated these to 'reliable' private firms, often managed by RPR supporters. Critics were quick to point out that the state's assets had been transferred not so much to the market as to the government's friends and that there was a real danger of seeing the RPR increasing its grip on major French assets.

Mitterrand used his constitutional prerogatives and his political skills to frustrate the government's privatisation programme. Worried about his slender majority in parliament and anxious to demonstrate to the country his government's ability to deliver, Chirac wanted to avoid lengthy parliamentary discussions. He asked the Assembly to approve in principle the privatisation programme, which would subsequently be fleshed out by executive rulings (*ordonnances*). However, such rulings constitutionally required the president's signature and Mitterrand withheld his. He was accused by Chirac of undermining the will and legitimacy of the newly elected Assembly. Mitterrand argued that Chirac deprived the Assembly of its right to discuss a crucial piece of legislation. There was a risk that French assets would pass into foreign control and that consumers' interests would be jeopardised by shareholders' pursuit of unbridled profit. Such matters could not be rushed without debate. Mitterrand delayed the implementation of the privatisation programme, which a year later was put on hold after the October 1987 stock-exchange crash. More importantly, he was able to present himself as the guardian of national interest and the voice of moderation. Although the *cohabitation* had reduced his power to impose his personal preferences, it left him with sufficient room for manoeuvre to improve his political credentials.

Law and order and immigration

The vigorous law and order policies introduced by Pasqua, Chirac's populist interior minister, were thought to be an electoral winning card. He also believed that toughening the government's stance on immigration would deprive the FN of its main electoral appeal. During the *trente glorieuses* France had encouraged immigration to increase its workforce and to sustain its economic growth. However, since the 1973 economic crisis, the legal entry of immigrant workers had been severely restricted and a policy of voluntary repatriation was designed under Giscard. Conversely, in 1981 the left had improved immigrants' rights and even thought of giving them the right to vote at local elections, although this was not implemented. In 1983 young **beurs** organised various marches through the country, to demand civic and political rights for immigrants and their children and better access to the job market. Expressing their desire to be part of the republic, they launched *SOS Racisme*, a pressure group determined to fight a new surge of racism. Indeed, from 1983, FN electoral successes compelled governing parties to make immigration a major national issue and to toughen their policies. In 1986 measures were taken to restrict immigrants' entry into the country, to facilitate the expulsion of illegal immigrants and to make it more difficult to obtain asylum status. A new **code de la nationalité** was devised, which made it more difficult for immigrants' children born on French territory to acquire French nationality.

Mitterrand exploited these controversial issues and denounced the 'threat of racially motivated exclusion pervading discussions about the new *code de la nationalité*'. He demonised the right as a set of parties, groups and factions whose intolerance was self-evident in their politcal programme. His 1988 presidential programme ('Lettre à tous les français') was a complete contrast to the 1981 *110 propositions*. Its strength was in its consensual tone. In particular, his famous

---

beurs

Slang term derived from the word *arabe* which refers to French nationals of North African origin. It acquired prominence in December 1983 with *la marche des beurs* against racism. The *beur* culture is now increasingly visible through cinema, rap music, literature and the radio station *Radio Beur*.

---

code de la nationalité

(regulations as to nationality) stipulates that: (1) all children born from French parents are French (*droit du sang*), and that: (2) all children born on the French territory are French (*droit du sol*). Changes introduced by Pasqua in 1986 and 1994 restricted the *droit du sol* and made it more difficult to obtain French nationality. In particular, children born in France from immigrant parents have to wait till the age of 18 to declare that they want to be French. During a crucial period of socialisation where norms and values are learnt, particularly at school, they remain 'foreigners'. As such, Pasqua made some concessions to the FN which argued that '*être français, ça s'hérite ou ça se mérite*'.

ni–ni (neither nationalisation, nor privatisation) revealed an attempt to smooth out ideological differences in the name of national unity and solidarity. Under the banner *La France unie*, Mitterrand comfortably won the elections (54 per cent) against Chirac in May 1988. The crumbling of the PCF (6.7 per cent) attested to the end of left-wing illusions whereas a good result for Le Pen (14.5 per cent) confirmed the extreme right's strength. However, in the ensuing general elections, the PS failed to obtain an absolute majority (276 deputies out of 577). In order to exercise power, the new government had to obtain the tacit support of the 27 communist deputies or cajole the 49 centre-right deputies who were ready to support moderate policies that rejected both neo-liberal and socialist dogmas. Polarisation was to be replaced by consensual politics.

Mitterrand's second term, 1988–95

Consensus and political malaise

Mitterrand appointed as prime minister Michel Rocard, a popular figure whom he personally despised. Coming from the PSU, Rocard had joined the PS in 1974 and defended a social-democratic ideal opposed to Mitterrand's electoral opportunism. His method of government rested on the search for consensus, based on negotiation with professional interests. Rocard sought to improve the efficiency and quality of the administrative machinery and its ability to deliver results. His government was open to personalities from the centre-right and from 'civil society' (Fouroux, Saint-Gobain ex-president, Kouchner from the charity *Médecins Sans Frontières*), symbolising a willingness to supersede 'artificial' political divisions among socially minded reformists and to favour expertise over political strife.

This *ouverture* mirrored growing uncertainty about ideologies. In 1991, 60 per cent of the French believed that the left–right divide had no relevance, compared with 33 per cent in 1981. The collapse of communism in 1989, the failure of Keynesianism symbolised by the PS U-turn in 1983, and the lack of clarity in the Gaullist message, marred by neo-liberal excesses, made it difficult for political leaders to explain what a better future would be. In 1990 *The Financial Times* claimed that Mitterrand had been more successful than Thatcher in controlling wage rises and congratulated the socialists for their conversion to market principles. The apparent global reign of liberal-democracy and market economy seemed impossible to challenge and reduced political action to pragmatic managerialism. The only alternatives were to be found in small or protest parties on each side of the political spectrum, such as the Greens and the FN. The share of votes that governing parties (PCF, PS, UDF and RPR) won at general elections declined throughout the period, from 93 per cent of the total vote in June 1981, to 74 per cent in March 1993 and 57 per cent in June 1997. This *vote éclaté* (scattered vote) conveyed disillusion with established political parties.

In this context, Rocard's ambition to rejuvenate the meaning of political action through dialogue was likely to fail. The consensus which started to prevail had no real positive content, but was rather a consensus by default, *faute de mieux*. Dialogue proved to be a strenuous exercise in a society where professional interests equated negotiation with an insidious attempt to challenge their interests. Public-sector workers, in particular, preferred to resort to strikes to ensure that the status quo was not challenged. Given that the economic context was rather good (strong economic growth, low inflation, stability of the French franc), it seemed that the over-cautious Rocard missed the opportunity to push further social and economic reforms. One of the only decisions which stood out for its originality was the creation of the *revenu minimum d'insertion* (RMI) or minimum benefit payment, designed to support the poorest members of society, to give them right of access to a wide range of social security benefits and to facilitate their integration into the job market. All parties supported the RMI, making it difficult to characterise it as a typical left-wing measure.

A series of financial scandals, affecting all parties and related to the illicit funding of their activities, did nothing to improve the prevalent political malaise. The 1990 amnesty law which cleared most politicians from previous wrong-doings gave the impression that deputies, from left to right, colluded to absolve themselves and eroded people's faith in the political elite. Corruption charges were all the more damaging as *les années fric et frime* coincided with a socialist presidency which had started in an atmosphere of moral uprightness and ended with the valorisation of profit and an upsurge in unemployment (3 million unemployed in 1992). When the Gulf War (1991) put an end to global economic growth, the pessimistic mood deepened. Mitterrand took this opportunity to sack Rocard and appointed the pugnacious Edith Cresson (May 1991). The appointment of a woman as prime minister was intended as a marketing coup. It failed. Her rash declarations ('The stock exchange? I don't give a damn about it'), her confrontational style, but most of all her inability to curb unemployment made her truly unpopular. Mitterrand, it seemed, had sacrificed leadership to a hazardous political marketing exercise. After less than a year, Cresson was replaced by Pierre Bérégovoy (April 1992), a previous finance minister with a solid reputation for orthodox economic policies. Bérégovoy's commitment to monetary stability and budgetary cautiousness, partly imposed by the EU (see below, pp. 191–2), were incompatible with generous social reforms and he was unable to prevent the 1993 socialist electoral melt-down. In the wake of the March 1993 general elections, interest groups from farmers to truck-drivers, nurses to public-sector workers besieged Matignon to defend their revenue and professional interests. The 1993 general elections were a disaster for the left, which failed to return more than 93 deputies (70 PS, 23 PCF). With 450 deputies (213 UDF, 247 RPR) out of 577, the right returned to power and opened a second period of cohabitation under Balladur's premiership.

Crises of identity: immigration and Europe

In the 1990s, around 4 million immigrants lived in France, 35 per cent of them originating from the Maghreb. Although this number had been fairly stable over the two past decades due to strict controls on immigration, the FN successfully whipped up fear, asserting that France was swamped by immigrants. The FN compelled other political leaders to toughen their stance on immigration and thus to legitimise its ideas. In 1991 Chirac complained about the unpleasant smells coming from immigrants' kitchens and warned the French that an 'overdose of immigrants' would be fateful. Giscard also made similar unsavoury remarks. Cresson herself did not exclude the use of summary measures to expel illegal immigrants. Lingering resentment of the Algerian War, the public perception that some Muslim countries, such as Iran, were France's enemies and the rise of Muslim fundamentalism made Maghrebis the prime target of the FN's rhetoric. They were not only responsible for unemployment and insecurity, but their values, traditions, music and religion also threatened to corrupt the soul of France. Increasingly, the debate became focused on the 'integration' of immigrants and their children into the national community.

In 1989 three Muslim girls from Creil were excluded from their school because they were wearing headscarves, as required by their religion. The republican principle of *laïcité* prescribed a strict separation between republican institutions (such as schools) and religion. Whether it was possible to be a Muslim and French at the same time became a major issue. The incident fuelled a debate about the French model of integration. The *Haut conseil à l'intégration*, set up in 1990, painfully defended a republican model which required immigrants to comply with the rules governing French society and to accept the republic's core values. Their 'fusion' into the national community was considered necessary to contribute to its harmonious development. Differences should be respected, but not exalted. The *Haut conseil* was therefore opposed to a multicultural model, *à l'anglaise*, which would divide the republic into distinctive communities, each celebrating its own values and defending its own rights, all potentially ignoring one another.

However, the equality of rights central to the French model of integration was blatantly ignored. In 1990–91, in the suburbs of Mantes-la-Jolie and Vaulx-en-Velin, young people from various ethnic backgrounds, mostly unemployed, burnt cars, ransacked shops and organised pitched battles against the police. Most of them, born in France of immigrant parents and therefore French nationals, felt they were treated as second-class citizens, due to the colour of their skin. These riots were also a good reminder that immigrant communities were the first to be affected by unemployment, educational failure, derelict housing and poor access to leisure activities. The *politique de la ville* launched in the early 1990s had failed to dispel the complex malaise affecting French suburbs. Several films, such as *L'état des lieux* (1995) and *La Haine* (1995), revealed the development of a counter-culture in the suburbs. They demonstrated the limits of the French integration model and the social damage of an economic policy generating exclusion. If a minority of the people with an immigrant background found solace in the most rigorous forms of Islam, most of them wished to be part of the national community without forgetting their roots. The growing popularity of *raï* singers, such as Khaled or Cheb Mammi, who mixed traditional Arabic melodies with jazz or pop music and French lyrics, the success of rap groups, such as Zebda, alternating the use of the French, Algerian and Kabyle languages, illustrated that there could be different ways of being French. When the *black, blanc, beur* French side won the 1998 football World Cup, it was hastily argued that France had finally recognised diversity as a winning card. However, when in 2002, during a friendly football match between France and Algeria in Paris, young people of Maghrebi origin, most of them French nationals, booed the *Marseillaise* and interrupted the game by invading the pitch and chanting 'Bin Laden, Bin Laden', it became all too clear that the immigration malaise had not been dispelled at all. The event played into the hands of the FN and made it easier for Le Pen to argue that non-European immigrants could not be integrated into the national community and that they were chiefly responsible for the collapse of law and order.

Uncertainties about French identity were also fuelled by European integration. In 1982 three successive devaluations had convinced Mitterrand that France's Keynesian policies isolated her from her European partners. From 1983, with the support of Jacques Delors, president of the European Commission, and Helmut Kohl, the German chancellor, Mitterrand made Europe a cornerstone of his *septennats* and became a major proponent of further European integration. He believed that the 1986 Single European Act (SEA), which created a common European market, required the development of common policies, notably social policies, and the creation of a common currency. The collapse of the Soviet bloc (1989) gave impetus to the furthering of European integration, leading to the signing of the Maastricht Treaty in 1992. The treaty made provisions for a growing convergence of economic and financial policies, the establishment of a European central bank and the introduction of a common currency for all member states. Provisions were also made to improve cooperation in the field of foreign and security policies, without infringing on national sovereignty. The treaty, however, did little to promote a social Europe.

The French usually viewed European construction as a desirable but distant objective whose complexity was better left to technocrats. However, the ratification of the Maastricht Treaty politicised and polarised the issue. The parliament could have ratified the treaty, but Mitterrand preferred to directly ask the French to do so and organised a referendum (1992). He anticipated that public opinion would approve the treaty *en masse*. His decision, however, was mainly motivated by domestic issues. At a time when his popularity was floundering, he hoped to derive political credit from his European policy and to expose publicly the internal divisions of the right on Europe. His strategy backfired. Part of the right, led by Séguin and Pasqua, revived traditional Gaullist themes and pointed out that the treaty undermined French national sovereignty. The introduction of a common currency and the constraints it imposed on French economic and social policy (low inflation, reduction of budgetary deficit and limited public borrowing) dangerously constrained France's ability to pursue her own policies. However, the left was equally divided. For the PCF, Maastricht Europe was essentially furthering economic deregulation, encouraging privatisation, threatening public services and neglecting social progress. More, the worrying drift towards a socio-economic 'Anglo-Saxon' model was denounced as an attempt to destroy French culture. The concept of subsidiarity did little to reassure those who, from wood pigeon hunters to film producers, feared that Brussels would 'subvert' French traditions. Chevènement broke away from the PS to create the *Mouvement des citoyens* (MDC), arguing that Europe worked on undemocratic principles and promoted market values which were incompatible with the republican ideal (solidarity). The FN saw Maastricht as the product of cosmopolitan 'Eurocrats' who engineered an anti-national plot to humiliate the French. Thus, the Maastricht Treaty was only ratified by a slim majority (51 per cent). This was a major rebuff to Mitterrand's political manoeuvring, but above all, it revealed that France felt insecure about her identity and her ability to shape her future to her own liking.

The second *cohabitation* (1993–95)

Uncertainties about the future nourished fascination with the past. The second *cohabitation* juxtaposed a president publicly revealing the ambiguous role he had played within the Vichy regime and a prime minister whose felt-hat and *vieille France* mannerisms exuded 1950s' bourgeois values. Mitterrand, who was dying of prostate cancer, seemed less interested in politics than in his posterity and was anxious to explain that as a young law student from a Catholic and provincial background, his flirtation with the Vichy regime was neither surprising nor incompatible with an involvement in the Resistance. By blurring the opposition between resisters and collaborators, a distinction that was pivotal to Gaullist and PCF mythology, Mitterrand's revelations threw France into a soul-searching exercise. The trial of Touvier, a French *milicien* who had been protected by the church, the assassination of Bousquet, the former Vichy police chief and one-time close friend of Mitterrand, and the growing pressure to prosecute Papon, a civil servant who in the 1970s became Giscard's budget secretary despite his active war involvement in the deportation of Jews, forced French people to confront the complexities of the occupation years.

Balladur's subdued style ensured that the second *cohabitation* was a serene and peaceful one. After the 1993 right-wing victory, Balladur agreed to lead the government. He thus allowed Chirac to distance himself from the humdrum of daily business to preserve his chances for the 1995 presidential elections. Balladur's considerate but firm conservatism led him to increase social benefits for the poorest and largest families, but also to toughen security and immigration controls. To reduce budget deficit, as required by the Maastricht Treaty, to boost employment and economic growth and to finance growing demands for social welfare, the government launched a new bond (*emprunt Balladur*). Trusting a prime minister who exuded confidence and competence, the French mobilised their private savings and the bond was oversubscribed. Further finance was obtained through the privatisation of nationalised companies. Bérégovoy had already authorised the partial privatisation of state companies (Elf-Aquitaine, Rhône-Poulenc) to improve the state's finances. Balladur went further and launched a vast privatisation programme, which proved popular with the French public. France seemed to turn into a nation of shareholders (Elf-Aquitaine: 3 million shareholders; Rhône-Poulenc: 2.9 million) and the left was unwilling to criticise privatisations on political grounds. Privatisation had become a necessary element of an economic logic dictated by external constraints, and no longer provoked ideological disagreements.

Further privatisations under later Gaullist or socialist governments would be uncontentious.

Balladur's popularity soon convinced him that he could become a better presidential candidate than Chirac. Acrimony grew between the two leaders. Chirac found it difficult to criticise the work of a fellow Gaullist prime minister, but he built his campaign around three powerful slogans which would eventually ensure his victory. *La pensée unique*, a derogatory expression, typified the continuity between Balladur and his immediate socialist predecessors, in particular a servile acceptance of market constraints. Chirac opposed to this logic *la volonté politique, art du possible*, asserting, without much practical explanation, the primacy of politics over economics. With an unemployment rate reaching 12.5 per cent and a growth in poverty, Chirac also condemned *la fracture sociale* which excluded a growing part of the population from the benefits of economic and social security. The lack of a credible socialist candidate to replace Mitterrand encouraged Chirac to develop ideas which could potentially attract left-wing voters.

In this context, Balladur failed to survive the first round of the 1995 presidential elections. Against all odds, Chirac was left to face Lionel Jospin, the candidate that the PS managed to appoint in desperation less than 3 months before the first ballot. Jospin, the socialist party secretary in the 1980s and former education minister under Rocard, was not ready to accept uncritically Mitterrand's heritage, his unprincipled political scheming and lack of commitment to social-democracy. He was willing to turn the page and give new impetus to the left. Given the perilous state of the left, his 47.4 per cent against Chirac (52.6 per cent) was something of an achievement.

Chirac's first term, 1995–2002 and *la gauche plurielle*, 1997–2002

Political will and its limits

When President Chirac announced in July 1995 that France would resume nuclear testing in the South Pacific, despite previous international commitments, he knew he would face criticism at home and abroad. However, he intended to show that France was still free to determine policy independently from external constraints and that political will could overcome the most stringent forms of resistance. The constitutional reforms introduced to enhance the powers of parliament in November 1995 also indicated a willingness to restore some measure of political debate. To reduce the *fracture sociale*, the budget devoted to fighting unemployment increased dramatically, but without much effect since the 140 billion FF thus spent did not prevent unemployment from reaching 12.7 per cent in 1996. Political will alone seemed unable to reduce *la fracture sociale* and it became clear that it was difficult to escape the constraints of *la pensée unique*. The prime minister, Alain Juppé, presented a series of audacious reforms to curb social security spending (health and pensions) and to reorganise public companies such as the SNCF in order to save labour costs. These reforms triggered massive opposition from public-sector workers worried about their *avantages acquis*. Juppé's technocratic and confrontational style did little to avert demonstrations and strikes. The actions of postal, electricity and railway workers paralysed France in December 1995 and compelled the government to ditch most of its reforms.

In March 1997 Chirac announced the dissolution of the National Assembly, a move which took most political pundits by surprise. Against the interest groups which regularly took to the streets to impose their views, the president argued that it was time to allow the French nation to express itself. He needed to find a new legitimacy to carry out necessary but painful reforms (reducing state and social security budget deficits) in order to meet the criteria imposed by the Maastricht Treaty if France wished to join the euro in 1999. Politically, a snap election could also take the left by surprise, rally the right around the president and heal the lingering animosity between *Balladuriens* and *Chiraquiens* which had weakened the RPR since the last presidential election.

It was a risky move given the unpopularity of the Juppé government and the prevalent impression that the promises of 1995 had been betrayed. The French voters could hardly be enthusiastic about the prospect of further budgetary cuts jeopardising social entitlements and a renewed economic *rigueur* which would invariably lead to job losses. The advantages of the euro were not clear at all and many voters were convinced that the EU, which had made little progress on social issues, endangered rather than protected their social rights. Finally, having concluded an electoral alliance with the *Verts*, the PCF and the MDC, Jospin was ready to oppose a united electoral front against the right. The June 1997 general elections represented a crushing defeat for the right, especially the RPR which lost 111 deputies. The *gauche plurielle* with 319 deputies out of 577, including 7 *Verts* and 38 communists, had a clear majority. However, the high abstention rate (32 per cent) and the success of the FN (15 per cent) revealed a persistent political malaise.

La gauche plurielle and the third cohabitation (1997–2002)

A battered Chirac had no alternative but to appoint Jospin as prime minister. The third cohabitation gave the prime minister 5 years to imprint his mark on France. Jospin appointed two communist and one Green ministers but marginalised socialists who had belonged to Mitterrand's faithful old guard. When Jospin declared that in an increasingly global world his room for manoeuvre was limited, it became clear that the government's originality was not to be found in the implementation of an audacious economic policy. The *gauche plurielle* privatised more companies than any previous government, without an eyebrow being raised, even by communist ministers. However, ambitious labour legislation was introduced to reduce the legal working week from 39 to 35 hours. *Les 35 heures* were primarily designed to increase labour flexibility and lower unemployment. By 1999 more than 11,500 companies had endorsed the scheme and it was estimated that 102,000 jobs had been created or protected. The national employers' federation (MEDEF) and right-wing parties attacked this legislation, arguing that it would increase production costs. Politically, they also resented the government's ambition to regulate the labour market through legislation, a method reminiscent of old-fashioned interventionism. Yet the government's determination to see a fall in unemployment, especially among the youngest generations, led to the creation of 150,000 *emploi-jeunes*. In 2000, and for the first time, unemployment fell below 10 per cent. Arguably, it was difficult to know whether this was due to government policy or to a propitious global context, which boosted economic growth (3.2 per cent GDP in 1998), helped to reduce deficits and facilitated entry into the euro-zone (1999).

The *gauche plurielle* accepted the principles of a market economy, but rejected a 'market society'. Equality and solidarity should prevail. So, in a country where women have been notoriously under-represented in elected bodies, it encouraged political parties to put forward an equal number of male and female candidates for each election (*la parité*). Political parties failing to do so would be financially sanctioned. Likewise, the government offered unmarried couples, regardless of their sexual orientation, the possibility to sign a contract officially recognising their union and protecting their mutual rights. The *Pacte civil de solidarité* (PACS) was criticised by the right as an attempt to legitimise homosexual 'marriage' and to degrade traditional family values. Finally, a new *couverture sociale universelle* (CSU) gave people who had been progressively excluded from the job market or lived in poverty better access to social security services, in particular health provisions.

The *gauche plurielle* was a fragile electoral coalition that had no common political programme. Cohesion was sometimes difficult to maintain. The 'republican' (MDC) interior minister, Chevènement, resigned when Jospin opened negotiations with Corsican nationalists. Chevènement argued that their methods (acts of terrorism that included political assassinations) and demands (greater autonomy, if not independence for Corsica) undermined the republic's authority. To treat Corsicans as a distinct group within the republic and to grant them special rights would introduce a dangerous form of 'communitarism', leading to the balkanisation of the republic. Communists opposed major green projects, such as the progressive phasing out of nuclear plants, deemed unrealistic and detrimental to employment. Finally, PS arrogance was criticised by all its coalition partners, each of them demanding greater recognition and increased participation in government.

The 2002 political earthquake

After 5 years of *cohabitation*, Chirac appeared as a weakened president. Between 1995 and 1997 he had not kept his election pledges. The

archives

In France access to government archive material is subject to strict laws. Different swathes of documents are released after 30, 40 and 50 years, although sensitive documents can be held back for 100 years. In a debate in the National Assembly in 2000 the PCF demanded an enquiry into the massacres of Algerians by the French police on 17 October 1961. Jospin rejected such a call but he did announce that access to the archives on the war would be widened. In an official circular dated 26 April 2001 he instructed the ministries of employment, justice, the interior, foreign affairs, defence and culture to ease access in particular for research by 'people from the scholarly or university communities'.

failure of the 1997 dissolution cast doubt on his political flair. The opportunist but amicable president, embroiled in several corruption scandals, and the upright but uncharismatic socialist prime minister, overconfident about the propriety of his policies, had acquired a common distaste for the *cohabitation* as a political solution. It deprived France of a firm and clear leadership and the constant search for a consensus between the two leaders prevented the emergence of bold and original solutions. Therefore, both supported the reduction of the presidential term from 7 to 5 years, to make it coincide with the span of the legislature, thus limiting the prospect of future *cohabitations.*

At first the 2002 presidential elections appeared as an unexciting contest between Chirac and Jospin, despite a record number of 16 candidates which indicated a general dissatisfaction with what the two main contenders had to offer. As the media and opinion polls entertained the idea that the outcome of the first round had already been decided, a large part of the electorate abstained (28 per cent). This high abstention rate, however, was also the result of Jospin's poor electoral strategy. Arguing that his presidential programme was not a socialist one, he disappointed a substantial number of left-wing voters who deserted him, choosing to stay at home or to support the *Verts* or one of the three Trotskyist candidates. Conversely, Chirac astutely played the law and order card, largely relayed by television programmes. The French were bombarded with images that gave the impression that order had collapsed and that France was hopelessly ridden with crime. Some voters believed that the situation was so dramatic that Le Pen, who clearly linked insecurity with immigration, would be a better prospect than Chirac. Le Pen also attracted voters, such as the unemployed, who had been disappointed with the 'system' and people worried by the future of French identity.

The first round's results provoked a political earthquake. Chirac only gathered a paltry 19 per cent of the votes and Le Pen achieved his best score ever (16.8 per cent), ousting Jospin (16.2 per cent) from the second round. In the name of republican values, nearly all candidates called voters to support Chirac in the second round. After two weeks of street demonstrations against Le Pen, Chirac was re-elected with 82 per cent of the votes. The second round of the presidential elections was transformed into a referendum against the FN. However, with 18 per cent of the vote, the FN could no longer be labelled a protest party, but must be acknowledged as an established party able to attract voters on a national-populist platform.

To dispel the prevalent political malaise, Chirac appointed as prime minister Jean-Pierre Raffarin, a politician with an unusual profile. President of the essentially rural but dynamic Poitou-Charentes region, Raffarin, unlike previous right- or left-wing prime ministers, was not a graduate of the ENA, did not belong to any partisan Parisian coterie and had not pursued a career in the civil service. A moderate liberal with a commercial background and a reassuring provincial *bon sense*, Raffarin cultivated a plain and simple political style which differed very much from Juppé's and Jospin's didactic and often patronising approach. Yet he often appeared to lack depth and substance and quickly became satirically known for his *raffarinades*, his ability to state the obvious and to make empty statements. Nevertheless, he remained a remarkably popular prime minister. He claimed to represent *la France d'en bas*, the ordinary, hard-working people whose efforts were stifled by an over-centralised bureaucracy and whose desire to lead a peaceful life was frustrated by rising crime rates and an ineffective judicial system. If these issues were properly addressed, it was argued, then the voters who had supported Le Pen might well shift their allegiance to the traditional right.

Raffarin's task was facilitated by two major political factors. First, in the June 2002 general elections the right won a massive majority (399 seats out of 577). With the presidency, the government, the National Assembly, the Senate and the vast majority of regional and local councils controlled by the right, the left had lost virtually all institutional resources to act as a counter-power, except the *mairie* of Paris, controlled by the charismatic but cautious Bertrand Delanoë since 2001. Secondly, under Chirac's impetus, the right finally overcame its partisan divisions. Despite the fierce opposition of François Bayroux, the leader of the UDF, many argued that no ideological differences now separated the RPR from the UDF and that the electoral hegemony of the right would be better served by the creation of a single party. Under the leadership of Juppé, the newly created *Union pour un mouvement populaire* (UMP) represented less the fusion of the diverse right-wing families than their absorption into the Gaullist machinery. The right was thus successfully *Chiraquisée*. The bewildered UDF lost most of its troops, and die-hard Gaullists such as Pasqua were condemned to the political wilderness.

The prime minister's endearing provincial simplicity must be contrasted with the political skilfulness of his young, tough and popular interior minister Nicolas Sarkozy. In the aftermath of the 2002 elections, Sarkozy played a key role in wooing back FN voters into the traditional right-wing fold. He argued that the success of the extreme right was due to three major factors. First, the rise of unpunished petty crime and unsociable behaviour led to a growing feeling of insecurity. Strict and tougher law and order policies were required to prevent the FN from appearing to be the only party to address these issues. Second, the development of overtly repressive law and order policies could help to dispel the illusion that there was no substantial difference between left- and right-wing governments. Such an illusion dangerously fuelled the FN's success as it provided Le Pen with the opportunity to present himself as the only alternative to the status quo. Finally, immediate and highly visible results were urgently needed, for the FN claimed that traditional parties never respected their electoral pledges and paid little attention to the plights of ordinary people. Thus, a series of laws were passed to curb and criminalise unsociable or threatening behaviour, from beggars, prostitutes, gypsies, teenagers and immigrants, today's *classes dangereuses*. The importance of the repressive function of the police and the judiciary system was reinforced. When visiting a police station in Toulouse in February 2003, Sarkozy rebuffed the local officer who had developed a series of social and education schemes to improve relations between his officers and the disaffected youngsters of the *banlieues*. Sarkozy reminded the officer that the objective of the police was to arrest criminals, not to play football with them.

In 2003 thorny domestic issues, such as improving labour flexibility and economic growth, lowering income tax, reviewing pensions policies and furthering the decentralisation process, were somewhat eclipsed by the second Iraq war. In the aftermath of 11 September 2001, US President Bush launched an attack on so-called rogue states – such as the Taliban regime in Afghanistan and Saddam Hussein's Iraq which, it was claimed, supported terrorist attacks against Western interests. Arguing that Saddam had consistently failed to comply with UN resolutions on weapons inspections and was producing weapons of mass destruction which threatened the West, President Bush was determined to use force against Iraq. Supported by the British and Spanish prime ministers and most Eastern and Central European countries which were about to join the EU, this bellicose approach led to a major diplomatic row with France.

Chirac took the view that the dismantling of the weapons of mass destruction should be done under the aegis of the United Nations by supporting the work of UN inspectors. Force should only be used in the last resort and only with the approval of the international community. On 18 March 2003 Chirac condemned Bush and Blair's unilateral decision to go to war as illegal and insisted that France, a permanent member of the UN security council, would veto any military action in Iraq which would take the form of an ultimatum. France's position was supported by the German chancellor, Schröder, and the Russian president, Putin. Chirac's stance was supported by French public opinion which had become highly critical of Anglo-Saxon hegemony. In the USA, anti-French demonstrations took place and the Bush administration did nothing to hide its anger, declaring that France would be punished for its opposition to American strategy. This major rift between NATO members called into question the way the West, and the EU in particular, pursued its defence and foreign policy. However, whether Chirac's essentially Gaullist position actually increased France's influence on the international stage is debatable. If he gained some prestige in the Third World, he also alienated many of the applicant states for the EU in Central and Eastern Europe, accusing them of being blindly pro-American. In this way the second Iraq war poisoned Franco-American relations as it rekindled major differences between French and American conceptions of their respective roles on the world stage.

Document 12a: L'echec des Beurs?

Entretien avec Nadia Zouareg, ex-marcheuse beur

Lors des marches des Beurs [entre 1983 et 1986], nous, les enfants d'immigrés, nous disions que nous ne voulions pas être les remplaçants de nos pères éboueurs ou balayeurs de rue. Ce n'était pas du mépris pour nos parents. Au contraire: ce sont eux qui nous ont poussés à faire des études. Ils voulaient que leurs enfants gravissent les échelons dans la société française. Pour casser les marches des Beurs, on a vu apparaître SOS Racisme [. . .] Ça a cassé le processus politique ouvert par les Beurs. Les gens de SOS Racisme ont intégré les rangs des socialistes [. . .] Les Beurs, ceux des marches, n'ont pas rejoint le PS; nous, on est retournés plus ou moins gentiment dans nos petites associations. SOS Racisme a fait l'éloge de la différence. Ils avaient raison: c'est vrai qu'on est tous différents, rien qu'au niveau de nos ADN. En fait, ils ont eu tort car, plutôt que de rassembler, ils ont creusé le fossé. Ça a servi le camp adverse. Ça a été négatif.

Nous, les Beurs, on disait: 'le mélange, c'est comme l'essence, ça fait marcher les mobylettes'. Et pas: 'Nous, on est beaux'. Pour moi, Beur n'est pas spécialement *beautiful*. [. . .] Aujourd'hui, ceux qui ont cru en cet élan des marches des Beurs sont aigris. Nous qui avions été éduqués à l'école française, égalitaire, laïque et républicaine, nous avons perdu nos illusions. Certains sont devenus complètement désabusés; d'autres ont été poussés vers des valeurs dites traditionnelles – mais qui, pour nous, je répète, élevés à l'école républicaine, n'avaient rien de 'traditionnel' – familiales et religieuses. C'est une marche arrière. Et aujourd'hui, comment veut-on que des jeunes à qui on dit qu'ils ont une identité différente, ne cèdent pas à d'autres sirènes? [. . .] Les jeunes ont le sentiment de ne pas exister. Ils doivent attendre 18 ans pour avoir la nationalité française? Qu'est-ce qu'on leur laisse comme marge? Tout casser.

© Périphéries, novembre 1998, www.peripheries.net/i-nadi.htm.

Document 12b: La normalisation de la gauche?

Le problème de Mitterrand fut de rendre la gauche majoritaire en la réunifiant, malgré un PCF puissant. Il y parvint en adoptant un programme ultra-socialiste et en laissant espérer une pratique modérée. Pour Jospin, il s'agit aujourd'hui de rendre la gauche majoritaire, malgré un PCF faible et après avoir pratiqué une politique modérée. L'idée d'une planification centrale a disparu, et même celle d'une 'planification démocratique'. L'appropriation collective des moyens de production s'est également évanouie. Le gouvernement Jospin a privatisé autant que ses prédécesseurs de droite. L'ouverture du capital des entreprises publiques est l'euphémisme qui permet de persévérer dans cette voie. L'autarcie, le protectionnisme et le volontarisme industriel ne sont plus de mise [. . .] L'Europe, le marché mondial et le déclin communiste auront été les professeurs de modération du socialisme français.

Jean-Claude Casanova, 'Présidentielle: l'état de la gauche', *Le Monde*, 22 mars 2002, pp. 1–20.

Document 12c: Le *Front National* en 2002

'*La France retrouvée*'. Profession de foi de Jean-Marie Le Pen: deuxième tour des élections présidentielles 2002

Je suis socialement à gauche, économiquement à droite et, plus que jamais, nationalement de France!

J'ai fait un rêve pour chacun d'entre vous. Le rêve d'une France retrouvée dans laquelle il ferait, à nouveau, bon vivre. N'ayez pas peur de rêver, vous, les petits, vous les exclus, vous les jeunes, vous les victimes du Système, vous dont on refuse d'entendre la voix. Ne vous laissez surtout pas piéger par les vieilles divisions de la gauche et de la droite. Vingt ans durant, ils vous ont menti sur l'insécurité, le

continued

chômage, l'immigration, sur l'Europe et sur le reste. Vous les ouvriers et les ouvrières de toutes les industries ruinées par l'Europe de Maastricht. Vous, les artisans, les commerçants et les entrepreneurs persécutés par le fisc. Vous, les fonctionnaires et les représentants des forces de l'ordre, bafoués par un État que vous vous acharnez à défendre. Vous les agriculteurs et les pêcheurs aux retraites de misères, acculés à la ruine et à la disparition. Vous, les parents qui tremblez pour vos enfants, même à l'école. Vous qui avez désormais peur de sortir le soir dans la rue. Vous, les retraités qui peinez à joindre les deux bouts. Vous, Françaises et Français, quelque soit votre race, votre religion ou votre condition sociale, je vous demande de donner à la France cette chance historique qu'elle a de se redresser enfin.

Homme du peuple, je serai toujours du coté de ceux qui souffrent. Orphelin de guerre, j'ai connu le froid, la faim, la pauvreté, j'ai été travailleur manuel, puis chef d'entreprise. Jeune député, j'ai combattu en Algérie, avec le contingent. Je veux redonner fierté et cohésion à notre grand peuple français. La France peut et doit devenir le centre d'un monde francophone, économique, social, culturel et politique de 400 millions d'hommes.

Chers compatriotes, si vous vous êtes abstenus ou si vous avez voté pour un autre candidat, au deuxième tour ne vous abstenez pas et votez pour moi, le seul candidat qui peut faire changer les choses. Ne vous laissez pas manipuler par les medias ou par les politiciens. Je ne vous ai jamais caché la vérité, même quand elle n'était pas agréable à entendre. J'ai toujours respecté mes engagements et je continuerai à le faire demain. Je n'ai qu'une ambition: la France et les Français!

Topics
FOR DISCUSSION

1   Why did Mitterrand win the 1981 presidential elections?
2   How did Mitterrand set out to transform France? To what extent was he successful?
3   What issues did the *marche des beurs* raise? To what extent does Document 12a defend a republican ideal?
4   Compare the strengths and weaknesses of the French left in 1981 and 2002. How does Document 12b help us to understand the changing nature of the French left?
5   What reasons could explain the rise of the FN? What are the political objectives of the FN? In Document 12c, who are 'France's enemies'? Why does Le Pen find it necessary to insist on his personal *parcours*?

CHAPTER 13

France since 2002

Timeline

2002
5 May   Jacques Chirac re-elected president (82%) against Jean-Marie Le Pen
June   Landslide victory in legislative elections for centre-right UMP. Chirac appoints Raffarin as PM
November   Widespread public sector strikes over government privatisation plans bring country to a standstill

2003
14 February   de Villepin's discourse to the UN against military intervention in Iraq
April–May   Muslims in France elect the first Conseil Français du Culte Musulman (CFCM)
May–July   Major industrial action against pension reforms

2004
15 March   Law prohibiting the wearing of signs or dress ostensibly displaying a religious affiliation in schools

2005
23 February   Parliament vote through a law recognising the positive benefits of colonisation
29 May   Referendum on EU constitution: the project is rejected by 54.7% of French voters. Prime Minister Raffarin resigns and is replaced by de Villepin
October   National strikes against welfare reforms, low pay and privatisation of public services
October–November   Paris suburbs are hit by riots following confrontation between youths of North African origin and the police.

The second round of the 2002 presidential elections opposing Jacques Chirac to Jean-Marie Le Pen marked a turning point in recent French history for two reasons. First, it was the last time that left-wing voters, under the banner of an anti-FN Republican Front, rallied behind the conservative candidate Jacques Chirac to crush Le Pen's presidential ambitions. Ten years later, this notion of a republican alliance had lost its political potency principally because ideas traditionally defended by the extreme right had made tremendous inroads into mainstream politics. A majority of conservative rank and files were keen to see their party concluding local alliances with the FN, whereas a substantial number of left-wing voters were attracted to the FN's programme of state intervention to defend vulnerable parts of the economy – a notion that the mainstream left had long disavowed. Second, the salience given to the Chirac–Le Pen duel deprived France of an in-depth debate about the future, which presidential campaigns usually bring to the fore. This was unfortunate, as the time was ripe to ask serious questions about the role of France in Europe and in the world, about the efficacy, sustainability and desirability of its socio-economic model, and the enduring relevance of its republican values, such as *laïcité*. At a time when global market forces, migratory and ecological

Unrest spirals out and spreads to other cities. Emergency measures are introduced to restore order

2006
March–April   Youth employment laws (CPE: Contrat Première Embauche) are scrapped after mass demonstrations across France

2007
*6 May   Nicolas Sarkozy wins presidential election (53.6%) against socialist candidate Ségolène Royal. Sarkozy appoints Fillon as PM
June   The UMP wins parliamentary elections
20 December   Sarkozy presents his controversial views on laïcité in a discourse delivered in the Lateran Basilica, Rome*

2008
October   France plans to inject 10.5bn euros into the country's six largest banks

2009
October   Launch of the 'grand débat sur l'identité nationale' by the Ministry of Immigration and National Identity

2010
*30 July   Sarkozy's tough discourse in Grenoble on immigration and law and order is seen as a lurch to the right. Illegal Roma camps are dismantled and their residents deported back to Romania and Bulgaria
September–October   Massive demonstrations against government plans to rise retirement age to 62*

2011
15 January   Sarkozy declares France's support to the democratisation process in Tunisia

trends, new ideas (about religion, for instance) and new technologies were clearly challenging the 'French model', the country voted massively for Chirac (with 82 per cent, the biggest landslide in a presidential election) as a way of blocking Le Pen, even though the incumbent president did not have a clear programme.

This chapter will explore debates about the weight of external constraints and what appears to be France's reluctance to embrace a market-led globalisation, often defined as an imposition of Anglo-Saxon values. Not that to reform is an impossible task in France, as it is often claimed, but overall the discourse about change and its desirability is more critical, less enthusiastic. The issue of how much control the nation should retain over its borders to preserve its identity has become a defining debate of the early twenty-first century, cutting right through the traditional left/right political cleavage. The chapter also seeks to situate France in its international environment and chart how it has sought to maintain its prestige on the world stage now that the country is resolutely a second-rank power. In doing so the chapter will examine how the idea of decline has become part of a national narrative that straddles the left/right divide and has become particularly important to the political ambitions of conservative leaders, such as Sarkozy.

2002–7 Chirac's second term

International relations

In terms of popularity Chirac's opposition to the Iraq War made spring 2003 into the high water mark of his two presidential terms. At home the right championed his stance as a sign of renewed international vigour, while the left supported him on the grounds of anti-imperialism: a moment of consensus that was a throwback to de Gaulle's strident foreign policy in the 1960s. Abroad Chirac received a hero's welcome in Algeria during an offi-

*March   France plays leading
role in enforcing no-fly zone
over Libya
3 March   Decree prohibiting
the concealment of the face
in public, often dubbed the
anti-burqa law
August–November   Drastic
austerity measures aimed at
reducing public deficit*

2012
*6 May   Socialist candidate
François Hollande wins the
presidential elections (51.6%)
against Sarkozy and appoints
Ayrault as PM
June   Socialists and their
allies win majority in
parliamentary elections*

2013
*January   French forces
intervene in Mali to help
government regain control
over the north of the country
seized by Islamists
May   France enters recession
after the economy shrank by
0.4% over the past 8 months.
Unemployment reaches 10.5%*

cial three-day visit beginning on 2 March 2003. Over half a million people lined the streets of Algiers as he made his way through the capital in an open top limousine. Accompanied by five cabinet ministers, the official visit was intended not only to cement a new era in Franco-Algerian relations, but also to send a clear international signal, namely that France was a voice of peace with strong support in the Arab World.

The Algerian connection was important in other ways too because in opposing invasion Chirac stressed to Blair the fact that he had been an officer in the Algerian War. So, unlike the British Prime Minister, he had first-hand knowledge of the devastating consequences of war. Such exchanges were a measure of deteriorating relations which, once the invasion began on 20 March, went from bad to worse. The Chirac–Blair dynamic became notoriously fractious, while in the USA anti-French feeling led a Republican dominated Congress to rename French fries as 'Freedom Fries' in the Congressional cafeterias in Washington, a ruling that spawned a nationwide movement.

By 15 April 2003 British and US forces, supported by a small Australian contingent, had seemingly defeated Saddam Hussein's forces and on 1 May Bush declared that the major combat operations were over. It was fantasy politics. In reality little thought had gone into post-invasion reconstruction and in the absence of a plan the country descended into chaos. By 2004 British and US forces were bogged down in a war against a number of insurgent groups; a situation made even worse by revelations about torture and human rights abuses carried out by the US army in Abu Ghraib prison in Baghdad.

Given this train of events, Chirac felt vindicated and continued to argue that intervention should have gone through the UN. While recognising that the Saddam's removal was positive, he was adamant that the invasion had made the world a more dangerous place, telling the BBC on 17 November 2004: 'There's no doubt that there has been an increase in terrorism and one of the origins of that has been the situation in Iraq. I'm not at all sure that one can say that the world is safer.'

As the events in Iraq unfolded, Chirac threw his weight behind a 'yes' vote in the referendum for a European Union constitution on 29 May 2005. In part his campaign was about political authority. With falling poll ratings, he wanted to reassert his presidential power. But it was also about legacy. With his tenure coming to an end, he wanted to be remembered as the leader who 'saved' the European project. In this respect Chirac played the anti-Anglo-Saxon card to the hilt, arguing that a 'no' vote would be in the interests of Anglo-Saxon powers who wished to stop 'European construction'. In contrast, he continued, a 'yes' vote, by endorsing a constitution that streamlined institutions and made decision making easier, would give the EU strength and prevent an uncontrolled free-market world dominated by the USA.

In party political terms Chirac's 'yes' camp was supported by the three main parties: the Centre, UMP and PS. The 'no' camp drew support from the left with the Greens, the PCF and the Trotskyist parties all denouncing the constitution as a 'capitalist's charter'. Significantly, too, the 'no' argument was bolstered by Laurent Fabius who broke with the PS line on the grounds that the constitution was a threat to France's social model. On the far right the FN attacked the constitution as a further erosion of French sovereign power, while Philippe de Villiers brandished the spectre of the 'Polish plumber'. Pointing towards the enlargement of the EU in 2004 to 25 countries, de Villiers portrayed the EU as an institution out of control. For him it was clear that this expansion eastwards would open the door to Eastern Europeans such as Polish plumbers who, as EU citizens, would flood the job market with cheap labour, in effect stealing French work. Furthermore, de Villiers argued, this was just the thin end of a wedge that would lead ultimately to Turkish accession, a prospect that, according to opinion polls, was widely unpopular in France.

Polls in autumn 2004 suggested a narrow 'yes'. But by the spring the 'no' vote had taken a clear lead. To convince voters Chirac put his reputation on the line, forcefully intervening with a succession of television and radio appearances. Underlining that the constitution had been endorsed in Spain by a wide margin, he argued that France must not become the 'black sheep' that sabotaged the European project. It was to no avail. The referendum on 29 May 2005 delivered a resounding 'no', with 55 per cent rejecting the constitution out of a 69 per cent turnout.

Three days later the Dutch followed suit. The constitution was in tatters – a personal humiliation for Chirac – and he quickly responded. Promising a government that would act, Chirac sacked Raffarin as prime minister and replaced him with Dominique de Villepin. Even more significantly, the new cabinet included the return of Sarkozy as Interior Minister who had stood down the previous summer as Finance Minister when he was elected the UMP leader.

Social issues

The referendum was a political verdict on Chirac and throughout the autumn his opinion ratings plummeted. This was because the economy was gripped by a terrible sameness. Unemployment remained stubbornly stuck at 10 per cent, disproportionately affecting young people and French people of African origin, while growth levels were sluggish.

It was in this context that large-scale urban riots broke out across the country during autumn 2005. Voices of discontent had emerged in early 2005 on the internet from a group proclaiming themselves to be the 'natives of the republic' (www.indigènes-république.fr). Their argument: French people of African descent were suffering from social exclusion because of slavery and colonial racism. This legacy, it was argued, meant they would always be seen as the 'natives' of the French Empire rather than as equal citizens.

Although the exact strength of the 'natives of the republic' was difficult to gauge, it was a tinder box atmosphere which was fuelled further when Sarkozy was pelted with stones and bottles during a visit to a police station in the run-down Paris suburb of Argenteuil on 25 October. Provocatively Sarkozy described the rioters as scum (*racaille*). Then two days later two teenagers, Zyed Benna and Bouna Traore, were fatally electrocuted as they hid from pursuing police in an electrical sub-station in Clichy-sous-Bois, another Paris suburb largely populated by North African immigrants and their French-born descendants. News of their deaths triggered riots in Clichy-sous-Bois which quickly spread, first to the rest of the Paris region and then the rest of France. By 8 November rioting had engulfed the poorer parts of many major towns and cities, including Amiens, Belfort, Bordeaux, Lille, Lyon, St Etienne and Toulouse. On one night alone 1,173 cars were burnt, 330 people arrested and 12 police officers injured.

The scale of the violence led the government to authorise Emergency Powers, a set of measures established in 1955 during the early stages of the Algerian War, and under them local authorities in more than 30 French towns and cities imposed curfews or restricted people's movements. By the middle of November the rioting finally began to subside as Chirac, accused of weakness by his political opponents, sought to regain the initiative and meet his critics head-on. In a televised speech he was clear that law and order had to be respected. Rioters would be brought to justice. But he also reached out to the rioters, describing them as 'the sons and daughters of the republic' and condemned racism in the clearest terms: 'How many CVs are thrown in the waste paper basket because of the name or the address of the applicant?...We will never build anything long-lasting without fighting this poison of racism'.

The government recognised that the root cause was unemployment. Its response was a flagship policy designed to create jobs in the poorer suburbs: the *Contrat Première Embauche* (CPE – First Employment Contract) which made it easier to fire under-26-year-olds. De Villepin's argument was that the labour market was too weighed down with restrictive laws. This meant that employers were reluctant to take young people on. Thus by making it easier to lay people off, de Villepin reasoned, the CPE would unlock jobs because employers would be willing to take more risks on young applicants.

Inevitably de Villepin's proposals immediately ran into hostility from trade unions, not least because of the way the government used the UMP majority to rush the legislation through the National Assembly, and on 18 March 2006 1.5 million people demonstrated across the country. Students in particular became the focus of opposition and soon, in the face of coordinated occupations, half the 84 universities were closed. It was the largest student protest since 1968 and, confronted with a protracted stand-off, neither de Villepin nor Chirac showed the appetite for a fight. Quickly the government back-pedalled and by April the CPE had effectively been shelved.

Decline?

In 2003, Nicolas Baverez's *La France qui tombe: un constat clinique du déclin français* became a best-seller: as an economic historian and member of the French employers' federation (MEDEF), Baverez argued that France needed a 'shock therapy', a set of radical reforms which would make her accept – and benefit from – the rules of global competition. He regretted the 'lack of courage' from centre-right governments and deplored their refusal to undertake such reforms. The economist Eric Le Boucher, in his weekly chronicle in *Le Monde*, lambasted Chirac's caution and in 2005 claimed that the French model was not only poorly adapted to global competition, but also failed to protect vulnerable people against unemployment and poverty, despite high levels of taxation and social security contributions. In the early 2000s, the prophets of doom were dominant: the number of books, pamphlets, reviews and special issues devoted to France's decline was such that the famous Parisian bookshop Gibert Jeune opened a section entirely dedicated to the subject. In July 2005, a survey revealed 66 per cent of the French thought that France was declining. For Sarkozy, Chirac had become a lame duck president defined by the absence of any meaningful programme. Equating Chirac's prudence with a lack of vision and a desire to avoid polarising public opinion, Sarkozy developed a confrontational political style that was partly moulded in reaction to Chirac's leadership.

Yet, for the pessimistic political commentators, the roots of France's decline ran deeper. In *Les Trente Piteuses (1968–1998)* Baverez clearly blamed the political and moral choices made in 1968 as the deciding factors in France's decline. This became one of the core polarising themes of Sarkozy's 2007 electoral campaign. For him, May 68's legacy, its intellectual and moral relativism, had to be 'liquidated' once and for all. This attack on May 68 provided a national political narrative to put forward neo-liberal criticisms

Le Minitel

From 1982, the Minitel, a small dun screen with a keyboard connected to a telephone landline, started to appear in French homes. A four digit dial connected users with a range of services, allowing them to book train tickets, review their bank accounts or seek online sexual thrills. As part of an ambitious drive to equip the country with cutting edge technology and assert its technological independence, the Ministry of Telecommunications sponsored the project and provided all subscribers with a Minitel terminal, free of charge. By 1995, there were more than 20 million Minitel users, who could access some 25,000 online services, the world's first large database accessible to the general public. Yet, its terminals were not computers: they could not store, analyse or search data. Licences to offer a service had to be approved by State agencies (France Télécom), which failed to turn a technological success into a global commercial venture. No other countries bought the Minitel. With the advent of the Internet and free market solutions, the Minitel's days were numbered. Amid a degree of nostalgia for state-sponsored technological grandeur, this 'Internet-in-one country' finally went offline in June 2012.

commonly found in 'Anglo-Saxon' countries, and for this reason, often perceived to be alien to France's culture. On these terms this anti-68 narrative underlined how May 1968 had eroded a strong work ethic, promoted dependency on an overly generous welfare state, and embedded a reluctance to embrace the rigour of a free-market global economy.

It is unlikely that Sarkozy's attack on May 68 was the determining factor in his electoral victory in 2007. After all, a survey published by CSA in March 2008 revealed that 78 per cent of the French thought that May 68 had been a source of progress rather than decline. Some even pointed with some relish that as a twice-divorced candidate, Sarkozy would not have been able to contest a presidential election if May 68 had not shaken to the core traditional family values. Yet Sarkozy's ambition to break away from the past, his attempt to polarise debates around a clear left/right cleavage and in doing so, to redefine the ideological and sociological contours of the French right proved to be successful. In May 2007, he won the presidential elections with 53 per cent of the vote. His opponent, the Socialist candidate Ségolène Royal, the first woman to reach the second round of a presidential election in France, appeared unprepared to face Sarkozy's well-choreographed campaign. By contrast Royal's programme lacked clarity and economic clout, and some of its authoritarian proposals – such as the incarceration of juvenile delinquents in military boot camps – were unpalatable to traditional left-wing voters. Above all, her campaign was undermined from within. The PS's elites, whose role in the campaign she decided to marginalise, only provided a lukewarm support, some even casting doubt on a woman's ability to do the job. Compared with the UMP, a redoubtable electoral machine entirely geared toward Sarkozy's victory, the PS could win scores of local and regional elections, but failed to rise to the requirements of a presidential campaign. Conversely, Sarkozy's results proved that he had attracted voters outside the traditional UMP's sphere of influence: in particular, he scored well among voters who had previously supported the Front National (FN): as Interior Minister, Sarkozy's controversial law and order policies and strong stance on immigration had convinced them that he could now implement what the FN had long advocated. It is estimated that in 2007, the FN lost some one million potential voters to Sarkozy. Neo-liberals, moral conservatives and ethno-nationalist voters thus formed a politically awkward, but electorally effective alliance which saw in Sarkozy a man ready to break France's pattern of decline.

Le Sarkozysme et la droite décomplexée

Le Sarkozysme has variously been analysed as a modern version of Bonapartisme given its authoritarian and nationalist tendencies; a Pétainiste mentality with its desire to overcome moral decline (rooted in May 68) and readiness to scapegoat particular sections of the population; and an awkward synthesis between the neo-liberal, Gaullist and extreme right-wing traditions. It has also been compared to Berlusconi's populism, for its brash political style, anti-intellectualism, business-oriented programme, incestuous relations with the media and obsession with celebrities, but also to American neo-conservatism for its virulent attack on left-wing principles and policies. Sarkozy himself had defined its political ambition in *Témoignage*, a book published at the start of his presidential campaign:

> I have worked hard to give back to the French right its self-confidence. [*Je me suis beaucoup mobilisé pour décomplexer la droite française*]. For a long time, it remained paralysed in face of the left which relished nothing more than occupying the moral high ground. And so the right, by remaining silent, became the accomplice in the obliteration of its own identity. Instead of defining what it stood for, it ended up defining itself by what it was not or was not anymore...this suicidal strategy explains in part the enduring success of the National Front.

Yet, Sarkozy's ability to attract FN voters in 2007 was not solely motivated by electoral opportunism but a willingness to operate a major ideological realignment of the French right. The overall project was a clear rupture with the past, or at least, with the Chirac years. There were differences of style: Sarkozy's personal taste for the limelight, expensive life-style, and presidential hyper-activism contrasted with Chirac's preferences for farmers' fairs, traditional regional food, and quiet but cunning leadership. Yet, the rupture was to be an ideological one: the creation of a right free from complexes (*une droite décomplexée*). Whether in practice this ideological re-orientation led to a major policy change is open to question.

Sarkozy's redefinition of the right first rested on the reactivation of the left/right cleavage which, throughout the 1990s, had increasingly become blurred. Under Sarkozy's presidency, the French right indulged in a flurry of controversial declarations, such as: the chemical castration of rapists; the use of DNA testing for visa applications by families; superiority of Western civilisation; inability of young Muslims to speak French properly. Divisive and polarising policies were also introduced, such as the creation of a Ministry for Immigration and National Identity, the expulsion of Roma or the ban of the burqa. Crucially, they also granted a strong degree of legitimacy to the FN's rhetoric.

Immigration and *laïcité*

This legitimisation of FN arguments is illustrated by the discourse that Sarkozy made in Grenoble in 2010. Following shootings between drug dealers and the police in Grenoble's suburbs in July 2010, drastic law and order measures were announced, some of which explicitly targeted immigrants or people who had recently acquired French nationality. For instance, Sarkozy demanded that juvenile offenders born in France from foreign parents be denied the right to automatically acquire French nationality when they reach adulthood. He also demanded that French citizens of foreign origin who deliberately sought to harm representatives of public authority, be stripped of their French nationality. By doing so, he defined *de facto* different categories of French citizens, opposing ethnic French people and others, and thus tapping into one of the most enduring obsessions of the extreme right. The objective was also to contest the FN's monopoly on the stigmatisation of Islam. When in 2011 Marine Le Pen compared Muslim street prayers to the Nazi Occupation of France, Sarkozy quickly called on the UMP to organise a national debate on the place of Islam in France. This initiative backfired and revealed strong divisions within UMP itself. Sarkozy's redefinition of right-wing values was not to everyone's taste within the UMP: Prime Minister François Fillon, for instance, expressed his staunch opposition to such policies, rejecting the stigmatisation of Muslims in France.

Similarly, Sarkozy intended to break with the past by redefining the ideological foundation of **la laïcité**. On 20 December 2007, he took up his duties as canon of Saint John Lateran Basilica in Rome, an honorific title granted by the Vatican to French rulers since King Henry IV (1598–1610). Sarkozy accepted the honour, as other presidents did before him, but turned a symbolic and usually discreet diplomatic ceremonial into a major political event: regretting the suffering that the French Republic once inflicted on the catholic clergy, he invited the French to rediscover the Christian roots of the nation that, he argued, an anti-clerical Republic had once wrongly tried to sever. He asserted that the actions of those who are inspired by transcendental values are inherently superior to those driven by secular motivations. He questioned the ability of state school teachers, untouched by divine grace, to transmit important values when compared to that of priests and pastors untainted by moral relativism. Finally, to declare, as he did, that religion should make a positive contribution to public debates and play an active role in the definition of a public morality was a major rupture with the traditional republican ideal. For a staunch republican, religious preferences are a matter of private choice. Reason and progress – that is neither faith, nor identity – are the basis for

la laïcité

There is no consensus on what *laïcité* is or should be. As defined by the 1905 law, *laïcité* refers to the separation of Church and State and the prohibition for one to run, influence or finance the other. The law guarantees freedom of conscience, the freedom to practise one's religion provided that the expression of a religious preference does not disrupt public order: places of worship must not become political forums. As such, *laïcité* is different from *sécularisation*, which indicates a growing indifference towards religion.

Laïcité may also be seen as the necessary condition to ensure that religion is not exploited for political reasons: religions may positively contribute to public debates (for instance on bio-ethics, or poverty) providing they accept pluralism as a pre-condition for their participation: this is the position of the French Catholic Church, which saw in Sarkozy's Lateran discourse a vindication of its own position. For others still, *la laïcité* is a politically oppressive idea: it is not enough for individuals to have the right to worship (religious freedom is constitutionally recognised by the Republic), but their belonging to a religious group should confer on them specific rights. In that respect, they often point to British multiculturalism as a desirable model. Finally, for neo-republicans, *la laïcité* is the spine of republicanism, the solution to a domestic war which had pitched the French against themselves: it warrants equality between individuals of different creeds (or without any), and prevents the nation from crumbling under the pressure of religious communities.

political action. The clerical tone of the discourse may have flattered part of Sarkozy's electoral base, but its core ambition was to redefine at the highest level the meaning of *la laïcité.*

It is customary to present the expulsion of three veiled French Muslim girls from their school in 1989 as the key moment when *laïcité* erupted into the public debate. The 2004 law which forbids the wearing of ostentatious religious articles (such as veils, kippas and crosses) in state schools did not, as intended, close the debate, as the issue resurfaced at regular intervals, but with a renewed intensity under Nicolas Sarkozy's presidency. Islam quickly became a key point of tension.

The promotion of a moderate Muslim elite who could diffuse more radical religious demands has been a major ambition shared by successive ministers of the Interior, from left and right since the late 1980s. In 2003, Nicolas Sarkozy as Minister of Interior announced the creation of the Conseil Français du Culte Musulman (CFCM). Specific tensions between Sarkozy and the CFCM soon mirrored wider issues concerning the relations between Islam and *laïcité.* Among the different groups represented with the CFCM, Sarkozy initially favoured the Union des Organisations Islamiques de France (UOIF), whose neo-conservative values, more rigorist religious interpretation of Islam and above all its desire to appear as a French-based organisation resonated with his political instincts. Sarkozy wished to encourage the formation of an 'electoral lobby' among Muslims which could supplement his conservative votes and act as a relay for his forceful law and order policy in French suburbs. Indeed, in 2004, the UOIF called Muslims to abstain from demonstrating against the law banning ostentatious religious symbols in schools and in 2005, when riots spread through some French suburbs, it issued a fatwa calling young Muslims to respect law and order. To conflate issues pertaining to the *banlieues* with Islam offended some Muslims who found that most of their official representatives showed too much loyalty towards their political masters. On the other hand, with no Muslim vote emerging in his favour, Sarkozy performed a U-turn and refocused his strategy on the defence of a French national identity endangered by Muslim values. The 2010 law banning the wearing of burqa in public places or controversies about the growing visibility of halal products, show that debates about *la laïcité* have become polarised and politicised.

Born with the republican left which sought to limit the influence of religion in the name of freedom and progress, hard-line *laïcité* has now become one of the battle flags of the FN, whose ultra-Catholic clientele once refused to recognise an impious republic. Islamophobia often serves to bridge differences between the extreme right, the mainstream right and the hard-line republican left; a form of political syncretism that is well illustrated, since 2007, by the website *Risposte laïque* where there is no clear differentiation between left and right on this issue, but rather a variety of complex positions cutting right across traditional political cleavages.

NATO, Europe and the Arab Spring

Sarkozy wanted to position himself as a mould breaker. Emulating Tony Blair, he sought to go beyond traditional notions of left and right in a way that would disorientate opponents. This was why he appointed Bernard Kouchner as Foreign Minister in his first government in May 2007. Kouchner was a household name as a man of the left who had co-founded the world famous *Médecins Sans Frontières* in 1971 and served as minister in a series of socialist governments between 1988 and 1999, notably as a Minister of Health from 1992 to 1993. As a Socialist Party member Kouchner had recently supported Royal's presidential bid, so for Sarkozy his appointment to such an impor-tant post was a statement. Sarkozy wanted to demonstrate that his was a different type government: one that was open to all political talents.

Kouchner's acceptance of the post produced outrage in the Socialist party which expelled him, but he justified his decision on the grounds that he would be able to fashion a foreign policy which focused on humanitarian issues. High profile initiatives though remained the privileged domain of Sarkozy. Thus it was Sarkozy who announced France's return to the NATO military command structure on 11 March 2009. By reversing de Gaulle's 1966 decision, it was a highly symbolic foreign policy gesture which, Sarkozy argued, reflected the realities on the ground. France was the fourth biggest contributor of troops to NATO, while French generals were already commanding operations in Kosovo and Afghanistan. Opinion polls showed that a clear majority, 58 per cent according to *Paris Match*, supported Sarkozy, but amongst his political opponents there was outrage. On the left and within the UMP critics denounced the move as a betrayal of the Gaullist tradition that would undermine France's ability to act as a counterweight to US influence in the world, in particular within the Arab world. Sarkozy was adamant, however. France, he maintained, needed to have a say in the future direction of NATO and in an effort to quash UMP dissent, François Fillon, the prime minister, made it into a matter of principle, stating that he would resign if the government lost the vote. One week later the decision was ratified by parliament by 329 to 238.

Through the NATO decision Sarkozy wanted to demonstrate that he was not a pris-oner of the Gaullist tradition. For him boldness was the key; a policy that was equally clear in the way in which he built bridges with the new Barack Obama administration in Washington, elected in November 2008, while also trying to assume leadership of the European Union. With the EU he sought to give fresh impetus to the Euro-Mediterranean initiative launched in 1995 which, through partnership between the EU and the coun-tries of the southern Mediterranean, aimed to turn the region into an area of dialogue, exchange and cooperation. Sarkozy also tried to reinvigorate the integration process through the elucidation of a simplified treaty that would replace the stalled European constitution. Indeed by the time France assumed the six-month EU Presidency in July 2008, he had outlined an ambitious agenda whose aim was to transform the EU into a global actor that could prevent ideological confrontation between Islam and the West; engage with emerging powers such as Brazil, China and India; and combat global warming. No less significantly Sarkozy underlined his opposition to Turkish member-ship, while also underlining the need for a co-ordinated defence and security strategy.

If Sarkozy was strident over NATO, Franco-US relations and the EU, he and his government were badly caught off guard by the Arab Spring in early 2011. The events that shook the Arab World began in Tunisia on 17 December 2010 when Mohammed

Bouazizi, a jobless graduate, set himself on fire after police confiscated his vegetable cart and spat in his face. On 4 January 2011 Bouazizi died from his injuries and his humiliation sparked widespread protests that toppled President Ben Ali ten days later. Given that the Ben Ali regime was one of the most repressive in the region, the Tunisian example gave encouragement to the rest of North Africa and the Middle East and soon Algeria, Egypt, Morocco, Lebanon, Oman, Syria and Yemen were witnessing opposition movements. In Algeria and Morocco the protests were contained by promise of reform, but in Egypt President Hosni Mubarak was overthrown on 11 February. In Libya protests broke out in the eastern part of the country against Muammar Gaddafi's regime on 15 February while in Syria security forces killed five protesters on 19 March, the gravest unrest in that country for years.

These movements were driven by young, educated, ambitious populations rising up against entrenched regimes. They wanted a different future and key to their action was use of the social media – Facebook, Twitter, YouTube, mobile phones – to outwit police and army repression. Yet, the way to which Sarkozy reacted to events showed the French government to be out of touch with the Arab world. Initially French ministers voiced support for Ben Ali, even offering advice on how to control the law and order situation. Only when Ben Ali had departed did Sarkozy admit mistakes in press conference on 23 January, stating that France had been too close to Ben Ali and thus unable to comprehend the situation clearly: 'Behind the emancipation of women, the drive for education and training, the economic dynamism, the emergence of a middle class, there was despair, a suffering, a sense of suffocation. We have to recognise that we underestimated it.'

This lack of understanding was underlined by Alain Juppé who replaced Kouchner as Foreign Minister in an autumn 2010 reshuffle. In a conference on the Arab Spring on 16 April 2011 at the Institute of the Arab World in Paris he admitted that the revolutions had come as a 'surprise': 'For too long we thought that authoritarian regimes were the only bastions against extremism in the Arab world. Too long, we have brandished the Islamist threat as a pretext for justifying to an extent turning a blind eye on governments which were flouting freedom and curbing their country's development.'

Juppé concluded that France must not be afraid of this 'Arab Spring', emphasising that the government intended to back the transition to democracy in North Africa and the Middle East. Thereafter Sarkozy tried to seize the high ground, firstly by calling on G8 countries to provide a financial aid package to post-revolutionary Egypt and Tunisia on 26 May 2011 and then by urging NATO intervention in support of the anti-Gaddafi opposition in Libya. Indeed when Gaddafi was finally overthrown Sarkozy, accompanied by David Cameron, made a dramatic visit to Tripoli where his intention was clear. By embracing the Libyan revolution as a personal victory, Sarkozy wanted to banish his earlier ambiguities over Tunisia and cast himself as a champion of the 'Arab Spring'.

Economic and social turmoil

Sarkozy's 2007 presidential campaign promised a major rupture with the remains of a planned economic culture, which had already been seriously eroded over the previous

25 years. His leading slogan 'work harder to earn more' (*travailler plus pour gagner plus*) was not only aimed at castigating the 35-hour week – the flagship reform of the Jospin government that Chirac never challenged – but to extol the virtue of hard work and enterprise. It echoed back to Guizot's slogan from the 1830s 'Enrich yourselves!' (*'Enrichissez-vous!'*) and satisfied the liberal instincts of the French Orleanist right (chapter 3). In 2007, he pledged to overhaul the French welfare state, arguing that it was financially too costly and discouraged work. His planned reforms of the labour market had a definite Anglo-Saxon flavour: he thought of scrapping the minimum wage to boost employment or to cut benefits for the unemployed who refused two jobs or further professional training. But apart from increasing the retirement age from 60 to 62, amidst a wave of strikes and demonstrations, no overtly neo-liberal reforms were introduced. In fact, one would be hard pressed to find any ideological consistency in Sarkozy's economic policy. In July 2007, the so-called TEPA law (*Loi en faveur du Travail, de l'Emploi et du Pouvoir d'Achat*) introduced a raft of fiscal measures favouring highest earners and property owners: a cap on tax paid by France's wealthy elite (*le bouclier fiscal*) combined with Sarkozy's taste for the glittering world of celebrities made it easier to compare him with Silvio Berlusconi than Margaret Thatcher. In fact, Sarkozy's credentials as a free-marketeer were soon challenged by the 2008 financial and economic crisis. In September 2008 in a major speech in Toulon, Sarkozy tapped into the Bonapartiste tradition to justify an interventionist approach: capitalism had to be tamed, 'moralised', its core activities re-oriented towards production rather than speculation; globalisation and the financial sector had to be regulated, the State given a new role in steering the economy in the right direction and the EU a more forceful part to play in the economic governance of the world. At the national level, as the TEPA had boosted neither employees' purchasing power, nor consumption and investment, and as the tax shield had become a 'symbol of injustice', they were scrapped in 2010. At the European level, the President

The fate of the working class

In 2011, Terra Nova, a centre-left think tank, argued that the electoral heart of the French left was now made up of young people who found it difficult to secure a first job, women who struggled to juggle professional and familial duties, and immigrants and sexual minorities who faced daily discrimination. All these outsiders put their faith in the state to help them overcome exclusion. By contrast, well-integrated workers and employees with a modest income but a stable job were now fearing the consequences of globalisation (erosion of industrial base, lower wages, unemployment, migration) and tempted to vote for right-wing populist parties to protect the little they had acquired: 30 years ago, they would have had voted for a left-wing party. Class has thus become less important than the outsider/insider cleavage. Controversies erupted when Terra Nova suggested that a coalition between the outsiders and the liberal middle-class, around values such as solidarity, tolerance and openness, should now form the political and electoral backbone of the left. However, Terra Nova was adamant that a nostalgic attachment to a declining working class with whom the left now shared few values would be a strategic mistake.

sought to play a leading role in the management of the crisis, dramatising his personal role in effecting the outcomes of the European Council's meetings, announcing in turn the end of the crisis or its severe deepening. Yet, his high energy style could not detract from his *de facto* alignment with German strategic objectives which were forcefully set out by the Chancellor Angela Merkel. For this reason '*Merkozy*' not only became a by-word for austerity, but also, in the eyes of Sarkozy's opponents, for France's blind con-formity to Berlin's policies. Significantly, this Merkel–Sarkozy alignment was not enough to prevent rating agencies from downgrading France of its AAA in January 2012 – a major blow for Sarkozy because these agencies justified this downgrade on the grounds that France's reforms of its socio-economic model had not gone far enough.

The on-going economic crisis had a damaging effect on Sarkozy's opinion rating and as France geared up for the presidential elections in May 2012 he was clearly trailing his main opponent, the socialist candidate François Hollande. Hollande himself ran a carefully constructed campaign that attacked Sarkozy's weak points. Understanding the way in which Sarkozy's support for the wealthy had significantly damaged the incumbent's popularity, Hollande declared 'I do not like the rich' ('*Je n'aime pas les riches*'), paraphrasing his mentor, the late François Mitterrand, who once had famously quipped 'I do not like easy money' ('*Je n'aime pas l'argent facile*'). By doing so, Hollande was tapping into French political culture's enduring aversion, not so much to money, but to its conspicuous display. Hollande also projected a more serene style of presidential leadership, pledging to be a 'normal' president who would avoid brash statements and provide measured responses to difficult problems. Allied to this, Hollande cast Sarkozy as the subordinate partner in the Franco-German alliance, proposing an alternative economic solution; one that would focus upon growth and break with German imposed austerity at all costs.

In the first round Hollande won 28.63 per cent against 27.08 per cent for Sarkozy, while Marine Le Pen came third with 18 per cent of the vote – the largest for a far-right candidate under the Fifth Republic whose message of patriotism, protectionism and state regulation played well to blue-collar workers who felt threatened by the economic crisis. Then in the second round Hollande won with 51.64 per cent of the vote against 48.36 per cent for Sarkozy. It was a clear mandate, but, given the dire economic prob-lems, there was no honeymoon period. Hollande wanted to privilege long-term objectives over quick fixes, but as he pondered a political and economic strategy during the summer of 2012, he was immediately being criticised for a lack of leadership. The arch-Gaullist Henri Guaino ridiculed Hollande's calculated normality as a throwback to the disastrous indecision of the Fourth Republic.

One year on from his victory and Hollande's opinion poll ratings had plummeted to the lowest of any modern political leader: his measured approach had proved unable to reverse the Europe-wide austerity drive, restore growth or cut unemployment which at 3.2 million has reached record levels. In 2013 pessimism was still the dominant mood but as French commentators look to the past to make sense of the future, it is less the Fourth Republic which is alluded to, than the 1930s. With the economic crisis wors-ening, with the prospect of deep and lasting cuts, with an unpopular president who appears powerless in the face of external constraints, with a political class riven with corruption scandals, with an extreme right-wing party that is on the ascendant, a sense of gloom is all pervasive about the viability of the French model. Yet, although France has substantially reformed its economic and welfare system over the past two decades, in line with other European countries, the French remain more sceptical than their neighbours about the benefits to be gained from neo-liberal reforms inspired by the EU or imposed by global markets. On this basis scepticism will be a source of such conflict for some time to come.

Document 13a :   Dominique de Villepin, Discours prononcé à l'ONU lors de la crise irakienne – 14 février 2003

[…] Il y a deux options:

- l'option de la guerre peut apparaître a priori la plus rapide. Mais n'oublions pas qu'après avoir gagné la guerre, il faut construire la paix. Et ne nous voilons pas la face: cela sera long et difficile, car il faudra préserver l'unité de l'Irak, rétablir de manière durable la stabilité dans un pays et une région durement affectés par l'intrusion de la force;

- face à de telles perspectives, il y a l'alternative offerte par les inspections, qui permet d'avancer de jour en jour dans la voie d'un désarmement efficace et pacifique de l'Irak. Au bout du compte, ce choix-là n'est-il pas plus sûr et le plus rapide?

Personne ne peut donc affirmer aujourd'hui que le chemin de la guerre sera plus court que celui des inspections. Personne ne peut affirmer non plus qu'il pourrait déboucher sur un monde plus sûr, plus juste et plus stable. Car la guerre est toujours la sanction d'un échec. Serait-ce notre seul recours face aux nombreux défis actuels?

[…] Dans ce contexte, l'usage de la force ne se justifie pas aujourd'hui. Il y a une alternative à la guerre: désarmer l'Iraq par les inspections. De plus, un recours prématuré à l'option militaire serait lourd de conséquences. L'autorité de notre action repose aujourd'hui sur l'unité de la communauté internationale. Une intervention militaire prématurée remettrait en cause cette unité, ce qui lui enlèverait sa légitimité et, dans la durée, son efficacité. Une telle intervention pourrait avoir des conséquences incalculables pour la stabilité de cette région meurtrie et fragile. Elle renforcerait le sentiment d'injustice, aggraverait les tensions et risquerait d'ouvrir la voie à d'autres conflits.

Nous partageons tous une même priorité, celle de combattre sans merci le terrorisme. Ce combat exige une détermination totale. C'est, depuis la tragédie du 11 septembre, l'une de nos responsabilités premières devant nos peuples. Et la France, qui a été durement touchée à plusieurs reprises par ce terrible fléau, est entièrement mobilisée dans cette lutte qui nous concerne tous et que nous devons mener ensemble. C'est le sens de la réunion du Conseil de Sécurité qui s'est tenue le 20 janvier, à l'initiative de la France. Il y a dix jours, le Secrétaire d'Etat américain, M. Powell, a évoqué des liens supposés entre Al-Qaida et le régime de Bagdad. En l'état actuel de nos recherches et informations menées en liaison avec nos alliés, rien ne nous permet d'établir de tels liens. En revanche,

continued

nous devons prendre la mesure de l'impact qu'aurait sur ce plan une action militaire contestée actuellement. Une telle intervention ne risquerait-elle pas d'aggraver les fractures entre les sociétés, entre les cultures, entre les peuples, fractures dont se nourrit le terrorisme?

La France l'a toujours dit: nous n'excluons pas la possibilité qu'un jour il faille recourir à la force, si les rapports des inspecteurs concluaient à l'impossibilité pour les inspections de se poursuivre. Le Conseil devrait alors se prononcer et ses membres auraient à prendre toutes leurs responsabilités. Et, dans une telle hypothèse, je veux rappeler ici les questions que j'avais soulignées lors de notre dernier débat le 4 février et auxquelles nous devrons bien répondre: En quoi la nature et l'ampleur de la menace justifient-elles le recours immédiat à la force? Comment faire en sorte que les risques considérables d'une telle intervention puissent être réellement maîtrisés?

En tout état de cause, dans une telle éventualité, c'est bien l'unité de la communauté internationale qui serait la garantie de son efficacité. De même, ce sont bien les Nations Unies qui resteront demain, quoi qu'il arrive, au cœur de la paix à construire.

Monsieur le Président, à ceux qui se demandent avec angoisse quand et comment nous allons céder à la guerre, je voudrais dire que rien, à aucun moment, au sein de ce Conseil de Sécurité, ne sera le fait de la précipitation, de l'incompréhension, de la suspicion ou de la peur. Dans ce temple des Nations Unies, nous sommes les gardiens d'un idéal, nous sommes les gardiens d'une conscience. La lourde responsabilité et l'immense honneur qui sont les nôtres doivent nous conduire à donner la priorité au désarmement dans la paix. Et c'est un vieux pays, la France, d'un vieux continent comme le mien, l'Europe, qui vous le dit aujourd'hui, qui a connu les guerres, l'occupation, la barbarie. Un pays qui n'oublie pas et qui sait tout ce qu'il doit aux combattants de la liberté venus d'Amérique et d'ailleurs. Et qui pourtant n'a cessé de se tenir debout face à l'Histoire et devant les hommes. Fidèle à ses valeurs, il veut agir résolument avec tous les membres de la communauté internationale. Il croit en notre capacité à construire ensemble un monde meilleur.

Topics
FOR DISCUSSION

1 In this speech, what are the interests and values shared between France and the US? And what keeps the two countries apart?

2 For de Villepin, what is the ideal that France must defend? How is the country supposed to achieve this? With the benefit of hindsight, has France done so successfully?

3 To what extent is this a 'Gaullist' discourse? Or is it a departure from Gaullism?

Document 13b: Texte du discours du Président de la République Française dans la Salle de la Signature du Palais du Latran. Discours de Nicolas Sarkozy à Latran le 20.12.07.

[…] Tout autant que le baptême de Clovis, la laïcité est également un fait incontournable dans notre pays. Je sais les souffrances que sa mise en œuvre a provoquées en France chez les catholiques, chez les prêtres, dans les congrégations, avant comme après 1905. Je sais que l'interprétation de la loi de 1905 comme un texte de liberté, de tolérance, de neutralité est en partie, reconnaissons le, […] une reconstruction rétrospective du passé. C'est surtout par leur sacrifice dans les tranchées de la Grande guerre, par le partage de leurs souffrances, que les prêtres et les religieux de France ont désarmé l'anticléricalisme; et c'est leur intelligence commune qui a permis à la France et au Saint-Siège de dépasser leurs querelles et de rétablir leurs relations. Pour autant, il n'est plus contesté par personne que le régime français de la laïcité est aujourd'hui une liberté: la liberté de croire ou de ne pas croire, la liberté de pratiquer une religion et la liberté d'en changer, de religion, la liberté de ne pas être heurté dans sa conscience par des pratiques ostentatoires, la liberté pour les parents de faire donner à leurs enfants une éducation conforme à leurs convictions, la liberté de ne pas être discriminé par l'administration en fonction de sa croyance.

La France a beaucoup changé. Les citoyens français ont des convictions plus diverses qu'autrefois. Dès lors la laïcité s'affirme comme une nécessité et oserais-je le dire, une chance. Elle est devenue une condition de la paix civile. Et c'est pourquoi le peuple français a été aussi ardent pour défendre la liberté scolaire que pour souhaiter l'interdiction des signes ostentatoires à l'école.

Cela étant, la laïcité ne saurait être la négation du passé. La laïcité n'a pas le pouvoir de couper la France de ses racines chrétiennes. Elle a tenté de le faire. Elle n'aurait pas dû. Comme Benoît XVI, je considère qu'une nation qui ignore l'héritage éthique, spirituel, religieux de son histoire commet un crime contre sa culture, contre ce mélange d'histoire, de patrimoine, d'art et de traditions populaires, qui imprègne si profondément notre manière de vivre et de penser. Arracher la racine, c'est perdre la signification, c'est affaiblir le ciment de l'identité nationale, c'est dessécher davantage encore les rapports sociaux qui ont tant besoin de symboles de mémoire. C'est pourquoi nous devons tenir ensemble les deux bouts de la chaîne: assumer les racines chrétiennes de la France, et même les valoriser, tout en défendant la laïcité, enfin parvenue à maturité. Voilà le sens de la démarche que j'ai voulu accomplir ce soir à Saint-Jean de Latran

Le temps est désormais venu que, dans un même esprit, les religions, en particulier la religion catholique qui est notre religion majoritaire, et toutes les forces vives de la nation regardent ensemble les enjeux de l'avenir et non plus seulement les blessures du passé. Je partage l'avis du Pape quand il considère, dans sa dernière encyclique, que l'espérance est l'une des questions les plus importantes de notre temps. Depuis le siècle des Lumières, l'Europe a expérimenté tant d'idéologies. Elle a mis successivement ses espoirs dans l'émancipation des individus, dans la démocratie, dans le progrès technique, dans l'amélioration des conditions économiques et sociales, dans la morale laïque. Elle s'est fourvoyée gravement dans le communisme et dans le nazisme. Aucune de

continued

ces différentes perspectives – que je ne mets évidemment pas sur le même plan – n'a été en mesure de combler le besoin profond des hommes et des femmes de trouver un sens à l'existence

[…] Longtemps la République laïque a sous-estimé l'importance de l'aspiration spirituelle. […] Je pense que cette situation est dommageable pour notre pays. Bien sûr, ceux qui ne croient pas doivent être protégés de toute forme d'intolérance et de prosélytisme. Mais un homme qui croit, c'est un homme qui espère. Et l'intérêt de la République, c'est qu'il y ait beaucoup d'hommes et de femmes qui espèrent. La désaffection progressive des paroisses rurales, le désert spirituel des banlieues, la disparition des patronages, la pénurie de prêtres, n'ont pas rendu les Français plus heureux. C'est une évidence. Et puis je veux dire également que, s'il existe incontestablement une morale humaine indépendante de la morale religieuse, la République a intérêt à ce qu'il existe aussi une réflexion morale inspirée de convictions religieuses. D'abord parce que la morale laïque risque toujours de s'épuiser quand elle n'est pas adossée à une espérance qui comble l'aspiration à l'infini. Ensuite et surtout parce qu'une morale dépourvue de liens avec la transcendance est davantage exposée aux contingences historiques et finalement à la facilité. […]

Dans la République laïque, l'homme politique que je suis n'a pas à décider en fonction de considérations religieuses. Mais il importe que sa réflexion et sa conscience soient éclairées notamment par des avis qui font référence à des normes et à des convictions libres des contingences immédiates. Toutes les intelligences, toutes les spiritualités qui existent dans notre pays doivent y prendre part. Nous serons plus sages si nous conjuguons la richesse de nos différentes traditions.[…]

Je mesure les sacrifices que représente une vie toute entière consacrée au service de Dieu et des autres. Je sais que votre quotidien est ou sera parfois traversé par le découragement, la solitude, le doute. Je sais aussi que la qualité de votre formation, le soutien de vos communautés, la fidélité aux sacrements, la lecture de la Bible et la prière, vous permettent de surmonter ces épreuves. Sachez que nous avons au moins une chose en commun: c'est la vocation. On n'est pas prêtre à moitié, on l'est dans toutes les dimensions de sa vie. Croyez bien qu'on n'est pas non plus Président de la République à moitié. Je comprends que vous vous soyez sentis appelés par une force irrépressible qui venait de l'intérieur, parce que moi-même je ne me suis jamais assis pour me demander si j'allais faire ce que j'ai fait, je l'ai fait. Je comprends les sacrifices que vous faites pour répondre à votre vocation parce que moi-même je sais ceux que j'ai faits pour réaliser la mienne. […]

En donnant en France et dans le monde le témoignage d'une vie donnée aux autres et comblée par l'expérience de Dieu, vous créez de l'espérance et vous faites grandir des sentiments nobles. C'est une chance pour notre pays, et le Président que je suis le considère avec beaucoup d'attention. Dans la transmission des valeurs et dans l'apprentissage de la différence entre le bien et le mal, l'instituteur ne pourra jamais remplacer le curé ou le pasteur, même s'il est important qu'il s'en approche, parce qu'il lui manquera toujours la radicalité du sacrifice de sa vie et le charisme d'un engagement porté par l'espérance.

Topics
FOR DISCUSSION

1   What are the domestic and international contexts in which this speech was made?
2   In this speech, what sort of *laïcité* does Sarkozy want to promote? To what extent does this mark a departure from previous understandings of the concept?
3   Find out how this speech was received. Who welcomed it, who criticised it and why?

Further reading

General books

Martin Alexander (ed.), *French History Since Napoleon*, London: Arnold, 1999.

Maurice Augulhon, *The French Republic 1879–1992*, Oxford: Blackwell, 1995.

Jill Forbes, Nick Hewlett and François Nectoux, *Contemporary France*, Harlow: Longman, 2001.

Brian Jenkins, *Nationalism in France: Class and Nation since 1879*, London: Routledge, 1990.

Roderick Kedward, *La Vie en Bleu: France and the French since 1900,* London: Allen Lane, 2005.

Michael Kelly (ed.), *French Culture and Society*, London: Arnold, 2001.

Maurice Larkin, *France Since the Popular Front*, Oxford: Clarendon, 1997.

Roger Magraw, *France 1815–1914*, London: Collins, 1983.

Margaret Majumdar (ed.), *Francophone Studies*, London: Arnold, 2002.

James McMillan, *Twentieth Century France: Politics and Society 1898–1991*, London: Edward Arnold, 1992.

Kevin Passmore, *The Right in France from the Third Republic to Vichy*, Oxford: Oxford University Press, 2012.

Roger Price, *A Concise History of France*, Cambridge: Cambridge University Press, 1993.

Charles Sowerwine, *France since 1870: Culture, Politics and Society*, Basingstoke: Palgrave, 2001.

Richard Vinen, *France, 1934–1970*, Basingstoke: Macmillan, 1996.

Journals

French History

French Cultural Studies

French Politics and Society

Modern and Contemporary France

L'Histoire

History Today

Francophone Post-Colonial Studies

International Journal of Francophone Studies

Chapter 1

Geoffrey Best (ed.), *The Permanent Revolution: The French Revolution and Its Legacy 1789–1989*, London: Collins, 1988.

Peter Campbell, *The Ancien Régime in France*, Oxford: Blackwell, 1988.

William Doyle, *The Origins of the French Revolution*, Oxford: Oxford University Press, 1999.

William Doyle, *The French Revolution: A Short Introduction*, Oxford: Oxford University Press, 2001.

Martin Evans and Ken Lunn (eds), *War and Memory in the Twentieth Century*, Oxford: Berg, 1997.

Alan Forrest, *The French Revolution*, Oxford: Blackwell, 1995.

François Furet, *Interpreting the French Revolution*, Cambridge: Cambridge University Press, 1981.

Robert Gildea, *The Past in French History*, New Haven: Yale University Press, 1994.

Georges Lefebvre, *The Coming of the French Revolution*, New York: Random House, 1957.

Simon Schama, *Citizens: A Chronicle of the French Revolution*, London: Viking, 1989.

Ronald Schechter (ed.), *The French Revolution: The Essential Readings*, Oxford: Blackwell, 2001.

Chapter 2

André Jardin and André Tudesq, *Restoration and Reaction, 1815–1848*, Cambridge: Cambridge University Press, 1983.

Pamela Pilbeam, *The 1830 Revolution in France*, London: Macmillan, 1991.

Pamela Pilbeam, *Republicanism in Nineteenth Century France, 1814–1871*, London: Macmillan, 1995.

René Rémond, *Les Droites en France*, Paris: Aubier-Montaigne, 1982.

James Roberts, *The Counter-Revolution in France: 1787–1830*, Basingstoke: Macmillan, 1990.

Chapter 3

Charles Ageron, *Histoire de l'Algérie contemporaine (1830–1994)*, Paris: Presses universitaires de France, 1994.

Robert Hervé, *Louis-Philippe et la monarchie parlementaire*, Paris: Denoël, 1990.

André Jardin and André Tudesq, *Restoration and Reaction, 1815–1848*, Cambridge: Cambridge University Press, 1983.

Pierre Rosanvallon, *Le Sacré du citoyen: histoire du suffrage universel en France*, Paris: Gallimard, 1992.

Chapter 4

R. J. W. Evans and Hartmut Pogge von Strandmann (eds), *The Revolutions in Europe 1848–1849: From Reform to Reaction*, Oxford: Oxford University Press, 2000.

Ruth Harris, *The Man on Devil's Island: Alfred Dreyfus and the Affair that Divided France*, London: Allen Lane, 2010.

Robert Gildea, *Children of the Revolution: The French, 1799–1914*, London: Allen Lane, 2009.

James McMillan, *Napoleon III*, London: Longman, 1991.

Pierre Miquel, *Le Second Empire*, Paris: Plon, 1992.

Pamela Pilbeam, *French Socialists before Marx: Workers, Women and the Social Question in France*, Teddington: Acumen Publishing, 2000.

Roger Price, *The French Second Empire: An Anatomy of Political Power*, Cambridge: Cambridge University Press, 2001.

Philippe Séguin, *Louis Napoléon le Grand*, Paris: Librairie générale française, 1992.

Robert Tombs, *France 1814–1914*, London: Longman, 1996.

Chapter 5

Robert Aldrich, *Greater France*, Basingstoke: Macmillan, 1996.

Eric Cahm, *The Dreyfus Affair in French Society and Politics*, London: Longman, 1996.

Robert Gildea, *France 1871–1914*, London: Longman, 1996.

Jean-Marie Mayer and Madeleine Reberioux, *The Third Republic 1871–1914*, Cambridge: Cambridge University Press, 1984.

Eugene Weber, *Peasants into Frenchmen*, London: Chatto and Windus, 1979.

Chapter 6

Jean-Jacques Becker, *The Great War and the French People*, Leamington Spa: Berg, 1985.

Martin Evans, *Empire and Culture: The French Experience, 1830–1940*, Basingstoke: Palgrave Macmillan, 2004.

Alistair Horne, *The Price of Glory: Verdun 1916*, London: Macmillan, 1962.

Douglas and Madeleine Johnson, *The Age of Illusion: Art and Politics in France 1918–1940*, London: Thames and Hudson, 1987.

John Keiger, *France and the Origins of the First World War*, London: Macmillan, 1983.

Jay Winter, *Sites of Memory, Sites of Mourning: The Great War in European Cultural History*, Cambridge: Cambridge University Press, 1998.

Chapter 7

Jean-Pierre Azema, *From Munich to the Liberation*, Cambridge: Cambridge University Press, 1984.

Philippe Bernard, *The Decline of the Third Republic, 1914–1938*, Cambridge: Cambridge University Press, 1985.

Julian Jackson, *The Popular Front in France*, Cambridge: Cambridge University Press, 1988.

Sian Reynolds, *France Between the Wars: Gender and Politics*, London: Routledge, 1996.

Chapter 8

Hannah Diamond, *Women and the Second World War in France, 1939–1948: Choices and Constraints*, Harlow: Longman, 1999.

Martin Evans, 'Robert Paxton: The outsider', *History Today*, September 2001, pp. 26–8.

Robert Gildea, *Marianne in Chains*, London: Macmillan, 2002.

Julian Jackson, *The Dark Years: France 1940–44*, Oxford: Oxford University Press, 2001.

Roderick Kedward, *Resistance in Vichy France*, Oxford: Oxford University Press, 1978.

Roderick Kedward, *Occupied France*, Oxford: Blackwell, 1985.

Roderick Kedward, *In Search of the Maquis*, Oxford: Clarendon Press, 1993.

Roderick Kedward and Nancy Wood (eds), *The Liberation of France: Image and Event*, Oxford: Berg, 1995.

Michael Marrus and Robert Paxton, *Vichy France and the Jews*, Palo Alto: Stanford University Press, 1995.

Robert Paxton, *Vichy France: Old Guard and New Order, 1940–1944*, New York: Columbia University Press, 1982.

Henry Rousso, *Le Syndrome de Vichy*, Paris: Seuil, 1987.

Chapter 9

Martin Alexander, Martin Evans and J. F. V. Keiger (eds), *The Algerian War and the French Army 1954–62: Experiences, Images, and Testimonies*, Basingstoke: Macmillan, 2001.

Claire Duchen, *Women's Rights and Women's Lives in France 1944–1968*, London: Routledge, 1994.

Martin Evans, *The Memory of Resistance: French Opposition to the Algerian War 1954–1962*, Oxford: Berg, 1997.

Martin Evans, *Algeria: France's Undeclared War*, Oxford: Oxford University Press, 2012.

Jean Fourastié, *Les Trente Glorieuses*, Paris: Fayard, 1979.

Robert Gildea, *France since 1945*, Oxford: Oxford University Press, 2002.

Alistair Horne, *A Savage War of Peace: Algeria 1954–1962*, London: Macmillan, 1977.

Jacques Marseille, *Empire colonial et capitalisme français: histoire d'un divorce*, Paris: Albin Michel, 1984.

Jean-Pierre Rioux, *The Fourth Republic*, Cambridge: Cambridge University Press, 1987.

Kristin Ross, *Fast Cars and Clean Bodies*, Cambridge, MA: MIT Press, 1995.

Pierre Vidal-Naquet, *Torture: Cancer of Democracy*, trans. Barry Richard, Harmondsworth: Penguin, 1963.

Pierre Vidal-Naquet, *La torture dans la république: essai d'histoire et de politique contemporaine*, Paris: Éditions de Minuit, 1972.

Irwin Wall, *The United States and the Making of Post-War France*, Cambridge: Cambridge University Press, 1991.

Chapter 10

Serge Bernstein, *The Republic of De Gaulle*, Cambridge: Cambridge University Press, 1993.

David Caute, *Sixty-Eight: The Year of the Barricades*, London: Hamilton, 1988.

Philip Cerny, *The Politics of Grandeur: Ideological Aspects of de Gaulle Foreign Policy*, Cambridge: Cambridge University Press, 1980.

Claire Duchen, *Feminism in France: From May '68 to Mitterrand*, London: Routledge and Kegan Paul, 1986.

Vladimir Fisera (ed.), *Writing on the Wall: France, May 1968*, London: Allison and Busby, 1978.

Patrick Seale and Maureen McConville, *The French Revolution 1968*, London: Heinemann, 1968.

Andrew Shennan, *De Gaulle*, London: Longman, 1993.

Chapter 11

Gill Allwood, *Women and Politics in France 1958–2000*, London: Routledge, 2000.

David Bell and Byron Criddle, *The French Communist Party in the Fifth Republic*, Oxford: Clarendon Press, 1994.

Claire Duchen, *Feminism in France: From May '68 to Mitterrand*, London: Routledge and Kegan Paul, 1986.

Bernard Esambert, *Pompidou: capitaine d'industries*, Paris: Éditions O. Jacob, 1994.

John R. Frears, *France in the Giscard Presidency*, London: Allen and Unwin, 1981.

Valéry Giscard d'Estaing, *Démocratie française*, Paris: Fayard, 1976.

Valéry Giscard d'Estaing, *Deux français sur trois*, Paris: Flammarion, 1984.

Andrew Knapp, *Gaullism since de Gaulle*, Aldershot: Dartmouth, 1994.

Eric Roussel, *Georges Pompidou 1911–1974*, Paris: J. C. Lattès, 1994.

Chapter 12

Edward Arnold, *The Development of the Radical Right in France: From Boulanger to Le Pen*, Basingstoke: Macmillan, 2000.

David Bell, *Presidential Power in Fifth Republic France*, Oxford: Berg, 2000.

David Bell, *French Politics Today*, Manchester: Manchester University Press, 2002.

Tony Chafer and Brian Jenkins (eds), *France: From the Cold War to the New World Order*, Basingstoke: Macmillan, 1996.

Alistair Cole, *François Mitterrand: A Study in Political Leadership*, London: Routledge, 1994.

Peter Davies, *The National Front in France: Ideology, Discourse and Power*, London: Routledge, 1999.

Julius Friend, *The Long Presidency: France in the Mitterrand Years, 1981–1995*, Oxford: Westview, 1998.

Alec Hargreaves, *'Race' and Ethnicity in Contemporary France*, London: Routledge, 1995.

Jack Hayward, *The State and the Market Economy: Industrial Patriotism and Economic Intervention in France*, Brighton: Wheatsheaf, 1986.

Nick Hewlett, *Modern French Politics: Analysing Conflict and Consensus since 1945*, Cambridge: Polity, 1998.

Mairi Maclean, *The Mitterrand Years: Legacy and Evaluation*, Basingstoke: Macmillan, 1998.

George Ross, Stanley Hoffmann and Sylvia Malzacher, *The Mitterrand Experiment: Continuity and Change in Modern Europe*, Oxford: Polity Press, 1987.

Chapter 13

John R. Bowen, *Why the French Don't Like Headscarves: Islam, the State, and Public Space*, Princeton: Princeton University Press, 2007.

Tony Chafer and Emmanuel Godin, *The End of the French Exception? Decline and Revival of the French Model*, London: Palgrave, 2010.

Tony Chafer and Gordon Cumming, *From Rivalry to Partnership? New Approaches to the Challenges of Africa*, London: Ashgate, 2011.

Pepper D. Culpepper, Bruno Palier and Peter A. Hall, *Changing France: The Politics that Markets Make*, Basingstoke: Palgrave Macmillan, 2008.

Martin Evans and John Phillips, *Algeria: Anger of the Dispossessed*, London: Yale University Press, 2007.

Martin Evans, *Algeria: France's Undeclared War*, Oxford: Oxford University Press, 2012.

Emmanuel Godin and Tony Chafer, *The French Exception*, Oxford: Berghahn, 2005.

Emmanuel Godin and Natalya Vince (eds), *France and the Mediterranean: International Relations, Culture and Politics*, Oxford: Peter Lang, 2012.

Nick Hewlett, *The Sarkozy Phenomenon*, Exeter: Societas, 2010.

Pascal Perrineau and Luc Rouban (eds), *Politics in France and Europe*, Basingstoke: Palgrave Macmillan, 2009.

Nicolas Sarkozy, *Témoignage*, Paris: XO Editions, 2006.

David Styan, *France & Iraq: Oil, Arms and French Policy Making in the Middle East*, London: Tauris, 2004.

Index

Page numbers in **bold** indicate a glossary box

110 propositions 180, 187
1830 Revolution *see* July Revolution
1848 Revolution 43–44

Abetz, Otto 120, 123
absolutism 4, 5, 6, 7–8, 9–10
Abu Ghraib 203
Action française 72, 99, 102, 118
Adenauer, Konrad 156
Afghanistan 175, 198, 211
African colonies **132**, 141, 156, 158, 174
  decolonisation 145, 150–53
  nationalist uprisings 142–43
Afrique équitoriale française 125
agriculture 55, 86, 98, 138, 139, 158
Aide-toi, le Ciel t'aidera 25
Airbus 167
Albania 81, 113
Albert, Martin 49, 50
alcoholism 144
Algeciras conference 80
Algeria 42, 50, 54, 56–57, 68, 73, 81, 103, **126**, 126, 128, 138, 144, 150, 203, 212
Algerian Assembly 145
Algerian Communist Party **146**
Algerian rebellion (1954) 17–18, 144
Algerian War **28**, **86**, **136**, **145**, 145–46, 150–53, 190, 205
  17 October 1961 protests **152**
  and May 1968 160
  and words **153**
Algérie française 144

Algiers, Battle of 146, **146**
Algiers expedition **27**
Algiers rebellion 161
Ali, Mehemet 42
Alleg, Henri **146**, 148
Alliance 124
Alphaville (film) 158
Alsace-Lorraine 63, 64, 69, 86, 116, 133
America 79, 99, 140, 181, 204
  Bretton Woods 136
  civil rights movements 161
  gay and lesbian rights 164
  and NATO 155
  New Deal 101
  and the Soviet Union 131–32, 136
  Vietnam War 155, 156, 161
  Wall Street Crash 97–98
  World War I 84, 85
  World War II 113, 122
America–France relationship 156, 211
  Compagnie générale transatlantique 54
  de Gaulle 125, 126, 128, 155–56
  Fourth Republic **135**, 136, 142
  Iraq wars 198, 203
  Marshall Aid 132, 135, 136, 138
  nouvelle vague **159**
  post-World War I 86, 88–89
  post-World War II 128
  Vichy regime 120
American Express Company 161
American republicans 26
American War of Independence 4, 6, 8

Amiens Charter 75
Amouroux, Henri 117
ancien régime 5, 9, 11, 21, 22, 24, 74
Angkor Wat 91
Anti-89 2
anti-capitalism 40, 74, 118, 179
anti-clericalism 24, 35, 37, 48, 57,
    65, 67–68, 68, 71, 73–74, 89,
    209
anti-communism 114, 120, 131–32,
    135, 142, 144, 168
anti-imperialism 202
anti-nuclear protests 171, **172**
anti-Semitism 70–71, 72, 99, 100, 102,
    106, 107, 118–19, 120, 123, 126,
    144
Arab-Israeli War (1967) 156
Arab Spring 211–12
Arago, Dominique 48
architecture 171
archives **195**
aristocracy 4, 6, 17, 21, 24
armaments 103, 115
army 24, 70, 72, 116, 127, 142, 145,
    146, 150, 151, 162, 163
  conscription 13, 22, 40, 68, 81, 102,
      151, 153, 168
  Gouvion Saint-Cyr law 22
  military service 17
  republicanised 153
  World War I 81–82
artisans 139
Artois 82
Artois, Comte d' *see* Charles X
Asia **132**, 143, 156
Ateliers nationaux **49**, 49, 50
Atlantic Alliance 136
Atlantic Revolution 4
Aubrac, Lucie **126**
August Decrees 10, 11
Aulagnier, Abbé 2
Auriol, Vincent 134
Aurore, L' 72
Aussaresses, Paul **146**

Australia 203
Austria 14, **23**, 42, 54, 108, 119
  Anschluss 106–7
  and the Balkans 80–81, 82
  Crimean War 56
  French Revolutionary wars 12, 13
  Napoleonic wars 16
  World War I 82
Austria-Hungary 85
  Treaty of The Three Emperors (1881)
      79
  Triple Alliance (1882) 79
authoritarianism 158, 161
autogestion **167**
Ayrault, Jean-Marc 203

Baker, Keith 5
Balkan League 81
Balkans 80–81, 82
Balladur, Edouard 186, 192–93
Bandung conference 143
Bank of France 15, 101, 103
banking reforms 54–55
Bao-Dai 142
Barre, Raymond 172–73
Barthes, Roland 160
Bastille Day **10**, 66, 69
Bastille, storming of 10
Baudelaire, Charles **57**
Baverez, Nicolas 206
Bedarida, François 124
Bedarida, Renée 124
Belgium 35, 56, 108, 114, 132
Ben Ali, Zine El Abidine 212
Ben Bella, Ahmed 144, 145
Ben Youssef, Mohammed 142
Benna, Zyed 205
Bérégovoy, Pierre 189, 192
Berlusconi, Silvio 207, 213
Berry, Duc de 22
beurs **187**, 198
Bidault, Georges 134
Birkin, Jane 2, **159**
birth rate 138

Bismarck, Georges, Otto von 58, 63, 69, 79

black, blanc, beur 190

Blair, Tony 198, 203, 210

Blanc, Louis 48, **49**, 50

Blanqui, Louis-Auguste 36, 41, 50, 55

bloc national 87, 88

Bloch, Marc 124

blocked society 158, 166

'bloody week' 64

Blum, Léon 101, 102, 103, 104–5, **105**, 106, 118, 133

Bokassa, Emperor 175

Bolland, Adrienne **103**

Bonapartism 15–16, 53–54, 57, 60, 207

Bonapartists 21, 22, 23, 26, 36, 48

Bonnet, Georges 107

Bosnia-Herzegovina 81, 82

Bouazizi, Mohammed 211–12

Boudiaf, Mohamed 144, 145

Boulanger affair 70

Boulanger, Georges 70, 72

Bourbon-Leblanc, Gabriel 29–30

Bourbon Restoration 19–31

bourgeoisie 4, 20, 24, **34**, 34, 37–41, 43, 47, 50, 57, **86**

Bourguiba, Habib 143

Bousquet, René 121, 123, 192

Brasillach, Robert 99, 124

Brazil 211

Bressy, Raymond 109

Brest-Litovsk 85

Breton, André **86**

Bretton Woods 136

Briand, Aristide 84, 88, 89

Britain 5, 8, 39, 98, 99, 102, 105, 117, 181
  EEC 155, 169
  gay and lesbian rights 164
  Indian independence 143
  and Russia 80, 81
  Soviet expansion 131–32

Britain–France relationship 123, 126, 145, 156
  American War of Independence 6
  colonial rivalry 79
  Crimean War 56
  de Gaulle 125, 155
  entente cordiale 42–43, 80, 81
  Free French 124, 125
  French Revolutionary wars 13
  Iraq wars 203
  July Monarchy 42
  Mers-el-Kebir incident (1940) 118
  post-World War II 128
  Spanish Civil war 105
  trading treaties 55
  Versailles Peace Treaty (1919) 86, 89, 102
  World War I 82, 83
  World War II 108–9, 113, 114, 122, 124–25

Brittany 52, 133, 158, 171, **172**, 172

Brousse, Paul 71

Brunschvicg, Cécile **103**

Buchez, Philippe 41

Bulgaria 81, 85

bureaucracy 16

Bush, George W. 197–98

cadres 139, 161

cafés **67**

cagoulards 106

cahiers des doléances 7

Cambodia 56, 91, 142

Cameron, David 212

Cameroon 91, 125

Campbell, Peter 9

canuts 36

capitalism 4, 42, 71, 74, 75, 89, 98, **99**, 118, 133, 134, 160, 171, 186, 213

Carné, Marcel **101**

Carnot, Sadi 71

cartel des gauches 89, 99

Catholic schools 137

Catholicism 37, 74, 122

Catholics **52**, 56, 57, 65, 70, 71, 89, 101, 105, 119–20, 124, 133, 210

Cavaignac, General 26, 50, 51

censorship 8, 22–23, 27, 36

Centre démocrate (CD) 190

Centrists 168

Chaban-Delmas, Jacques 144, 166–68, 169

Chabrol, Claude **159**

Challe, Maurice 150, 151, 152

Chamber of Deputies 21–22, 23, 26, 27, 28, 65–66, 70

Chamberlain, Neville 107

Chambord, Comte de 65

chambre bleu-horizon 87

chambre introuvable 21–22, 23

chambre retrouvée **21**, 23

Champagne 82

Charbonnerie, la 23

Charles X **21**, 21, 23–24, 26–27, 28, 34, 35, 36, 65

Charter (Louis XVIII) 20–22, 23, 24, 25, 26–27, 28–29, 34

Chateaubriand, François-René 23–24, **24**, 25

Chautemps, Camille 106

Cheb Mammi 190

Chevaliers de la Foi **21**

Chevènement, Jean-Pierre 184, 191–92, 195

China 142, 156, 160, 161, 211

Chinoise, La (film) 158

Chirac, Jacques **84**, 162, 169, 172, 173, 174, 175, 185, 186, 188, 190, 192, 193–98, 201, 202–6, 208, 213

Christian Democrats 133

church 21, 72

   Charles X 23–24

   Civil Constitution of the Clergy 11

   Concordat 15

   and education 24, 51, 57, 68, 209

   Gallicans **52**

   July Monarchy 37

   and the MRP 133

Sarkozy 209

Second Republic 48

separation from state 74

Third Republic 67, 68, 71, 73–74, 89

Ultramontains **52**

Vichy regime 119–20

and women 74

church property 15

Churchill, Winston 124, 125, 131

cinema **101**

   nouvelle vague **159**

Citoyens 61 154

Citroën 183

Civil Code (1804) 15

Civil Constitution of the Clergy 11

civil liberties 24

Civil Service 21

Clair, René **101**

class conflict 4–5, 20, 50, 67, 87, 101, 104

classes dangereuses 197

Clémenceau, Georges 75, 84, 86, 88, 93–94, 108

clergy 6

Club Jean Moulin 154

Cobban, Alfred 4

code de la nationalité **187**

cohabitation **185**,

   1986–88 185, 186

   1993–95 192–93

   1997–2002 194–95

Cohn-Bendit, Daniel 161, 162

Cold War **132**, 133, 135, 155

collaboration 115, 118, 121–22, 123–24, 192

Colonial Exhibition (1931) **86**, 91

colonial postcards 91

colonialism *see* empire

Combat 124

Commission of Jewish Matters 119

Committee of Public Safety (Algiers) 146, 150

Committee of Public Safety (French Revolution) 14

Common programme 169
Communards 67
communism 5, 87, 101, 102, 118, 120, 123, 125, 135, 136, 156, 174
collapse of 188
Communist International 88
communists 100, 103, 104, 107, 126, 133, 134, 142, 151, 155, 163
communitarism 195
Compagnie générale transatlantique 54
Compagnon de la Libération **126**
Concordat 15
Condorcet, Marquis de 2
Confédération générale du travail (CGT) 71, 135, 158, 161, 162
Amiens Charter 75
merges with CGTU 102
World War I 82
Confédération générale du travail unifiée (CGTU) 102
Congo 68
Congress de Tours 88
conscription 13, 22, 40, 68, 81, 102, 151, 153, 168
Conseil Français du Culte Musulman (CFCM) 210
Conseil national de la résistance (CNR) 126, 127
Conseil national des femmes françaises (CNFF) 87
Conseil national des indépendants et paysans (CNIP) 137, 139–40
conseil régional 181
conservatism 17, 42, 50–52, 65, 66, 67, 71, 72, 73, 168, 192
conservatives 87, 89, 105, 107, 114, 121, 133, 150, 163, 167, 168, 172, 201, 207
Constant, Benjamin 25
Constituent Assembly 49–50
constitutional monarchy 8, 10, **20**, 26, 33
failure (Louis XVI) 11–13
fall of (Louis-Philippe) 43–44
foundations (Louis XVIII) 20–22

Consulate 15
Consultative Assembly 126
consumerism 138, 160
Contract Première Embauche 205
Convention 13–14, **15**, 17
corporal punishment 49
Corps législatif 52, 57–58
corruption scandals 215
Corsica 172, 195
cottage industries 55
Coty, François 99
Coty, René 144, 146
couches nouvelles 67
Council of Europe 136
Council of the Republic 134
Couve de Murville, Maurice 163
couverture sociale universelle (CSU) 195
credit crises 6
Crédit Lyonnaise, le 54
Crédit mobilier, Le 54
Crémieux Decrees 118
Cresson, Edith 189, 190
Crime de Monsieur Lange, Le (Renoir) **101**
Crimean War 56
Croix-de-Feu 100, 105
Croix, La **72**
Crozier, Michel 158
Cuba 156
Cuban Missile Crisis (1962) 156
Cuénat, Hélène 140
cultural origins, French Revolution 9
Czechoslovakia 107, 108, 113
communist control of 132
Soviet invasion of 156

Daladier, Edouard 100, 101, 106–8, 114
Danton, Georges 13, 14
d'Argenlieu, Thierry 142
Darlan, Admiral 120, 123, 126
Darnand, Joseph 123, **127**
Daumier, Honoré 37, **37**
Davies, Norman 113
Dawes, Charles 88

Dawes Plan 88
de Beauvoir, Simone **136**, 140, 151, 171
de Brinon, Fernand 123
de Broglie, Duc 37, 65
de Gaulle, Charles 57, 115, 125–26,
    127, 127–28, 134, 135–36, 137,
    140, 146, 149–64, 165, 166, 167,
    169, 174, 175, 179, 185, 203, 211
de Gouges, Olympe **15**
de la Rocque de Severac, François
    99–100, 104, 105–6
de la Vigerie, Emmanuel d'Astier 124
de Laclos, Choderlos **8**
de Maupeou, Chancellor 9
de Villepin, Dominique 204, 205, 215–16
de Villiers, Philippe 2, **3**, 3, 204
Déat, Marcel 121, 123
death penalty 21, 49, 181
Debord, Guy **160**
Debray, Régis 158
Debré, Michel 150
Decazes, Elie 22
decentralisation 181–82
Declaration of the Rights of Man and the
    Citizen 2, 10, 17, 18
decline 202, 206–7
décrispation 170
Defectors 25
Defferre, Gaston 145, 181
Defferre reforms 145, 150
Delanoë, Bertrand **152**, 197
Délégation du térritoire (DATAR) 158
Delors, Jacques 166, 191
democracy 14, 33, 35, 44, 47, 48, 49,
    50, 51, 53, 57, 82, 86, 98, 99, 101,
    107, 167, 169–70, 181, 212
Démocratie française 170
demographics 6, 122, 138, 153, 158
Deneuve, Catherine 171
Denmark 114, 169
Depression 97, 98–99
Déroulède, Paul 70, 73
Derrida, Jacques 160
Deschanel, Paul 88

despotism 9, 25
Deuxième Sexe, Le 140
Devil's Island 72
diamonds affair 175
diaries **124**, 129
Directory 14–15
dirigisme 134, 170
discours de Cochin 174
divorce law (1975) 171
Doctrinaires, les 22, 26
Dollfus, Engelbert 55
Doriot, Jacques 123–24
Douaumont **83**
Doumergue, Gaston 100, 101
Dreyfus Affair 72–73, 99
Drieu la Rochelle, Pierre 106
Droits de la femme, les (de Gouges) **15**
Drumont, Edouard 70–71
Duclos, Jacques 166
Ducos, Roger 15
Dunbar, Sly **14**
Duras, Marguerite 171

Eastern Europe 131, **132**, 133, 198
economic depression 6
economic expansion 170
economic liberalism 40, 42, 48
economic policy
    Barre 172–73
    Chaban-Delmas 167
    cohabitation (1986–88) 186
    de Gaulle 156–58
    Giscard 170, 172–74
    grande alternance 175, 180–83
    Popular Front 101–2
    Sarkozy 212–15
economic recession 35
economic reform 215
economy 75, 137, 153, 166
    AAA rating 214
    budget deficits 106
    crises 6–7, 43, 69, 89, 97, 98–99,
        134–35, 165, 172–74, 181, 187,
        204, 212–15

and the empire 68, 91, 141
euro 191, 194, 195
Fourth Republic 138–40
French Revolution 5–6, 13
local, development 181
Napoleon III 54–55
and the state 213
trente glorieuses **138**, 138–39, 165,
    168, 187
Wall Street Crash 97–98
war debts 86, 88, 123
Edict of Fraternity 13
éditions de Minuit **146**
education 166
Algerians 144
and church 24, 51, 57, 68, 209
higher 159, 162, 167
law (1833) 39
Muslims 68
private 168, 184
public 184
Second Republic 49, 50
secondary 170
state control of 68
vocational training 170
women 140
Egypt 80, 131, 212
Elba 16
electoral system 23, 25, 42, 43, 137,
    150, 154, 184
see also suffrage
Elle 140
Elysée Treaty 156
émigrés 15, 21, 23, 24
empire 54, 137, **153**, 153, 155
decolonisation 138, 140–46, 150–53
and the economy 68, 91, 141
expansion 42, 56–57, 68–69, 80, 91
importance 91, 108, 115
Napoleonic 16
Popular Front 103
support for de Gaulle 125
entente cordiale 42–43, 80, 81
environment 171

épanouissement personnel 170
equality 11, 14
Ere nouvelle, L' 48
Estates General 6–7, 9, 17
État des lieux, L' (film) 190
Ethiopia 102
euro 191, 194, 195
Euro-Mediterranean Partnership
    Initiative (EMPI) 211
European central bank 191
European Coal and Steel Community
    (ECSC) 89, 136
European Council 174
European Defence Community 136, 143
European Economic Community (EEC)
    145, 155, 156, 169
European integration 136, 138, 174,
    191–92
European Monetary System 174
European Parliament 174
European Union 189, 194, 198, 204,
    211, 213–14, 215
European Union constitution 203–4
exode 115, 117
Express, l' 154

Fabius, Laurent 183, 184, 204
Fabre-Luce, Alfred 106
Facebook 212
family 16, 163, 171, 207
Family Code (1939) 108, 139
fascism 100, 101, 102, 105, 106, 108,
    120–21, 123, 136
Faure, Edgar 143, 144
*Fédération de la gauche démocratique et
    socialiste* (FGDS) 154
feminism 165, 167, 171, 175–76
Ferdinand, Franz, Archduke 82
Ferdinand, King of Spain **23**
Ferry, Jules 68–69, 71
Fifth Republic 149, 154, 156, 165, 167,
    175, 179, 214
Figaro, Le **14**, 26
Fillon, François 209, 211

financial crises 43, 104
causes of French Revolution 6–7
financial scandals 189
Finland 114
First Republic 49
Flaubert, Gustave **57**
Force ouvrière 135
Foreign Legion **28**
foreign policy 106
  Briand 89
  Chirac 202–4
  de Gaulle 155–56, 203
  Giscard 174
  July Monarchy 34–35, 42
  Napoleon III 56–57
  Pompidou 168–69
  Popular Front 102
  president's supremacy 185
  Sarkozy 210–11
Foucault, Michel 160
Fourastié, Jean **138**
Fourcade, Marie-Madeleine **126**
Fourrier, Joseph 41
Fourth Estate **72**
Fourth Republic 18, 115, 133–37,
    140–46, 150, 156, 179, 214
Fourth Republic Constitution 140
fracture sociale 193
franc 98, 99, 104, 183, 189
  collapse (1923) 88, 89
Franc-Tireur 124
France, Battle of 114–15
France Juive, La 70
Franco, General 104–5, 108, 117
Franco-Prussian War 58, 63, 70, 136
Franco-Russian Treaty (1891) 79–80
Franco-Soviet Pact 102
Free French 124, 125, 126, 127
free market 204, 207
free trade 42, 55, 138
freemasons 7, **21**, 72, **74**, 100, 118,
    143
Frenay, Henry 124
French Academy 21

French Africans 205
French Guiana 72
French Revolution **11**, 15, 19, 20, 21,
    24, 25, 34, 67, 75, 118, 137
French Revolutionary calendar 14
French Union 140–43
Freud, Sigmund **86**
Front de libération nationale (FLN) 144,
    145, 146, 150, 151, 152, **152**, 160
Front national (Resistance movement)
    125
Front national (FN, Le Pen) 3, **153**, 184,
    187, 188, 190, 191, 192, 194, 196,
    197, 199–200, 201, 204, 207, 208,
    210
Furet, François 4–5, 7–8

Gabin, Jean **101**
Gabon 56
Gaddafi, Muammar 212
Gainsbourg, Serge **14**, **159**
Gallicans **52**
Gambetta, Léon 57, 67
Gamelin, Maurice 114
Garaud, Marie-France 167–68
Garçonne, La (Margueritte) **87**
GATT trade agreement 136
gauche plurielle 193–95
Gaullism 125, **127**, 136, 144, 149–64,
    165–69, 171, 186, 192, 197, 198,
    207, 211
Gaullists 137, 143, 169, 172, 173, 174,
    184, 193
gay and lesbian rights 164, 181, 195
George III 8
Gerlier, Pierre-Marie, Cardinal 120
German Democratic Republic 132
Germany 70, 72, 75, 100, 105, 108, 113,
    117, 119, 124, 127
  Anschluss 106–7
  and the Balkans 80–81, 82
  diplomatic isolation 79
  East-West division 132
  invasion of Denmark 114

invasion of Norway 114
invasion of Poland 109
invasion of Soviet Union 121, 122, 125
Moroccan crisis 80
Napoleonic Empire 16
Non-Intervention Pact (1936) 105
occupation of Czechoslovakia 113
Treaty of The Three Emperors (1881) 79
Triple Alliance (1882) 79
unification of (1871) 58, 63
war on America 122
see also West Germany
Germany–France relations 174
1931–39 102
economy 214
Elysée Treaty 156
European Defence Community 136, 143
invasion 114–15
Locarno Treaty (1925) 89
reparations 88–89, 98
Versailles Peace Treaty (1919) 86–87
Vichy collaboration 115, 118, 121–22, 123–24
World War I 82–85
World War II 118, 123
Gibert Jeune 206
Giraud, Henri, General 126
Girondins 12, 13–14, 43
Giscard, d'Estaing, Valéry 155, 163, 165, 169–75, 179, 180, 187, 190
global warming 211
globalisation 202, 206, 207, 213, 215
Godard, Jean-Luc 158, **159**
Goude, Jean-Paul 1, 3
Gouin, Félix 134
Gouvion Saint-Cyr law 22
Grain Board 103
grande alternance 175, 180–83
grandes écoles 140
grandeur 155, 174
grands magasins **55**, 55

Great Fear 10
Great Revolution 9, **24**, 43, 51
Greece 81, 108, 132
Green party *see Verts*
Grenelle agreements 162
Grenier, Fernand **126**
Grévy, Jules 70
Grynszpan, Herschel 107
Guaino, Henri 214
Guderian, Heinz 114
Guernica (Picasso) **105**
Guesde, Jules 71, 82
gueules cassés **86**
Guizot, François de 22, 39, 42–43, 45, 48, 213

Hached, Ferhat 143
Haine, La (film) 190
Haiti **15**
Hardy, Françoise **159**
harkis 150, 152, **153**, 153
Haussmann, Georges-Eugène, Baron **54**
Haut conseil à l'intégration 190
Haute-Savoie 133
Hawks, Howard **159**
Hebert, Jacques 14
Henry IV 209
Herriot, Edouard 89, 99
Heydrich, Reinhard 121
history and memory **3**
Hitchcock, Alfred **159**
Hitler, Adolf 2, 98, 101, 102, 105, 106, 107, 109, 117, 118, 120, 124
Ho Chi Minh 142
Hobsbawm, Eric 79
Hoffmann, Stanley **99**
Holland 108, 132, 204
    French Revolutionary wars 13
Hollande, François 214
Holocaust 121–22
House of Peers 21, 24
housing 140
Hugo, Victor 37
Humanité, L' 101, 114

Hungary 107, 160
    see also Austria-Hungary
Hunt, Lynn 5
Hussein, Saddam 198, 203

immigration 108, 138, 139, 158, 159,
    184, 187–88, 189–91, 207, 208–9
    and citizenship 208
    and law and order 191, 208, 210
independents 71
India 6, 56, 131, 143, 211
Indo-China 56, 68, 91, 145
Indo-China War 135, 142
industry 5, 39–40, 54, 55, 57, 75, 98,
    134, 138, 162, 168, 172, 173, 182
    autonomy 167
    car 123, 158, 162–63
Institut français de l'opinion publique
    (IFOP) **108**
Institute of the Arab World 212
intellectualism, causes of French
    Revolution 7–8
intellectuals **136**, 151
International Communist Movement
    (Comintern) 101, 106
International Exhibition (1937) **105**
Iraq wars
    (1991) 189
    (2003) 197–98, 202, 203
Ireland 169
iron curtain 131, 132
Islamophobia 210
Israel 156
Istiqlal 142
Italian Communist Party 160
Italy 14, 42, 57, 98, 100, 102, 105, 113,
    120
    invasion of Albania 113
    invasion of Ethiopia 102
    military intervention in 56
    Napoleonic Empire 16
    nationalism 35
    Non-Intervention Pact (1936) 105
    Triple Alliance (1882) 79, 80

Italy–France relations
    colonial rivalry 79
    Versailles Peace Treaty (1919) 86
    World War I 83
    World War II 114, 122
Ivory Coast 143

Jacobinism 14, 181
Jacobins 13, 17, 22, 26, 36
Japan 113, 122
Jaurès, Jean 71, 72, 74–75, 82
je suis partout 124
Jesuits 23, 24, 68
Jeunesse agricole chrétienne (JAC) 133
Jeunesse communiste révolutionnaire
    (JCR) 159
Jeunesse ouvrière chrétienne (JOC) 133
Jeunesses étudiante chrétienne (JEC) 133
Jeunesses patriotes 99
Jews 2, 11, 108, 143, 192
Joan of Arc 106
Joffre, Joseph 83
Joliot-Curie, Irène **103**
Jospin, Lionel **84**, 193, 194–95, 196
journalists 161
Juillard, Jacques 2–3
Juillet, Pierre 167–68
July Monarchy 19, **27**, 28, 33–47, 65
July Revolution 27, 33–35
Juppé, Alain 193–94, 197, 212

Kellog–Briand Pact (1928) 89
Kellog, Frank B. 89
Keynesianism 181, 188
Khaled 190
Kohl, Helmut 191
Kosovo 211
Kouchner, Bernard 211, 212
Kristallnacht 107
Krivine, Alain 159

La Bourdonnye, François de 21, 25
La Fayette, General 26, 27, 28
Labour Charter (1941) 118

labour parliament 49
labour reforms
  Chaban 167
  Contract Première Embauche 205
  equal pay 171
  gauche plurielle 193–95
  Labour Charter (1941) 118
  'labour parliament' (1848) 49
  les 35 heures 194
  lois auroux **182**
  Matignon Agreements 103, 104
  minimum wage 167
  paid holidays 103, **104**, 182
  Sarkozy 212–14
  SMIC 167
labour relations
  'battle for production' 133
  strikes and unrest 75, 87, 88, 103–4,
      106, 107–8, 135, 144, 158,
      161–63, 189, 193–94
  working conditions
Lacordaire, Jean-Baptiste 48
Lacore, Suzanne **103**
Lacoste, Robert 145, 146
Laffitte, Jacques 35, 37
laïcité **209**, 209–10
Lainé law 22
Lamartine, Alphonse de 43, 48
language
  Corsican 172
  French 68
Laos 142
Larzac plateau 168
Latin America **132**, 156
Laval, Pierre 100, 102, 106, 114, 115,
      120, **127**
Lavigerie, Charles, Cardinal 71
law and order 6, 10, 127, 168, 187, 191,
      196, 197, 204–5, 207, 208, 210
  and immigration 191, 208, 210
Le Boucher, Eric 206
Le Pen, Jean-Marie 3, 184, 188, 191,
      196, 197, 199–200, 201, 202
Le Pen, Marine 209, 214

League of Nations 86, 88, 89
Leagues, the 99–100, 103
Lebanon 91, 212
Lebrun, Albert 100, 106
Leclerc de Hauteclocque, Philippe,
      General 142
Ledru-Rollin, Alexandre-Auguste 43, 48
Lefebvre, Georges 4
left–right opposition 17, 51, 161, 163,
      170, 173–74, 183–84, 188, 197,
      202, 207, 208
Léger, Fernand 133
Legion of French Volunteers against
      Bolshevism (LVF) 123, 124
Legion of Honour 70
légitimistes, les 36
Lenin, Vladimir 85
Leo XIII 71
Lesseps, Ferdinand 70
Liaisons dangereuses, Les (de Laclos) **8**
liberal reforms (1974–81) 170–72
liberalism 17, 26, 48, 57–58
liberals 21, 22, 25–26, 33, 169
Liberation 124, 127–28, 134
liberation movements 164
Libération-Nord 124
Libre Parole, La 70
Ligue des patriotes 70
Ligue patriotique des françaises 87
Lip *affaire* **167**
literacy 8
Locarno Treaty (1925) 89
loi anticasseurs (1973) 168
loi de la double vite 23
loi Dexonne 172
loi Haby (1975) 170
loi veil, la 175–76
Loubet, Émile 72
Louis-Napoleon *see* Napoleon III (Louis-
      Napoleon)
Louis-Philippe, Duc d'Orleans 27, 33–35,
      37, 37, 41, 43–44, 65
Louis XVI 5, 8, 9–10, 11–12, 13, 20, 27
Louis XVIII 20–22, 28–29

L'Ouverture, Toussaint **15**
Lusitania 84
Luxembourg 56, 132
Lyautey, Louis Hubert 91

Maastricht Treaty (1992) 191–92, 194
Macedonia 81
MacMahon, Patrice de, Marshal 64, 65, 66
Madagascar 56, 68, 142
Madame Bovary (Flaubert) **57**
Maginot Line 114, 115
Maistre, Joseph de 25
Manchuria 113
Mandouze, André 124
Manifeste des 343 salopes 171
Manuel 23
maquis 126–27
Marat, Jean-Paul 13
Marchais, Georges 173
Marchandeau law (1938) 118
Marcuse, Herbert 160
Margueritte, Victor **87**
Marianne 17, 67
Marie-Antoinette 8
market economy 170, 188, 195
Marne, Battle of 82
Marseillaise, La (national anthem) 1, **14**, 66, 191
Marseillaise, La (Renoir film) 3
Marshall Aid 132, 135, 136, 138
Marshall, George 132
Martignac, Vicomte 26
Marx, Karl 41, **49**, 71
Marxism 4, 5, 64, 75, 133, 179, 180, 183
Masson, André **86**
Massu, Jacques, General 146, **146**, 150, 151, 163
Mathiez, Albert 4
Matignon Agreements 103, 104
Mauroy, Pierre 181
Maurras, Charles 72, 99, 102, 107, 117, 125, **127**

May 1968 4, 158–63, 165, 166, 168, 179, 206–7
Mayer, René 144
Médecins Sans Frontières 1–18, 211
media **152**, 160, 161, 170, 181
Mendès-France, Pierre 101, 137, 142, 143–44, 145, 149, 166
mental institutions 160
meritocracy 11, 15
Merkel, Angela 214
Mers-el-Kebir incident (1940) 118
Messmer, Pierre 168
Mexico 56
Michelet, Jules 43
middle classes 68, 71, 74, 100, 101, 103, **104**, 144, 212
Milice 123, 124, 127
military service 17
Millerand, Alexandre 74
milliard des émigrés 24
Ministériels 22
Ministry for Immigration and National Identity 208
Minitel **206**
Mirabeau, Honoré Gabriel Riqueti, comte de 2
Mitterrand, François 2–3, 18, 144, 149, 154, 163, 164, 168, 169, 173, 175, 179–93, 214
modernisation 170, 174, 183–84
Mollet, Guy 133, 144–46, 151
monarchists *see* royalists (monarchists)
Mongolia 113
Monnet, Jean 138
Montagnard republicans 26
Montesquieu, Baron de 8
Montmorency, Mathieu de **21**, 25
Morocco **86**, 91, 212
    Algeciras conference 80
    decolonisation 142, 143, 145
Moulin, Jean 125–26, **155**
Mouvement de libération des femmes 171
Mouvement des citoyens (MDC) 192, 194

Mouvement républicain populaire (MRP) 137, 144, 146, 154, 190, 195
  female vote 139
  Third Force 136–37
  tri-partite alliance 133–35
Mouvements unis de la Résistance 125–26
Mubarak, Hosni 212
Munich Agreement 107, **108**
Muslims 57, 68, 144, 150, **153**, 190, 208, 209
  Arab Spring 211–12
  headscarf incident (1989) 190, 210
  women, suffrage 144
Mussolini, Benito 102, 106, 107

Nanterre 159, 161
Napoleon I (Bonaparte) 14, **15**, 21, **24**, 41–42, 52
Napoleon III (Louis-Napoleon) 36, **37**, 51–52, 54–55, 55, 56, 57–58
Napoleonic Code 15
Napoleonic Empire 16
Nasser, Gama Abdel 145
National Assembly 9
National (Constituent) Assembly **15**, 18, **34**
  Fifth Republic 149, 163, 166, 167, 168, 180, 184, 186, 194, 197, 205
  Fourth Republic 134, 135, 145
  French Revolutionary period 9, 10, 11, 12, 13
  Second Republic 44, 48, 49–50, 51
  Third Republic 63, 65, 75, 82, 84, 87, 88, 100, 107
  Vichy regime 117
National Guard 12, 13, 24, 27, 34, **34**, 35, 36, 43, 64
national identity 68, 192, 210
  immigration and Europe 189–92
national independence 155–56, 174
National, Le 26
national parks 171
National Revolution 117–20, 119, **124**, 126

national sovereignty 17, 20, 21, 26, 53, 128, 136, 191
nationalisation 134, 138, 168, 173, 188
  arms industry 101, 103
  banks 182
nationalism 34–35, 42, 56, 72, 82, 99, 100, 105, 120
'natives of the republic' 204–5
Nazi-Soviet Pact 109, 114, 125
Nazism 3, 100, 102, 105, 107, **108**, 113, 118, 119, 120, 123–24, 133
Neo-Destour 143
neo-liberalism 181, 184, 186, 188, 206–7, 213, 215
Netherlands 13, 108, 132, 204
New Caledonia 56, 64, 125
New Deal 101
Ney, Marshall 21
Nivelle, Robert, General 83–84
nobility *see* aristocracy
Nora, Pierre 166
Norman, Jesse 1
Normandy 158
North Africa 98, 108, 122, 123, 126, 138, 139, **153**, 158
North Atlantic Treaty Organisation (NATO) 132–33, 136, 143, 155, 174, 198, 211, 212
Norway 114
notables, les **39**, 39, 44, 47, 49, 50, 53, 55, 149
Nouvel Observateur, Le 154
nouvelle vague **159**
nuclear energy 171, 173, 195
nuclear weapons 115, 155, 156, 168–69, 174, 193
nuns **74**

Obama, Barack 211
Oberg, Carl, General 121
Occupation 113–30, 136
oil crises
  1973 **138**, 165, 168
  1979 173, 175

Oman 212
opportunists 67, 70, 73
Organisation civile et militaire 124
Organisation de l'armée secrète (OAS) 152, 154
Organisation for European Cooperation 136
Orleanism 37–39, **39**, 65, 213
Ottoman Empire **27**, 42, 56, 80, 91
Oudinot expedition 51

Pacific Islands 125
Pacte civil de solidarité (PACS) 195
paid holidays 103, **104**, 182
Painlevé, Paul 84
Palestine 131
Palmerston, Henry Lord 42
Panama 70
Panama Canal Company 70, 71
Papon, Maurice **152**
Paris, construction project **54**
Paris Commune
    1792 13, 106
    1871 63–64
Paris, Comte de 65
parlements 6, **7**, 9
parliamentarism **25**
Parti communiste français (PCF) 4–5, **86**, 108, 115, 133, 136, 140, 142, 144, 149, 150, 154, 168, 174, 180, 188, 189, 191, 192, 194, 204
    Algerian War 146, 151, 160
    female vote 140
    formation 88
    gauche plurielle 193–94
    and May 1968 160, 161–62, 163
    persecution 108, 114, 118
    Popular Front 100–106
    and the Resistance 125
    Third Force exclusion 136–37
    tri partite alliance 133–35
    Union de la gauche 168, 169, 173
parti de la résistance 34, 35–36
parti de l'ordre 51

parti du mouvement 33, 35
Parti ouvrier français (POF) 71
Parti populaire français 108, 123
Parti social français (PSF) 105–6, 108
Parti socialiste de France (PS) 165, 174, 179–80, 188, 189, 193, 204, 207, 211
    formation of 168
    gauche plurielle 193–94
Parti socialiste français (PSF) 71
Parti socialiste unifié (PSU) 154, 160
Pasqua, Charles 187, 191, 197
passive obedience 16
paternalism 55, 159
patriotism 214
Paul-Boncour, Paul 110
pauperism 6, 40, 48
pauvres couillons du front **86**
Paxton, Robert 120–21
Peace of Amiens 15
peasantry 4, 10, 17, 39, 49, 50, 51, 53–54, 55, 67, 68, 74, 119, 122, 144
pensée unique 193
Pentarques 50
Périer, Casimir 35–36, 37
Persia 80
Pétain, Philippe 83, 84, 100, 114, 117–20, 123, **124**, 125, 126, 127, **12**7, 133, 137
Peter I 81
petite alternance 169–70
Pflimlin, Pierre 146, 151
phalansteries 41
Phoney War 113–15
Picasso, Pablo **105**, 133
pied-noir **153**
Pinay, Antoine 137, 146
Pinton, Auguste **124**, 129
Pius V 11
Pius VII 15
Pivert, Marceau 109–10
plebiscites 15, 16, 51, 53, 57, 154, 169
Pleven, René 136

Plogoff **172**
Poher, Alain 166
poilus **83**
Poincaré, Raymond 81, 82, 88–89
Poland 86, 98, 107, 108, 109, 113, 114, 115, 121
  Napoleonic Empire 16
  nationalism 35
Polignac, Jules de, Prince 26
politique de la ville 190
politique de relance 181–82
Pompidou, Georges 154–55, 162, 163, 165, 166–69, 171
Popular Front 100–106, 107–8, 118, 144
popular government of democratic union 163
popular revolutions 4, **11**, 13–14
Portugal 139, 158
Possibilists 71
Poujade, Pierre 143–44, 150
prefects 15, 21, 23, 51
  new roles (1982–83) 181
press freedom 25
prison 160
privatisation 186, 188, 192–93
pro-natalism 87, 108
protectionism 40, 55, 138, 214
Protestants 11, 21, 72
provisional government, Second Republic 48–50
Prussia 6, **23**, 42
  Crimean War 56
  Franco-Prussian War 58, 63, 70, 136
  French Revolutionary wars 12, 13
  Napoleonic wars 16
Pucheu, Pierre 106, 123
Putin, Vladimir 198

Quebec separatism 156
Question, La (Alleg) **146**, 148

racism 98, 106, 118, 119, 153, 184, 187, 205

Radical Party 73–74, 75, 81, 89, 100, 107, 114, 118, 133, 144, 146, 150, 154, 169, 171, 190
  cartel des gauches 89
  female vote 140
  Popular Front 100–106
  Third Force exclusion 136–37
radicalism 74, 179
radicals 43, 50, 51, 70, 72, 137
Raffarin, Jean-Pierre 196–97, 204
raï music 190
railways 54, 55, 83, 186
ralliement 71
Ramadier, Paul 134–35
Rassemblement du peuple français (RPF) 143
  female vote 139
  launch 135–36
Rassemblement national populaire (RNP) 123
Rassemblement pour la république (RPR) 173, 174, 180, 186, 188, 189, 194, 197
  Third Force exclusion 136–37
rationing 135
Reagan, Ronald 181
Rebatet, Lucien 99
Red Hand 143
regionalism 165, 167, 171–72, 181
Renault 123, 162–63
Renoir, Jean 3, **101**
reparation 88–89, 98
républicains indépendants 169
Républicains indépendants party 155
Republican Front 144–46
republicanism 14, 57, 58–59, 67, 69, 133, 190, 192
republicans 26, 36, 51, 64–66, 71, 72, 184, 209
  républicains de la veille 49
  républicains du lendemain 49–50
Resistance 120, 122, 123, 124–27, **126**, **127**, 133, 169, 192
Resistance Charter (1944) 126

revenu minimum d'insertion 189
révolte des canuts 36
Revolutionary Tribunal 13–14
Reynaud, Paul 114, 125
Ribot, Alexandre 84
Richelieu, Armand, Duc de 22
right–left opposition *see* left–right
    opposition
Riposte laïque 210
Rivette, Jacques **159**
Robespierre, Maximilien 13, 14
Rocard, Michel 188–89, 193
Rohmer, Eric **159**
Roma 208
Romania 56, 108, 162
Roosevelt, Franklin D. 101, 125
Rosenberg, Ethel **136**
Rosenberg, Jules **136**
Rouget de Lisle, Joseph **14**
Rousso, Henry **127**
Royal, Ségolène 207, 211
royalists (monarchists) 2, 4, 13, 14, 20,
    51, 52, 64–66, 67, 70, 99, 120
    see also Ultras
Royer-Collard, Pierre Paul 22, 26
Russia 6, 16, **23**, 54
    and the Balkans 80–81, 82
    Franco-Russian Treaty (1891) 79–80
    Treaty of The Three Emperors (1881)
        79
    World War I 82
Russia-France relationship
    Crimean War 56
    Franco-Russian Treaty (1891) 79–80
Russian Revolution 4, 84–85, 87, 88, 105

Sacré-Cœur **65**
Sagan, Françoise 151
Saint-Domingue **15**
Saint-Simon, Claude Henride Rouvroy de
    40
*salaire minimum indexé sur la
    croissance* (SMIC) 167
Salan, Raoul, General 146, 150, 152

Salut les Copains **159**
sancturisation **174**
sans-culottes 13, **13**, 14, 17, 106
Sarkozy, Nicolas 197, 204, 205, 206,
    217–18
    Témoignage 208
Sarraut, Albert 102
Sartre, Jean-Paul **136**, 142, 151
Savary, Alain 184
Schama, Simon 5
school-leaving age 103
Schröder, Gerhard 198
Schuman, Robert 133, 135, 143
Schuster, Jean **86**
scrofula 117
Secher, Reynald 2
Second Empire 19, 52–58
Second Republic 19, 47–52
*Section française de l'Internationale
    ouvrière* (SFIO) 140, 143, 144, 150,
    154
    cartel des gauches 89, 99
    female vote 140
    formation 74–75
    internal divisions 88
    Popular Front 100–106
    Third Force 136–37
    Tri-partite alliance 133–35
Séguin, Philippe **84**, 191
Séguy, Georges 162–63
semaine des barricades 151
Senate 65, 66, 87, 104, 106, 166, 197
Senegal 56
September laws 36
Serbia 81
service du travail obligatoire (STO) 123,
    126
Seven Years War 6
Shakespeare, Robbie **14**
shopkeepers 139, 144
Sieyès, Abbé 7, 15
Signoret, Simone 151
Simon, Jules 65
Single European Act (SEA, 1986) 191

Sismondi, Jean de 40
Situationists **160**
slavery 5, **15**, 49, 205
Soboul, Albert 4
social media 212
socialism 4, 17, 20, 75, 120, 134
socialist movement 71, 74–75
socialists 48–49, 50, 57, 67, 72, 81–82,
    89, 100, 101, 104, 107, 114, 118,
    124, 137, 181
société des amis du peuple 36
Société des Saisons 36
Société du spectacle (Debord) **160**
Solidarité français 99
Sorbonne University 4, 159, 161, 162
SOS Racisme 187, 198
Soustelle, Jacques 144
Soviet Union 79, 88, 101, 109, 113, 117,
    133, 140, 142
  and America 136
  and Atlantic Alliance 136
  intervention in Hungary 160
  invaded by Nazi Germany 121, 122,
    125
  invasion of Afghanistan 175
  invasion of Czechoslovakia 156
  invasion of Finland 114
  Kellog–Briand Pact (1928) 89
  Nazi–Soviet Pact 109, 114, 115
  Non-Intervention Pact (1936) 105
  post war expansion 131–32
  post-World War II 128
  Vichy regime 120
  World War II 113
Soviet Union–France relations 155–56,
    174
  Franco–Soviet pact 102
Spain 54, 105, 108, 117, 119, 158, 204
Spanish Civil war 104–5, 113, 115
Spanish expedition **23**
Spanish Popular Front 105
Special Operations Executive 124
Spitzer, Gérard 160
St Helena 16

St-Laurent, Yves 153
stalemate society **99**, 139
Stalin, Joseph 2, 109, 117, 132
Stalinism 3
state 72
  control of education 68
  control of media 167, 170, 181
  culture of dialogue 166–67
  and the economy 213
  intervention 181–82, 184, 201
  and local government 181
  planning 138
  regulation 214
  separation of church from 74
Statut des Juifs (1940) 118–19
Stavisky Affair 100
Stresemann, Gustav 88
Suez Canal 70, 145
Suez expedition (1956) 145
suffrage 25, 35, **37**, 48, 154, 181
  18 year-olds 169
  Algerians 103
  immigrants 187
  universal male 13, 14, 21, 22, 47, 48,
    49, 50, 51, 57, 65
  women 68, 74, 87, **103**, **126**, 139
  women, Muslim 144
suffragette movement 39
surrealism **86**
Switzerland 42, 82, 108
Syria 42, 91, 120, 212

Taliban 198
Tapie, Bernard 183
taxation 6, 7, 8, 9, 10, 21, 43, 74, 89,
    137, 180, 183, 186, 197, 206, 213
technology **72**, 138, 140, 158, 167, 173,
    182, 184, 202
  computers 157, 158, 184
  Minitel **206**
Témoignage chrétien **124**, 124
Temps, Le 42
Temps modernes, Les **136**
Tennis Court Oath (1789) 9

TEPA law 213
Terra Nova **213**
Terror, the 3, 14, 49
terrorism 203
Texcier, Jean 124
Thatcher, Margaret 181
'theory of nationalities' 56
Thiers, Adolphe 27, 41–42, 43, 57, 67
    and the Paris Commune 63–64
    royalist republic 64–65
Third Estate 6–7, 9, 17
Third Force 136–37
Third Republic 3–4, 63–77, 100, 101,
    106, 117, 118, 133, 134, 149
Third World 156, 160, 174, 198
Thorez, Maurice 101, 103, 154
Tiananmen Square 1
Tocqueville, Alexis de 37, 43
Togo 91
Tonkin 69
torture 146, **146**, 148
tourism 171
Tous les garçons et les filles **159**
trade unions 55, 67, 71, 75, 102, 103,
    108, 124, 135, 139, 158, 161, 167,
    169, 173, 205
Trafalgar 16
Traore, Bouna 205
Treaty of Frankfurt 63–64
Treaty of London 42
Treaty of Rome 145
Treaty of The Three Emperors (1881) 79
trente glorieuses **138**, 138–39, 165, 168,
    187
Triple Alliance (1882) 79, 80
trois glorieuses 27
Truffaut, François **159**
Truman Doctrine 132
Truman, Harry S. 131, 132
Tunisia 68, 142–43, 145, 146, 211–12
Turkey 85, 204
Turreau, Louis Marie, General 2
Twitter 212
two-speed society 158

Ultramontains **52**
Ultras **21**, 21, 22, 23, 24–25, 26, 28,
    29–30, 35
unemployment 6, 35, 47, 98, 102, 161,
    172, 173, 175, 179, 182, 183, 184,
    186, 189, 190, 193, 194–95, 204,
    205, 206, 213, 214
*Union de défense des commerçants et
    artisans* (UDCA) 143–44
Union de la gauche 168, 169, 173
*Union démocratique et socialiste de la
    résistance* (UDSR) 143, 144
Union des démocrates pour la V (UDV)
    154
*Union des Organisations Islamiques de
    France* (UOIF) 210
union nationale 100
Union nationale des étudiants de France
    (UNEF) 159, 160
Union pour la défense de le république
    (UDR) 163, 166, 173
Union pour la démocratie française
    (UDF) 173, 174, 180, 188, 189, 197,
    204
Union pour la nouvelle république (UNR)
    150, 154
Union pour un mouvement populaire
    (UMP) 197, 204, 207, 209, 211
union sacrée 82–85
United Nations 156, 198, 203
Universal Declaration of Human Rights
    (1948) 2
universalism 17
universities 21, 23, 163, 205
utopian socialism 40–41, **41**, 71

Vallat, Xavier 103
Varennes 12
Veil, Simone 171
Vendée 2, 3, 11, 13, 23, 36
Vercors 151
Verdun, Battle of 83, 117, 145
Versailles Peace Treaty (1919) 85–88, 89,
    102

Verts 188, 194, 195, 196, 204
Vian, Boris 147
Vichy regime 137, 192
   and the church 119–20
   collaboration 115, 118, 121–22,
      123–24
   and the Holocaust 121–22
   World War II 115–21, 123–24
Vichy syndrome **127**
Vietnam Solidarity Committee 161
Vietnam War 155, 156, 161
Villèle, Jean-Baptiste, Comte de **21**, 24,
      25, 26
Viviani, René 84
voie sacrée 83
volonté politique, art du possible 193
Voltaire 8
vom Rath, Ernst 107

Waldeck-Rousseau, René 73, 74
Wall Street Crash 97–98
war and memory **84**
'war guilt cause' 87
Warsaw Pact 133
Waterloo 16, 21, 26, 34
welfare state 134, 138, 189, 192, 193,
      207, 213, 215
West Africa 141, 143, 145, 158
West Germany 132, 136, 143, **174**
Western Alliance 155, 156
Western Europe 156
Weygand, Maxime, General 115
White Terror 21
Wilhelm II 79, 80
Wilson, Daniel 70
Wilson, Woodrow 86
wine crisis 75
women 130, 163
   abortion and birth control 108, 171
   and the church 74

education 140
emancipation 212
employment 140, 158
femme au foyer 119
femmes tondues **127**
feminism 165, 167, 171, 175–76
les pétroleuses 64
marginalisation of 17
Muslim, *loi Veil* 175–76
Muslim, suffrage 144
new woman **87**
and the Occupation 122
Parité 195
in politics 139, **147**, 171, 204
Popular Front **103**
and the Resistance **126**
suffrage 68, 74, 87, **103**, **126**,
      139–40
Vichy regime 119
women's rights **15**, 16
   Fourth Republic 139–40
   Giscard 171
   Mitterrand 154
   post-World War I 87
   Second Republic 48
working classes 47, 54, 55, 57, 64, 71,
      75, **101**, 101, **104**, 133, 135, 139,
      161, 162–63, **213**
World Cup (1998) 191
World War I 81–85, 91, 114, 136
World War II 108–9, 115–21, 123–24,
      131

yé-yés **159**
Yemen 212
Young, Owen D. 89
YouTube 212

Zebda 190
Zola, Émile 72